Early Medieval Theology

General Editors

John Baillie (1886–1960) served as President of the World Council of Churches, a member of the British Council of Churches, Moderator of the General Assembly of the Church of Scotland, and Dean of the Faculty of Divinity at the University of Edinburgh.

John T. McNeill (1885–1975) was Professor of the History of European Christianity at the University of Chicago and then Auburn Professor of Church History at Union Theological Seminary in New York.

Henry P. Van Dusen (1897–1975) was an early and influential member of the World Council of Churches and served at Union Theological Seminary in New York as Roosevelt Professor of Systematic Theology and later as President.

THE LIBRARY OF CHRISTIAN CLASSICS

Early Medieval Theology

Edited and Translated by
GEORGE E. MCCRACKEN
PhD, FAAR

In collaboration with
ALLEN CABANISS
PhD, FRHS

Westminster John Knox Press
LOUISVILLE • LONDON

© 1957 The Westminster Press

Paperback reissued 2006 by Westminster John Knox Press, Louisville, Kentucky.

All rights reserved. No part of this book may be reproduced or transmitted in any form or by any means, electronic or mechanical, including photocopying, recording, or by any information storage or retrieval system, without permission in writing from the publisher. For information, address Westminster John Knox Press, 100 Witherspoon Street, Louisville, Kentucky 40202-1396.

Cover design by designpointinc.com

Published by Westminster John Knox Press
Louisville, Kentucky

This book is printed on acid-free paper that meets the American National Standards Institute Z39.48 standard.♾

PRINTED IN THE UNITED STATES OF AMERICA

Library of Congress Cataloging-in-Publication Data is on file at the Library of Congress, Washington, D.C.

ISBN-13: 978-0-664-23083-8
ISBN-10: 0-664-23083-0

GENERAL EDITORS' PREFACE

The Christian Church possesses in its literature an abundant and incomparable treasure. But it is an inheritance that must be reclaimed by each generation. THE LIBRARY OF CHRISTIAN CLASSICS is designed to present in the English language, and in twenty-six volumes of convenient size, a selection of the most indispensable Christian treatises written prior to the end of the sixteenth century.

The practice of giving circulation to writings selected for superior worth or special interest was adopted at the beginning of Christian history. The canonical Scriptures were themselves a selection from a much wider literature. In the Patristic era there began to appear a class of works of compilation (often designed for ready reference in controversy) of the opinions of well-reputed predecessors, and in the Middle Ages many such works were produced. These medieval anthologies actually preserve some noteworthy materials from works otherwise lost.

In modern times, with the increasing inability even of those trained in universities and theological colleges to read Latin and Greek texts with ease and familiarity, the translation of selected portions of earlier Christian literature into modern languages has become more necessary than ever; while the wide range of distinguished books written in vernaculars such as English makes selection there also needful. The efforts that have been made to meet this need are too numerous to be noted here, but none of these collections serves the purpose of the reader who desires a library of representative treatises spanning the Christian centuries as a whole. Most of them embrace only the age of the Church Fathers, and some of them have long been out of print. A fresh translation of a work already translated may shed much new light upon its meaning. This is true even of Bible translations despite the work of many experts through the centuries. In some instances old translations have been adopted in this series, but wherever necessary or desirable, new ones have been made. Notes have been supplied where these were needed to explain the author's meaning. The introductions provided for the several treatises and extracts will, we believe, furnish welcome guidance.

JOHN BAILLIE
JOHN T. MCNEILL
HENRY P. VAN DUSEN

CONTENTS

(An asterisk marks the sections translated and edited by Allen Cabaniss.)

	page
LIST OF ABBREVIATIONS	14
GENERAL INTRODUCTION	15

THE NATURE OF DIVINE TRUTH

VINCENT OF LÉRINS	23
The Commonitory	36
PASCHASIUS RADBERTUS OF CORBIE	90
The Lord's Body and Blood (Selections)	94
RATRAMNUS OF CORBIE	109
Christ's Body and Blood	118
*A REPLY TO THE THREE LETTERS (Selections)	148
Text	154

GOD'S WORD IN HOLY SCRIPTURE

GREGORY THE GREAT	179
The Commentary on Job (Selections)	183
ALCUIN OF YORK	192
Commentary on the Epistle to Titus (Selections)	195
* CLAUDIUS OF TURIN	211
Commentary on Galatians (Selections)	221
Defense and Reply to Abbot Theodemir	241
* RUPERT OF DEUTZ	249
Commentary on Saint John (Selections)	257
On the Victory of God's Word (Selections)	269

THE VOICE OF THE PREACHER

GUIBERT OF NOGENT 285
   How to Make a Sermon 287
RABANUS MAURUS OF MAINZ 300
   Five Sermons
      I. Sermon Before Our Lord's Nativity . 302
      VII. Sermon on the Lord's Epiphany . . 304
      XXII. Sermon on the Day of Pentecost . . 305
      XLV. Sermon on Faith, Hope, and Love . 307
      LVII. Sermon on Contempt for the World and
            on Future Reward. . . . 310
IVO OF CHARTRES 314
   Two Sermons
      XXII. Sermon on the Lord's Prayer . . 317
      XXIII. Sermon on the Apostles' Creed . . 323
*AGOBARD OF LYONS 328
   *On the Truth of the Faith and the Establishment of All
   Good* 334
   On Divine Psalmody 363

IDEALS OF THE PRIESTHOOD

ANONYMOUS 371
   Address to the Clergy 374
THEODULPH OF ORLÉANS 379
   Precepts to the Priests of His Diocese . . 382
THE VENERABLE BEDE 400
   On Bishop Aidan 407

INDEXES 411

ACKNOWLEDGMENTS

Valuable assistance on thorny points has been received from the Rev. Professors Joseph C. Plumpe, Leo F. Miller, J. N. Bakhuizen van den Brink, Albert C. Outler, and Robert M. Grant. Part of the text was read by my colleague, Professor S. W. Houston. Thanks are also due to the librarians of Drake University, the State University of Iowa, the Divinity School of the University of Chicago, and the Union Theological Seminary, for their assistance in providing rare books for my use.

Much of the drudgery of typing the manuscript has been done by my wife.

G. E. McC.

LIST OF ABBREVIATIONS

ACW	*Ancient Christian Writers*
CE	*Catholic Encyclopaedia*
CSEL	*Corpus scriptorum ecclesiasticorum Latinorum*
DTC	*Dictionnaire de théologie catholique*
EC	*Enciclopedia Cattolica*
EpKA	*Epistulae Karolini Aevi*
KL	Wetzer and Welte's *Kirchenlexikon*
LCC	*Library of Christian Classics*
LTK	*Lexikon der Theologie und Kirche*
MGH	*Monumenta Germaniae Historica*
MPG	Migne, *Patrologiae cursus completus*, Series Graeca
MPL	Migne, *Patrologiae cursus completus*, Series Latina
NPNF	*Nicene and Post-Nicene Fathers*
NSH	*New Schaff-Herzog Encyclopaedia of Religious Knowledge*
OL	Old Latin
PLAC	*Poetae Latini Aevi Carolini*
RE	*Realenzyklopädie für protestantische Theologie und Kirche*
TU	*Texte und Untersuchungen*
V	Vulgate (in Scripture references only)

General Introduction

DARK AS THE SEVEN CENTURIES SPANNED BY THE selections in this volume are commonly supposed to have been, those who investigate them more than superficially will discover that in this period the church of Christ was ever endeavoring to lift aloft a light which the darkness did not overcome.

One must not, of course, expect to find in the early Middle Ages all the characteristics that in our own age are regarded as signs of high achievement. This was a time when men thought much less of the originality of their own productive genius than of the preservation in an age of turmoil of the values transmitted to them in mysticism and morality out of the Christian past. Their attitude toward this inheritance was loyalty to its admittedly high standards, rather than a self-centered conviction that it was their privilege, much less their duty, to develop the faith in novel directions.

Our medieval forebears in the church must be evaluated in the light of the types and intensities of the evils which they faced. Theirs was a time of great political instability in which nations hitherto beyond the frontiers of civilization were attempting to assimilate cultural and spiritual treasures which had come to them with the breakdown of late antiquity. When no central authority extended its power beyond relatively narrow boundaries, it was natural that barbarous violence should be widespread and that the security for which the men of that era would yearn was literal safety from the arrow that flies by night and the destruction that wastes at noonday.

To cope with this situation the church strove to provide for the Western world such security as it could, and this it did principally by using two forces at its disposal. First, it continued to furnish pastoral instruction in doctrine, liturgy, and morality for the laity through the agency of parish priest and diocesan bishop. This theme runs throughout the volume but appears most vividly in the selections taken from the unknown bishop (perhaps Caesarius of Arles), Theodulph, and Bede.

Secondly, it provided for those who would make learning their vocation by establishing for them, as refuges from the tribulations of medieval life, great monastic foundations like Lérins, Corbie, Fulda, Tours, and Jarrow, which at one time or another housed most of our authors. We here refrain from further discussion of the great contributions of monasteries of this period to its inner life and religious culture only because another volume (XII) in this series has been planned to cover this theme more exhaustively.

The sources from which our writers drew their principal inspiration were two in number, the Bible and the Fathers—not, however, thought of as representing different traditions of divine truth but pouring forth in one and the same mighty stream of revelation. Not yet had anyone conceived that truth could be preserved relatively unchanged in the written form of the Scriptures, while at the same time ecclesiastical tradition might differ from it. Recourse to support from the sacred writings is constant, as will be seen from the frequency of citations in the texts. In this period the Bible was no closed book, at least not to the learned, and if the common people could not read God's Word for themselves, this was because literacy itself was relatively rare, not that reading of the Scriptures was deemed dangerous and forbidden to them. The Bible was read deeply and profoundly and, what is more, it was remembered. How otherwise when it was everywhere recognized, that in the memorable words applied by Gregory the Great to The Book of Job, its Author was the Holy Spirit himself?

That the Bible required interpretation was no more overlooked in medieval times than now. Most of the writers in this volume, and many another of their contemporaries, turned out long series of commentaries on the sacred books. The *catena*, or chain, of patristic comments on the Scriptures and the gloss in one form or another were favorite medieval compositions. Of more formal commentaries we have included part of Alcuin's commentary on the Epistle to Titus as typical of the less original exegesis of the period—more than half is borrowed verbatim from Jerome. Although largely unoriginal, Claudius' commentary on Galatians demonstrates a certain vigor of thought and idea which he had learned intimately enough to make his own. Observe, however, in the selection that we translate that he made little of the famous passage that impressed Luther so profoundly. Three centuries later Rupert and his era were sufficiently emancipated from slavish adherence to authorities for his works to bear the mark of strong individuality.

The men of the Middle Ages further developed the method of exegesis inherited from the fathers in a fashion peculiarly their own. They expanded the two senses in which Scripture may be expounded: the literal or historical, and the spiritual or allegorical. For Gregory the Great there were now three senses: the historical, the allegorical, and the moral, but John Cassian's list, most clearly expressed in the selection from Guibert of Nogent, has four: the historical, the allegorical, the tropological, and the anagogical. The difference between the last three is perhaps difficult for modern man to detect: what these were is shown by a couplet long circulated:

> "*Littera gesta docet, quid credas allegoria,*
> *Moralis quid agas, quo tendas anagogia.*"

The literal sense gives the historical data of revelation; the allegorical, that which we may believe about it; the tropological, rules of conduct; and the anagogical, the direction of our spiritual progress. A fine example of the application of the method to the word "Jerusalem" will be found in our selection from Gregory the Great. Though the terminology used here is not much encountered nowadays, the methods are still to be found in commentaries of one school or another.

That there may, however, be varieties of interpretation on given points mutually in conflict was acutely realized by that charming and subtle thinker, Vincent of Lérins, in his *Commonitory*, with which we open our examination of medieval Christianity. For him, divine truth is to be found within the Scriptures, a fact fundamental to his thought though often lost sight of because he may at times appear in the sequel to range himself with those who declare truth to be what the church may teach, even though seemingly in opposition to Biblical teaching. If there be various interpretations by various men, as, of course, there are and were, how, then, is the Christian to distinguish between them? Vincent's answer is to examine them in the light of the church's teaching, which should reveal the truth, but because there were doubtless many points conceivable to Vincent on which the church had not yet spoken through the pronouncements of a universal council, then recourse must be had to the principles of ecumenicity, antiquity, and agreement, that is, in the words of the now famous formula bearing his name, Christian truth is what has been believed everywhere, always, and by all men. This formula did not at once win wide acceptance, probably because it was promulgated in connection with a veiled attack upon Augustine's doctrine of predestination, and the great prestige of the bishop of Hippo caused his views to triumph, at least for a time. Yet in the Reformation and also in modern times, particularly in our own day, when the ecumenical movement grows increasingly strong and there are many champions of Christian unity bearing witness, the great formula has had deep significance.

Our second and third selections concern one of the ninth century doctrinal controversies still of high interest in modern times. It is curious that until that relatively late date no theologian had as yet devoted a single treatise to the paramount doctrine of the Eucharist. This was left to be done first by a learned and humble monk, Paschasius Radbertus, abbot of Corbie, in a work bearing the title of *The Lord's Body and Blood*. As this is too long for full translation, we have attempted to render in English enough of the argument to enable the reader to understand Paschasius' relation to his more original fellow monk, Ratramnus. He, in the work which we have translated *in toto* as *Christ's Body and Blood*, courteously rejects the Radbertian thesis that the body of Christ on the altar is the same body that was conceived of the Holy Spirit, born of the Virgin Mary, suffered, died, and ascended into heaven. Thus, Ratramnus denied that part of Paschasius' doctrine which doubtless was later developed into transubstantiation.

This work of Ratramnus has had as amazing a history as any book known. Though marked with considerable originality, a feature present in Ratramnus' other writings, and a dangerous quality in an age so largely devoted to the preservation of the *status quo*, it did not win for its author the condemnation that might have been expected. Not until the Eucharistic controversy associated with the name of Berengarius of Tours, two centuries later, was the book condemned, and then under the quite mistaken notion that it was the product of that rare spirit John Scotus Eriugena, a man eccentric for his day and thus largely misunderstood by the Latin temperament in the West. At the dawn of the Reformation, the first printed edition of

"Bertramus," as was then supposed to be the true name of the author, aroused so great a disturbance among supporters of the now firmly entrenched doctrine of transubstantiation that it was suspected of being either an interpolated text or even the fabrication of some member of the reforming party. On the other hand, it gave much illumination to many of the early Protestants of varying shades of opinion, as will be seen. Now universally accepted as a genuine work of the ninth century, the little book remains to our day a controversial document of first importance to systematic theology.

Associated with the same monastery and in the same age was another controversy on the doctrine of predestination which had an entirely different outcome. The monk Gottschalk, searching for peace of mind in the writings of Augustine, fastened upon that doctrine in which the bishop of Hippo was himself extreme, namely, his doctrine of predestination, forged on the anvil of the controversy against the Pelagians and the so-called Semi-Pelagians, the latter represented in this volume, of course, by Vincent of Lérins' *Commonitory*. Poor Gottschalk's sensitive personality attracted both devotion and opposition and the dogma of predestination received wider attention in the ninth century than at any time between Augustine and the Reformation.

Ratramnus also took part—here, however, in accord with the prevailing view of the Western church—in two other controversies. The first of these has to do with the use of images in worship and the controversy is represented in this volume by the reply of Claudius of Turin to the Abbot Theodemir. The other was occasioned by the doctrine of the "Double Procession of the Holy Spirit." The church in the West, inserted into the Niceno-Constantinopolitan Creed the words "*Filioque*" (and from the Son) to show that the Holy Spirit proceeds from the Son as well as the Father. The innovation, made without the sanction of a general council and without consultation of the East, has since then been universally defended by the Latin church, and remained in the creed when adopted by the Reformers. Hence, it is today one of the chief obstacles to union of the Orthodox churches with both Rome and the Protestants.

While writers like Vincent and Ratramnus were dealing on highest levels of thought with questions of theological import, other churchmen were producing a rich body of homiletical material in which the Word of God was preached to the faithful. Our selection from Guibert of Nogent is not properly a sermon but rather a manual for the preacher, as the title suggests, and also an exhortation against the sin of laziness among the clergy and particularly reluctance to engage in this active phase of the pastoral ministry. Those who are inclined to think preachers dull, as doubtless some preachers are, will be surprised at the wit of Guibert and also at the sparkle to be found in the medieval sermons here presented. As typical examples, we have selected five sermons preached by that able churchman Rabanus Maurus to his monks at Fulda. Three are on the important feasts of Christmas, the Epiphany, and Pentecost; one is an exposition of I Corinthians, ch. 13, and the last is on a topic of great popularity in the Middle Ages, contempt for the world and the hope of future reward. From the sermons of Ivo of Chartres, much better known as an authority on canon law, we have chosen characteristic homilies on the Lord's Prayer and on the Apostles' Creed. The only extant sermon of Agobard of Lyons is a discursive treatment of a wide range of Christian doctrine with special emphasis on the two communities, the redeemed and the damned. His short work *On Divine Psalmody*, which we include here also, exhibits a sturdy loyalty to Scripture as the standard by which to judge the liturgy, and, by implication, all of faith, life, and conduct.

The other phase of the Christian ministry, the work of the parish pastor, received great attention, and it was in this field that Gregory the Great wrote his *Pastoral Rule*, one of the most popular products of the early Middle Ages, and one which might have been included were it not for its length and the availability of good and recent translations.

Less well known and therefore the more welcome are two works on the pastoral office, one of which is the anonymous *Address to the Clergy* made by an unknown bishop and widely used by many another bishop as a guide for his own clergy. Whoever its true author was, he was a man of no literary pretension but keenly aware of the problems met with by the typical pastor, and with a strong desire to improve the cure of souls in the diocese entrusted to him. A later work by Theodulph of Orléans is in the same form but markedly different in tone and spirit, particularly with reference to style. Finally, we conclude with a short selection from the foremost work written in England during the Middle Ages, Bede's *Ecclesiastical History of the English People*, which gives an impressive picture of the life of the saintly missionary and bishop Aidan.

THE NATURE OF DIVINE TRUTH

Vincent of Lérins: The Commonitory

INTRODUCTION

THE AUTHOR OF *THE COMMONITORY* ATTRIBUTED to Vincent of Lérins furnishes us with scant information concerning himself. He is the monk Peregrinus, now residing in an unnamed monastery far from urban centers. The Council of Ephesus (which took place in 431) is now three years past. The bishop of Rome is a Sixtus identifiable with Pope Sixtus III (who reigned 432–440) and Cyril is bishop of Alexandria—he reigned from 412 to 444. This gives us the year 434 for the completion of the work.

External evidence on the life and work of the author is contained principally in a notice concerning him in the book *On Famous Writers*[1] which, late in the fifth century of our era, the presbyter Gennadius of Massilia compiled as a continuation of Jerome's work *On Famous Men*[2]:

"Vincent, a native of Gaul and presbyter in the monastery of the island of Lerina[3]: a man learned in the Holy Scriptures and well informed as to the church's doctrines, he composed in a very polished and lucid style, for the purpose of shunning heretical sects, a most powerful treatise to which, suppressing his own name, he gave the title *Peregrinus Against Heretics*. After the greater part of the second book had been lost as the result of the theft of its rough draft

---

[1] *De illustribus scriptoribus*, ed. E. C. Richardson, TU 14 (1896) 83, tr. by him, NPNF, 2d ser., 3.396. Here the chapter is 65; other editions have 64. See B. Czapla, *Gennadius als Literarhistoriker* (Münster i. W., 1898); H. Koch, TU, 31 pt. 2; J. Madoz, *Estud. Ecles.* 11 (1932) 484.
[2] *De viris illustribus*, sometimes called *Catalogus Scriptorum*, tr. by Richardson, NPNF, 2d ser., 3.349–384.
[3] Lerina, now called St. Honorat, is the smaller and seaward of the two islands off Cannes. The monastery was famous for centuries. The larger island is now called Ste. Marguerite. See A. C. Cooper-Marsdin, *The History of the Islands of the Lérins* (Cambridge, 1913).

by parties unknown, he summarized its substance briefly, appended it to the first book, and published both in one volume. He died in the reign of Theodosius and Valentinian."[4]

Vincent's name appears in the Roman martyrology and he is commemorated on May 24, but we do not have the details of his death. His contemporary and fellow monk Eucherius,[5] afterward bishop of Lyons, calls Vincent "pre-eminent alike for eloquence and wisdom" and "a jewel shining with inner splendor," adding the detail that Vincent's brother was Lupus (probably the later bishop of Troyes). So far as we are aware, the identification of Peregrinus with Vincent has been universally accepted. "Peregrinus" is therefore a pseudonym, if, indeed, it is to be read as more than a synonym for monk. The description of the book given by Gennadius neatly conforms to the state in which the work has come down to us, but no one has been convinced by Poirel's attempt[6] to identify Vincent with Marius Mercator.

Though not the only work composed by Vincent, *The Commonitory* represents his chief claim to fame. The unusual word does not appear as the title in the manuscripts but is taken from the preface, in which Peregrinus tells us that he intends to write a commonitory, a reminder of his own views and for his own use, to jog the memory or supply the defects of a poor one.

The book bears throughout ample evidence of its author's acquaintance with Scripture and with the doctrinal controversies of the first four centuries. Moreover, Gennadius' favorable comments on the style are hardly exaggerated in any respect: Vincent always is clear and forceful, often brilliant, never dull. The claim that Peregrinus will write in a plain and unadorned style is a conventional pretense, for he writes, not in the language of his day, but very much better than, for example, his contemporary Sulpicius Severus. Vincent obviously had had a good education in rhetoric. Frequently there are phrases taken from authors of the best classical periods.[7]

[4] The period of joint reign is 425-450.
[5] MPL 50.711 = CSEL 31.193; MPL 50.773 = CSEL 31.66. That Vincent was son of Epirochius and born at Tullie Leucorum in Prima Belgica is claimed by Hewison (Scottish Text Society 22.152) but we do not know the evidence.
[6] R. M. J. Poirel, *De utroque commonitorio* (Nancy, 1895) and in his edition (Nancy, 1898), refuted by Koch (*Theol. Quartalschr.* 81 [1899] 426-428).
[7] Terence, Cicero, Lucretius, Sallust, Horace, and Ovid, are all ultimate sources of phrases which appear. On this topic see J. Madoz, *Rech. de Sc. Rel.* 39 (1951) 461-471.

The original intent must have been to write two books. The first contains a preface and a concluding summary, followed by the following sentence of an editor: "The second commonitory has intervened but nothing more of it has survived than the last part, that is, only the summary given below." The summary, however, repeats the argument of *both* books, that for the second seven times longer than that for the former. Finally, there is another conclusion to the whole work.

Gennadius' claim that the second book was stolen is nothing short of an attempt to explain the curious condition of the manuscript as he read it, that is, the same condition in which we too find it. We are thus left with a perplexing problem of why the second book is missing, for which no satisfactory answer has been made.

What Vincent intends to discuss is the method for telling what catholic truth is. He begins[8] with the Holy Scriptures as the source of all true doctrine, but since it is interpreted variously by various men, one needs some guide for distinguishing between the various interpretations. Here the solution is that one must examine them in the light of the church's teaching, but if the church has not yet spoken through the conclusions of some universal council, then one must use the principles of ecumenicity, antiquity, and agreement, in the words of the now famous "formula of St. Vincent of Lérins," catholic truth is *quod ubique, quod semper, et quod ab omnibus creditum est*, that is, what has been believed everywhere, always, and by all men. The catholic searches for what is both ancient (*antiquitas* or *vetustas*—the words are synonymous) and ecumenical (*universitas*), but Vincent is well aware that even in these there may be some divergence, and so he adds agreement (*consensus*). The agreement, then, of the ancient and ecumenical church —the catholic church, that is—is his rule. Opinions not ancient in time, opinions of one or of a few—these are to be disregarded, and only opinions of those who have remained faithfully in communion with the catholic church may be accepted.

Does this not prevent Christian progress or development? Not true progress (*profectus*), says Vincent, but it does prevent change (*alteratio*); that which produces something new, not found in antiquity, not ecumenical, is condemned, but what is clearly to be derived from antiquity may be developed. To explain his meaning he draws analogy from organic growth in

[8] So also in the *Excerpta*, mentioned below.

the world of nature. What was present in the organism at conception may develop, often changing its outward appearance but never its essential nature. Old men are not what they were as infants, so far as outward appearance is concerned, but they are the same persons.

He illustrates his rule from the heresies, though this is no history of heresies. Some of them he mentions merely in passing, but three heretics, Photinus, Apollinaris, and Nestorius, he discusses at some length, these chosen, doubtless, because they were all involved in the Christological controversy, and the last was recent. It is clear also that though Vincent has no intent to expound the whole of Christian doctrine, he has a strong interest in the doctrines of the Trinity and incarnation, and he lets us know this by inserting, in what he calls merely a digression, his views on this important dogma (Chapters XII–XVI). Here he is in accord with the position of that creed which bears the name of Athanasius, the *Quicumque Vult*. Indeed, at times his language recalls that of the creed so vividly that he has been thought by some[9] to have been its author. While the parallels are striking and it is perfectly clear that there is some sort of relationship between this creed and *The Commonitory*, the best explanation is that the unknown author of the creed was familiar with *The Commonitory*. In any case, since the *Quicumque* is only one third as long as Vincent's discussion of the incarnation, it cannot be the longer work promised us by Vincent.

The Commonitory marks an important point in the doctrinal controversy in modern times called Semi-Pelagian,[10] though the only designation by which it was known in its own day was "the relics of the Pelagians" (*reliquiae Pelagianorum*), a phrase found in Prosper.[11] The movement was found chiefly in southern Gaul, principally among the clergy of Massilia and Lérins, and its leading proponents, besides Vincent, were John Cassian and,

---

[9] Joseph Anthelmi, *Nova de symbolo Athanasiano disquisitio* (1693); G. D. W. Ommanney, *The Athanasian Creed* (London, 1880), and his *Dissertation on the Athanasian Creed* (London, 1897). See G. Morin, *Revue Bénédictine* 44 (1932) 205–219.

[10] On this controversy and Vincent's part in it see Moxon's edition (xxii–xxxii); F. Loofs (NSH 10.347–349); J. Pohle (CE 13.703–706); B. B. Warfield (NPNF, 1st ser. 5.xxi); E. Amann (DTC 14.1796–1850); W. Koch (LTK 9.460 f.); G. DePlinval (EC 11.286–288); Miller (RE 14.94); R. Rainy, *The Ancient Catholic Church* (New York, 1902) 485–493; P. DeLetter (ACW 14.3–6 and notes 7–17 on pp. 158 f.).

[11] Prosper to Augustine in the latter's letter 225 (MPL 33.1106).

later, Faustus of Riez. The "Semi-Pelagians" themselves would have been quite horrified to learn that they were destined to be called such, for they were in their own estimation vigorous opponents of all that Pelagius and Caelestius had stood for, and they were strongly convinced that their own view was wholly orthodox and that Augustine's extreme view, to which they were opposed, was error, if not heretical, as Vincent boldly calls it. The controversy had broken out in the closing years of Augustine's life and he was thus far the only writer among their opponents. Though by 432, to be sure, a bishop of Rome had taken up the fight on Augustine's behalf, there was not as yet— and there was not to be for another century—any official condemnation by a church council.

Briefly, it may be stated that Pelagius' teaching denies the necessity of divine grace in effecting man's salvation. By free will man may choose to ask for salvation, divine grace being, though helpful, not necessary. This view, emphasizing the importance of man's part in the process, is the direct opposite of the Augustinian doctrine of grace and free will, in which prevenient grace is regarded as an absolute necessity before man can hope for salvation; so great a necessity, indeed, that Augustine goes one step farther and expounds his doctrine of predestination, whereby God predetermines who shall be saved (the elect) and who shall not (the damned).

As the Semi-Pelagians understood Augustine, his view was too rigid, too extreme, and it must be admitted that after his death, later theologians, perhaps as a result of the work of the Semi-Pelagians, took a somewhat less extreme position.[12] The Semi-Pelagian point of view may perhaps be stated as follows: first, Pelagius and his confreres were absolutely and unequivocally heretical—the Council of Carthage had said so; secondly, the beginning of faith (*initium fidei*), the asking for salvation by man, is the result of the power of free will, but the faith itself and its increase (*augmentum fidei*) are absolutely dependent upon God; thirdly, while the gift of divine grace is a doctrine to be maintained against Pelagius in so far as every strictly natural merit is excluded, this does not prevent nature and its works, that is, man alone, from having a certain claim to grace; fourthly, perseverance, that is, continuance in the faith after the initial act, is not a special gift of grace,

---

[12] DeLetter (ACW 14.5) speaks of a "partial withdrawal of the Augustinians expressed in the *Capitula seu praeteritorum Sedis Apostolicae episcoporum auctoritates de gratia Dei*" (MPL 51.205–212).

since the justified man may of his own power persevere to the end.

The Gallic clergy had probably first heard of Augustine's views on this subject from a reading of his works *On Grace and Free Will* and *On Rebuke and Grace*,[13] which were written in 426 or 427, and, though not addressed to them, doubtless had been circulated widely. The earliest surviving statement of the Semi-Pelagian position occurs, probably, in a work of John Cassian, the *Conference XIII with the Abbot Chaeremon*,[14] but Augustine was informed of the Semi-Pelagian doctrines by two letters[15] about them which came to him from Prosper and Hilary, laymen in the Gallic church. In his book *On the Predestination of the Saints*, written about 428 or 429, he refers to the Semi-Pelagians in not unkindly vein, in Chapters 2 and 38. At about the time when John Cassian was writing, Vincent must have been busy on a work known to us as the *Objectiones Vincentianae*, now extant only in the form in which it appears in Prosper's counterattack, *Replies to the Sections of the Vincentian Objections on Behalf of Augustine's Teaching*.[16] That the "Objections" are the work of our Vincent was long doubted, but the fifth objection bears such certain evidence of being by the same hand as *The Commonitory* that it is now believed that our Vincent wrote them. Another work of the same period and same doctrinal point of view, the *Capitula Calumniantium Gallorum*, has not yet been certainly proved to be his, though it is of the same school of thought.[17]

In the end Prosper became the most determined Gallic

[13] The Augustinian works to be consulted are: (a) Epist. 217 *ad Vitalem* (MPL 33.978–990 = CSEL 57.403–425), not tr. in NPNF; (b) Epist. 194 *ad Sixtum* (MPL 33.874–891 = CSEL 57.176–214), not tr. in NPNF—the Sixtus was afterward Pope Sixtus III; (c) *De gratia et libero arbitrio* (MPL 44.881–912, not in CSEL), tr. NPNF, 1st ser. 5.425–465; (d) *De correptione et gratia* (MPL 44.915–946, not in CSEL), tr. NPNF, 1st ser., 5.467–491; (e) Epist. 225 *Prosper ad Augustinum* and Epist. 226 *Hilarius ad Augustinum* (MPL 33.1102–1112 = 51.61–74 = CSEL 57.454–481), not tr. in NPNF; (f) *De praedestinatione sanctorum* (MPL 45.959–992, not in CSEL), tr. NPNF, 1st ser., 5.493–519; (g) *De dono perseverantiae* (MPL 45.993–1034, not in CSEL), tr. NPNF, 1st ser., 5.521–552.
[14] *Collatio XIII Abbatis Chaeremonis* (MPL 49.887–954 = CSEL 13.361–396), tr. NPNF, 2d ser., 11.422–425. See Owen Chadwick, *John Cassian, a Study in Primitive Monasticism* (Cambridge, 1950) 111–120; L. Christiani, *Jean Cassien* (Paris, 1946).
[15] Epist. 225–226.
[16] *Pro Augustini doctrina responsiones ad capitula objectionum Vincentianarum* (MPL 45.1843–1850 = 51.177–186).
[17] MPL 45.1835–1844 = 51.155–174. See also *ibid.*, 51.185.

defender of Augustinianism. With Hilary he went to Rome and succeeded in interesting Pope Celestine I (422–432) in writing to a group of Gallic bishops that letter which Vincent cites in *The Commonitory* (Ch. XXXII) for his own purposes. Prosper also wrote a *Letter to Rufinus on Grace and Free Will Against the Conferencer* (John Cassian),[18] a work long thought to be by Augustine. Not content with this, he even took to verse and composed a poem of some thousand hexameters to which he gave the Greek title of *Peri Achariston*[19] and also two *Epigrams Against Augustine's Traducer*.[20] In his *Call to All Nations*,[21] and subsequently, he "devoted the utmost pains to soften down with noble tact the roughness and abruptness of many of his master's propositions,"[22] but Semi-Pelagianism, though now rebuked by a bishop of Rome, was not dead, and was not officially condemned by any council until the Synod of Orange, convoked by Caesarius of Arles on July 3, 529, adopted twenty-five canons which declared the view heretical.

This brings us to the part played in the controversy by *The Commonitory* itself. Frequently throughout the work there are covert allusions to Augustine, though never by name, and most of them would probably not have been noticed by anyone had there not been in Chapter XXVI a specific allusion to an unnamed heresy clearly identifiable with Augustine's views. Moreover, the letter[23] already mentioned, which Celestine wrote to the Gallic bishops at the instance of Prosper and Hilary, directed beyond the slightest shadow of doubt against the Semi-Pelagians of southern Gaul, is actually cited by Vincent as a praiseworthy example of a bishop of Rome who gave a directive to other bishops to suppress a heresy in their dioceses.

[18] *Epist. ad Rufinum de gratia et libero arbitrio contra collatorem* (MPL 45. 1795–1802 = 51.213–276).
[19] MPL 51.91–148. The Greek title is ironically Latinized as *De ingratis*, "On the Graceless Ones," and there is a deliberate pun here. See F. J. E. Raby, *Hist. of Christian Latin Poetry* (Oxford, 2d ed., 1953), pp. 84 f., where two elegiacs are set as if a stanza.
[20] *Epigrammata in obtrectatorem Augustini* (MPL 41.149–202).
[21] *De vocatione omnium gentium* (MPL 51.647). It also appears in the earlier edition of MPL among Ambrose' works but in the 1879 edition (MPL 17.1167) it is excluded, though noted. The question of the authorship has been debated. P. DeLetter, who has recently translated it in ACW 14 (1952), accepts it as by Prosper, and in his dissertation J. J. Young has studied its style (*Cath. Univ. Patr. Stud.* 87 [1952]), concluding that the *clausulae* show it to be by Prosper. [22] So Pohle.
[23] Cited by Vincent (XXXII), printed MPL 50.528–537 as Epist. 21 *ad Episcopos Galliarum*; dated by Madoz between June, 431 and July, 432. See D. M. Cappuyns, *Rech. de Théol. Anc. et Med.* 1 (1929) 319, n.

He does not tell us what this heresy was. One would suppose it was one which he himself opposed, but the truth is that it was a view that he had espoused in the *Objectiones Vincentianae* and also at least once, then clearly, in *The Commonitory*. Vincent's position here seems a bit equivocal, and he may also be equivocal in citing the letter of Capreolus of Carthage to the Council of Ephesus, for though we do not know Capreolus' precise views on the doctrine of grace, they were probably influenced by Augustine.

The question therefore arises as to whether *The Commonitory* was written primarily to cloak an attack upon Augustine, or whether the chief purpose was the ostensible one of providing a rule for distinguishing heresy when it arises, and the allusions to Augustine merely incidental to the main purpose. This unsolved question has been further complicated by a recent discovery. Many years ago Lehmann had printed a reference to an unknown work by Vincent contained in an anonymous medieval compendium of passages drawn from Cassiodorus[24]:

"The book of Vincent, priest of the island of Lérins, which he composed from the works of the blessed Augustine and sent to Saint Sixtus the Pope, is useful. On this account I have reread it."

No notice was, however, taken of this passage by any student of Vincent until in 1940[25] Father Madoz published the news that he had found in a manuscript formerly in the library of Ripoll in Spain a florilegium of Augustinian quotations, with a preface and a conclusion that clearly bear the stigmata of Vincent's style, namely, "excerpts gathered from all of Augustine of blessed memory by Vincent, priest of the island of Lérins, of holy memory." Not only can there be no doubt that the author of *The Commonitory* and the author of the excerpts are one and the same, but it is also undeniable that whereas the former contains a sharp attack upon Augustine, the latter contains only admiration for him.

How, then, can these conflicting points of view be reconciled? Madoz' answer to this perplexing question is this: in *The Commonitory*, Vincent is discussing doctrines (grace and predestination) on which he differed markedly from the bishop of Hippo, whereas in the excerpts he is discussing the Trinity and the incarnation, concerning which he was in wholehearted agreement with Augustine. Hence, the different tone.

It is not our purpose to present here a full account of the

[24] P. Lehmann (*Philologus* 73 [1914–1916] 268).
[25] J. Madoz (*Gregorianum* 21 [1940] 75–94).

influence of *The Commonitory* on the whole course of subsequent thought. It goes without saying that a work embodying, as it does, in its great formula, a principle so closely in accord with the practice of the medieval church toward new doctrines, would have been expected to be read and cited again and again in medieval writers. Yet *The Commonitory* appears to have been neglected in that period, and is not cited in any of the medieval catalogues. The reason for this neglect lies probably in the fact that its author bore the taint of a doctrine condemned after 529 as heretical.

The Commonitory was, however, of influence among the forces at work for Christian unity at the time of the Reformation, though Madoz calls it "the apple of discord." Its point of view was adopted as his own by an irenical writer of the Erasmian school, George Cassander (1513–1566).[26] His plea for unity was on the basis of the "fundamental articles" of the faith, ascertainable in Scripture and the Fathers, and essentially comprised in the Apostles' Creed. Authority for him, as with his contemporary, George Witzel, stops with the first five centuries, so far as what is requisite for unity is concerned. A little later another writer of much the same point of view as regards tradition was Peter Meiderlin (1582–1651), who added to his chief doctrine of the Spirit and of Love such doctrines as the church has approved through decisions of valid councils, in which case he too can accept the formula of Vincent.[27] So also Hugo Grotius (1583–1645) argued for abandonment of the controversial figures of the Reformation like Luther and Calvin, and for a turn to irenic figures like Erasmus and Melanchthon, or, better still, to the witness of the early church, specifically to *The Commonitory* and its formula.[28]

In the Church of England, Vincent has always found his supporters, especially among those within it who have put emphasis on the claim that it has deep roots within the early church. For example, Richard Baxter (1615–1691) in his *Gildas Salvianus: The Reformed Pastor* says:

"We must learn to difference well between certainties and uncertainties, necessaries and unnecessaries, catholic verities—

---

[26] See John T. McNeill, *Unitive Protestantism* (New York, 1930) 271, and in Ruth Rouse and S. C. Neill, *History of the Ecumenical Movement* 1517–1948 (Philadelphia, Westminster Press, 1954) 38; P. Tschackert (NSH 2.348 f.).
[27] See Martin Schmidt in Rouse and Neill, *op. cit.*, 82.
[28] See Schmidt, *op. cit.*, 94; also Carl Bertheau in NSH 7.287 *s.v.* "Meldenius, Rupertus," which was Meiderlin's pseudonym.

quae ab omnibus, ubique et semper sunt retentae—and private opinions; and to lay the stress of the church's peace upon the former and not upon the latter."[29]

In this connection, also, Newman should be consulted, particularly his *Apologia pro Vita Sua* and his *Essay on the Development of Christian Doctrine*.[30]

Among Roman Catholics since the Reformation, Vincent has enjoyed a varied repute. Baronius calls *The Commonitory* a "little work clearly of gold"; Cardinal Bellarmine, "Small in size but very large in virtue"; the Benedictine Mabillon, "A little book not large but golden, and to be committed to memory."[31] Pope Benedict XIV remarked in 1748 that if in Vincent and Hilary anything human [i.e., unorthodox] appeared, they were to be excused, since in their time catholic doctrine had not yet been defined.[32] A catechism printed in the diocese of Würzburg during the pontificate of Leo XII (1823-1829) contained a question to which Vincent's formula was given as the answer, but the Roman censors commented on this that the rule of Vincent was not the only criterion of dogma, nor a particular one, nor was it a definition of the church.[33] The formula played its part at the Vatican Council of 1870,[34] and in the conversations at Malines.[35] Recently, however, the French Dominican Congar has this to say in his remarkable book *Divided Christendom*[36]:

---

[29] See John T. Wilkinson's edition (London, Epworth Press, 1939), p. 141. Baxter was, of course, quoting the formula from memory.

[30] C. F. Harrold, ed., J. H. Newman, *Apologia pro Vita Sua* (New York, 1947), pp. 98, 178; *An Essay on the Development of Doctrine* (New York, 1949), consult index *s.v.* Saint Vincent. On Vincent's formula in other Anglican writers, see R. S. Moxon, *Modernism and Orthodoxy: An Attempt to Re-Assess the Value of the Vincentian Canon in Regard to Modern Tendencies of Thought* (London, 1924); Robert M. Grant, *The Bible in the Church, A Short History of Interpretation* (New York, Macmillan, 1948), 94-97.

[31] C. Baronius, *Martyrologium Romanum* (Ambères, 1613) p. 220; R. Card. Bellarmine, *De Scriptoribus Ecclesiasticis* 440 (Naples, 1862) p. 56; J. Mabillon, *Tractatus de studiis monasticis* (Venice, 1770) 1.2, ch. 4, p. 87; cf. also the title of Winzet's translation of *The Commonitory*.

[32] Benedict XIV, *Littera apostolica de nova martyrologii editione*, July 1, 1748, n. 31, cited by Madoz (88).   [33] H. Kihn, in KL 12.987 f.

[34] See J. B. Card. Franzelin, *De Divina Traditione et Scriptura* (Rome, 1st ed., 1870; 3d ed., 1882), thesis 24; T. Granderath, *Geschichte des vatikanischen Konzils* (Freiburg i. Br. 1906), 2.631 n.

[35] Lord Halifax, *The Conversations at Malines 1921-1925* (London, 1930) 281 f.

[36] M. J. Congar, *Divided Christendom: A Catholic Study of the Problem of Reunion*, tr. from *Chrétiens Désunis* by M. A. Bousfield (London, 1939),

"Now this 'canon,' which can be clearly understood in a perfectly [Roman] Catholic sense, is here put into the hands of historians, who make use of it on the normal lines of historical study. The mistake of those who set it up, thus interpreted, as the ultimate standard of ecclesiastical faith, is to subject that faith in the last analysis to the judgment of professors and not of the apostolic succession of the magisterium regarded as such. If this 'canon' were really the standard of Catholicism, then the supreme magisterium would reside with historians, for it is their business to say, from a *study of the texts*, what has been believed always, everywhere, by everyone. The magisterium, always living in the Church by the twofold principle of the apostolic succession and the assistance of the Holy Spirit, simply declares what *is* the belief of the universal Church. The past may be known by the fact of the present; the present is not determined by a reference to the past. Here we touch upon a decisive issue between the Protestant Reformation and the Church, for the very idea of reformation is involved. Is the nature of the apostolic Church such that, having fundamentally erred, she can be brought back to the truth and reformed by professors in the name of critical study? Protestantism only exists in virtue of an affirmative answer to this question, justified by the Vincentian 'canon.'"

The Jesuit Madoz, the foremost patristic scholar in Spain and the living authority who has studied Vincent most intensively, points out what he considers Vincent's defects: The point of view is negative and the solution is individualistic. Moreover, from the Roman point of view, it is faulty to omit any reference to the dogma of apostolic succession.

The Commonitory has been extremely popular. It has been printed, so DeLabriolle tells us, more than a hundred and fifty times, counting Latin texts and translations into the various vernaculars. The present translation was made from the text of the excellent edition by Reginald Stewart Moxon in the *Cambridge Patristic Texts* (Cambridge, 1915). This was based on collation of all four manuscripts and nine editions, and is the only edition thus far to have an adequate introduction and full commentary in English.

A complete bibliography would occupy many pages. Of Latin texts the only ones that are still of much value are the following: Etienne de Baluze, three editions (Paris, 1663, 1669, 1684), the third often reprinted, especially in J. P. Migne's *Patrologiae cursus completus*: Series Latina (Paris, 1844), Vol. 50; in H. Hürter's *SS Patrum Opuscula Selecta* 10 (Innsbruck, 1880),

p. 183. The spirit of this work is marvelously irenic: Christians not in communion with Rome are treated as brothers.

and R. M. J. Poirel's *Vincentii Peregrini seu alio nomine Marii Mercatoris Lerinensis Commonitoria duo* (Nancy, 1898). Joseph Jessing printed a Latin text *in usum scholarum* (Columbus, Ohio, 1898), from a Milan edition of 1805. G. A. Jülicher published his revision of Sichard's *editio princeps* (Basle, 1528) in Krüger's *Sammlung ausgew. kirch. u. dogmengesch. Quellenschrifte* 10 (Leipzig, 1st ed., 1906; Tübingen, 2d ed., 1925); and G. Rauschen gave us a fresh examination of the manuscripts in his *Florilegium Patristicum* (Bonn, 1906).

Ninian Winzet *alias* Wingate (1518–1592), a Roman Catholic opponent of John Knox (see *Dict. of Nat. Biogr.* 21.707 f.), issued at Antwerp in 1563 *A richt goldin buke written in Latin about XI C zeris passit and neulie translated in Scottis be Niniane Winzeit a catholik Preist*, reprinted as "Certaine Tractates . . . and a Translation" by James K. Hewison for the Scottish Text Society (Edinburgh–London, 1887–1890), Vols. 15, 22. This was dedicated to Mary, Queen of Scots. The language is intelligible to English readers with the help of Hewison's notes.

E. B. Pusey included in his *Library of the Fathers* (London–Oxford, 1837; reprinted, London–Belfast, 1874) a revision of a 1651 anonymous translation preserved in a Bodleian manuscript (8vo D. 261 Linc.). Later translations include one by J. Stock (London, 1879), with notes; another by C. A. Heurtley (NPNF, 2d ser., 11.123–159 [New York, 1894]); a third by T. H. Bindley in *Early Christian Classics* (London–New York, 1914), and, most recently, still another by Rudolph E. Marcus in *Fathers of the Church* (New York, 1949) 7.255–332 (Rauschen's text is followed, with some of his notes).

On Vincent's life and work the most useful discussions, besides Moxon's introduction, are the following: G. Bardy, article in DTC 15.3045–3055; P. DeLabriolle, *Histoire de la littérature latine chrétienne* (Paris, 2d ed., 1924) 568–570, tr. by H. Wilson (New York, 1925) 425 f.; the 2d ed. revised by G. Bardy (Paris, 1947) 2.649–655; G. A. Jülicher, article in RE 20.670–675, revised and abridged in NSH 12.192–194; H. Kihn, article in KL 12.985–989; Hugo Koch, "Vincentius von Lerinum und Marius Mercator" (*Theol. Quartalschr.* 81 [1899] 396–434), and his "Vincenz von Lerin und Gennadius" (TU 31 = 3d ser., 1[1907] 37–58); Jules Lebreton, "Saint Vincent de Lérins et saint Augustine" (*Rech. de Sc. Rel.* 30 [1940] 368 f.), and the following, all by José Madoz S.J.: "Contra quien escritio San Vicente de Lerins su Conmonitorio" (*Estudios Ecles.* 10 [1931] 534); "El testimonio de Gennadio sobre s. Vicente de

Lerins" (*ibid.* 11 [1932] 484); "El concepto de la tradicion en S. Vicente de Lerins" (*Analecta Gregoriana* 5 [Rome, 1933], by far the ablest discussion in any language); "El Conmonitorio de San Vicente de Lerins" (Madrid, 1935), a Spanish translation; "Un tratado desconocido de San Vicente de Lerins" (*Gregorianum* 21 [1940] 75–94); and "Cultura humanistica de San Vicente de Lerins su Conmonitorio" (*Rech. de Sc. Rel.* 39 [1951] 461–471).

Vincent of Lérins: The Commonitory

THE TEXT

PEREGRINUS' TREATISE ON BEHALF OF THE ANTIQUITY AND ECUMENICITY OF THE CATHOLIC FAITH AGAINST THE PROFANE NOVELTIES OF ALL HERETICS

1. Preface

"Ask your fathers and they will tell you; your elders, and they will speak" (Deut. 32:7, OL).

"Fit your ear to the words of the wise" (Prov. 22:17, OL).

"My son, forget not these speeches but let your heart keep my words" (Prov. 3:1, OL).

Remembering these words of counsel from Scripture, I, Peregrinus, who am the least of all the servants of God, think that it would be of no slight value, and certainly, in view of my own weakness, very necessary, should I entrust to writing what I have faithfully received from the holy fathers.[37] Thus, I should have readily available the means of supplementing the defects of a poor memory by constant reading of it. I am encouraged to undertake this task, not only by the fruit of the labor, but also by consideration of time and the opportunity of place: by consideration of time, because as time snatches away everything human, we in turn ought also to snatch from it what may advance us toward life eternal, particularly since "a fearful prospect of the approach of judgment" [38] divine exacts from us zeal for religion, and the cunning of new heretics imposes upon us much anxiety and attention. The opportunity of place stimulates me because, shunning as we do the crowdedness of cities and their throngs, we now reside in a small farmhouse belonging to the monastery, and relatively secluded, where, apart from every distraction, there can exist that quiet peace of which the psalmist sings, "Be still and see that I am Lord."[39]

---

[37] Tertullian, *De praescript. haer.* for which see LCC, vol. 5.
[38] Heb. 10:27.
[39] Ps. 46:10 (45:10, V). The reading is Old Latin.

In addition, it well suits our purpose. Though for some little time we were tossed about in the many storms of this life's warfare, at last we have brought ourselves, thanks to Christ's favoring gale, into religion's haven, a harbor ever most safe for all men. Having stilled the blasts of vanity and pride, propitiating God by the sacrifice of Christian humility, we can escape not only the shipwrecks of this present life but the fires of the age to come.[40]

Now, in the Lord's name, however, I shall attempt the task which presses me on, that is, to write down, with the fidelity of a recorder rather than the presumption of an author, what has been handed down[41] by the men of earlier time and entrusted to our keeping, taking care to observe, as I write, the principle of not reporting everything that might be said but limiting myself to the essential points, and to present even these, not in language that is flowery and measured, but in simple and everyday speech, with more truth implicit than explicit. Let those write elegantly and with close attention to style who are impelled to this task either by confidence in their ability or by fulfillment of duty. I shall myself be content with having stimulated my memory, or rather my forgetfulness, by providing myself with a commonitory. This, however, I shall daily attempt to correct and supplement, little by little, while working over what I have learned, the Lord being my helper. I have set down this warning at the outset, so that, if by chance the manuscript should slip into the hands of holy men, they will not hastily criticize it, when they see in it what should be corrected by the promised polishing.

II. The Standard Test for Orthodoxy

1. As often, then, as I have made earnest and diligent inquiries of men outstanding for their holiness and learning, seeking to distinguish, by some sure and, as it were, universal rule, between the truth of the catholic faith and the falsity of heretical perversity, I would get from almost everyone some such answer: Should I or any other person wish to unmask the frauds of heretics as they arise, and avoid their snares, and in healthy faith to remain sound and whole, we would, with the Lord's help, doubly fortify our own faith, first, of course, by the authority of the divine law, and, second, by the tradition of the catholic church.

---

[40] Cf. Salvian, *De gub. Dei* 8 (to end). [41] Tradition, oral and written.

2. Here someone may possibly ask: Since the canon of the Scriptures is complete, and is abundantly sufficient for every purpose, what need is there to add to it the authority of the church's interpretation? The reason is, of course, that by its very depth the Holy Scripture is not received by all in one and the same sense, but its declarations are subject to interpretation, now in one way, now in another, so that, it would appear, we can find almost as many interpretations as there are men.[42] Novatian[43] expounds it in one way, Sabellius in another, Donatus in another; Arius, Eunomius, Macedonius, in another; Photinus, Apollinaris, Priscillian, in another; Jovinian, Pelagius, Caelestius, in another; finally, Nestorius, in still another. For this reason it is very necessary that, on account of so great intricacies of such varied error, the line used in the exposition of the prophets and apostles be made straight in accordance with the standard of ecclesiastical and catholic interpretation.

3. Likewise in the catholic church itself especial care must be taken that we hold to that which has been believed everywhere, always, and by all men.[44] For that is truly and rightly "catholic,"[45] as the very etymology of the word shows, which includes almost all universally. This result will be reached if we follow ecumenicity,[46] antiquity, consensus. We shall follow ecumenicity if we acknowledge as the one true faith what the whole church throughout the world confesses. So also we shall follow antiquity if we retreat not one inch from those interpretations which, it is clear, the holy men of old and our fathers proclaimed. Likewise, we shall follow consensus if in antiquity[47] itself we earnestly strive after the pronouncements and opinions of all, or certainly almost all, the priests[48] and teachers alike.

---

[42] Cf. *quot homines, tot sententiae* (Terence, *Phorm.* 2.4.14; Cicero, *De fin.* 1.5.15).

[43] The persons named in this paragraph are all well-known heretics. On Donatus see G. G. Willis, *Saint Augustine and the Donatist Controversy* (London, 1950); W. H. C. Frend, *The Donatist Church: A Movement of Protest in North Africa* (Oxford, 1952). For a recent appraisal of Nestorius, see Aubrey R. Vine, *An Approach to Christology* (London, 1948).

[44] The famous formula: *Quod ubique, quod semper, et quod ab omnibus.*

[45] From καθ' ὅλου, *on the whole.* The earliest application of this phrase to the church is in Ignatius, *Ad Smyrn.* 8.

[46] *Universitas* corresponds to *ubique* in the formula.

[47] *Vetustas* and *antiquitas* are normally synonymous in Vincent.

[48] *Sacerdos* (pl., *sacerdotes*), in Vincent and many other authors, can mean either *priest* or *bishop*, sometimes clearly one or the other, at other times

III. A Rule for Evaluating Dissent

4. What, then, will the catholic Christian do if some small part of the church cuts itself apart from the communion of the universal faith? What, certainly, except to prefer the health of the whole body to the diseased and injured part?[49] What if some new contagion should try to infect not only this insignificant part but the whole church likewise? Then he will watch out that he cling to antiquity, which no longer can be led astray by any new deception.

What, however, if in antiquity itself error be unmasked in two or three men, or even in one city or in some province? Then, to be sure, he will carefully oppose the rashness or ignorance of the few with the decrees of a universal council, arrived at universally, in olden times, if such there be. But what if some such error should arise on which no pertinent decree can be found? Then he will undertake to examine and investigate the views of the forefathers and to compare them with each other, yet only of those who, though living in different times and places, yet steadfastly remained in communion and faith with the one catholic church, and stand out as teachers worthy of acceptance. Whatsoever he discovers that not one or two alone, but all together, with one and the same agreement, openly, often, and continually, have held, have written, have taught, let him also understand that he must believe this without any hesitation.

IV. Effects of the Donatist and Arian Heresies

To make our meaning clearer, however, we must illustrate it by individual examples, amplify it a bit more fully, lest hasty discussion and overcondensation may cause matters of real importance to be lost.

5. In the time of Donatus, from whom the Donatists take their name, when great numbers in Africa hurled themselves headlong into the madness of their error, and when, without regard for their name, their religion, their profession, they set a higher store on the profane boldness of one man than on the church of Christ, then those who throughout Africa, detesting the profane schism, remained steadfast in communion with all

not clearly distinguishable. We call attention to this word wherever it occurs.
[49] Cf. Matt. 18:8.

the churches in the world, alone of them all could be safe within the sacred precincts of the catholic faith, leaving to posterity a remarkable example of how thenceforth the moral wholesomeness of all should be preferred to the madness of one or, at any rate, of a few.

6. So, too, when the poison of the Arians had infected, this time not some small part of the world but almost all the bishops[50] of the Latin tongue, preventing them from seeing the best course to follow in such great confusion, whoever then stood out, a true lover and worshiper of Christ, preferring the ancient faith to the new sort of unbelief, remained unspotted by this new contagion.

The danger of this period abundantly demonstrated how much calamity is introduced by the appearance of a new doctrine. Then not only concerns of smallest import but even of the highest are ruined.[51] Not only relationships by marriage and by blood, friendships, families, but cities, provinces, nations—even the whole Roman Empire—were shaken and uprooted from their foundations.

For when this godless innovation of the Arians, like some Bellona or some Fury, had first of all taken captive the emperor,[52] and had then subjected to new laws the palace officials, thenceforth it never ceased to create confusion everywhere, involving in it everything public and private, sacred and profane, with no respect for what was good and true, but striking down whomsoever it pleased as if it itself enjoyed a higher position of authority. Then wives were violated,[53] widows stripped of their weeds, virgins profaned, monasteries demolished, clergy ejected, deacons scourged, bishops (*sacerdos*) exiled; workhouses, prisons, mines, filled with saints, of whom the greater part, banned from the cities, thrust forth and exiled, amidst the deserts,[54] caves, wild beasts, and rocks, afflicted with nakedness, hunger, and thirst, were worn out and destroyed. Was there any other cause of all this than that in place of

---

[50] More than four hundred bishops were present at Ariminum on October 10, 359. The resultant creed is printed in LCC, vol. 3, pp. 341 f. See Jerome, *Dial. adv. Lucif.* 19; Sulpicius Severus, *Chron.* 2.43 (NPNF, 2d ser., 11.116 f.). The situation was doubtless worse in the East.
[51] Cf. Sallust, *Bell. Iug.* 10.
[52] Constantius II (son of Constantine the Great) was emperor in the East 337–350, sole emperor 350–361.
[53] Possible sources: Ambrose, *De fide*; Hilary's book against Constantius; Jerome, *Dial. adv. Lucif.* 19, and Athanasius, *Epist. Encycl.*, esp. 3.6.
[54] Cf. Heb. 11:38.

heavenly doctrine human superstitions are inaugurated, that well-founded antiquity is being overthrown by wicked innovation, that the institutions of our predecessors are being destroyed, that the decrees of the fathers are being rescinded, that the decisions of our ancestors are being brought to naught, that within the most pure bounds of hallowed and uncorrupt antiquity, the lust of a wicked and novel inquisitiveness does not confine itself?

V. The Martyrs' Defense of the Ancient Faith

7. But perhaps we invent these stories out of hatred for the new and love for the old? Let him who thinks so hearken at least to the blessed Ambrose who, in the second book he addressed to the Emperor Gratian, complaining of the bitterness of the times, says:

> "O Almighty God! Sufficiently have we now by our banishment, by our blood, expiated the slaughter of the confessors, the exiles of bishops (*sacerdos*), and the crime of such great impiety. Sufficiently has it become clear that those who have violated the faith cannot be safe."[55]

Likewise in the third book of this same work, he says:

> "Let us preserve the teachings of our predecessors, and let us not rashly and rudely break the seals[56] we have inherited from them. That sealed book of the prophets[57] no elders,[58] no powers, no angels, no archangels have dared open. To Christ alone has been preserved the right to explain it. Who of us may dare to unseal the sacerdotal book, sealed by the confessors and hallowed already by the martyrdom of many? They who had been forced to unseal this, nevertheless, afterward sealed it again, condemning the fraud practiced upon them; they who had not dared to tamper with it became confessors and martyrs. How can we deny the faith of those whose victory we proclaim?"[59]

We proclaim it clearly, I say, O venerable Ambrose! We proclaim it clearly, and marvel at it as we praise. For who is that man so crazy that, though he is unable to overtake, does not long to take after those whom, from defending the faith of

---

[55] Ambrose, *De fide* 2.16.141 (NPNF, 2d ser., 10.242), written in 378.
[56] Cf. Rev. 5:2. [57] Cf. Rev. 5:1–5. [58] *Seniores*, not *presbyteri*.
[59] Ambrose, *De fide* 3.15.128 (NPNF, 2d ser., 10.260).

our predecessors, no power repelled, no threats, no blandishments, not life, not death, not the palace, not the imperial guards, not the emperor, not the empire, not men, not demons? These, I say, in return for their steadfastness to the ancient religion, the Lord judged worthy of so great a reward that through them[60] he restored churches that had been laid low, brought back to life peoples that were spiritually dead; set back on the heads of bishops (*sacerdos*) crowns[61] that had been torn off; washed away those wicked blots,[62] not letters, of the novel impiety, with a fountain of faithful tears poured from heaven upon the bishops; lastly, when almost the whole world was overwhelmed by a fierce hurricane of sudden heresy, summoned it back to the ancient faith from the new kind of faithlessness, to the ancient sanity from the new madness, to the ancient light from the new blindness.

8. But in this divine virtue of the confessors, as it were, the point we should mark especially is that the defense they then undertook in the case of the ancient church was not of some part of it but the whole. It was not right that men so important and of such character should, with so great an effort, support the false and inconsistent notions of one or two men, or should contend on behalf of some conspiracy in any little province, but favoring the decrees and definitions[63] of all the bishops (*sacerdos*) of holy church, heirs of catholic and apostolic truth, they preferred to surrender themselves rather than to surrender the faith of ecumenical antiquity. For this reason they deserved to reach such great renown as to be justly and deservedly considered not only confessors but even chiefs among the confessors.

VI. The Question of Rebaptizing Heretics

9. Great, therefore, is this example of these same blessed men, and clearly divine, worthy of being cherished by all true catholics in unwearied contemplation. Like the seven-branched

---

[60] E.g., Athanasius, Hilary, Eusebius of Vercellae. Cf. Jerome, *Dial. adv. Lucif.* 19.
[61] Bishops, as such, wore no crowns but the word was sometimes used by metonymy in addressing the pope and other bishops (by Priscillian, Jerome, Paulinus of Nola, etc., cited in *Thesaurus Linguae Latinae* 4.984). Cf. Rev. 2:10.
[62] *Lituras*, making a pun with *litteras*, a play also used by Ovid, *Tristia* 3.1.15.
[63] *Decreta*, decisions with reference to practice, *definitiones*, those with reference to doctrine (so Moxon).

candlestick[64] shining with the sevenfold[65] light of the Holy Spirit, they exhibited to posterity a very clear example of how thenceforth, through the list of empty babblings of errors, the boldness of the profane innovation might be crushed by the authority of hallowed antiquity. This, of course, is nothing new. Indeed, the character of the church has always been so strong that the more a man is devoted to religion, the more is he ready to oppose innovations. Numerous examples exist, but in order not to prolong the discussion unduly, let us take one and, most preferably, one from the Apostolic See,[66] so that all may see clearer than day with how much force, how much zeal, how much energy the blessed successors of the blessed apostles have always defended the integrity of the religion they received.

Once upon a time, then, Agrippinus,[67] bishop of Carthage, a man of venerable memory, was the first of all human beings to hold the view that men ought to be rebaptized,[68] a contention contrary to the divine canon, contrary to the rule of the universal church, contrary to the opinions of all his fellow bishops,[69] contrary to the custom and institutions of the forefathers. This view brought in so much evil that not only did it furnish an example of sacrilege to all heretics, but even a cause for error by certain catholics[70] as well. When, therefore, from all sides all men cried out against this innovation, and all the priests (*sacerdos*) everywhere were restrained each only by his own zeal, then Pope Stephen, of blessed memory, bishop[71] of the Apostolic See, with others indeed as his confreres, yet nevertheless, prior to them, withstood it, thinking it proper, as I suppose, that he ought to surpass all the others in devotion to the faith as he was superior to them by prestige of place.[72] Well,

[64] Cf. Ex. 25:31–40.   [65] Cf. Rev. 1:12.
[66] A term applicable to any see founded by an apostle or possessing an apostolic letter (Augustine, *De doctr. Christ.* 2.13), but Vincent doubtless means Rome.
[67] Agrippinus preceded Donatus (not the Great) who was Cyprian's predecessor as bishop of Carthage. He held the first Council of Carthage, c. 213–225, or even earlier, at which seventy bishops were present. The question discussed was rebaptism.
[68] An oversimplification of a thorny problem: whether those baptized by a heretical sect, e.g., Novatian's followers, should again be baptized. Rome did not follow the practice, the church in Africa and Asia did. The question was settled at the Council of Arles (314).
[69] *Consacerdotes.* See note 48, p. 38.   [70] E.g., Cyprian.
[71] *Antistes*: in pagan Latin *priest* but in ecclesiastical Latin generally applied to a bishop worthy of special respect. This bishop was Stephen I (254–257), participant in the rebaptism controversy.
[72] *Loci auctoritate.*

in the letter which was at that time sent to Africa, he gave his sanction as follows: "Nothing ought to be renewed except what has been handed down."[73] That holy and wise man knew that the plan of piety admits of nothing else than that everything in the faith which has been received from our fathers should be handed on in faith to our sons; that it is our duty not to lead religion where we wish but to follow where it leads; that it is the peculiar quality of Christian modesty and gravity, not to hand down to posterity its own accomplishments, but to preserve what it has received from our predecessors. What, then, was the result of all this? What but the usual and customary one? Antiquity was, of course, retained; novelty was hissed off the stage.

10. But perhaps the side of innovation then lacked defenders? On the contrary, it had at hand so great a force of talent, such great streams of eloquence, so great a number of supporters, so much appearance of the truth, such great citation from the oracles of the divine law—though naturally interpreted in a new and erroneous sense—that it appears to me that that whole conspiracy could not have been destroyed without the destruction of the sole cause of this endeavor, that very thing so undertaken, defended, praised, the profession of novelty. What happened in the end? What effect did that African Council[74] or decree itself have? Through God's gift, none at all. The whole business was abolished, destroyed, trodden down, as if a dream, as if a fable, as if unnecessary.

11. O marvelous reversal of the situation! The authors[75] of this same doctrine are adjudged catholics, the followers heretics. The teachers are absolved, the disciples condemned. The writers of the books will be "sons of the Kingdom,"[76] the supporters will receive punishment in hell. For who is so mad that he would doubt that that most blessed light of all the saints and bishops and martyrs, Cyprian, with his other colleagues,

---

[73] Quoted also by Cyprian, *Epist.* 74.1.2 (*ad Pompeium*), in slightly different form: "If they come to you from any heresy, let nothing be renewed except what has been handed down, namely, the hand should be placed on them for penitence, since the heretics themselves do not baptize any who come to them, but only communicate with them."

[74] The third of three councils held under Cyprian, this one in 256, reported by Augustine, *De baptismo contra Donatistas*, Books 6–7. Cf. Cyprian, *Epist.* 69–75.

[75] Both Cyprian and Agrippinus had affirmed the necessity of rebaptizing heretics but were not condemned.

[76] Matt. 13:38.

will reign forever with Christ? Or who, on the other hand, is so sacrilegious as to deny that the Donatists and other pests who, on the authority of that council, keep boasting that they rebaptize, will burn eternally with the devil?

VII. HERETICS QUOTE SCRIPTURES

This judgment seems to me to have been promulgated with divine sanction particularly because of the fraud of those who plot to deck out heresy under a name not its own, often try to lay their hands on the works of some ancient worthy written a bit vaguely, which, owing to the obscurity of their own doctrine, agree, so it might seem, with it, so that they seem not to be the first or even the only ones who believe that vague belief which they advance. Their wickedness I judge to be worthy of a double hatred, both because they have no fear of setting before others the poisoned cup of heresy; and because their godless hands fan the embers, now deadened into ash, of the memory of each saintly man, and any features of his career which ought to be buried in silence they revive by defaming them abroad, following completely the steps of Ham[77] as their precedent. He not only failed to cover the nakedness of Noah, who ought to have been treated with tactful respect, but even reported it to others to be laughed at. For this reason Ham so deserved punishment for his offense against filial duty that even his descendants[78] were involved in the curse deriving from his sin. Far, far different was the lot of those blessed brothers of his who were unwilling to defile with their own eyes the nakedness of their respected father, nor to allow any others to do it, but covered him, as it is written, walking backward. That is, the sin of the holy man[79] they neither approved nor betrayed, and for this reason they were rewarded with a blessed benediction for their descendants. But let us return to the matter we proposed to discuss.

12. We ought, with great fear, to dread the sin of altered and polluted faith, a crime from which we are deterred not only by the teaching of the church's constitution but also by the authority of apostolic censure. It is known to all how seriously, how gravely, how vehemently, the blessed apostle Paul inveighs against certain persons who with wondrous fickle-

---
[77] Gen. 9:22.
[78] Canaan, son of Ham, ancestor of the Canaanites (Gen. 9:18, 25).
[79] Perhaps a veiled allusion to Augustine.

ness had been too soon removed from Him "who called them into the grace of Christ," to " that gospel which was not something else" [80]; "who had accumulated for themselves teachers to suit their own likings, turning them away from listening to truth and causing them to turn toward myths" [81]; "incurring condemnation for having violated their pledge" [82]; who had been deceived by those of whom the same apostle writes to his Roman brethren: "I ask you, brethren, to observe those who create dissensions and difficulties in opposition to the doctrine which you yourself have learned, and to avoid them. For such persons do not serve the Lord Christ but their own belly, and by fair speeches and blessings they seduce the hearts of the innocent" [83]; "who enter into households and capture weak women burdened with sins, who are led by various impulses; always learning and never arriving at a knowledge of the truth" [84]; "empty talkers and deceivers who upset whole families, teaching what they have no right to teach, for the sake of base gain" [85]; "men of corrupt mind, of counterfeit faith" [86]; "proud, yet knowing nothing, but are listless about controversy and disputes about words; who are bereft of truth, imagining that godliness is a means of monetary gain" [87]; "at the same time they learn also to be idlers, gadding about from house to house, and are not only idlers but gossips and busybodies saying what they should not" [88]; "who rejecting a good conscience have made shipwreck of their faith" [89]; "whose profane and vain babblings are conducive to ungodliness and their talk creeps in like cancer." [90] Quite properly, also, is it written of them, "But they will not get very far, for their folly will be plain to all, as was that of those men." [91]

VIII. Exegesis of Galatians 1:8

When, therefore, certain people of this sort went about among the provinces and the cities, carrying with them their errors for sale, and had come to the Galatians, and when the Galatians, upon hearing them, were nauseated,[92] as it were, by the truth, and vomited up the manna of apostolic and catholic doctrine, and were pleased by the garbage of the new heresy,

---

[80] Gal. 1:6, 7.   [81] II Tim. 4:3, 4.   [82] I Tim. 5:12.
[83] Rom. 16:17, 18.   [84] II Tim. 3:6, 7.   [85] Titus 1:10, 11.
[86] II Tim. 3:8.   [87] I Tim. 6:4, 5.   [88] I Tim. 5:13.
[89] I Tim. 1:19.   [90] II Tim. 2:16, 17.
[91] II Tim. 3:9: "those men" are Jannes and Jambres.
[92] Cf. Num. 21:5.

the authority of apostolic power put itself forth, so that with the greatest severity he [Paul] made his pronouncement: "If we," he says, "or an angel from heaven should preach to you a gospel contrary to what we have preached to you, let him be accursed."[93]

What does he mean by, "If we"? Why not rather, "If I"? Because, though Peter, though Andrew, though John, though, finally, the whole company[94] of the apostles "should preach to you a gospel contrary to what we have preached to you, let him be accursed."

A tremendous severity, on account of his steadfast adherence to the faith that was first delivered,[95] he has spared neither himself nor his fellow apostles! And this is a small part of it. He says, "Though an angel from heaven should preach a gospel to you contrary to what we have preached to you, let him be accursed." It was not enough, for the preservation of the faith once delivered, to have mentioned the nature of man's condition, unless he also included the superior state of the angels also. "If we," he says, "or an angel from heaven." Not that the holy angels in heaven can now sin, but what he says is this: If, he says, what cannot happen comes to happen, whoever tries to alter the faith once delivered, let him be accursed.

13. But perhaps he spoke carelessly and with human impetuosity poured forth the decree, rather than with divine guidance? Perish the thought! For he continues in the following verse and emphasizes the very point by tremendous reiteration: "As we said before, so now I say again: If any person should preach to you a gospel contrary to what you have received, let him be accursed."[96] He did not say: If any man should preach contrary to what you have received, let him be blessed, let him be praised, let him be accepted, but he said, "Let him be accursed," that is,[97] separated, segregated, excluded, lest the dire contagion of a single sheep infect the blameless flock of Christ by poisonous contact when intermingled with them.

IX. THE WARNING TO THE GALATIANS APPLIES TO ALL

But perhaps these teachings were for the Galatians only? Very well, but in that case those commandments stated in the following chapters of the same epistle apply to the Galatians only, such as: "If we live by the Spirit, let us also walk in the

---

[93] Gal. 1:8. [94] Cf. Cyprian, *De mortal.* 26; also the Te Deum.
[95] Cf. Jude 3. [96] Gal. 1:9. [97] Excommunication, not eternal death.

Spirit. Let us not become desirous of vain glory, provoking, envying one another," [98] et cetera. If this is absurd, and the commandments apply equally to everyone, then it follows that just as these injunctions which relate to conduct, so also those provisions concerning faith apply to all men in equal fashion.

14. And just as it is unlawful for any men to provoke one another, or to envy one another, so it is unlawful for anyone to receive any gospel contrary to what the catholic church everywhere preaches.

Or perhaps when it was said that anyone who preached contrary to what had been preached should be accursed, the directive was meant to be in force then, but there will be no command to curse in the present time. Very well, but then that which he also says there, "But I say, walk by the Spirit and do not gratify the desire of the flesh," [99] was in that case applicable to those times, but now will not apply. If, however, it be wrong and wicked to believe this, then it follows of necessity that as these injunctions are to be observed in all ages, so also those commandments which forbid the changing of the faith are also for all ages. To preach something to catholic Christians contrary to what they have received never was lawful, never is lawful,[1] never will be lawful, and to put under the ban those who preach anything other than what was once received, never was unlawful, never is unlawful, never will be unlawful.

Since this is so, is there anybody so bold as to preach contrary to what was preached under the auspices of the church, or so fickle as to receive contrary to what he received from the church? That man, that "chosen instrument,"[2] that "teacher of the Gentiles,"[3] that trumpet of the apostles, that herald of all the earth, that one with knowledge of the things in the heavens,[4] cries out, and again cries out, to all men, and always, everywhere, through his epistles, that if any man should preach some new doctrine, he should be accursed. On the other hand, the frogs, and gnats and flies,[5] about to die, such as are the Pelagians,[6] cry out, and even to catholics, saying, "Take us for

---

[98] Gal. 5:25, 26. [99] Gal. 5:16.
[1] Cf. Horace, *Ars Poetica* 58 f. [2] Acts 9:15 (σκεῦος ἐκλογῆς = *vas electionis*).
[3] II Tim. 1:11. [4] Cf. II Cor. 12:2.
[5] Cf. Ex. 8:6, 16, 21; Eccl. 10:1 (where *dying* flies, not flies *about to die*, are mentioned; a text used in the Donatist controversy by several writers, e.g., Jerome, Augustine, Optatus, Fulgentius, and Gelasius, all of whom, like Vincent, have *about to die*).
[6] Vincent does not approve of the Pelagians, even if he did not wholly approve of the Augustinian view.

your authorities; take us for your leaders; take us for your expositors; condemn what you used to hold; hold what you used to condemn; throw away the ancient faith, the institutions of your fathers, the deposit of your forebears, and accept"—what? I shudder at the thought of uttering it, for it is so arrogant a set of doctrines that not only could it not be stated as a fact but also could not even be refuted without incurring some sort of guilt.

X. Why New Doctrines Are Sometimes Permitted in the Church

15. But some will say: How then does it happen that certain excellent persons who are in the church are often divinely permitted to preach new doctrines to catholics? A proper question and one quite worthy of more careful and fuller treatment, but it must be answered, not on the basis of one's own ability, but with reliance on the authority of divine law, the pattern of the church's teaching.

Let us listen to the holy Moses and let him teach us why learned men and those who on account of their knowledge are even called prophets by the apostle,[7] are sometimes permitted to produce new doctrines which the Old Testament is wont to call, in an allegorical sense, "other gods"—this because, of course, the heretics give as much veneration to their opinions as the pagans do to their gods. In Deuteronomy the blessed Moses writes,[8] "If there should arise among you a prophet or one who says he has had a dream"—that is, a teacher appointed in the church, whose disciples or whose hearers believe he speaks by a revelation—what then? He continues, "And he should describe a sign or wonder, and what he has said should come to pass"—certainly some great teacher of such knowledge that he can appear to his own followers to know, not only things human but also things superhuman, such as their disciples boast were Valentinus, Donatus, Photinus, Apollinaris, and others of that stripe. What then? "And should say to you, 'Let us go and follow other gods whom you do not know, and let us serve them.'" What are these "other gods" but strange errors? "Whom you do not know," that is, new ones and unheard of? "And let us serve them," that is, let us believe them, follow them. What does he say in the end? "You shall not listen to the words of that prophet or dreamer."

And why, I ask you, does God permit to be taught what he

[7] I Cor. 14:3, 37.   [8] Deut. 13:1, 2.

does not permit to be listened to? He says: "Because the Lord your God is testing you to make it known whether or not you love him with your whole heart and with all your soul." [9] Clearer than broad daylight is the reason why sometimes divine Providence suffers teachers of the churches to preach new doctrines: "That the Lord your God," he says, "may test you." Assuredly, it is a great testing when the one you think a prophet, a disciple of the prophets, a teacher and supporter of the truth, whom you have embraced with the greatest respect and affection—when he, suddenly and secretly, insinuates harmful errors which you are neither able quickly to detect, because you are led on by the prestige of his former authority, and cannot early decide to condemn, because you are fettered by affection for your old teacher.

XI. Nestorius, Photinus, Apollinaris

16. Here possibly someone may insist that the views supported by the words of the holy Moses be illustrated by examples drawn from the church. This is a just demand, one that cannot long be disregarded.

I shall begin with examples of most recent date and the most incontrovertible. What a trial do we think that recently was when that wretch Nestorius, suddenly transformed from a sheep into a wolf, began to rend the flock of Christ, while those he was gnawing at still in large part believed him still a sheep and therefore laid themselves open all the more to his sharp teeth? For who could easily imagine him to wander from the path who he saw was chosen by the mighty judgment of the emperor,[10] and attended by so great a zeal on the part of the priests?[11] when he was known to enjoy the great affection of the saints, the highest favor with the people? who daily expounded the divine books, and refuted the harmful errors of both Jews and pagans? How could any man fail to give proof that he was teaching aright, preaching aright, and believing aright, when, to gain an opening for his own single heresy, he kept attacking the blasphemies of all heresies?[12] This was, however, the situation that Moses speaks of: "The Lord your God is testing you to make it known whether or not you love him."

---

[9] Deut. 13:3. [10] Theodosius II.
[11] *Sacerdotes*, probably *priests*, here.
[12] Socrates (*Hist. Eccl.* 7.29) quotes him as saying to the emperor, "Give me the world pure from heretics and I shall give you heaven in return."

Passing on from Nestorius, in whom there was always more to excite admiration than profit, more renown than real knowledge, a man whose natural endowments—not divine grace—had for a time created the belief among the people that he was great, let us make mention of those who, endowed with great merits and with great energy, became no small trial for the catholics. Such a man was Photinus who, in Pannonia, in the memory of our fathers, is reported to have tried the church of Sirmium,[13] where, with the approval of everyone, he had been advanced to the office of bishop[14] and for some time administered it as a catholic, suddenly, like that wicked "prophet or dreamer" whom Moses means, he began to persuade God's people that were entrusted to him, to follow "other gods," that is, strange errors, which it did not know before. There was nothing unusual in this: the particular danger was that, to accomplish so great a crime, he made use of no ordinary aids. For he had great natural ability, was outstanding in learning, and very eloquent, able to debate and write, as he was, fluently and powerfully in both languages, as is shown by his monumental works which he wrote partly in Greek and partly in Latin.[15] But fortunate it was that those of Christ's sheep who were entrusted to him, ever on guard and wary for the catholic faith, quickly turned their gaze to those admonitory words of Moses, and if they were impressed by the eloquence of their prophet and shepherd, were yet not unaware that they were being tested, for thenceforth they began to flee from him as a wolf whom hitherto they had followed as the ram of the flock.

Not only from the example of Photinus but also from that of Apollinaris do we learn the danger of that great trial of the church and are given warning at the same time about the necessity of guarding with greater care the faith that must be preserved. For he himself gave rise among his disciples to great burning questions and great perplexities, since the authority of the church was drawing them one way, the association of their teacher withdrawing them the other, so that, wavering and vacillating between the two, they knew not which was better to accept.

But possibly the man was one of such a sort as to be easily ignored. On the contrary, he was so powerful and of such character that on most topics he was too quickly believed. What could surpass his acuteness, his skill, his learning? How

[13] Sirmium was an important city in Lower Pannonia, near Mitrovitz.
[14] *Sacerdotium.* See note 48, p. 38.   [15] None survives.

many heresies in how many books did he crush! How many errors hostile to the faith did he refute! The proof is that work in no fewer than thirty books, a very famous and monumental undertaking, in which he, with a great mass of proofs, reduced to naught the mad calumnies of Porphyry. To mention all his[16] works would require a long time. These certainly could make him the peer of the greatest builders of the church, had his passion for heretical inquisitiveness not led him to devise something new, which polluted, like leprosy, all his labors and caused his teaching to be called, not the church's edification, but its temptation.

XII. Errors of Photinus, Apollinaris, and Nestorius

At this point I may be requested to explain the heresies which I have mentioned above, that is, those of Nestorius, Apollinaris, and Photinus. This is not, indeed, pertinent to the question at issue. We have not entertained the thought of tracing completely the errors of each heretic but of adducing examples of a few who illustrate well and clearly the remark of Moses to the effect that if ever some teacher in the church, himself a prophet in interpreting the mysteries of the prophets, should try to introduce something new into the church of God, divine Providence then suffers this to happen for our trial.

17. As a digression,[17] therefore, it will be useful to give a brief exposition of the views of the above-mentioned heretics, that is, of Photinus, Apollinaris, Nestorius.

The doctrines of Photinus are as follows: He says that God is single[18] and mere man,[19] and should be regarded as the Jews regarded him. He denies the fullness of the Trinity and does not think there is any such person[20] as God the Word or as the Holy Spirit. Christ he regards as no more than a mere man[19] who got his beginning, according to Photinus, from Mary. And he propounds it to be in every way Christian teaching that one should worship only the person[20] of God the Father and

---

[16] Apollinaris', not Porphyry's.
[17] Vincent's exposition of the Trinity extends to the end of Ch. XVI.
[18] I.e., "one," a strongly monotheistic view, as opposed to the trinitarian concept.
[19] *Solitarius.*
[20] Throughout this passage the word *person* has the technical sense drawn from the theater, i.e., it connotes the idea of impersonation not found in the English word normally.

that Christ should be cherished only as a man. So much for Photinus' views.

Apollinaris boasts, however, that he is in harmony with the church on the unity of the Trinity, though not even in this respect with full soundness of faith, but on the doctrine of the Lord's incarnation he blasphemes in open fashion. For he says that in the very flesh of our Saviour there existed, either no human soul at all, or that he was not possessed of a rational soul. Moreover, this same flesh of the Lord did not come into being from the flesh of the holy Virgin Mary, but, he said, came down from heaven into the Virgin; and ever vacillating and in doubt, he kept preaching at times that it was coeternal with God the Word, at others that it was created out of the divinity of the Word. He would not have it that in Christ there are two substances, one divine, the other human, the one from the Father, the other from the mother, but he thought that the very nature of the Word was split, as if some part of it remains in God, and the other part was changed to flesh, and although truth says that of two substances Christ is one, he, contrary to the truth, maintains that of the one divinity of Christ two substances were created. Such are the views of Apollinaris.[21]

On the other hand, Nestorius, suffering from a disease the opposite of Apollinaris', while he pretends to distinguish between two substances in Christ, all at once he brings in two persons, and with unheard-of wickedness wants to have it that there are two Sons of God, two Christs, one of them God, the other, man; one derived from the Father, the other from the mother.[22] And so he maintains that the holy Mary ought to be called not the *Theotokos*[23] but *Christotokos*,[24] because, of course, she gave birth, not to that Christ who is God but to that one who was man. But if any man thinks that in his writings[25] he says there is one Christ and preaches that there is one person of Christ, let him not believe it hastily. For either he

[21] This is not what Apollinaris taught but what Vincent derived from his teaching, probably through Augustine and Epiphanius.
[22] Hostile inferences derived from Nestorius' teaching, denied by Nestorius.
[23] Greek for *God-bearer*, a term used for the Virgin after the Council of Ephesus in 431. Cf. John Cassian, *De incarn. Christi* 2.2 (MPL 50.51–57).
[24] *Christ-bearer*.
[25] Most are preserved only in fragments. In 1889, however, there was discovered in the archives of the Nestorian Church a Syriac manuscript of which the text was published in 1910 by the Lazarist Paul Bedjan and, among other translations, one in English by G. R. Driver and Leonard Hodgson in 1925: *Nestorius: The Bazaar of Heracleides*. This is a Syriac translation, probably from a Greek original, of Nestorius' own apology.

thought this up as a clever trick in order to deceive, so that through good things he might more readily persuade evil, as the apostle says, "Through good he produced death for me" [26] —either, as we have said, for the sake of deceit, in some places in his writings he boasts that he believes there is one Christ and one person of Christ—or he asserts that after the Virgin had been delivered of her child the two persons were united in one Christ, although at the time of the conception, or of the delivery, and for some little time thereafter, he asserts, there were two Christs. So that, although, of course, Christ was born an ordinary man and only that[19] and was not yet allied in unity of persons with the Word of God, afterward there descended into him the person of the Word assuming flesh; and though now the person assumed may abide in God's glory, for some time there was no difference it seems, existing between him and other men.

XIII. The Trinity and the Incarnation

18. This is the way that those mad dogs, Nestorius, Apollinaris, and Photinus, bark against the catholic faith: Photinus, by not admitting the Trinity; Apollinaris, by saying that the nature of the Word was mutable,[27] by not admitting that there are two substances in Christ and either denying the whole soul of Christ or at any rate the intelligence and reason in the soul, and maintaining that the Word of God took the place of thought; Nestorius, by claiming that there either always were, or for a time there were, two Christs. The catholic church, however, having right beliefs concerning God and our Saviour, commits neither blasphemy in the matter of the mystery of the Trinity nor in the incarnation of Christ. For she worships one divinity in the fullness of the Trinity and the equality of the Trinity in one and the same glory, and one Christ Jesus, not two, and she confesses that he is equally God and man. That, indeed, there is in him one person, but two substances, and she believes that there are two substances but one person: two substances because the Word of God is not mutable, so as to be convertible into flesh; one person, lest by professing two Sons, she might seem to be cherishing a quaternity, not a Trinity.

19. It will be, however, worth-while if we, again and again,

---

[26] Rom. 7:13.
[27] Mutable in a comprehensive sense which might even include the possibility of death or of moral alteration.

strip off the husks of the kernel of truth and examine it more distinctly and explicitly. In God is one substance but three persons; in Christ two substances, but one person. In the Trinity, different persons,[28] not different substances;[29] in the Saviour, different substances,[29] not different persons.[28] How in the Trinity are there different persons,[28] not different substances?[29] Because, of course, there is one person of the Father, another of the Son, another of the Holy Spirit. Nevertheless, the Father, Son, and Holy Spirit are not of different natures but one and the same. How in the Saviour are there different substances,[29] not different persons?[28] Because, of course, one substance is of divinity, the other of humanity. Nevertheless, the divinity and the humanity are not different persons[30] but one and the same Christ, one and the same Son of God, and one and the same person of one and the same Christ and Son of God, even as in man the flesh is one thing, and the soul another, but one and the same man is soul and flesh.

In Peter and Paul the soul is one thing, the flesh another, yet there are not two Peters, flesh and soul, or one Paul that is soul and another flesh, but there is one and the same Peter and one and the same Paul, consisting of the double and distinct nature of spirit and body.[31]

So therefore in one and the same Christ there are two substances, but one is divine, the other human; one from the Father, God, the other from the mother, the Virgin; one coeternal and equal with the Father, the other temporal and inferior[32] to the Father; one of the same substance[33] as the Father, the other of the same substance[33] as the mother, yet there is one and the same Christ in both substances.

There is not therefore one Christ who is God, another man; not one uncreated, the other created; not one incapable of suffering, the other capable of suffering;[34] not one equal with the Father, the other inferior[32] to the Father; not one from the Father, the other from the mother; but one and the same Christ is God and man, the same not created and created; the same immutable and incapable of suffering, the same both equal to and inferior to the Father; the same begotten of the

---

[28] *Alius atque alius.*   [29] *Aliud atque aliud.*   [30] *Alter et alter.*
[31] Synonyms for "soul" and "flesh."
[32] If Vincent meant "co-eternal" and "equal," above, to be synonyms, then this word should be "younger," not "inferior."
[33] *Consubstantialis* = ὁμοούσιος.   [34] Cf. Ignatius, *Epist. ad Polycarp.* 3.

Father before the ages began, the same born of the mother in time, perfect God, perfect man. In God is the highest divinity, in man the full humanity. Full humanity, I say, since it has both soul and flesh, but real flesh, our flesh, the mother's flesh; the soul endowed with understanding, powerful in mind and reason.

There is, therefore, in Christ, the word, the soul, the flesh, but all this is one Christ, one Son of God, and one Saviour and one Redeemer of us all. One, however, not by some corruptible mélange of divinity and humanity, but by a whole and single unity of person. For that union has not converted and changed one thing into another, which is the error peculiar to the Arians, but has rather so compacted both into one that while in Christ there always remains the singleness of one and the same person, there also forever endures the characteristics of each nature, by which, of course, God never begins to be body, nor at any time does the body cease to be body.

This may also be demonstrated by the example of the human status. Not only in the present life, but in the future also, each man will consist of soul and body, yet never will the body be turned to soul or the soul to body, but as each man will live eternally, so in each man will remain eternally and of necessity the difference of each substance. In Christ also the characteristic of each substance must remain its own forever, yet with the unity of person not diminished.

XIV. Jesus Christ, True Man, Not Appearance

20. But when we rather often use the word "person" and say that God became man through person, there is great reason[35] to be apprehensive lest we seem to say that God undertook the form of the Word only in imitation of human action, and that whatever of human intercourse this is, is as if suggested, not as if a real man did it, as happens usually in theaters when one man by quick changes plays several roles, none of them the man himself. For as often as some imitation of the action of another person is undertaken, so often the duties and deeds of another are undertaken, but those who act the part are not themselves the ones whose part they act. So, to make use of an example drawn from worldly life [and from the Manichaeans],[36] when a tragic actor plays the part of a

---

[35] Because of the dramatic sense of *persona* in Latin. The Manichaeans thus maintained that the Lord merely played a part.

[36] The bracketed words are probably a gloss.

priest[37] or king, he is not the priest or king. When the action ceases, the personality he had assumed ceases likewise. Far be from us so wicked and nefarious a mockery! Let it be that folly of the Manichaeans, who, preachers of illusion,[38] say that the Son of God, God, represented the person of man, not substantively, but simulated it in some pretended action and character.

The catholic faith says, however, that the Word of God was so made man that he undertook our nature, not deceptively by suggestion, but in reality and truth, and performed human actions, not as if imitating someone else, but rather as if performing his own, and certainly as if he was the person whose part he acted. So also, in what we ourselves speak, know, live, exist, we are not imitating men but are men. Peter and John, to choose them as examples, were not men by imitating men but by being men. Paul did not feign to be the apostle or pretend to be Paul, but he was the apostle and he really was Paul. So also, God, by assuming the form of the Word and having flesh, speaking, doing, suffering through the flesh, yet with no corruption of his own nature, certainly deigned not to imitate a perfect man or feign one, but deigned to perform so as not to appear or be thought to be a true man but to be one in reality.

As the soul, united to the body, is nevertheless not turned into flesh, does not imitate a human being, but is a human being not by pretense but by substance, so also God the Word—apart from any conversion of himself—uniting himself with man, was made man, not by confusion, but by imitation, but by really being man.

Abandon, then, this idea of that person that it is assumed by feigning imitation, where always one thing is and another is pretended, where he who acts is never he whom he acts. Far be it from us to believe that God the Word assumed the person of man in this deceitful manner, but rather that, while his unchangeable substance remained and while he took upon himself the nature of perfect man, he really was flesh, really man, really the person of man, not pretended but true, not imitative but substantive, not, finally, what would cease with the action but what thenceforth would remain in substance.

[37] *Sacerdos*, certainly *priest*. See note 48, p. 38.
[38] Docetism, the view that Christ merely appeared to be man, was the basis for the Manichaean Christology.

XV. Union of the Incarnation in Christ's Conception

This union of person in Christ was therefore not produced after his birth of the Virgin, but was accomplished and perfected in the very womb of the Virgin.

21. We ought to take particular care to confess not only that Christ is one but that he is always one, because it is an intolerable blasphemy for you to maintain, though you grant he is now one, that once upon a time he was not one but two, namely, that he was one following the time of his baptism, but two at the time of his birth. We shall be unable to avoid this great sacrilege unless we confess that the man was limited to God—in unity of person, of course—not from the ascension nor from the resurrection, nor from the baptism, but already in his mother, already in the womb, already, in short, in the very act of the Virgin's conception. On account of this unity of person, it comes about that the characteristics which are God's are ascribed to man and also that the characteristics of the flesh are attributed to God, without distinction and in union together.[39] This is why, by divine inspiration, he is said in the Scriptures both as Son of Man to have descended from heaven and as Lord of Glory to have been crucified on earth.[40] This is also why, when the flesh of the Lord was made, the flesh of the Lord was created, the very Word of God is said to have been made, the very wisdom is said to have been created, filled with knowledge of God, just as in foreknowledge his hands and his feet are reported as pierced.[41]

Through this unity of person, I say, it has come about by virtue of a like mystery that, since the flesh of the Word comes to birth from a mother yet perfectly chaste, the belief that God the Word himself was born of a Virgin is most strikingly catholic,[42] and its denial is most wicked. Since this is the case, God forbid that anyone should try to cheat holy Mary of her prerogatives of divine grace or of her peculiar[43] glory. For by an unusual gift of the Lord and our God, who is also her own son, she should be acknowledged most truly and most blessedly to be the *Theotokos*, but not in the sense in which a certain

---

[39] *Communicatio idiomatum* (partnership of properties).
[40] John 3:13, I Cor. 2:8. *Dominus maiestatis*, instead of *dominus gloriae*, is an Old Latin reading.
[41] Ps. 22:16 (21:17, V).
[42] *Catholicissime*, an adverb cited in *Thesaurus Linguae Latinae* 3:1618 only for this occurrence, is to be found also in Vincent's *excerpta* (see Introduction).
[43] *Specialis*.

wicked heresy[44] imagines which maintains that she ought to be called the mother of God only because, to be sure, she gave birth to a man who afterward became God, just as we say "the mother of a priest" or "the mother of a bishop,"[45] not because she bore a priest or bishop but because she brought to life a man who afterward was made priest or bishop. Holy Mary was not, I say, the *Theotokos* in such a sense, but rather because, as was said above, already in her hallowed womb that most sacred mystery was performed on account of that unparalleled and unique unity of person, as the Word in the flesh is flesh, so also the man in God is God.

XVI. Summary of the Digression on the Trinity

22. But now, to recapitulate for the purpose of refreshing our memory, let us repeat more briefly in condensed form the points made concerning the heresies which were mentioned about the catholic faith, so that when repeated they may be more fully understood, and when pressed home, they may be more firmly held.

Accursed be Photinus for not accepting the full Trinity and for preaching that Christ was only a mere man.

Accursed be Apollinaris for maintaining that the divinity in Christ is corrupted when changed and for doing away with his characteristic of perfect man.

Accursed be Nestorius for denying that God was born from the Virgin, for asserting that there are two Christs, and having rejected faith in the Trinity, for introducing to us the "quaternity."

But blessed be the catholic church which now worships one God in the fullness of the Trinity and likewise the equality of the Trinity in one Divinity, so that the individuality of substance of the persons does not destroy their distinguishing characteristics and the distinction of the Trinity does not split the unity of the Deity.

Blessed, I say, be the church which believes that in Christ there are two true and perfect substances but one person of Christ, so that neither does the distinction of the natures divide the unity of person nor the unity of person destroy the difference of the substances.

Blessed, I say, be the church which, though it confesses that Christ is and always has been one, professes that the man was

---

[44] Not identifiable.   [45] *Presbyter* and *episcopus*.

united with God, not after birth, but already in the very womb of his mother.

Blessed, I say, be the church which understands that God was made man not by a conversion of nature but by reason of a person, though not of a person pretended and temporary but one that has reality and permanence.

Blessed, I say, be the church which preaches that this unity of person has so much power that on its account, by a marvelous and indescribable mystery, it attributes divine attributes to the man and human attributes to God. On its account she does not deny that man came down from heaven following God and believes that God following man was made on earth, suffered, and was crucified. Because of it, finally, she confesses both that man is Son of God and that God is Son of the Virgin.

Blessed, then, and to be worshiped, hallowed, and consecrated, and a confession[46] worthy in every way to be compared with that heavenly praise[47] of the angels which glorifies the one Lord God with a threefold repetition of the word "holy." For this reason she preaches most emphatically the unity of Christ so as not to go beyond the Trinity.[48]

This has been said as a digression. Some other time, if God should please, the subject should be treated and explained at greater length.[49] Now let us return to the main argument.

XVII. Origen a Great Trial to the Church

23. We were saying above[50] that in the church of God the error of the teacher is the testing of the people and that the testing is the greater in proportion to the learning of the one who errs. This we taught first by the authority of Scripture; secondly, by examples from the church, that is, by mentioning

---

[46] Not a written creed but confession of the Trinity. With this whole passage compare Leo the Great's "Tome," i.e., *Epist.* 28 (*ad Flavianum*), tr. NPNF, 2d ser., 12.38–43, which had its mighty effect upon the Council of Chalcedon in 451.

[47] The Sanctus: Isa. 6:3, another form in Rev. 4:8. Cf. also the later Te Deum.

[48] By making a quaternity.

[49] In 1693, Joseph Anthelmi claimed in his *Nova de symbolo Athanasiano disquisitio* that Vincent was the author of the *Symbolum quicumque vult*, the so-called Athanasian Creed. Some parallels are printed by Heurtley (NPNF, 2d ser. 11.157, appendix 1), still more by Moxon (pp. lxvi–lxxiii). The latter concludes that the author of the *Quicumque* borrowed ideas from Vincent. The creed is not the work promised.

[50] Ch. X.

those who had been at one time held to be of sound faith, but in the end had fallen away into the false doctrines of others or had themselves founded their own heresy.[51] This is an important point, certainly, useful for learning, and necessary to be remembered. We ought again and again to demonstrate it by accumulation of examples and to drive it home, so that all who are truly catholics ought to know that when in the church they accept the teachers, they should not with the teachers desert the faith of the church.

My opinion is that although we are able to adduce many examples of this type of trial, there is almost no instance comparable to the trial brought on by Origen,[52] in whom there were many features so excellent, so unparalleled, so marvelous, that at first sight one would judge quite easily that credit should be given to all his pronouncements. If the facts of his life gain credence, he had great energy, great chastity,[53] patience, endurance. If his ancestry or his learning mean anything, what is more noble than, first of all, that he was born into a family made illustrious by a martyrdom?[54] or the fact that later, bereft not only of his father but also of his riches, in the midst of the adversities of holy poverty he climbed so high that he was often, so they say, persecuted[55] for his confession of the Lord's name? These were not the only qualities in him which afterward, all of them, became a source for trial, but his genius was so deep, so keen, so choice, that he far outstripped by many laps almost all. So great was the magnitude of his doctrine[56] and of all his learning that there were few areas of sacred philosophy and almost none of human of which he was not a complete master. When Greek had yielded to his knowledge, he worked on Hebrew. What should I say of his eloquence, so pleasing, so pure, so sweet a style that I think there flowed from his mouth not words but drops of honey? What perplexities did he not illumine by the powers of his discourse? What was

[51] Augustine is meant.
[52] The source may be the long sketch by Jerome, *De vir. ill.* 54 (NPNF, 2d ser., 3.373–374). On Origen, whose importance is scarcely exaggerated by Vincent, see J. Daniélou, *Origène* (Paris, 1948); R. Cadiou, *La jeunesse d'Origène* (Paris, 1935), tr. by John A. Southwell as *Origen: His Life at Alexandria* (St. Louis-London, 1944).
[53] An allusion to Origen's extreme application of Matt. 19:12, the reason adduced for not making him *presbyter*.
[54] His father, Leonidas, was martyred in 202.
[55] In the Decian persecution of 250 he was imprisoned, tortured, but escaped death.
[56] Vincent distinguishes between his theological and secular learning.

hard to accomplish that he did not make to seem very easy? But perhaps his assertions were but a web of argument? On the contrary, it is clear that no teacher ever employed more proofs drawn from divine law.

"But, I suppose, he wrote few works, then?"[57] Nobody ever wrote more—so much, I think, that his works not only cannot be read through;[58] they cannot even all be found. Moreover, that he might not lack the means of utilizing his knowledge, he enjoyed an abundance of long life.[59] Perhaps he was unhappy in his students? Who was happier? From his bosom, of course, were produced doctors[60] unnumbered, priests (*sacerdos*) unnumbered, confessors and martyrs. How much admiration he excited in everybody, how much fame he enjoyed, how much esteem—who could now describe it all? Who, devoted to the faith more than another, did not fly to him from the uttermost parts of the world? What Christian did not venerate him almost as a prophet, what philosopher not as a master? How he was respected not only by private persons but also by the imperial family itself is declared by the histories,[61] which say he was summoned by the mother[62] of the emperor Alexander, moved by the heavenly wisdom, with love of which both he and she were afire. His letters which he wrote to the emperor Philip,[63] first of the Roman emperors to be a Christian, composed with the authority of a Christian teacher, also offer testimony supporting the same view. As for his unbelievable erudition, if anyone has not accepted Christian testimony as reported by us, let him at least take the admission of pagans at the hands

---

[57] The reader.
[58] Epiphanius (*Haer.* 64.63) says he was popularly supposed to have written six thousand works, but Jerome cuts this to about a third. Of course, many ancient works would now be called articles.
[59] Aged sixty-nine at death.
[60] E.g., Gregory Thaumaturgus of Neo-Caesarea, Dionysius of Alexandria, Theognostus, Pierius, and Firmilian of Caesarea in Cappadocia.
[61] Probably Eusebius, *Hist. Eccl.*, Book 6, in Rufinus' Latin version.
[62] Alexianus, son of Gessius Marcianus and Julia Mammaea, was adopted at the age of thirteen by the emperor Elagabalus. As Alexander Severus, he became emperor in 221–222 and died in 235. The meeting with Origen probably took place c. 232, though the date has been much discussed and Moxon declares for 218. Cf. Eusebius, *Hist. Eccl.* 6.21.3 (NPNF, 2d ser., 1.269).
[63] Julius Verus Philippus, surnamed the Arab, emperor 244–249, and, with his son, slain at Verona. The claim that he was a Christian, made not only by Vincent but by Eusebius (*Hist. Eccl.* 6:34; Jerome, *De vir. ill.* 54), is not borne out by the facts. He was neither baptized nor a catechumen, participated in official paganism, but was probably lenient to Christians.

of the philosophers who witness to it. That wicked Porphyry[64] says that when but a boy, aroused by Origen's fame, he took himself to Alexandria, and there saw him, already aged but clearly of such character and so great a man that he had built the citadel of universal knowledge. Night would quickly fall before I could touch even briefly on only a small part of what was outstanding in this man, all of which not only made its contribution to the glory of religion but also increased the magnitude of the trial. Who would quickly desert a man of so great genius, so great doctrine, so great influence, and would not prefer to apply to himself the common remark that he would rather be wrong with Origen than be right with others?[65] What more is needed? It turned out that it was not the human virtues of so great a person, so great a doctor, so great a prophet, but, as the sequel showed, his too dangerous trial led many astray from the integrity of the faith.

Therefore, this Origen, so great and of such a character as he was, insolently abusing the grace of God, coddling too much his own genius, trusting too much in himself, yet giving little weight to the ancient simplicity of the Christian religion, presuming that he knew more than all men, despising the traditions of the church and the teachings of the men of old,[66] expounds certain passages of the Scriptures in a novel fashion,[67] has earned for himself what was said to the church of God: "If there should arise among you a prophet . . ."[68] and a bit later it says, "You shall not listen to the word of that prophet," and also it says, "Because the Lord your God is testing you whether or not you love him."

It was really not only a trial but even a great trial, without warning to draw away, gradually and little by little, from the old religion to a new profanity, that church which was devoted to him, and hung upon him from admiration for his genius, knowledge, eloquence, manner of life, and influence, having no suspicions of him, no fear of him.

---

[64] Cf. Eusebius, *Hist. Eccl.* 6:19, but Vincent exaggerates. Origen had left Alexandria before Porphyry was born and died when the latter was twenty-one.
[65] Cicero, *Tusc. Disp.* 1.17.39: *Errare mehercule malo cum Platone . . . quam cum istis sentire.*
[66] This is not in accord with Origen's own position. See his *Contra Celsum* 1.7, 6.6; *De princip. praef.* 2, where Origen's words as translated by Rufinus may be rendered as: "That truth alone must be believed which in no respect is out of harmony with the tradition of the church and the apostles."   [67] The allegorical method.   [68] Deut. 13:1.

But somebody will say that Origen's books are corrupted—this I shall not deny but even favor this view,[69] and it has been handed down orally and in writing, not only by catholics but also by heretics, but we should note the point that, though he himself is not a great trial[70] to us, the books published under his name are, swarming, as they are, with many wounds of blasphemies, read and loved, not as the works of someone else but as his works, so that although there was originally no suggestion of error in Origen's concept, Origen's prestige appears capable, however, of inducing men to be in error.

XVIII. TERTULLIAN A GREAT TRIAL TO THE CHURCH

24. The situation is the same with Tertullian. As, of all our writers, Origen must be judged among the Greeks to be easily first in rank, so among the Latins Tertullian has this honor, for who is more learned than he, who more accomplished in matters both divine and human? With remarkable mental capacity he embraced with his interest all philosophy and all the schools of the philosophers, and the founders and supporters of the schools, and all their teachings and all their varied histories and studies. Did he not so excel in intellectual power and force that there was almost nothing which he proposed for himself to attack that he did not sharply penetrate or crush with weight? Who can adequately praise his style, which was so woven with powerful cogency that it forced men to assent even though it did not persuade them?[71] Almost every word he uttered was an epigram, and every sentence was a victory.[72] This the Marcions[73] know, the Apelleses, the pagans, the Gnostics, and the rest, whose blasphemies he blasted with the mighty weight of his many great works, as with so many

---

[69] Jerome, *Epist. ad Pammach.* 84:10, thinks the suggestion stupid, but Rufinus contended that this had happened.
[70] If here Origen is meant to stand for Augustine, then the latter was no longer a trial, being dead, but his books were still troublesome to those of the Semi-Pelagian belief.
[71] Persuasion was not Tertullian's method—he used the bludgeon.
[72] A bon mot appropriated from Jerome *Epist.* 48.13, who applies it to Plato, Theophrastus, Xenophon, and Aristotle.
[73] Tertullian wrote polemics against Marcion, Apelles, Praxeas (who, as Dr. E. Evans suggests in his edition of the work, pp. 184 f., may not be a real person but a pseudonym), and Hermogenes, as well as against the Jews (*Adversus Iudaeos*), the pagans (*Ad nationes, Apologeticum,* and *De idololatria*), and the Gnostics (*Adversus gnosticos scorpiace, De carne Christi, De resurrectione carnis*).

thunderbolts. Yet he also, after all these accomplishments that have been mentioned—this Tertullian, I say, clinging too lightly to catholic doctrine, that is, to the ecumenical and ancient faith, far more eloquent than faithful, at last changed his faith and did in the end what the blessed confessor Hilary writes in a certain passage[74] about him: "By his later error he withdrew prestige from his writings that can be approved."

He also has been a great trial in the church, but about him I wish to say no more. This only shall I mention that, contrary to the teaching of Moses, by affirming as true prophecies, as they arose in the church, those novel furies of Montanus, and those mad dreams of new doctrine dreamed up by mad women, he deserved to have it said of him and of his writings, "If among you a prophet should arise . . . you will not listen to the words of that prophet." Why? "Because," it says, "the Lord your God is testing you whether or not you love him."

XIX. Lessons from These Examples

To the force, then, of these and other examples drawn from the church, so many and so great, we ought to give close attention and to understand clearer than day, according to the rules in Deuteronomy, that if at any time some teacher in the church should wander from the faith, divine Providence suffers this to occur for our testing "whether we love God or not in our whole heart and in our whole soul."

XX. The Marks of a True Catholic

25. Since this is so, he is the true and full[75] catholic who loves the truth of God, who loves the church, who loves the body of Christ,[76] who puts nothing before divine religion, before the catholic faith: not before the prestige of any man, not love, not genius, not eloquence, not philosophy, but despising all these, and planted in faith, unmoving, steadfast, decides that whatever he has learned has been held ecumenically in ancient times by the catholic church, this alone he ought to hold and believe.

Whatever new and unheard-of thing he learns has been introduced subsequently by any single person in addition to or contrary to all holy men, this he understands belongs not to

---

[74] Hilary of Poitiers (d. 367), *Comm. in Matt.* 5:1 (MPL 9:943).
[75] *Germanus* normally means full brother, blood brother, not half-brother or step-brother.
[76] Cf. Eph. 1:23.

5—E.M.T.

religion but to the trial, especially instructed by the remarks of the blessed apostle Paul; for this is what he writes in the First Letter to the Corinthians, "There must be heresies so that the approved may be made known among you."[77] This is as if he were to say: For this reason the authors of heresies are not divinely rooted out, in order that those approved be made known, that is, how tenacious and faithful and steadfast each lover of the catholic faith may appear.

Really, when each novelty bubbles up, immediately one sees the difference between the weight of the grains and the lightness of the chaff.[78] Then what was held by no weight within the threshing floor is with no great effort shaken away. Some completely fly away at once; others, only shaken out, are afraid of perishing and blush to return though wounded, half dead, half alive. They have, of course, drunk so much poison that it neither kills nor is assimilated. It neither forces them to die nor lets them live, a wretched condition! On how many waves of care, in how many whirlpools are they shaken about! Now they are snatched along wherever the wind drives them, when the error is aroused; again, turned back, they strike against themselves, like waves flowing in the opposite direction. Now they give their approval with rash assumption to what seems uncertain; again, with unreasoning fear, they dread even what is certain; uncertain where to go, where to return; what to seek, what to avoid; what to hold, what to let go.

Indeed, this affliction of a hesitating and badly vacillating heart is a remedy granted them by divine compassion, if they have any sense. For this reason they, though outside the most safe harbor of the catholic faith, are shaken about, beaten about, and almost killed by the blasts, so that they may furl the sails of their concept, shaken out upon the deep, which they had ill set before the winds of novelties, and may bring themselves back and hold themselves within the most trustworthy haven of their good and calm mother,[79] and may vomit up those bitter and stormy floods of errors they first had swallowed, so that thenceforth they may be able to quaff the streams of fresh and living water.[80] Let them learn well what they had learned not well, and from the whole doctrine of the church let them grasp what they can grasp with understanding, believe what they cannot grasp.

[77] I Cor. 11:19.
[78] Cf. Matt. 3:12; Tertullian, *De fuga*.
[79] See Joseph C. Plumpe, *Mater Ecclesia*, in Cath. Univ. Stud. in Christ. Ant. 5 (Washington, 1943).
[80] Cf. John 4:10.

XXI. Exegesis of I Timothy 6:20

26. Since this is so, turning it over in my mind repeatedly, I cannot sufficiently express my surprise at the monstrous madness of certain men, at the huge impiety of their blinded mentality, finally, at their passion for error so keen that they are not satisfied with the rule of faith handed down and once for all received from ancient days, but day by day they are seeking innovation after innovation, and they constantly long to add something new to religion, to change something, or remove something, as though the doctrine of letting what was once revealed suffice was not of heavenly origin but was earthly teaching, which could not otherwise be perfected without constant revision, without, rather, adverse criticism, although the divine oracles cry out, "Remove not the ancient landmarks which your fathers have set,"[81] and, "Judge not the judge above you"[82] and "Whoever breaks through a fence will be bitten by a serpent,"[83] and the apostle's dictum, by which all the cursed novelties of all the heresies often have been and always must be hewn to pieces, as with a spiritual sword, "O Timothy, guard what has been entrusted to you, avoiding the godless chatter of novelties and the contradictions of what is falsely called knowledge, professing which, some have missed the mark as regards the faith."[84]

After such statements as these, will any be found so hard in head, with such anvil-like impudence, with such adamantine pertinacity, as not to fall before the mass of these great declarations of heaven, as not to crack under such weight, as not to crash under such mighty sledge hammers, as not, finally, to be crushed out by such thunderbolts? "Avoid," he says, "the godless chatter of novelties." He has not said "the ancient" or "the old." Rather, he clearly shows what on the contrary he ought to follow. For if novelty is to be shunned, antiquity is to be held, and if novelty is godless, antiquity is sacred. He says, "And contradictions of what is falsely called knowledge"—truly "falsely called" as applied to the teaching of the heretics, where ignorance masquerades under the name of knowledge, fog under that of sunshine, shadows under that of light—"professing which," he says, "some have missed the mark as regards the faith." Professing what, did they miss the mark? Nothing but some new and unknown doctrine?

[81] Prov. 22:28 (OL).
[83] Eccl. 10:8 (OL).
[82] Ecclesiasticus 8:14 (8:17, V).
[84] I Tim. 6:20.

You may hear some of them saying: "Come, O silly wretches, who are now commonly dubbed catholics, and learn the true faith which, except for us, nobody understands, which many centuries ago was hidden, but recently has become known and is revealed. But learn it secretly and by stealth: you will like it! And also, when you have learned it, teach it on the quiet, lest the world hear it, the church know it. To few has it been granted to receive the secret of so great a mystery." Are these not the words of that harlot who, in The Proverbs of Solomon, "calls to her the passers-by who keep going straight on their way, 'Whoever of you is most stupid, let him turn to me.'"[85] The weak in sense she exhorts and says, 'Take gladly of the hidden loaves, and drink by stealth the water sweet.'"[86] What next? It says, "But he does not know that creatures of earth perish with her."[87] Who are these creatures of earth? Let the apostle explain: They are those "who have missed the mark as regards the faith," he says.

XXII. Fuller Exegesis of I Timothy 6:20

27. But it is worth-while to treat at greater length that whole passage of the apostle. "O Timothy," he says, "guard what has been entrusted to you, avoiding the godless chatter of novelties." The "O" is an exclamation both of foreknowledge and of love, for he foresaw the future errors which he also lamented. Who is today's Timothy but either the universal church in a general sense or, taking the word in a special sense, the whole body of the episcopacy[88] which ought both to possess for itself and to pass on to others a knowledge of divine learning that is pure? What does "Guard what has been entrusted" mean? "Guard," he says, because of thieves, of enemies, lest, while men are sleeping, they sow weeds over that seed of good wheat which the Son of Man had sown in his field.[89] He says, "Guard what has been entrusted." What does "has been entrusted" mean? It is what has been entrusted to you, not what has been found by you; what you have received, not what you have thought up yourself; a matter, not of genius, but of teaching; not of personal adoption, but of public tradition; a matter brought to you, not brought out by you, in which you ought to be not the author but the guardian, not the initiator but the adherent,[90] not

---

[85] Prov. 9:15–18, also 4, 13, 14 (OL). [86] Prov. 9:5, 17.
[87] Prov. 9:18.   [88] *Praepositi* = *episcopi*.   [89] Cf. Matt. 13:24, 25, 37.
[90] Just possibly: "Not the teacher but the disciple."

leading, but following. He says, "Guard what has been entrusted to you"; preserve inviolate and unimpaired the talent[91] of the catholic faith. Let what you have been given as a trust remain with you, be handed on by you. You have received gold, return gold. I do not wish you to substitute for me one thing for another. I do not want you to counterfeit real gold by brashly and dishonestly offering lead or brass.[92] I do not want gilt but the real metal.

O Timothy! O priest! (*sacerdos*) O expounder![93] O doctor! If the gift of God has made you sufficient in genius, in skill, in learning, be the Bezalel[94] of the spiritual tabernacle, engrave the precious stones of divine dogma, fit them carefully, decorate them wisely, add to them splendor, attractiveness, beauty. Under your exposition, let what was hitherto believed, though vaguely, now be clearly understood. Let posterity, through you, joyfully receive with understanding what antiquity respected without understanding. The very same that you have learned, that teach, but when you say it anew, say nothing new.

XXIII. Progress in Christian Teaching

28. But perhaps someone will say, "Shall the church of Christ make no progress in religion?" Yes, indeed, it should, as great as possible. Who is there so ungenerous toward men, so full of hatred toward God, that he would try to forbid it? Let it, however, be *progress*, not alteration of the faith.[95] Involved in the idea of progress, of course, is the principle that the subject itself be increased, but in the idea of alteration, the principle is that something be changed from one form to another. Therefore, there should be a great increase and a vigorous progress, in individuals and in the whole group, in the single man as well as in the entire church, as the ages and the centuries march on, of understanding, knowledge, wisdom, but, at least, in its own kind, in the same doctrine, that is, in the same sense, in the same meaning.

29. Religion in the souls is analogous to reason in the bodies, which, though in the succession of years they develop and increase their elements, nevertheless remain what they were. There is a great deal of difference between the flower of

---

[91] Matt. 25:15.   [92] Tableware, not coinage, is the figure.
[93] Souter defines the word as sometimes exegete, commentator; oftener, perhaps, homilist, preacher.
[94] Ex. 31:1–5.   [95] Here Vincent makes a crucial statement.

boyhood and the ripeness of old age, but the very same persons become old men who had been youths. Although the stature and the outward appearance of one and the same man is changed, he is still, however, no less one and the same nature, one and the same person. The parts of infants are small, those of youths large, but they are nevertheless the same. Men have as many powers as they had when they were children, and if there are any such powers which are brought to birth in riper age, these were already in existence in the seed, so that nothing new appears in old men which was not latent long before in the boys.[96]

There is thus no doubt that this is the proper and right rule of progress, the unalterable and most beautiful order in growth, if the full measure of age in the older completes the web of those parts and forms which the wisdom of the Creator had in the children first tied upon the loom.[97]

If, however, the human appearance should later be changed into the likeness, not of its own kind, or, at least, if anything be added to or subtracted from the number of the parts, the whole body would necessarily either fall to ruin or become a monstrosity or at any rate be weakened.[98]

So also the doctrine of the Christian religion must follow the laws of progress, so as to be strengthened by the years, amplified by time, grow taller with age, yet remain uncorrupted and unimpaired, complete and perfect in all the measurements of its parts, and, as it were, in all its numbers and its proper senses, permitting, especially, no change, no wasting of its distinctive character, no variation in its outline.

30. For example, in olden times our forefathers sowed the church's field with seeds of the wheat of faith. It would be very wrong and out of harmony if we, their descendants, should harvest, in place of its true product, the grain of truth, the spurious weeds of error. On the other hand it would be right and quite in harmony if there should be no disparity between the first activity and the last. From the growth of the wheatlike teaching we should reap the doctrine of the same grain, so that when in course of time something is developed from those

---

[96] Vincent is in accord with all biological teaching before mid-nineteenth century when the principle of preformation was abandoned for that of epigenesis. My colleague in biology, Dr. L. P. Johnson, informs me that currently biologists have reverted to a modified preformation in which some change is regarded as possible.

[97] The figure is taken from the initial act of weaving.

[98] This phrase allows for the surgeon's knife.

original seedings, and now brings joy and is carefully tended, there is, however, no alteration in the qualities truly inherent in the seeds. The appearance, shape, beauty, may undergo a change so long as the basic nature of each species still endures. God forbid, I say, that those nurseries of the rosebushes of catholic interpretation be converted into thistles and brambles.[99] God forbid, I say, that, in that paradise[1] of the spirit, from cinnamon and balsam, darnel and wolfsbane should suddenly shoot forth.

Whatever, then, that in this church, God's husbandry,[2] was sown by the faith of the fathers, the same thing ought to be cultivated and nurtured by the energy of the children, the same should blossom and ripen with age, the same advance and be perfected. It is right that those ancient doctrines of the heavenly philosophy should in the progress of time be given complete care, be refined, polished,[3] but it is wrong for them to be changed, wrong for them to be mutilated, to be marred. Let them get proof, illumination, definition, but they must still retain their fullness, their integrity, their natural characteristics.

31. If once this license of wicked fraud is let in, I shudder at the thought of saying how great the danger which may ensue of splitting asunder and destroying religion. Once let any one part of catholic doctrine be abandoned, then will be abandoned another, and also yet another, at last another and another, in accordance with the precedent permitted. When at length the parts have been individually repudiated, what else will come about in the end but that the whole will be in the same way repudiated? On the other hand, if what is new begins to be mixed in with what is old, strange with familiar, profane with sacred, this habit will creep in, of necessity, so that after that, nothing in the church will remain untouched, nothing unimpaired, nothing whole, nothing spotless, but where formerly there was a sanctuary of pure and uncorrupted truth, there will at last be a brothel[4] of wicked and shameful errors. May God's goodness avert this wrong from the minds of his people—let this rather be the madness of the wicked.

32. The church of Christ, however, careful and alert guardian of the doctrines transmitted to it, never makes any change in them, no diminution, no addition; prunes away no

---

[99] Cf. Gen. 3:18. [1] Cf. Ecclesiasticus 24:15, 16.
[2] Cf. I Cor. 3:9. [3] The figure now is from the lapidary art.
[4] On adultery used to describe unfaithfulness, see Jer. 2:2; 3:14; 13:27; 31:32; Hos. 8:9; Matt. 12:34; 16:4; Mark 8:38.

essential, grafts on nothing that is not; never loses her own properties, appropriates none from others; but bends every energy upon this one task, by expounding faithfully and wisely the ancient truths, if any there are which in olden times were shapeless or left only begun, to care for them and polish them; if there be any already defined and revealed in their essentials, to strengthen them and fix them firmly; if there be any already strengthened and defined, to guard them. Finally, what else have the councils ever striven to accomplish by their decrees but that what was formerly believed with simplicity, that afterward should be believed more diligently; that what was formerly preached without concern, that afterward should be preached more urgently; that what was formerly cultivated with complacence, that same thing afterward should be nurtured with concern? This, and nothing else, I say, is what the catholic church, roused by the innovations of the heretics, has brought to fruition by the decrees of its councils. What she had earlier received from the oral tradition of the forefathers alone, this thenceforth she transmitted in written form to their descendants, compressing a great amount of meaning into a few words, and often, to provide more light for understanding, redesignating with a new name[5] a doctrine of the faith that is not new.

XXIV. Exegesis of I Timothy 6:20 Continued

33. Let us return to the apostle. "O Timothy," he says, "guard what has been entrusted to you, avoiding the godless chatter of novelties."

Avoid them, he means, as if they were a viper, as if a scorpion, as if a basilisk, lest they strike you, not only with their touch, but even with their gaze and breath.[6] What does "to avoid" mean? "Not even to eat with such."[7] What does "avoid" mean? He says, "If anyone comes to you and does not bring this doctrine..." What doctrine but the catholic and universal doctrine which remains one and the same, uncorrupted in the oral tradition of truth through the several successive generations, and will so remain for ages without end. What comes next? "Do not," he says, "receive him into the house or say 'Good morning' to him, for he who says 'Good morning' to him shares in his wicked works."[8]

[5] He is alluding to ὁμοούσιος as promulgated by Athanasius.
[6] The basilisk was a fabulous animal having these properties.
[7] I Cor. 5:11. [8] II John 10, 11.

"The godless chatter of novelties," he says. What does "godless" mean? What involves nothing sacred, nothing religious, what is wholly apart from the innermost holy of holies, which is God's temple.[9] He says, "The godless chatter of novelties." Chatter, that is, of novelties, of doctrines, subjects, opinions, which are contrary to the ancient faith and to the faith of old,[10] to receive which requires the violation, certainly in great part if not completely, of the faith[11] of the blessed fathers. All the faithful of all ages, all the holy, all the pure, the chaste, the virgins, all the clergy, the deacons and priests (*sacerdos*), so many thousands of confessors, such great hosts of martyrs, such vast numbers of cities and of nations; so many islands, provinces, kings, tribes, kingdoms, nations; almost, finally, the whole world, through the catholic faith, incorporated with Christ as Head,[12] must necessarily be stated to have been ignorant, through so long a tract of time to have made mistakes, to have blasphemed, have not known what to believe.

34. He says, "Avoid the godless chatter of novelties," to receive and to pursue which was never the part of catholics, but always of heretics. And really what heresy has ever bubbled up except under a definite name, in a definite place, at a definite time? Who ever has taught a heresy who did not first separate himself from agreement with the ecumenicity and the antiquity of the catholic church? The truth of this statement is made clearer than day by examples. Who before that godless Pelagius[13] granted to free will so much power that he did not think God's grace was needed to aid it in well-doing through every single act? Who before that monstrous[14] disciple of his, Caelestius, ever denied that the whole human race was implicated in the guilt arising from Adam's transgression?[15] Who before that sacrilegious Arius ever dared to destroy the unity of the Trinity? Who before that scoundrel Sabellius ever dared to confound the Trinity of the Unity? Who before that most cruel

---

9 I Cor. 3:16, 17.
10 *Vetustas* and *antiquitas* are ordinarily synonyms in Vincent. If a distinction must be found, perhaps the former connotes existence in past and present, the latter existence only in the past.
11 Here *fides* is that which is believed, though elsewhere Vincent uses it to mean trustworthiness, conviction, trust, and faith in the Christian sense.
12 Cf. Eph. 4:15; Col. 1:18.
13 This disclaims sympathy with the Pelagians.
14 Perhaps allusion to the allegation that Caelestius was a eunuch. Cf. Marius Mercator, *Comm. super Cael. nom.* 11: *Caelestius quidam, eunuchus matris utero editus.*
15 Cf. Rom. 5:14.

Novatian ever said that God is cruel in that he preferred the "death of the dying" to "his recovery and life"?[16] Who before Simon Magus,[17] the one struck down by the apostle's reprimand, from whom that ancient torrent of vilenesses[18] has, without interruption and in secret, continually flowed on even to Priscillian in these last[19] days—who before Simon ever dared to say that God the Creator is the author of evils, that is, of our crimes, wickednesses, and shameful deeds? That man, indeed, asserts that He created with his own hands a human of such a nature that, on its own initiative and by the impulse of its own will, governed by necessity, it can do[20] nothing else, can will to do nothing else, but sin, in view of the fact that, tossed about on the furies of every vice, and set aflame, it is carried along by its own limitless desire into every abyss of vileness?

Countless are the examples we might cite, but we pass over them for brevity's sake. All of them, however, clearly and irrefutably demonstrate that in the case of almost all the heresies there is a sort of established and legal rule that they always take delight in godless innovations, loathe the decisions of antiquity, and "through contradictions of knowledge, falsely so named, suffer shipwreck from the faith."[21]

On the other hand, however, it really is the characteristic of the catholics to preserve what is handed down and entrusted to them from the holy fathers, to condemn the godless innovations, and so the apostle has said and preached, not once but often, "If any man should proclaim to you contrary to what has been received, let him be accursed." [22]

XXV. Even Heretics Appeal to Scripture

35. Here perhaps someone will ask whether or not the heretics make use of testimonies derived from divine Scripture? They certainly do make use of them and vigorously, for you

---

[16] Ezek. 18:32.

[17] This famous figure, mentioned in Acts 8:5–24, and in the apocryphal Acts of Peter, as a sorcerer, appears also in early Christian literature in many other forms: as a Samaritan, a Jew, a pagan, a Christian, a Christian philosopher; a heresiarch, a pseudo apostle, pseudo Messiah. The connection here with Priscillian is, of course, that they were both sorcerers.

[18] Gnosticism.   [19] He was executed about a half century earlier.

[20] Cf. the fifth of the *Objectiones Vincentianae* (MPL 45.1843–1850): *quae naturali motu nihil possit nisi peccare.* See H. Koch, *Vincenz von Lérins und Gennadius* (Leipzig, 1907).

[21] I Tim. 1:19.   [22] Gal. 1:9.

may see them scamper through every single book of the holy law, through the books of Moses, through the books of Kings, through The Psalms, through the apostles, through the Gospels, through the prophets. With their own people or with others, in private or in public, in conversations or in books, at banquets or on the streets, they almost never adduce any argument of theirs which they do not try to darken in words of Scripture also.[23] Read the pamphlets of Paul of Samosata, of Priscillian, of Eunomius, of Jovinian, and of the rest of the pests. You may see a mountainous heap of proof texts, hardly any page without camouflage drawn from the sayings of the New and Old Testaments. They are, however, the more to be avoided and feared, as they lurk secretly the more under the shadow of divine law. For they know that their stenches will hardly please anyone if they breathe them out simply as they are. Therefore, they sprinkle them with the perfume of some heavenly saying in order that he who would easily spurn error that is human may not easily despise the oracles of God. They do just what people do when, about to give to children some medicine which has a bitter taste, they first smear the edges with honey, so that as soon as the unsuspecting child gets a taste of the sweetness, he will have no fear of the bitterness.[24] They also take care to do what poisoners do, who, in advance, disguise venomous herbs and harmful liquors, so that hardly anyone who reads the antidote described in the label will suspect the poison.

36. For this reason it was that the Saviour used to cry out, "Beware of false prophets who come to you in sheep's clothing, but inwardly are ravening wolves." [25] What does "sheep's clothing" mean except the preaching of the prophets and apostles with which they covered themselves as fleeces with the guilelessness of sheep, for that "spotless Lamb" [26] that "takes away the sins of the world." [27] Who are the "ravening wolves" but the wild and rabid opinions of the heretics who continually molest the sheepfolds[28] of the church and tear to bits the flock of Christ wherever they can? To creep more stealthily upon the unsuspecting sheep, they lay aside their wolfish guise, though keeping their wolfish fierceness, and they wrap themselves in

---

[23] See Tertullian, *De praescript.* 38-40.
[24] The same idea appears in Lucretius, *De rerum natura* 1:936-941, repeated 4.11-16. See M. Schuster, *Philologische Wochenschr.*, 1926, p. 157.
[25] Matt. 7:15 (OL). [26] I Peter 1:19.
[27] John 1:29, 36. [28] Cf. John 10:12.

the pronouncements of divine law like fleeces, so that when the softness of the wool is felt by anyone, he may not fear the sting of the fangs.

What does the Saviour say? "By their fruits you will know them." [29] That is to say, when they have begun not only to cite these divine words but also to expound them; not only, as up to now, to flaunt them, but also to interpret them, then will that bitterness, that acerbity, that rage be understood; then will that poison of the innovations be exhaled; then will the godless novelties appear; then you first may see the hedge pierced, the boundary posts of the fathers moved, the catholic faith cut down, the doctrines of the church torn to pieces.

37. These were the ones the apostle Paul strikes at in his Second Letter to the Corinthians when he says, "For such men are false apostles, deceitful workmen, disguising themselves as apostles of Christ." [30] What does "disguising themselves as apostles of Christ" mean? The apostles produced precedents from The Psalms, and so did these men. The apostles produced passages from the prophets, and these men did no less. But when they had begun to interpret in a different manner what they had produced in the same manner, then the sincere were indistinguishable from the hypocritical, the uncamouflaged from the camouflaged, the straight from the crooked, the true apostles, in the end, from the false apostles. "And no wonder," he says, "for Satan himself disguises himself into an angel of light. So it is not strange if his servants also disguise themselves as servants of righteousness."[31]

Therefore, according to the teaching of the apostle Paul, as often as the false apostles or the false prophets or the false doctors produce passages of divine law, by the improper interpretation of which they try to bolster up their own errors, there is no doubt that they are pursuing the clever devices of their author,[32] which certainly he never would have contrived, had he not known that there is altogether no easier way to deceive than that, when the fraud of wicked error is introduced, there the prestige of divine words is pretended.

XXVI. In Quoting Scripture Heretics Emulate the Devil

But someone will say, "Where do we find proof that the devil commonly employs the authority of proof texts taken from the

[29] Matt. 7:15 (OL).   [30] II Cor. 11:13.
[31] II Cor. 11:14, 15.   [32] The devil.

sacred law?" Let him read the Gospels, in which it is written, "Then the devil took him," that is, the Lord Saviour, "and set him on the pinnacle of the Temple and said to him, 'If you are the Son of God, throw yourself down, for it is written that he has given his angels charge of you that they guard you in all your ways. In their hands they will bear you up, lest you strike your foot against a stone.'" [33]

What will he do to men, poor fellows, as they are, when he attacked even the Lord of Glory himself with Scriptural quotations? "If," he says, "you are the Son of God, throw yourself down." Why? He says, "For it is written." The teaching of this passage should be carefully examined and remembered that, following the great example of the authority of the Gospel, when we see certain men producing passages apostolic or prophetic against the catholic faith, we have not the slightest doubt that the devil is speaking through them. For as then the head spoke to the Head, so now the members speak to the members, the members of the devil, that is, to the members of Christ, infidels to faithful, sacrilegious to religious, in a word, heretics to catholics.

What, finally, do they say? "If," he says, "you are the Son of God, cast yourself down." That is, if you wish to be a son of God and to receive the inheritance of the Kingdom of Heaven, throw yourself down, that is, throw yourself down from that teaching and tradition of the sublime church which is thought to be also the temple of God.[34] And if anybody asks one of the heretics when he gives this advice, "Where do you get the proof by which you teach that I ought to throw down the ecumenical and ancient faith of the catholic church?" he will at once reply, "For it is written." And right away he produces a thousand testimonies, a thousand proof texts, a thousand precedents, from the law,[35] from The Psalms, from the apostles, from the prophets, by which, interpreted in a new and wrong fashion, the poor soul may be cast down from the catholic citadel into the heretical abysses. But now with those promises which follow along, the heretics have in marvelous fashion grown accustomed to deceive the unwary. For they dare to promise and to teach, that in their church, that is, in the coterie of their communion, there is a great and special and wholly personal grace[36] of God, so that without any effort, without any

---

[33] Matt. 4:5, 6 (OL).   [34] I Cor. 3:16, 17.
[35] The only example in Vincent of *lex* as the Pentateuch.
[36] Vincent nowhere mentions the leading opponent of heresy in his day,

zeal, without any industry, though they neither ask, nor seek, nor knock,[37] those who belong to their number have some sort of arrangement with God, that borne up in the hands of angels, that is, protected by the preservation of the angels, they never can dash their feet against a stone, that is, never be ensnared by evil.[38]

XXVII. THE RULE FOR INTERPRETING SCRIPTURE

38. But someone will say, "If the divine pronouncement, sentiments, promises are appropriated by the devil and his disciples, of whom some are false apostles, others false prophets and false teachers, and all without exception are heretics, what shall the catholics and the sons of mother church do? How shall they distinguish truth from falsehood in the Holy Scriptures?" They will, of course, take great pains to follow the advice which at the beginning of this *Commonitory* we said the holy and learned men[39] had handed down to us, namely, to interpret the divine canon according to the oral traditions of the ecumenical church, and in close accordance with the rules of catholic doctrine. In this catholic and apostolic church, likewise, they must follow the principles of ecumenicity, antiquity, and consensus. And if at some time a part should rebel against the whole, innovation against antiquity, dissent of one or of a few in error against the consensus of all or, in any case, of nearly all the catholics, then they should set greater store on the preservation of ecumenicity than on the corruption of the part. In this same ecumenicity they must prefer the religion of antiquity to the godless innovation; likewise, in that very antiquity, to the rashness of one or of a few, the general decrees of a universal council, if any there be. Then, after that, if there are none, let them follow the next best, the harmony of the concordant opinions of many and great teachers. Having with the Lord's help, faithfully, seriously, earnestly, followed

---

Augustine, who died some four years before he wrote. This passage certainly appears, as has been claimed, to be a covert attack on the characteristically Augustinian doctrine of grace and predestination, opposed to the Gallic group to which Vincent belonged. See Introduction.

[37] Matt. 7:7; Luke 11:9. These words became the motto of the Semi-Pelagians.

[38] Vincent warns catholics that the predestinarianism of Augustine was being exaggerated into fatalism.

[39] Not only Irenaeus, Tertullian, Cyprian, and Augustine, but the men of Lérins as well.

these authorities, we shall, with no great trouble, unmask the harmful errors of the heretics as they arise.

XXVIII. How to Detect Heretical Innovations

39. Here now I see, as a necessary consequence, that I must prove by examples how the godless innovations of the heretics may be uncovered and condemned by producing and comparing with each other the harmonious beliefs of the teachers of olden times. Nevertheless, this ancient consensus of the holy fathers must be most zealously searched for and followed, not in every petty question[40] of divine law but only, at any rate particularly, in matters pertaining to the rule of faith. This method of attack should not be used always or in the case of all the heresies, but only in the case of the new and fresh ones when they first make their appearance, that is, as long as they are forbidden by the lack of time itself from falsifying the rules of the ancient faith, and before they try to corrupt the works of the forefathers, while the poison is seeping in. Heresies that have already gained much ground and are of long standing should never be approached in this way because the passing of much time has afforded them ample opportunity to pilfer[41] from the truth. Therefore, we should not refute those older profanities of schisms or of heresies, if need exists, by any other method than on the authority alone of the Scriptures,[42] or, at any rate, they should be avoided as long ago refuted and condemned by all the councils of catholic bishops (*sacerdos*). So, when first the rottenness of each wicked error begins to break out, and for its defense to filch some words of the sacred law, and to interpret these craftily and deceitfully, at once the opinions of the forefathers in expounding the canon must be collected. By them the innovation, whatever it is that arises, and therefore the godlessness, may be revealed without any doubt and be condemned without any hesitation. In doing this, however, use should be made, for comparison, of the opinions of only those fathers, who, living, teaching, enduring, righteously, wisely, and constantly, in the catholic faith and

---

[40] *Quaestiunculis.* If the force of the diminutive can be pressed at all, then it must mean questions petty in that they do not involve doctrine.
[41] That is, to exploit it improperly. Cf. John 10:1, 8.
[42] The Bible is the first and last appeal in refutation of heresies not yet condemned by a general council, but Tertullian (*De praescript.* 19) thought otherwise because the result would be, in his opinion, uncertain.

communion, have earned the reward of dying in Christ by faith or of being put to death for Christ with happiness.[43] Yet even these are to be believed only on the condition that whatever is confirmed by all of them or by a majority of them, constituting, as it were, a council of teachers in harmony with each other, receiving, holding, and transmitting in one and the same sense, clearly, frequently, and persistently—this should be taken to be indubitable, certain, established. Whatsoever, on the other hand anyone, though he be holy and learned,[44] though he be a confessor and a martyr, should believe apart from all or even contrary to all, let this be, among his personal and unpublished and private idiosyncrasies of thought, kept separate from the authority of the common, public, and general opinion, lest with the greatest danger to our eternal salvation, following closely the sacrilegious practice of heretics and schismatics, abandoning the ancient truth of the universal doctrine, we pursue the novel error of one man.

40. Lest anyone should possibly suppose that the holy and catholic agreement of these blessed fathers should have little value set upon them, the apostle says in First Corinthians: "And certain men, indeed, God has placed in the church, first, apostles,"[45] of whom he was one; "second, prophets": such was Agabus of whom we read in The Acts of Apostles[46]; "third, doctors," who are now called "tractators," whom this same apostle at times calls "prophets," because through them the mysteries of the prophets are revealed to the peoples. Whoever, therefore, sets little value on these men when they are in agreement in Christ in their interpretation of some one point of catholic doctrine, established, as they were in the church of God in different times and places, "disregards, not man, but God."[47] Lest there be variance from their unity in truth, the same apostle more earnestly protests when he says, "I appeal to you, brethren, that you all say the same thing and that there be no schisms among you, but that you be perfect in the same opinion and the same judgment.[48] If, however, anyone disagrees with the unanimity of their judgment, let him hear this passage from the same apostle, "God is not the God of dissension but of peace"[49]—that is, not of him who makes a defection

---

[43] The thought is that these have endured to the end and are therefore worthy of approval. Living authorities and those who have fallen away in later life are to be avoided.
[44] Augustine.   [45] I Cor. 12:28.   [46] Acts 11:27–30; 21:10–12.
[47] I Thess. 4:8.   [48] I Cor. 1:10.   [49] I Cor. 14:33.

from the unity of belief but of those who steadfastly remain in the peace of agreement. "As," he says, "in all the churches of the holy, I teach," [50] that is, churches of the catholics, which, therefore, are holy because they remain steadfast in unanimity of faith.

And lest anyone, with disregard for others, should possibly make the claim that he alone is heard, he alone believed, a bit later the apostle says, "Did the Word of God originate with you or are you the only ones it has reached?" [51] And to prevent anyone from taking this lightly he adds, "If anyone seems to be a prophet or spiritual, let him know that what I am writing to you are the Lord's commands." [52] As for these commands of the Lord, unless anyone is a prophet or spiritual, that is, a teacher of spiritual matters, let him be with the greatest zeal a worshiper of impartiality and unity, that is, not preferring his own opinions to those of others, and not departing from the views of all. "Who does not recognize these commands," he says, "will not be recognized." [53] That is, who either does not learn what is unknown, or sets little value on what is known, shall be not recognized; that is, he will be held unworthy to be divinely regarded among those united in faith and made equal to each other by humility, and I know not whether there is any evil that can be thought more bitter than this one. It was, however, this evil which, in accordance with the warning of the apostle, we see happened to Julian the Pelagian,[54] who either failed to associate himself in the belief of his fellows or dared to disassociate himself from it.

But now it is time for us to produce the promised proof, where and how the opinions of the holy fathers have been gathered, so that, in accordance with them, by the decree and authority of a council, the rule of the church's faith may be established.

For the sake of convenience, however, let this *Commonitory* end here, and let us make a fresh beginning with the following one.

[50] The Greek text has no word for "I teach," which appears in the Vulgate.
[51] I Cor. 14:36.   [52] I Cor. 14:37.   [53] I Cor. 14:38.
[54] Julian of Eclanum, the most gifted champion of Pelagianism was born 380–390, died 425–455. He was consecrated bishop of Eclanum in Italy by Innocent I (416–417), deposed in 418 with seventeen others, and exiled because he refused to sign the circular letter of Zosimus condemning Pelagius and Caelestius. He was a vigorous opponent of Augustine and drew forth from the bishop of Hippo more than one polemic.

6—E.M.T.

[*The Second Commonitory* came in this interval, but of it nothing more remains but the last part, that is, only the concluding summary.] [55]

XXIX. Summary

41. Since this is so, it is now time for us to summarize the argument of these two *Commonitories* in this conclusion of the second.

We have said above that it has always been and today still is the practice of the catholics to prove the true faith by these two means: first by the authority of the divine canon; secondly, by the tradition of the catholic church. Not that the canon alone is not sufficient on every point, but that the majority of people interpreting the divine words in accordance with their own way of thinking, produce various beliefs and errors, and therefore it is necessary that the understanding of the divine Scripture be set straight by the single standard of the church's interpretation, particularly in those subjects of inquiry on which the foundations of the whole catholic doctrine rest.

We likewise have said that, on the other hand, in the church itself there must be due examination of the agreement between ecumenicity and antiquity, so that we may not be broken off from the integrity of unity into the direction of schism, or from the religion of antiquity be hurled headlong into the innovations of heresy. We likewise have said that in the very antiquity of the church two points ought to be vigorously and zealously observed by those who wish not to be heretics. First, if there has been decided in ancient times anything bearing on the matter involved with the authority of a universal council by all the bishops (*sacerdos*) of the catholic church; secondly, if any new question arises, where no such pronouncement is to be found, recourse must then be had to the opinions of the holy fathers, provided that they were, each in his time and place, remaining steadfast in the unity of communion and faith, accepted as teachers worthy of approval, and whatever is found to have been held in one sense and consensus, this should be judged the church's true and catholic belief, free from every difficulty of doubt.

To prevent our appearing to have advanced this view on the

---

[55] This appears in the manuscripts.

basis of our own presumption rather than on ecclesiastical authority, we appealed to the example of the holy council which about three years ago was held at Ephesus[56] in Asia in the consulship of Their Excellencies,[57] Bassus and Antiochus. There, when there was a dispute concerning the ratification of the rules of faith, to prevent the possibility of any godless innovation creeping in by stealth as it did in perfidious Ariminum, all the bishops (*sacerdos*) who had assembled there, numbering nearly two hundred,[58] gave approval to this as the most catholic, most faithful, and best source of action, namely, that the opinions of the holy fathers should be brought in, some of them martyrs, others confessors, but all, it was agreed, had been and continued to remain, catholic bishops (*sacerdos*), so that, of course, from their agreement and decision, the reverence due the ancient doctrine might be duly and solemnly confirmed and the blasphemies of godless innovations be condemned.

When this was done, that wicked Nestorius was lawfully and deservedly adjudged to be opposed to catholic antiquity, but the blessed Cyril[59] to be in harmony with sacred antiquity. Accordingly, in order that there be no doubt about the matter, we also listed the names and number—though we had forgotten[60] the order—of those fathers, in accordance with whose harmonious and unanimous judgment, both the preliminaries of sacred law were expounded and the rules of divine doctrine were established, and to strengthen our memory it will be necessary to go through the list here again.

---

[56] The Third Ecumenical Council met at Ephesus in the Church of St. Mary on June 22, 431, summoned by Theodosius II, who did not himself attend. Cyril of Alexandria presided but would not wait for the delayed arrival of Bishop John of Antioch who, when he did reach Ephesus with his bishops, met in what would now be called a "rump session." The picture of sweetness and light which Vincent paints is not borne out by modern studies of the council.

[57] *Viri clarissimi*, i.e., senators.

[58] The deposition of Nestorius was signed by 198 bishops, but others later joined them and Prosper (*Chron. ad annum* 431) says there were more than two hundred.

[59] Cyril of Alexandria, made archbishop 412, died June 27, 444. He was nephew of his predecessor Theophilus, both of them men of domineering personality.

[60] The true order of the ten authorities whom Vincent remembers—there were two he has forgotten—is: Peter, Athanasius, Julius, Felix, Theophilus, Cyprian, Ambrose, Gregory of Nazianzus, Basil, Gregory of Nyssa. See MPL 50.680, n. 1.

XXX. THE COUNCIL OF EPHESUS

42. These are the men whose writings were recited in that council[61] either as those of judges or of witnesses: the holy Peter,[62] bishop of Alexandria, a most eminent doctor and a most blessed martyr; the holy Athanasius,[63] bishop[64] of that same city, most faithful teacher and most eminent confessor; the holy Theophilus,[65] bishop also of that same city, a man very famous for his faith, life, knowledge, who has been succeeded by the venerable Cyril, who now adorns the Alexandrian church. And lest perchance it be thought that this was the doctrine of one city and province, recourse was had also to those lights[66] of Cappadocia, the holy Gregory,[67] bishop and confessor of Nazianzus; the holy Basil,[68] bishop and confessor of Caesarea in Cappadocia; and the other holy Gregory,[69] bishop of Nyssa, in faith, character, integrity, and wisdom most worthy of his brother Basil. But to prove that not only Greece or the East but also the West and the Latin world have always had the same opinion, there were read there also certain epistles addressed to certain men by the holy Felix,[70] a martyr, and the

---

[61] Extensive but incomplete extracts of the proceedings appear in NPNF, 2d ser., 14.191–242; for the complete minutes, see P. Labbe, *Sacrosancta Concilia* (Paris, 1671) 3.1–1213.

[62] Peter of Alexandria, made bishop c. 300, martyred 311. Three short extracts of his book on the divinity of Christ were read. In these he took exception to such a view of the κένωσις as would suppose the Word to have parted with the power or glory of the divinity when he became man.

[63] Athanasius, born 293, died May 2, 373, became bishop of Alexandria in 326. He was exiled five times in his long career of controversy with the Arians. The selections read were two, one from his book against the Arians, *Oratio* 4, and the other from his letter to Epictetus.

[64] *Antistes*.

[65] Theophilus of Alexandria was uncle to Cyril. He succeeded Timotheus in 385 as twenty-second bishop and died in 412. Vincent's judgment of this opponent of Chrysostom is too favorable. The extracts read, from the fifth and sixth paschal letters, affirm the reality of Christ's body.

[66] The three Cappadocians were leading warriors in the battles against Arianism, Macedonianism, and Apollinarianism.

[67] Gregory, bishop of Nazianzus in Cappadocia, was born c. 329, died c. 390. His father was also bishop of Nazianzus. The selection read was from his *Epist. I ad Cledonium*.

[68] Basil the Great, born c. 330, died Jan. 1, 379, became bishop of Caesarea in Cappadocia in 370. The quotation read at Ephesus was from his *De spiritu sancto*.

[69] Gregory of Nyssa, brother of Basil the Great, was bishop of Nyssa in Cappadocia from 371 to 395. His commentary on Phil. 2:5 was read.

[70] This was Felix I, bishop of Rome 269–274, but he did not die a martyr. Vincent probably is confusing him with Felix II, bishop 355–358, who

holy Julius,[71] bishops of the city of Rome. And so that not only the head but also the sides might be used as support for the judgment, from the South was used the most blessed Cyprian,[72] bishop of Carthage and a martyr; from the North, holy Ambrose,[73] bishop of Milan.

All these, then, at Ephesus, to the sacred number of the decalogue,[74] were called as teachers, counselors, witnesses, and judges. And that blessed synod, holding their doctrine,[75] following their counsel, believing their testimony, obeying their judgment, without malice, without presumption, without favoritism, made its pronouncement concerning the rules of faith. Although a much greater number of the forefathers might have been adduced, it was unnecessary. The time of the sessions should not have been taken up with a great host of witnesses, and no one had any doubt that those ten had any different feeling from all their other colleagues.

XXXI. UNANIMITY OF THE FATHERS AT EPHESUS

After all this we added the opinion of the blessed Cyril, which is included in these same ecclesiastical proceedings. When the letter of the holy Capreolus,[76] bishop of Carthage,

died at Porto (Ostia) on Nov. 20, 365, also by natural death. From the sixth century on, Felix II was, however, thought to have been a martyr. The extract read was from the *Epist. ad Maximum de incarnatione Verbi* of Felix I, tampered with, in an Apollinarian sense, in the fourth century.

[71] Julius I, bishop of Rome 337–352, notable for his defense of Athanasius. The extract read at the council was from his letter to Docimus, not otherwise preserved.

[72] Cyprian, bishop of Carthage 248–258, a martyr. The extract was from his tractate *De eleemosyna*.

[73] Ambrose, bishop of Milan 374–397. Two extracts from his *De fide* (1.16 and 2.4) were read.

[74] There were twelve, not ten, fathers whose works were read. The two omitted were Atticus of Constantinople (406–425–7) and Amphilochus of Iconium (374–400). Labbe found one MS. in which their names were in a different place from the others, and Vincent may have used such a source.

[75] The writers were for the most part all relatively recent and Milman remarks that the passages had very little bearing on the question.

[76] Capreolus (bishop of Carthage 431–435) became involved in the council in a curious way. Theodosius II had sent Augustine an invitation to participate, but the letter reached Hippo after Augustine's death (Aug. 28, 430). It found its way to Capreolus as primate of Africa, but he declined to undergo the dangers of the journey, which were then great, owing to the Vandal invasion, but sent a priest named Besula with a letter preserved in both Greek and Latin (the latter in MPL 53.843 and MPL

was read, who had no other purpose or plea but that innovation should be defeated and antiquity defended, then Bishop Cyril proposed and carried what may not be out of place to include here. He says at the end of the proceedings, "The letter of the reverend and very devout Bishop Capreolus of Carthage has been read and will be inserted into the authentic acts.[77] His meaning is clear, for he wants the doctrines of the ancient faith to be confirmed, but the innovations which have been unnecessarily invented and wickedly advertised, to be condemned and refuted. All the bishops cried out: 'These are the words of all. So say we all. This is the wish of all.'" What do "the words of all" and "the wish of all" mean except that what was handed down from ancient times should be held; what was recently invented, destroyed?

After this we gave expression to our admiration for the humility and sanctity of that council in which, though the number of bishops[78] was so great, almost a majority from metropolitan sees, of such great learning and such great doctrine that nearly all could discuss the doctrines; men who, seeing that they had assembled for this very purpose, might have been emboldened by this fact to dare something on their own initiative and to establish it, yet they devised nothing new, made no presumption, arrogated to themselves positively nothing, but took every care to hand down nothing to posterity which they themselves had not received from the fathers, and not only did they settle the matter then currently at issue in proper fashion but also furnished an example to their successors in the future of how they too should cherish the doctrines of sacred antiquity, and condemn the inventions of profane novelty.

We also directed our attack against the wicked presumption of Nestorius, who boasted that he was the first and the only one to understand the sacred Scriptures, and that all were ignorant

---

50.682 n. 2) which we translate: "I desire your holiness to be asked again and again, that, with the collaboration of the Holy Spirit who, I doubt not, will be present in your hearts, in everything which you shall do, new doctrines and those unaccustomed to the ears of the church, you will expel from you, instructed by the strength of ancient authority, and that thus you will resist any new errors."

[77] This is doubtless taken from the official minutes. See NPNF, 2d ser., 14.218.

[78] *Sacerdotes*. If this should, instead, be here rendered as *priests*, then *metropolitani* should be *bishops*. Augustine was the only bishop not of metropolitan rank who was invited.

who, before him, endowed with the gift of teaching, had expounded the divine writings; that is, mark you, the entire body of bishops (*sacerdos*), the entire body of confessors and martyrs, some of whom had expounded the law of God, others agreed with those who had expounded it, or believed them. Finally, he even went so far as to maintain that the whole church was now in error and always had been, since it had followed and was still following, as he thought, unlearned and misguided teachers.[79]

XXXII. Celestine and Sixtus Against New Doctrine

43. All this, of course, was enough and more than enough to uproot and put out the profane innovations, yet so that nothing might seem lacking to the fullness of the task, at the end we added the twin authority of the Apostolic See—the one, of course, that of the holy Pope Sixtus,[80] the venerable father who now adorns the Roman church; the other, of his predecessor of blessed memory, Pope[81] Celestine—which now we have decided should be interpolated here.

Holy Pope Sixtus, in the letter which he sent to the bishop of Antioch,[82] speaks as follows about the Nestorian affair: "Therefore, because, as the apostle says, the faith[83] is one— evidently the faith which has also triumphantly prevailed— let us believe what ought to be said and say what ought to be held." What are the things that ought to be believed and said? He continues: "Let nothing further be conceded to innovation because it is proper to add nothing to antiquity. Let the clear faith and belief of our forefathers not be clouded with any muddy mixture." Spoken in every way like an apostle! He

---

[79] In defense of Nestorius, see F. Loofs, *Nestorius and His Place in the History of Christian Doctrine* (Cambridge, 1914); Aubrey R. Vine, *An Approach to Christology* (London, 1948) 31–55.
[80] Sixtus III (432–440) was concerned in restoring peace to the church, but was not interested in Christological problems. The purpose of citing him was, of course, to conciliate him and perhaps to win his help in attacking Augustinianism.
[81] Celestine I (422–432) was primarily concerned with political problems, but participated in the proceedings which led to the Council of Ephesus and the deposition of Nestorius.
[82] John, bishop of Antioch 429–448, took part in the proceedings at Ephesus, but was a friend of Nestorius and opponent of Cyril. The pope's letter referred to is printed in MPL 50.609, dated Sept. 15, 433. It was written to express joy at the reconciliation of John with Cyril.
[83] Cf. Eph. 4:5.

brightens the belief of the forefathers with the light of clarity but describes the novel profanities as a muddy mixture.

Holy Pope Celestine in like manner and with like meaning, in the letter which he sent to the bishops of the Gauls, charging them with conniving with error in that through their silence they failed the ancient faith and were allowing the profane innovations to arise, says: "The indictment rightly refers to us if we foster error by our silence. Therefore, rebuke this sort of people. Let them not have freedom to speak at will." [84] At this point, possibly, someone may not be fully sure who these people are whom he would forbid to have freedom to speak at will, the preachers of antiquity or the inventors of the new. Let Celestine tell, let him himself remove the readers' doubt. He goes on to say, "If it is a fact" (that is, if it is a fact, as some [85] charge before me against your cities and provinces, that by your harmful negligence you cause them to assent to certain novel beliefs)—"if it is a fact, let novelty then cease to assail antiquity." This, then, was the blessed opinion of the blessed Celestine, not that antiquity should cease to uproot novelty, but rather that novelty should stop assailing antiquity.

XXXIII. Summary of Both Commonitories

Whoever resists those apostolic and catholic decrees first of all must necessarily insult the memory of holy Celestine, who decreed that novelty should stop assailing antiquity, and, secondly, he must make fun of the decisions of holy Sixtus, who gave as his conclusion that nothing further be conceded to innovation because it is proper to add nothing to antiquity. Moreover, he also sets little value on the rule of blessed Cyril, who gave high praise to the zeal of the venerable Capreolus because he desired the doctrines of the ancient faith to be confirmed but new inventions to be condemned. So also he stamps his foot upon that synod of Ephesus, that is, upon the judgments of almost all the holy bishops of the East, who gave their vote

---

[84] This letter is printed in MPL 50.528–537, the part quoted in col. 530. The bishops addressed were Venerius of Massilia, Marinus, Leontius, Auxonius, Arcadius, Filuccius, and others. The letter was one of the last official acts of this pope. In appealing to the authority of such a letter, Vincent fails to reveal what the heresy was against which the pope wrote—for the reason, of course, that it was Semi-Pelagianism. In other words, Vincent appropriates a passage from a letter which, if quoted *in toto*, would give confirmation to his opponents.

[85] They were Prosper and Hilary, as the whole letter shows.

under divine guidance to the decree that nothing else should be believed than what the sacred and in Christ harmonious antiquity of the holy fathers had held; who, loudly crying out, with one voice, witnessed that these were the voices of all, that all wished this, that all thought this: that as almost all the heretics before Nestorius, setting little value on antiquity and supporting novelty, had been condemned, so also Nestorius himself, the author of this innovation and the assailant of antiquity, should be condemned.

If their assent, inspired by the gift of sacred grace from heaven, displeases anyone, what else is his object here except to claim that the condemnation of Nestorius' godlessness was not right? Finally, he despises as refuse[86] the whole church of Christ and its teachers, apostles, and prophets, and particularly the blessed apostle Paul. The church he despises because she has never withdrawn from her duty of cherishing and preserving the faith once handed down; the apostle, because he wrote: "O Timothy, guard what has been handed down to you, avoiding the godless chatter of novelties," and again, "If any man should announce to you contrary to what you have received, let him be accursed." But if neither apostolic decisions nor ecclesiastical decrees are to be dishonored, by which, in accordance with the most sacred consensus of ecumenicity and antiquity all heretics always in the past, and in these last days Pelagius, Caelestius, Nestorius, have justly and deservedly been condemned, then certainly it is the duty thenceforth of all catholics who are eager to prove themselves legitimate sons of mother church, to adhere to the holy faith of the holy fathers, to be welded to it, to die in it, but, as for the godless innovations of the godless, to hate them, shudder at them, extirpate them, persecute them.

These are the topics which have been discussed at greater breadth in the two *Commonitories*, but now, by way of summary, have been confined to somewhat smaller space, in order that my memory, to aid which we have composed them, may be supplemented by continually referring to them, without being worn out by their excessive length.

[86] Cf. I Cor. 4:13.

Paschasius Radbertus of Corbie: The Lord's Body and Blood (Selections)

INTRODUCTION

IN THIS SELECTION AND THE NEXT WE PRESENT two works bearing, in the manuscripts, the same title, *The Lord's Body and Blood*, both written during the first half of the ninth century at the Benedictine abbey of Corbie near Amiens, yet representative of opposing points of view.

The first of these contemporary writers is Paschasius Radbertus,[1] a native of the region of Soissons, who entered the newly founded monastery of Corbie while the first abbot, Adalhard, cousin of Charlemagne, was still living. Here his learning soon won for him the post of teacher, which he held for many years. He was well read not only in the Scriptures and the fathers but also in the pagan classics, at least those in Latin, and there is some reason to think he may also have known Greek. He was, however, a man of such remarkable humility, being fond of calling himself "of all monks the scum," that when in 844, upon the death of the third abbot Isaac, he was chosen in his stead, he refused advancement from deacon to presbyter.

The post proved to be no sinecure, for there were disturbances in the monastery, the general nature of which we can guess with a fair degree of probability. Among the monks were the unfortunate Gottschalk[2] and also Ratramnus, both of whom showed marked independence of thought. With the latter, Paschasius was destined to engage in polemics, not only on the

---

[1] See Jean Mabillon in MPL 120.9–24; also Bishop Engelmodus' verses to Abbot Radbertus (MPL 120.25–28), and the official *Privilegium monasterii Corbeiensis, Radberto abbati concessam a synodo Parisiensi anno* 846 (MPL 120.27–32: the date 866 is a misprint).

[2] On Gottschalk, see the *Reply to the Three Letters*, below.

Eucharist, which is our concern here, but also on the Virgin birth. Whatever the cause, Radbertus resigned as head of the abbey about 853 and retired to a life of study.

To the field of Biblical exegesis belong several works: twelve books of commentary on Matthew's Gospel[3]; an exposition of Psalm 44[4]; and five books on Lamentations.[5] Among the shorter works is one *On the Virgin Birth*,[6] another on *Faith, Hope, and Charity*,[7] a third on *The Passion of Saints Rufinus and Valerius*,[8] as well as two biographical compositions, one a life of Saint Adalhard[9] and the other a symposium in memory of Adalhard's brother Wala,[10] who succeeded him as abbot of Corbie.

The year of Paschasius' death is uncertain, but he died on April 26, probably about 865. On his deathbed, we are told, he humbly forbade his monks to compose his biography. The body lay in the church of St. John at Corbie until July 12, 1073, when the remains were transferred to the church of St. Peter.

Radbertus' book *The Lord's Body and Blood* not only is his earliest extant work but is also the first by any author ever to be devoted to the Eucharist. Prepared originally about 831, it was then dedicated to Radbertus' pupil Placidius, afterward Abbot Warin of New Corvey in Westphalia, in the founding of which monastery Radbertus had taken part in 822. The prologue addressed to Placidius[11] survives, as do also fifteen hexameters of an acrostic poem on this work.[12] About the year 844, however, Radbertus determined to send a revision of the treatise to King Charles the Bald. To this he prefixed both another poem of twenty-one hexameters,[13] invoking the Muses, and also a prose letter[14] which makes it clear that the book was intended

---

[3] *Expositio in evangelium Matthaei* (MPL 31.994), addressed to the monk Guntland.
[4] *Expositio in Psalmum* 45 [=44 (R.S.V.)] (MPL 120.993–1060), addressed to the poor nuns of St. Mary at Soissons who had given Radbertus his early education.
[5] *In threnos sive lamentationes Ieremiae libri v* (MPL 120.1059–1256), addressed to Odilmannus Severus.
[6] *Opusculum de partu Virginis* (MPL 120.1365–1386), addressed to a nun of Soissons.
[7] *De fide, spe et charitate libri iii* (MPL 120.1387–1490), addressed to Warin, abbot and archimandrite of [New] Corvey. This is preceded by an acrostic poem ("RADBERTUS LEVITA").
[8] *De passione SS Rufini et Valerii* (MPL 120.1489–1508).
[9] *Vita Sancti Adalhardi Corbeiensis abbatis* (MPL 120.1507–1556).
[10] *Epitaphium Arsenii seu vita venerabilis Walae abbatis Corbeiensis in Gallia* (MPL 120.1557–1650).
[11] MPL 120.1263–1268.   [12] MPL 120.1261–1264.
[13] MPL 120.1259–1260.   [14] MPL 120.1259–1260.

as a Christmas gift for the king. In both poem and preface the modesty of the man is again made abundantly manifest. Finally, when an old man, he again defended his views on the Eucharist in a letter to Frudegard.[15]

For this series our interest in the work resides primarily in the fact that Ratramnus (see next selection) presents a different view. Since Radbertus' work is too long for complete translation, selections have been chosen chiefly to provide a comparison with Ratramnus. During the next centuries Radbertus' views managed to dominate the field, particularly during the controversy associated with Berengarius of Tours, and though Roman Catholic writers are now not unwilling to see faults in Radbertus, he remains to them quite orthodox.

Citations from the Scriptures are naturally frequent but of the fathers he cites by name only Gregory the Great. This is the more surprising since in the prologue he has promised citations from Cyprian, Ambrose, Hilary [of Poitiers], Augustine, John [Chrysostom], Jerome, Gregory, Isidore [of Seville], Isicius [Hesychius], and Bede. Scholars have, however, detected his indebtedness also to Ambrose, Jerome, and Augustine. He also is fond of pious anecdotes, one example of which has been included in the translation.

The chief difference between the concepts of the Eucharist expressed by Radbertus and Ratramnus is that for the former the bread and wine on the altar become, after consecration by the priest, the true body and blood of Christ, whereas for the latter they are symbolically such. Radbertus is also very explicit that the true body and blood are identical with the natural body and blood visible during the Lord's life on earth and now reigning in heaven, another belief on which Ratramnus takes precisely the opposite view. That Radbertus is in error on this point is admitted by the Roman Catholic theologian Pohle,[16] who suspects that Radbertus inclined to "a grossly carnal Capharnaite-like apprehension." More than a century later, Radbertus' work is mentioned in the *Dicta de corpore et sanguine Domini*, formerly ascribed to Gerbert (Pope Silvester II, 999–1003), now believed to be by Hériger of Lobbes (d. 1007).

For Radbertus *figura* means "outward appearance" and *veritas*, "what faith teaches," though the latter to Ratramnus is "what is perceptible to the senses" and the former "what faith teaches."

[15] *Epistola de corpore et sanguine Domini ad Frudegardum* (MPL 120.1351–1366).
[16] CE 11.518.

Radbertus also gives attention to a number of interesting questions involved in the rite, for example: why bread and wine are used for the rite; why water is mixed with the wine; whether celebration by a bad priest invalidates the rite; why the elements undergo no visible change in appearance (though he cites instances where they are reported to have appeared otherwise to the eyes of persons of great faith); what are the words of consecration; whether the benefit from Communion varies with the size of the piece of bread received; why a fragment of the bread is dipped in the wine; and why, though Christ instituted the Lord's Supper *after* a meal, the church now prescribes complete fast before Mass.

Paschasius is quoted by Rathier of Verona (MPL 136.444–450) and by Gezo of Tortona (MPL 137.371–373).

This *Lord's Body and Blood* was first edited for print by a Lutheran, Hiobus Gast (Hagenau, 1528), whose edition has been much castigated by Roman Catholic theologians, in particular by Nicolaus Mameranus, who accuses Gast of expunging anything not fitting his own theological position and of interpolating Lutheran beliefs. The work was first printed under Roman Catholic auspices by Guillaume Ratus in 1540, and Mameranus' edition appeared at Cologne in 1550, John Vlimmerus' at Louvain in 1561. From the complete edition of Radbertus' extant works, edited in 1618 by the Jesuit Jacques Sirmond, the *abbé* Migne drew the text of most of volume 120 of his *Patrologiae cursus completus*: Series Latina, but for this work he used, instead, E. Martène and U. Durand's *Veterum Scriptorum et Monumentorum Amplissima Collectio*, vol. 9 (Paris, 1724–1733). While this edition[17] is occasionally supplied with critical notes which have superior readings, the text itself is very corrupt and the task of translation unusually hard. There seems to have been no previous version into English and the only translation into any language, this into German, is contained in P. M. Hausherr's *Der heilige Paschasius Radbertus: eine Stimme über die Eucharistie vor tausend Jahren* (Mainz, 1862), which we have not seen. Consult Eugène Choisy, *Paschase Radbert: Étude historique sur le IXe siècle et sur le dogme de la cène* (Paris, 1888); C. Gliozzo, *La dottrina in Paschasio Radberto e Ratramno, monaci di Corbia* (Palermo, 1945); Henri Peltier, *Pascase Radbert, abbé de Corbie: contribution à l'étude de la vie monastique* (Amiens, Duthoit, 1938); his article in DTC 13.1628–1639, and J. Pohle's article in CE 11.518.

[17] MPL 120.1267–1350, with critical notes.

Paschasius Radbertus of Corbie: The Lord's Body and Blood (Selections)

THE TEXT

I, 2. It is . . . clear that nothing is possible outside the will of God or contrary to it, but all things wholly yield to him. Therefore, let no man be moved from this body and blood of Christ which in a mystery are true flesh and true blood since the Creator so willed it: "For all things whatsoever he willed he did in heaven and on earth,"[18] and because he willed, he may remain in the figure of bread and wine. Yet these must be believed to be fully, after the consecration, nothing but Christ's flesh and blood. As the Truth himself said to his disciples: "This is my flesh for the life of the world,"[19] and, to put it in more miraculous terms, nothing different, of course, from what was born of Mary, suffered on the cross, and rose again from the tomb. . . . If our words seem unbelievable to anyone, let him note all the miracles of the Old and New Testaments which, through firm faith, were accomplished by God contrary to natural order, and he will see clearer than day that for God nothing is impossible, since all things that God wills to be, and whatsoever he wills, actually take place. . . .

4. . . . For the will in no respect acts without power, nor is the power without wisdom, because God's will is power and wisdom. Therefore, whatever he wills comes to be as he wills, and in no respect is faulty. Because he wills all things in his wisdom, his very wisdom is his will, and for this reason he wills no evil, nothing impossible for himself. Thus, because he so willed that his flesh and blood be this mystery, never doubt it, if you believe God, but with true faith always remember that this is that true flesh which was offered for the life of the world. Whoever eats of it in worthy fashion will never see death

[18] Ps. 115:3 (113:2:2, V).   [19] John 6:51.

through all eternity. For Christ left to his church in a mystery nothing greater than this sacrament and that of Baptism, as well as the Holy Scriptures in all of which the Holy Spirit, who is the pledge of the whole church, inwardly works the mysteries of our salvation unto immortality. But in them nothing miraculous is offered unbelievers, nothing better to believers, nothing more miraculous and nothing richer in this life, not that they may appear visible to the sight of the eyes but that in faith and understanding they may smell sweetly in the divine mysteries and that in them eternity and participation in Christ may be granted to men in the unity of his body.

5. For this reason therefore this mystery is far different from all those miracles which have occurred in this life, because they all occurred so that this one may be believed, that Christ is truth, yet truth is God, and if God is truth, whatever Christ has promised in this mystery is in the same way truth. Therefore the true flesh and blood of Christ, which anyone worthily eats and drinks, have eternal life abiding in them, but in corporeal appearance and taste they are not on this account changed, as long as faith is exercised for righteousness. And because of faith's desert the reward of righteousness is achieved in it. For the other miracles of Christ confirm this one of his Passion, and so the elements are not outwardly changed in appearance on account of the miracle but inwardly, that faith may be proved in spirit. Most truly we confess that because "the just man lives from faith" [20] he should have the righteousness of faith in the mystery, and through faith receive the life abiding in it, by which, the more securely mortal man has fed on immortality, the faster he speeds to the immortal, where he arrives, not on his feet, but through faith with good works.

6. In every way it is clear that as in paradise there was the tree of life from which the state of man might have continued forever, had he kept the commandments, and immortality, so in the church this mystery of salvation is provided; not that it is like that tree in nature, but an invisible power works inwardly through something visible. So in that visible sacrament of Communion, the divine virtue sustains us unto immortality by its invisible power, as if from the fruit of the tree in paradise, both by the taste of wisdom and by virtue, and through it we are immortal in spirit providing we take it worthily, and at last we are carried for the better to immortality. For this then "the Word was made flesh and dwelt among us," [21]

[20] Rom. 1:17. [21] John 1:14.

and that, through God the Word made flesh, the flesh might progress to God the Word, the Word's flesh, of course, becomes food in this mystery. And the food of the faithful, while it is believed to be the flesh for the life of the world and nothing else than the flesh of Christ's body from which Christ remains in us, and that we through it might be transformed into Him who was made nothing else than God's flesh deigning to dwell in us. If, then, it dwells in us so that we might remain members of his body in it, it is right that we are in it so that from it we might live and thus feed upon the flesh of the Word and drink his blood. This is, I say, the strengthening of our faith, this, its unity and sharing of life, where if the order of nature is sought, reason fails, and yet the truth of the fact remains outside human reason, so that in the reasoning of faith the force and power of the Godhead is believed in every way effective, because the doubting mind, though he who has the doubt be of good life, excludes it, so as not to reach an understanding of this sacrament.

II, 1. Of the sacrament of the Lord's body and blood daily celebrated in the church, no one of the faithful ought to be ignorant or unaware what in it pertains to faith and what to knowledge, because faith in the mystery is not rightly defended without knowledge, nor is knowledge nurtured without faith which it does not yet receive, yet sometime may perceive. For this reason the power of so great a sacrament must be examined, and Christ's teaching must be learned by faith, so that we may not be thought therefore unworthy, at least if we do not sufficiently discern this and do not understand how very worthy is the mystical body and blood of Christ, and how mighty in power, and how distinct from what may be corporeally tasted that it transcends every sacrifice of the Old Testament.

2. Whoever does not know this is undiscerning and should fear that from ignorance what has been provided us for our cure should end in ruin for those who receive it. Thence the Lord says in Leviticus: "If a man eats of a holy thing unwittingly, let him add a fifth part with what he ate and he will give it to the priest for the sanctuary. You will not profane the holy things of the Children of Israel which they offer to the Lord lest possibly they bear the iniquity of their crime when they have eaten holy things." [22] And he added: "I am the Lord who sanctify them." Then "they are the holy of holies." [23] There, surely, the mystery of Christ's body and blood is meant, of

---

[22] Lev. 22:14.   [23] Not an exact quotation of any passage.

which no one has the power to eat—not only no foreigner, sojourner, or hireling, but not even one who is blinded by ignorance of so great a mystery. Through ignorance, however, he who is completely ignorant of its power and value and the nature of the sacrament itself, perceives this. He does not truly know what the Lord's body and blood may be according to the truth, though in the sacrament it is received through faith. Indeed, he receives the mystery but does not know the power of the mystery, whence Solomon—no, through him, rather, the divine Spirit—commands us: "When you sit down at the table of a powerful man, to eat with a prince, pay careful attention to what are placed before you, since you know that you ought to prepare such things," [24] that is, to preach the death of Christ in the body that daily must be carried about. Carefully understanding and worthily perceiving the spiritual sacraments by the soul's palate and the taste of faith is like adding the fifth part to what one had earlier eaten through ignorance, when our inner man through Christ's grace receives the divine with understanding and by that power of faith is embodied in Christ. In some other manner the law would order that a fifth part be added to what any man had unwittingly eaten, although now no longer was anything in existence to which something could be further added. For something is not added to what does not exist but to what already exists. The Seventy [25] rightly order the fifth part to be added in addition to itself. For its fifth part is then rightly added to what was formerly unwittingly received, if the five senses of the body are inwardly converted to what are spiritually intelligible, because we know aright or perceive aright, the divine spirit which is in us is also enhanced by that same grace and teaches and increases those senses of ours to perceive them. So also, of course, to entice inwardly to the mystical reality not only taste but also sight and hearing, as well as smell and touch, in some manner it reveals that nothing is felt in them save the divine, nothing save the heavenly elements, and that something very terrifying is communicated. Thus how well is it put: "Let him add a fifth part on top of it," or, as other manuscripts have it, "with it and will give it to the priest." And because we should know that every sanctification of the mystical sacrifice is in some way efficacious, a thing capable of intelligible perception through the senses is divinely transformed by God's power through the Word of

[24] Prov. 23:1, quoted also by Ratramnus.
[25] Vulgate: *cum eo* = Sept. ἐπ' αὐτό.

Christ into his flesh and blood, and those who communicate in it through these are spiritually nourished. Everything should be universally attributed to Christ, indeed, who is the true and high priest, and everything marked with his virtue and his power. Because, of course, he frees us from all ignorance and removes us from the carnal attractions of this life, and he permits nothing earthly or vile to be seen there, but to know spiritual and mystical things in them so that our bodily senses may be more eagerly transferred to sanctifying them, if in any way the human element can be called more pre-eminent. "My heart and my flesh have cried out to the living God." [26]

3. Rightly then does every man cry out to the living God because everyone may daily eat the flesh and blood of Christ, yet the Lamb himself remains alive and whole, for he does not die: "Death has no further dominion over him." [27] He is truly, however, sacrificed each day in the mystery, is consumed for the washing away of sins. Thus the statement in the law is brought to bear: "I am the Lord who sanctify them." [28] He sanctifies, however, those who through these elements properly approach the sanctifying God and prayerfully receive them in the manner they ought. Because of sanctification and not contamination, he has proposed to the reborn in Christ: in some other way "he will bear the iniquity of their sin." [28] As the law says, "Whoever shall contaminate what is holy, unwittingly eating or seeking it in unworthy fashion out of contempt," hence they who receive the sacraments of life ought to be taught that if any man by chance is through sloth unaware of the salutary teachings of faith, he himself may be completely pardoned by the Lord.

III, 1. A sacrament is anything handed down to us in any divine celebration as a pledge of salvation, when what is visibly done accomplishes inwardly something far different, to be taken in a holy sense. They are called sacraments either because they are secret in that in the visible act divinity inwardly accomplishes something secretly through the corporeal appearance, or from the sanctifying consecration, because the Holy Spirit, remaining in the body of Christ, latently accomplishes for the salvation of the faithful all these mystical sacraments under the cover of things visible. By this divine power he teaches the souls of believers about things invisible more than if he visibly revealed what inwardly is

[26] Ps. 84:2 (83:3, V).   [27] Rom. 6:9.
[28] Lev. 22:16.

effective for salvation: "For we walk by faith and not by sight."[29]

2. Christ's sacraments in the church are Baptism and anointing,[30] and the Lord's body and blood, which are called sacraments because under their visible appearance the divine flesh is secretly hallowed through power, so that they are inwardly in truth what they are outwardly believed to be by the power of faith. There is a legal sense of the word "sacrament," that is, an oath, in which after choosing sides each person takes an oath concerning what he has determined by his agreement. This is called a sacrament because secretly invisible faith, through consecration by prayer to God or through something sacred, is grasped, because outwardly by sight or hearing the voice of the one swearing is heard. The birth of Christ, therefore, and all that dispensation of humanity, becomes, as it were, a great sacrament, because in the visible man the divine majesty inwardly for the sake of our consecration worked invisibly those things which came into being secretly by his power. Thus the mystery or sacrament, which is God made man, is rightly so called, but the word "*mystērion*" is Greek for what has in it a hidden and secret character. It is a sacrament in the divine Scriptures wherever the sacred Spirit accomplishes something in them inwardly by speaking. But instructed by the sacrament of the Scriptures, we are divinely fed from within, and, being fed, we are instructed to fulfillment of Christ's teaching. In the sacrament of his birth and humanity, however, we are also redeemed unto pardon, and the Scriptures are revealed unto understanding, and through it a way is shown to us and power is bestowed on us that we may pass from the condition of servants into that of adopted children. Furthermore, in the sacrament of Baptism a door for entering into adoption is opened for believers, that thenceforth in Christ's members, through that same rebirth freed from evil, we may be made one body. In this baptism, of course, and afterward, the Holy Spirit is poured forth upon the soul of the one being reborn, so that the whole church of Christ may be quickened when a single spirit has been received, and it may be made one body. Because as all members of our body are

[29] II Cor. 5:7.
[30] In this sentence "anointing" is part of the baptismal rite. Radbertus recognizes but two sacraments, Baptism and the Eucharist. His contemporary Rabanus Maurus includes with these extreme unction. The list of seven sacraments came to acceptance only with the Scholastics under the influence of Peter Lombard (d. 1164).

animated and guided by one soul, so that from the union of the parts one body results, so the parts of the whole church are guided and animated by one Holy Spirit that they be made one body of Christ. "Because if any man have not the Spirit of Christ, he is not his." [31]

3. No one therefore doubts that each of us, still in his mother's womb, receives a soul secretly, that is, to the end that he be made man with a living soul. So, meanwhile, the mother does not know when, through her, before birth, he enters life. In the same way, of course, no one ought to doubt that in the womb of Baptism, before the babe rises from the fount, the Holy Spirit enters into one reborn, although not seen; that the divine power is no less provident and efficacious for the regeneration of holy adoption than it was previously in the birth by flesh, to quicken the sown members of a man, though conceived in sin. Wherefore, we have no doubt that God, who surveys all things and is powerful over them, always grants grace that is capable of preventing what he has ordained from being changed. If within the father's lust and the sin of the mother the seed of passion becomes the members of a living man, so in times and places when the Holy Spirit is present, because he fills the whole earth, he offers himself rather to everyone reborn through faith, so that through him the members of Christ may feel themselves one, and that all of them may become one body.

4. But on the journey through this life we only feed upon and drink the sacrament of the body and blood so that nourished from it we may be made one in Christ, that being invigorated by tasting him we may be prepared for things immortal and eternal. While we are now fed on angelic grace we may be quickened spiritually. For us, however, in all these sacraments the divine Spirit works. If, indeed, in the Holy Scriptures he illumines our hearts, because "neither he who plants nor he who waters is anything but it is God who gives the increase." [32] Of this Ezekiel says: "For the Spirit of life was in the wheels," [33] and John says: "Let him who has ears for hearing hear what the Spirit says to the churches." [34] But in Christ the same Spirit is at work because Christ is believed to have been conceived from Him and the Virgin Mary.[35] In like manner, in the baptism

---

[31] Rom. 8:9.   [32] I Cor. 3:7.   [33] Ezek. 1:21.   [34] Rev. 2:7 (OL).
[35] MPL 120.1277 reads, "Mary ever Virgin," but Martène admits in the note that the majority of codexes do not have the adverb, which he interpolates from a marginal note in one codex only.

through the water we are from him all regenerated, and afterward we daily feed upon Christ's body and drink his blood by his power. No wonder that the Spirit which without seed created the man Christ in the womb of the Virgin, from the substance of bread and wine daily creates the flesh and blood of Christ by invisible power through the sanctification of his sacrament, though outwardly understood by neither sight nor taste. But because they are spiritual things, they are fully received as certainties by faith and understanding, as the Truth foretold.

IV, 1. That in truth the body and blood are created by the consecration of the mystery, no one doubts who believes the divine words when the Truth says: "For my flesh is truly food, and my blood is truly drink." [36] And that when his disciples did not rightly understand, he clearly identified what flesh he meant, what blood: "He who eats my flesh and drinks my blood, abides in me and I in him." [36] Therefore, if it is truly food, it is true flesh, and if it is truly drink, it is true blood. How else will what he says be true: "The bread which I shall give, my flesh, is for the life of the world," [37] unless it be true flesh? and the "bread which came down from heaven," [38] true bread? But because it is not right to devour Christ with the teeth, he willed in the mystery that this bread and wine be created truly his flesh and blood through consecration by the power of the Holy Spirit, by daily creating it so that it might be mystically sacrificed for the life of the world; so that as from the Virgin through the Spirit true flesh is created without union of sex, so through the same, out of the substance of bread and wine, the same body and blood of Christ may be mystically consecrated. It is plainly of this flesh and blood that he says: "Verily, verily, I say to you, except you eat of the flesh of the Son of Man and drink his blood, you will not have eternal life in you." [39] There, certainly, he is speaking about no other flesh than the true flesh and the true blood, that is, in a mystical sense. And because the sacrament is mystical, we cannot deny the figure, but if it is a figure, one must ask how it can be truth. For every figure is the figure of something, and always has reference to it in order that it might be a true thing of which it is the figure. That the figures of the Old Testament were shadows, no one who reads the sacred literature is in doubt, but this mystery is either truth or a figure and in the latter case a shadow. One should certainly inquire whether all this

[36] John 6:55, 56.   [37] John 6:51.   [38] John 6:51.   [39] John 6:53.

can be called truth without a shadow of falsity, though a mystery of this sort must be called a reality. But it seems to be a figure when it is "broken," when something is understood in visible appearance other than what is sensed by the sight and taste of the flesh, and when the blood in the cup is at the same time mixed with water. Furthermore, that sacrament of faith is rightly called truth; truth, therefore, when the body and blood of Christ is created by the power of the Spirit in his word out of the substance of bread and wine; but a figure when, through the agency of the priest at the altar, outwardly performing another thing, in memory of his sacred Passion, the Lamb is daily sacrificed as he was once for all.

2. If we truthfully examine the matter, it is rightly called both the truth and a figure, so that it is a figure or character of truth because it is outwardly sensed. Truth, however, is anything rightly understood or believed inwardly concerning this mystery. Not every figure is a shadow or falsity, whence Paul, speaking to the Hebrews about God's only Son, says, "Since he is the splendor of glory and the figure of his substance, bearing all things by the word of his power, making purification of sins."[40] In these words, certainly, he declares that there are two substances in Christ, each of them true. For when he says, "Since He is the splendor of the glory," of divinity, he proclaims him as consubstantial. But since the figure or character of his substance marks the human nature, where the fullness of divinity dwells corporeally, nevertheless, the one and true Christ is universally represented as God. For this reason he takes one thing for the demonstration of two substances and calls it the figure or character of substance, because as through characters or the figures of letters we as small children first progressed gradually to reading, later to the spiritual senses and understanding of the Scriptures, so also there is a progression from the humanity of Christ to the divinity of the Father, and therefore it is rightly called the figure or character of his substance. What else are the figures of letters than their characters, that through them force and power and utterance of spirit are demonstrated to the eyes? So also the Word is formed flesh that through flesh we as small children may be nourished to the understanding of divinity. Yet the characters of the letters are not falsity, nor are they anything but letters. Neither can the man Christ be called false nor anything but God, with the result, of course, that the figure may rightly be

---

[40] Heb. 1:3.

called the character of the divinity's substance. Because he advances us small children through himself to things spiritual, which must be understood inwardly and by our senses, he shows himself in visible form while we receive what is in it. But because he, after the flesh had to penetrate to heavens, so that, through faith, those reborn in him might with greater boldness seek, he has left us this sacrament, a visible figure and character of flesh and blood, so that through them our soul and our flesh are richly nourished for grasping things invisible and spiritual by faith. This which is outwardly sensed is, however, the figure or character but wholly truth and no shadow, because intrinsically perceived, and for this reason nothing else henceforth than truth and the sacrament of his flesh is apparent.

3. As it is the true flesh of Christ which was crucified and buried, truly is it the sacrament of his flesh, which is divinely consecrated through the Holy Spirit on the altar by the agency of the priest in Christ's word. The Lord himself proclaims, "This is my body."[41] Do not be surprised, O man, and do not ask about the order of nature here; but if you truly believe that that flesh was without seed created from the Virgin Mary in her womb by the power of the Holy Spirit, so that the Word might be made flesh, truly believe also that what is constructed in Christ's word through the Holy Spirit is his body from the Virgin. If you ask the method, who can explain or express it in words? Be assured, please, that the method resides in Christ's virtue, the knowledge in faith, the cause in power, but the effect in will, because the power of divinity over nature effectively works beyond the capacity of our reason. Therefore, let knowledge be held in the teaching of salvation, let faith be preserved in the mystery of truth, since in all these "we walk by faith and not by sight."[29]

V, 1. That that sacrifice of the lamb was a figure of Christ's Passion and of our participation in it, no one of the faithful is rightly unaware. But the difference between the two sacraments should, I think, be investigated: whether between the food which came down from heaven, and the water which flowed from the rock, or between that spiritual and divine exchange, especially since the blessed apostle proclaims that "all our fathers ate the same spiritual food and all drank the same spiritual drink."[42] If they received the same food and the same drink, why was it necessary for what it was to be changed and to be given under a different guise, if it were nothing more?

[41] Luke 22:19. [42] I Cor. 10:3.

From this it must be admitted that that food and that drink was the same that we now receive, and that rock from which the waters flowed was what is now preached, in the apostle's words, as Christ. Of course it was the same food, because to those who spiritually received it the manna was the type of the food of Christ's body, and that water which had flowed from the rock was drink and the figure of blood. If, indeed, in the prefiguration the shadow of the body and its original were the same, but not the same in the fulfillment of truth, because what was then foreshadowed in the symbol of things to come was the image of truth, now, however, the mystery of truth fulfilled and the Eucharist, the flesh of Christ, has been created out of the resurrection. The flesh of Christ was at an earlier time through the lamb or through that same heavenly food prefigured to believers. Of this bread David sang in the proverbs, "Man has eaten the bread of angels." [43] Otherwise that bread, that one which came down from heaven, and the drink, because it was corporeal, was not fitting for angels, but undoubtedly that bread and drink by which Christ was foreshadowed is the food of angels, and this sacrament is his true flesh and blood which man spiritually eats and drinks. And therefore man lives on what the angels live on because everything is spiritual and divine in what man receives.

2. It is clear, then, that both that lamb of the law and the manna, and everything of this kind which bore the figure of the flesh and blood of Christ, because he once suffered in the Passion, and each day on the altar is sacrificed in the morning and the evening, possessed nothing except the figure of that mystery; and if any power to be hallowed lay hidden in these, it has shone forth completely from the faith we enjoy. This they shared, to be sure, sighing, as it were, for the promise, through faith, and they understood from the figures the sacrament of truth. We, however, have now long received this grace promised to the fathers, and having received it we venerate it, and venerating it we are fed and watered from it. In the mystery we take the true flesh and blood of Christ, not foreshadowed, indeed, by figures drawn from puzzles in the law, but when these are solved and removed, we enjoy truth alone. Thus the Saviour says: "My flesh is truly food and my blood is truly drink. He who eats this flesh and he who drinks this blood has life eternal." [44] But the Lord says to the Jews, "Your fathers ate

[43] Ps. 78:25 (77:25, V).
[44] John 6:54, 55.

manna in the desert and died." [45] Shall we not also, who eat these things, die in this life even as they? We shall die but not, however, as they did, in the soul, because, eating carnally, they died eternally. We, however, know nothing carnal in it, but, understanding everything spiritual, shall spiritually remain in Christ. Therefore, concerning those who rightly perceive, he himself proclaims, "He who eats this bread shall live forever." [37] We do not spiritually take the flesh and blood for the sake of this life so that we may not die temporally, but for the sake of life eternal, upon which life, of course, they did not embark who formerly perceived these things worthily in a figure until the promised grace should come to us and to them in like fashion.

3. It is clear, therefore, that there is a great deal of difference, although the same food and the same drink are preached by the apostle, yet they are not actually the same but in appearance and in a figure in which the promise of truth was inherent. From this the spiritual understanding and the sacrament of faith which were to come were shared by them, so that they lacked nothing in the spirit which now they drank in hope, nor do we, remembering them, lack what is profitable for strengthening of faith and laying hold on life. Both we and they, however, being spiritual, are quickened by receiving, because they drank from the spiritual rock that followed them, meaning that after them Christ would come. Likewise, we also spiritually drink and eat the spiritual flesh of Christ, in which eternal life is believed to be. To know otherwise is death after the flesh, but spiritually to receive the true flesh of Christ is life eternal.

VI, 1. This, of course, Christ explains: "Who eats my flesh and drinks my blood remains in me and I in him." [36] This [46] it is to eat that flesh and to drink that blood, if he remains in Christ and Christ can remain in him who receives it worthily. He therefore remains in Christ who, reborn from water and Spirit, is held guilty of no mortal offense, and in him [remains] Christ who opened to him the door of faith through consecration by the Holy Spirit, so that he might be a member in his body, and he is a temple of the Holy Spirit. Because "if any man does not have the spirit of Christ, he is not his." [31] He who is not his, however, cannot truly be in him nor in his body, and he who does not remain in him, nor the life of the spirit live in his body, neither is Christ in him nor can he be in Christ, because in every way Christ is life. He, however, who is guilty

[45] John 6:49. See Ratramnus, note 96, below.
[46] Cf. Augustine, *In Ioann. ev. tract.* 26:18 (NPNF, 1st ser., 7.173).

of a mortal sin is far separated from life. This is the reason why He says, "Who eats my flesh and drinks my blood remains in me and I in him"; [36] otherwise unless he first remains in me and I in him, he cannot eat my flesh or drink my blood.

2. And what is it that men eat? They all eat, without distinction, what they often receive as sacraments of the altar. They receive them, of course, but one man spiritually eats the flesh of Christ and drinks his blood; another man, however, does not, although he may seem to receive the wafer from the hand of the priest. And what does he take, when there is a consecration, if he does not take the body and blood of Christ? Truly, because a wicked man takes it unworthily, as the apostle Paul says: "He eats and drinks judgment for himself, not first testing himself nor discerning the Lord's body." [47] See what a sinner eats and what he drinks—not flesh and blood of value to himself, but judgment. He may, of course, seem to take the sacrament of the altar with the others. Why? Because he does not test himself nor discern the Lord's body. Let the man without faith consider that, unworthy as he is, he can receive worthy and sacred things, not, indeed, expecting anything except what he sees, nor understanding anything other than he feels with his lip. Vainly, then, does he believe or understand what or how great is the judgment he incurs, because, of course, he visibly sees them all eating together from one substance, and if there is any further power in it he does not sufficiently taste it by faith. On this account the power of the sacrament is withdrawn from him and in the same he is doubly condemned because of his presumption. Of this the apostle speaks: "Let a man test himself first and so eat of that bread and drink from the cup." [48] Having observed these two rules, he may see whether he can take it worthily, namely, that he discerns the Lord's body, what the sacrament is, or how great it is, what sort of power it has, because it is divine and spiritual. Then let him test himself whether he is in Christ's body, or if Christ remains in him. Otherwise, except he discerns that spiritually and tests whether he is fit to receive it, he eats judgment for himself, because he makes a bad use of something good. In that case he does not take it for life, but in it condemnation to punishment.

3. And to confirm our statements by more certain proofs, let us tell what happened afterward to a certain man without faith who, not discerning the Lord's body nor testing himself according to the apostle, presumed to take this mystery unworthily.

[47] I Cor. 11:29. [48] I Cor. 11:28.

When the blessed Syrus,[49] first bishop of Pavia, was celebrating Mass in the church of the martyrs Gervasius and Protasius,[50] which he had himself dedicated, there were present a great number of his children whom he had begotten for God, to use the words of the apostle.[51] Into these devoutly holy mysteries there boldly entered a certain Jew,[52] who was put up by an evil spirit to try to take the Lord's body and to spit it out on a dunghill. In the throng of the faithful receiving the holy Eucharist from the hand of the bishop he approached the hands of the man of God with wicked daring, and with unclean lip took the Lord's body, and opened his mouth to spit it out. Struck with fitting punishment, he began loudly to cry out, but his words were unintelligible, in the sight and hearing of everyone. He attempted to shut his lips but could not; he tried to speak but his stiff tongue would not function properly and, as if he were carrying a burning dart in his mouth, he was tortured with mighty pain. The whole church rang with the clamor of his bawling, and the company of the faithful rejoiced at the power of so extraordinary a miracle of Christ, and the saying, "He himself scoffs at the scoffers"[53] was fulfilled; also what the apostle says, writing to the Galatians: "Do not make a mistake. God is not mocked for whatever a man sows, that he will also reap"[54]; also, what the Truth himself proclaims in the Gospel when he says: "With what measure you measure it shall be measured out to you again."[55] This unbelieving Jew must have neither heard nor read these preachings of the Scriptures if he thought he could play a trick on Christ and the Holy Spirit. The man of God directed him to be brought into his presence and, when he had come, said to him: "Soul who art without faith and full of perfidy, why have you fulfilled the plan of the wicked adversary to make you think the body of Christ very cheap? Look, what secret enticer has seduced you, poor man, to make you do this has been shown to all his faithful by divine power." The Jew, however, worsted by the great pain, never ceased uttering cries that could not be understood, so long as he had in his throat the pain of his evil, because, according to the

[49] An obscure figure, of whose dates nothing is certainly known.
[50] Martyred at Milan in the reign of Nero. Cf. Ambrose, *Epist.* 22; Augustine *Conf.* 9.7; *Acta Sanctorum*, June, 3.817–846; NSH 4.477. The church no longer exists at Pavia.
[51] Perhaps allusion to I Cor. 4:15.
[52] The story has been included as typical of Radbertus' attitude.
[53] Ps. 59:8 (58:9, V). Neither Vulgate nor Septuagint is followed closely.
[54] Gal. 6:7.   [55] Mark 4:24.

prophecy of most holy Simeon,[56] as to the faithless the Word of God is danger and destruction, so to his faithful he is life and exaltation. To those who looked carefully, the Lord's body seemed to hang in the Jew's mouth, neither settling down beneath the tongue nor from above clinging to the palate. When all the faithful begged mercy for him, the Lord's man Syrus stretched forth his hand and withdrew the mystery of the holy Eucharist from the sacrilegious mouth and said: "Look now, unbeliever, you have been freed. From now on take care not to do anything similar or to repeat this, lest something worse happen to you." The Jew, having thrown himself at his feet, said that he would believe in the Lord Christ if the water of sacred Baptism should pour upon him, and he would unite with the pious throng, and he confessed what he had intended to do when rashly presuming to take the Lord's body, also the sin of his former unbelief, and, lastly, said that he would hold to the firmness of true faith. "O God the Omnipotent Father," said the blessed bishop Syrus, "to thee I give thanks, who hast not disdained to correct Jewish treachery but convertest it to faith in thy only-begotten Son in full piety." When the man was baptized, many of the Jews, also believing on Christ, were reborn with him in sacred Baptism and were joined to Christ's faithful and the spiritual assembly. We have inserted this story of divine punishment into this little book of ours so that no unbeliever, before he discerns what the Lord's body is, or anyone guilty of a mortal crime, before he reconciles himself to Christ in peace, testing himself through penitence, should presume to eat of this bread or drink of this cup rashly and carelessly.

[56] Luke 2:25.

Ratramnus of Corbie: Christ's Body and Blood

INTRODUCTION

THE SECOND WORK ON THE EUCHARIST PRODUCED at Corbie in the ninth century was written by Ratramnus, priest and monk, of whom little is known save that he was still living at Corbie in 868 and was on terms of intimacy with King Charles the Bald. The main facets of Ratramnus' character were, first, an excellent knowledge of the Scriptures and the fathers; secondly, a clear and lucid style, undecorated, however, with classical allusions; and, thirdly, remarkable independence of thought.[1]

Several other works of his have come down to us, the order of composition being uncertain. The earliest may have been the book *On the Nativity of Christ*,[2] perhaps written in reply to Radbertus' *De partu Virginis*.[3] A second, *On the Predestination of God*,[4] is in two books and defends predestination to salvation and damnation, rejects predestination to sin. Though the work which we here translate now gives Ratramnus his chief claim to fame, it was the four books *Against the Objections of the Greeks who Slandered the Roman Church*[5] which probably seemed to contemporaries his principal achievement, a reply to the attack made upon the Western church by Photius, twice Patriarch of Constantinople (858–867, 878–886), and are concerned with the "Filioque Controversy." The first three books are devoted to demonstration from, respectively, the Bible, the councils, and the fathers, of the so-called doctrine of the double procession,

[1] The subsidiary materials in Bakhuizen's edition, cited below, have been found very helpful.
[2] *De nativitate Christi* alias *De eo quod Christus ex Virgine natus est* (MPL 121.81–102).
[3] MPL 120.1365–1386.   [4] *De praedestinatione Dei* (MPL 121.11–80).
[5] *Contra Graecorum opposita Romanam ecclesiam infamantium* (ibid. 223–346).

while the fourth consists of justification of distinctively Western usages, e.g., celibacy and the tonsure. In the most curious *Letter on the Dog-headed Creatures*,[6] Ratramnus again shows his independence by departing from the commonly accepted view that these fabulous creatures are animals. Since they appear to possess reason, he sees no objection to thinking them descendants of Adam, and he also takes occasion to condemn the book of the blessed Clement (doubtless the "Clementine Recognitions") as not in accord with the doctrine of the church. There are also two works *On the Soul*: the first in opposition to a certain Macarius Scotus, has only recently been published.[7] The second, *On the Quantity of the Soul*, refutes the theory that the soul is circumscribed or restricted by limitations of space. Six letters[8] to and from Ratramnus have survived, but there was a defense of the Trinity, now lost, written in opposition to Hincmar's proposal to revise the wording of the hymn "Sanctorum meritis inclyta gaudia" from *te, trina Deitas unaque*[9] to *te, summa Deitas*, a change smelling, to Ratramnus' nostril, of Sabellianism. Ratramnus was not afraid to express his own convictions.

The work with which we have here to deal is usually known by the same title as the corresponding work by Paschasius Radbertus, namely, *The Lord's Body and Blood* (*De corpore et sanguine Domini*), but though this phrase does appear in it more than once, the author much more frequently favors the phrase *corpus et sanguis Christi* (Christ's body and blood) and to help to distinguish the two works, we have adopted that title. Though certainly, at least in part, an irenic attack on Paschasius' eucharistic position, no reference is made to the mighty opposite, save allusion to views of certain persons not named. From the opening and closing paragraphs it is clear that the occasion for writing was a request for the author's opinions on the Eucharist made by a monarch, now identified as Charles the Bald, King of the West Franks from 840 onward, and Roman emperor from 875 to 877. It is likely that the date of composition was not long after Paschasius had sent a revised text of his book to Charles in 844.

[6] *Epist. de cynocephalis ad Rimbertum presbyterum scripta* (ibid. 1153-1156).
[7] A. Wilmart, "L'opuscule inédité de Ratramne sur la nature de l'âme" (*Revue Bénédictine* 43 [1931] 207-223). On Macarius Scotus, see James Kenney, *Sources for the Ecclesiastical History of Ireland*, §356, pp. 549 f.
[8] MGH *Epist.* 6.149-158: letter 10 is merely the epistolary parts of the *De corpore et sanguine Domini*.
[9] See Hincmar's *De una et non trina Deitate* (MPL 125.473-618).

Ratramnus' position may be briefly summarized as follows: the bread and wine on the altar are mystic symbols of Christ's body and blood in commemoration of him. They become such through sacerdotal consecration but they do not lose their outward appearance, remaining to the senses merely bread and wine. Within them, however, resides a power perceived only by faith and this is what makes them effective. They are *not* Christ's body and blood *in truth*, a phrase which to Ratramnus regularly means "perceptible to the senses," nor is this Christ's historical body which was born of the Virgin, suffered, was crucified, died, and was buried, and having ascended into heaven, now sits on the right hand of the Father. They are, therefore, Christ's body and blood *in a figure*, that is, symbolically. This doctrine is, of course, supported by appeal to the Scriptures and by citations from Ambrose, Jerome, Augustine, Fulgentius of Ruspe, and Isidore of Seville, as well as from two prayers found in the missal of Ratramnus' day.

In contrasting the *true* and the *figurative* senses, respectively, as "that which is seen by the eyes of the flesh" and "that which is seen only by faith," Ratramnus reverses the meaning of *veritas* and *figura* as used by Paschasius Radbertus. The work thus naturally represents a view largely at variance with that of Paschasius and may have been one of the causes of the disturbance that led to the abbot's retirement from his control of the monastery.

We hear, however, of no movement to condemn the work or its author, though Ratramnus' contemporary, the unfortunate Gottschalk, did suffer deeply for the independence of his views. Yet *Christ's Body and Blood* has had a strange history through the ages, and there have been times when the historicity of Ratramnus was even doubted.

In the next century Flodoard of Reims (d. 966) knew of the book,[10] and there is still extant from the same period an Anglo-Saxon sermon "On the Paschal Lamb and on the Sacramental Body and Blood of Christ," written by the Abbot Ælfric of Eynsham[11] (Aelfricus Grammaticus). Even the most cursory

---

[10] *Hist. Eccl. Rem.* 3.15 (MPL 135.181).
[11] The original Anglo-Saxon with a modern English version appears in B. Thorpe's *Homilies of the Anglo-Saxon Church* (London, 1844–1846) 2.262–283: "A Sermon on the Sacrifice on Easter Day"; a 1623 translation is in the Baltimore edition of Ratramnus (pp. 89–105). See S. Harvey Gem, *An Anglo-Saxon Abbot: Ælfric of Eynsham* (Edinburgh, 1912) 86–111 on Ælfric's debt to Ratramnus. M. De la Taille, *Mysterium Fidei* (Paris, 3d ed., 1931) calls both of them heretics.

reading of this sermon would amply demonstrate that Ælfric had known of Ratramnus' argument and had made it his own. A manuscript must surely have been sent from Corbie to Britain.

The collection of comments on the Eucharist first printed by the Jesuit Louis Cellot[12] and thus long known as the Anonymus Cellotianus was for a time believed to be the work of Gerbert of Aurillac (afterward Pope Silvester II, 999–1003),[13] but is now with good reason ascribed by Dom Morin to Hériger of Lobbes (d. 1107).[14] Hériger tells us that the eucharistic doctrine of Paschasius Radbertus was expanded by Rabanus Maurus and by a "certain Ratramnus in a book composed for King Charles" and that both writers distinguish the Lord's body in the Eucharist from the flesh born of the Virgin. In a later passage Hériger cites a text of Jerome borrowed from Ratramnus (§71). It is clear that Hériger had read the book and we know which copy he read. The catalogue made in 1049 of the Library at Lobbes[15] lists a manuscript which is certainly Codex Lobiensis 909, still extant in the library of the University of Ghent.

The same century saw the little book suffer in the controversy involving the heresy of Berengarius of Tours (d. 1088),[16] who as archdeacon of Tours began to have his doubts as to the correctness of Paschasius' position on the Eucharist. It was probably in 1050 that Berengarius addressed a letter to the celebrated Lanfranc, prior of Bec (d. 1089), in which he declared himself opposed to Paschasius and in favor of the views in our book which, however, he wrongly supposed to be the work of John Scotus Eriugena, Ratramnus' Irish contemporary at the court of Charles. This letter was laid by Lanfranc before Pope Leo IX, and, as a result, at a synod held at Vercelli in September of that year Berengarius was condemned *in absentia* and Ratramnus' book ordered destroyed. Doubtless one copy

[12] L. Cellot, *Historia Gotteschalci* (Paris, 1655), pp. 539 f. = MPL 121.9.
[13] See MPL 139.187 (among Gerbert's works); B. Pez, *Thesaurus anecdotorum novissimus* (Augsburg, 1721) 1.1, pt. 2, p. 133.
[14] G. Morin, "Les dicta d'Hériger sur l'Eucharistie" (*Revue Bénédictine* 25.1 ff.).
[15] Now in the British Museum.
[16] M. Cappuyns, "Bérenger de Tours" (*Dict. d'Hist. et de Géogr. Ecclés.* 8.385–407); A. J. MacDonald, *Berengar and the Reform of Sacramental Doctrine* (London, 1930). See the passage wherein Wyclif attacks those who condemned Berengarius, translated by Ford Lewis Battles (LCC 14.67 f.). Wyclif, in showing that transubstantiation is out of accord with the confession forced upon Berengarius, comes close to the view of Ratramnus.

was destroyed, but the book, of course, survived this persecution and also a similar fate which awaited it and Berengarius at a similar council in the Lateran in 1059. There has been much debate as to whether the book condemned at Vercelli was a forgery of Eriugena by Ratramnus, a forgery of Ratramnus by Eriugena, or quite unconnected with Ratramnus at all, but it is most probable that the truth is as we have stated. Throughout his difficulties Berengarius never gave Ratramnus' name as his source nor did any of his accusers: the book to them was by Eriugena.

Sigebert of Gembloux (d. 1112) mentions Ratramnus in his work on ecclesiastical writers (ch. 96) which he finished c. 1111,[17] but of six manuscripts of Sigebert used by his first editor, Suffridus Petri,[18] two wrongly gave Ratramnus' name as "Bertramus." Despite the preponderance of the evidence for what was the correct name, the incorrect one was adopted, and this error has had great hardihood, being repeated from time to time and as late as 1880.[19]

When the so-called Anonymus Mellicensis,[20] a writer formerly thought to have lived at Melk, whence the name, but now identified as Wolfger of Prüfening, composed his list of ecclesiastical writers, he included Ratramnus' work under the right name but shows that he had not seen a copy.

Four centuries now ensued in which we naturally hear next to nothing of Ratramnus, though there is no lack of works on the Eucharist in which he might have been mentioned if known. In this period Paschasius dominated the field. Though Thomas Aquinas (1225–1274)[21] says nothing of Ratramnus, Duns Scotus (d. 1308)[22] knew a little about him. The general silence was first broken late in the fifteenth century by brief mention in two works of Joannes Trithemius of Spanheim.[23]

[17] MPL 160.569.
[18] Suffridus Petri, *De illustr. eccles. scriptoribus*, part 5 (Cologne, 1580), p. 356.
[19] W. F. Taylor's reprint of *The Book of Bertram* (Rouen, 1673).
[20] MPL 213.961. See E. Ettlinger, *Der sog. Anonymus Mellicensis, De script. eccles.* (Karlsruhe, 1896) p. 72; see also Fichtenau (*Mitteil. Oesterr. Inst. für Geschichtsforschung* 51 [1937], 313).
[21] *Summa Theol.* 3, qu. 75, a. 1 *ad corpus*, corrected in the commentary *ad loc.* by Francisco Suarez, *Opera Omnia* (Paris, 1861) 21.4, where Ratramnus is mentioned.
[22] Duns Scotus, *Opera Omnia* (Paris, 1894) 17.155.
[23] *De script. eccles.* (Cologne, 5th ed., 1546) p. 120 = MPL 160.74, first ed. printed at Mainz, 1494; *Annales Hirsaugienses*, ed. Mabillon (*Mon. Sacr. Galliae*, 1696) 1018.

8—E.M.T.

In 1527, John Fisher, the bishop of Rochester, destined to be martyred in 1535 with Sir Thomas More, refers to "Bartramus Strabus" (p. 365) in his work on the Eucharist directed against Oecolampadius, the *De veritate corporis et sanguinis Christi in eucharistia* (Cologne, 1527) and places him among writers of the seventh and eighth centuries. Such a confusion of the name with that of Walfrid Strabo indicates that Fisher could hardly have known the work directly, though it has been alleged that he used it with interest. Moreover, he was writing at least four years before a printer of some prominence, John Prael, published at Cologne in 1531 the *editio princeps*: "*Bertrami Presbyteri de corpore et sanguine Domini Liber ad Carolum Magnum Imperatorem, iam recens aeditus.*" Again the name is wrong and the wrong king is mentioned, but the little book was influential. This Latin text was copied in every reprinting for the next century and a half. Whether Reformers had any hand in producing the edition is not certain but by February of the next year a German version had been prepared at Zurich by Leo Judä, and a copy of this was sent by Bullinger with his letter to the Margrave of Brandenburg.[24]

In the other party, of course, readers found Ratramnus astounding, and it was soon being alleged that the text was mutilated and even falsified in the interests of the Reformed point of view. Sixtus of Siena,[25] of the next generation, was only one of several who suggested either that "Bertramus" was merely a pseudonym for Oecolampadius, or that the propagators of the work had forged a false place of publication (Cologne) for the true one (Basle), in order to protect themselves. The ascription of the work to Oecolampadius was really ironic, since if he knew the book at all, he was at pains not to mention it. Yet all doubts that the work was an honest attempt to print a genuine medieval document were permanently laid to rest nearly fifteen decades later when in 1672 the great Benedictine Mabillon visited Lobbes and transcribed the text of Codex Lobiensis, mentioned above. *Christ's Body and Blood* was no fabrication of the sixteenth century.

Bakhuizen van den Brink has included with his now definitive edition of the text printed in 1954 a detailed account of the subsequent history of our work. We ourselves can here spare room for mention of only a few who found in the book something to admire or to carp at. The St. Gallen Reformer, Joachim

[24] Bakhuizen, pp. 64 f.
[25] Sixtus Senensis, *Bibliotheca Sancta* (Venice, 1566), pref. vi, n. 196.

Vadian, for example, speaks of Ratramnus with respect,[26] but the Magdeburg Centuriators saw in it the "seeds of transubstantiation."[27] Matthaeus Flacius did not see fit to mention Ratramnus in his famous *Catalogue*,[28] but the defect was remedied in Simon Goulart's revision thereof.[29] Albert Rizaeus Hardenberg, writing to Melanchthon from Worms on October 26, 1567, expressed the belief that "Bertramus' book" seemed to him not a bad means for patching up the peace in Christendom. The book figured in the eucharistic controversy between Peter Martyr Vermigli and Bishop Stephen Gardiner of Winchester.[30]

At his trial in Oxford in 1555 the martyr Bishop Nicholas Ridley said of Ratramnus:

"This man was the first that pulled me by the ear, and forced me from the common error of the Roman church to a more diligent search of Scripture and ecclesiastical writers on this matter. . . ."[31]

While imprisoned, however, he did not mention Ratramnus in the *Brief declaration of the Lord's Supper, or a Treatise Against the Error of Transubstantiation*,[32] though he did cite Augustine's *De doctrina Christiana* 3.16, a passage also quoted by Ratramnus.

Use of Ratramnus by Ridley and other non-Roman writers doubtless helped to intensify the opposition on the part of those who remained in the Roman church. In 1559 the book was condemned by the Council of Trent as a heretical work of Scotus Eriugena. The Antwerp Index under Pius IV (1570) lists it, and the so-called Belgian Index prepared at Douai (1571) does also, but declares that, if emended, the book can be

[26] Bakhuizen, p. 66.
[27] *Nona centuria ecclesiasticae historiae* (Basle, 1565), chs. 212, 355.
[28] *Catalogus testium veritatis* (Basle, 1556, rep. 1562, 1672).
[29] Lyons-Geneva, 1608.   [30] Bakhuizen, pp. 86–88.
[31] Glocester Ridley, *Life of Dr. Nicholas Ridley* (London, 1763) 685; in the *Praefatio et Protestatio* (p. 681) "Bertram" is listed as one of a number of authorities supporting Ridley's position. See also Baltimore edition of Ratramnus (cited below), p. xix.
[32] First printed at Zurich after Ridley burned in the same year; repr. by H. Christmas, *Works of Nicholas Ridley, D.D.*, The Parker Society 39 (Cambridge, 1843), pp. 1–45. See also p. 159, where Ridley speaks at the trial: "Sir, it is certain that others before these have written of this matter; not by the way only and *obiter*, as for the most of all the old writers, but even *ex professo*, and their whole books entreat of it alone, as Bertram . . . [who] . . . propoundeth the same which is now in controversy, and answereth so directly, that no man may doubt but that he affirmeth that the substance of bread remaineth still in the sacrament."

tolerated and makes specific suggestions for correction. On August 23, 1685, a royal edict was registered with the Parlement at Paris and condemned "*Ratram ou Bertram, Prestre, de l'Eucharistie avec un avertissement.*" This was doubtless the anonymous French translation printed at Quévilly, a suburb of Rouen, in 1672, now attributed with probability to Marc-Antoine de la Bastide.[33] Despite these prohibitions, however, the book continued to be read and even often printed under Roman Catholic auspices, though it was not actually removed from the Index until in the edition of 1900; when many works of early date were removed, it also was passed over in silence. The prohibition of the reading of heretical works, it would seem, has been generally directed more sharply against sixteenth century writers than against ancient and medieval heretics.

The first edition containing a Latin text independent of the *editio princeps* appeared in 1686, edited by Jacques Boileau, doctor of the Sorbonne and brother of the poet Nicolas Boileau-Despréaux. With it he published a new French translation, and a voluminous commentary, the purpose of which was to eliminate every contradiction and to wrest Ratramnus from the Calvinists. This last he tried to do by showing that both Ratramnus and Paschasius were completely in agreement and orthodox. Boileau's second edition, published in 1712, was reprinted in Migne's *Patrologia latina* 121.125–170, and is notable for a new refutation of the old charge that Scotus Eriugena was the author which had recently been renewed by the Jesuit Hardouin.[34] Boileau's text was reprinted also at Oxford and London in 1838 with a new English version by H. W. and W. C. C., and this text and translation, the text often superior to that in Migne, appeared at Baltimore in 1843, together with an American preface by the bishop of Maryland, W. R. Whittingham, and the 1623 translation of Ælfric's homily. We have found the Baltimore edition useful.

The translation below was made originally from Boileau's text in the Migne reprint, revised by comparison with the Baltimore edition. Further revision, however, was made after the appearance of the much better text in the critical edition of the distinguished Dutch scholar, Prof. J. N. Bakhuizen van den Brink, *Ratramnus: De corpore et sanguine Domini—texte établi d'après les manuscrits et notice bibliographique* (in "Verhandelingen

---

[33] Bakhuizen, 81.
[34] Boileau's second edition made, he says, a "friendly, honest, and literary refutation" of Jean Hardouin's *De sacramento altaris* (see MPL 121.103).

der koninklijke Nederlandse Akademie van Wetenschappen, Afd. Letterkunde," Nieuwe Reeks, Deel 71, No. 1 [Amsterdam: North-Holland Publishing Co., 1954]). Bakhuizen's text is unlikely to be superseded; our translation conforms to it.

Bakhuizen's edition is also invaluable for his fine discussion of Ratramnus' importance in church history but he does not attempt to relate him to systematic theology. For that the reader is to be referred to an excellent dissertation by John J. Fahey, *The Eucharistic Teaching of Ratramnus of Corbie* (St. Mary of the Lake Seminary, 1951). See also J. Geiselmann, *Die Eucharistielehre der Vorscholastik* (Paderborn, 1926); C. Gliozzo, *La dottrina in Paschasio Radberto e Ratramno, moaci di Corbia* (Palermo, 1945), 81–189; Joseph Martin, *Ratramne: une conception de la cène au IXe siècle* (Paris, 1891); A. Naegle, *Ratramnus und die hl. Eucharistie zugleich eine dogmatisch-historische Würdigung des Abendmahlstrettes* (in "Theol. Stud. der Leo-Gesellschaft" 5 [Wien, 1903]); Henri Peltier, *Pascase Radbert, abbé de Corbie: contribution à l' étude de la vie monastique* (Amien, 1938), esp. pp. 268–272; and the articles by L. Backes (LTK 8.642 f.), Michael Ott (CE 12.659 f.), and Antonio Piolanti (EC 10.549 f.). Despite their age, the sketches by Jacques Boileau and J. A. Fabricius, printed in MPL 121.9–12, 103–222, are still of some value.

Ratramnus of Corbie: Christ's Body and Blood

THE TEXT

1. You order me, glorious prince, to make known to your majesty my views on the mystery of Christ's blood and body, a command as fitting to your magnificent principate as most difficult for one endowed, like myself, with but feeble powers. For what is more consonant with a king's providence than to possess catholic wisdom concerning the sacred mysteries of Him who has deigned to grant him his royal throne, and that his subjects must not be permitted to hold variant opinions concerning Christ's body, upon which, it is agreed, the whole of Christian redemption rests?

2. While certain of the faithful say that in the mystery of the body and the blood of Christ, daily celebrated in the church, nothing takes place under a figure, under a hidden symbol, but it is performed with a naked manifestation of truth[35] itself, others bear witness, however, that these elements are contained in the figure of a mystery, and that it is one thing which appears to the bodily sense and another which faith beholds. No small divergence is to be distinguished between them. And though the apostle writes[36] to the faithful that they should all hold the same views and say the same things, and that no schism should appear among them, yet they are divided by great schism when they utter different views concerning the mystery of Christ's body and blood.

3. Wherefore your royal highness, motivated by zeal for the faith, not looking upon this situation with complacency, and

---

[35] In this work *veritas* and its cognates appear always to connote truth in a completely physical sense as opposed to any figurative or symbolical sense, not opposed to falsity.

[36] I Cor. 1:10.

desiring that, in accordance with the apostle's teaching, all may think the same and say the same, diligently searches out the hidden truth so that it may be able to call back to it those wandering from the path. For this reason you condescend to seek out the truth of this matter from most humble persons, aware that they know nothing of the mystery of so great a secret except perhaps by divine revelation which, without respect of persons, has shown the light of its truth through whomsoever it has chosen.

4. Pleasant as it is for one of our insignificance to be obedient to your command, so is it hard to discuss a topic most remote from the human senses, and one that cannot be fathomed except through the instruction of the Holy Spirit. Subject, therefore, to your majesty's command, yet relying on the permission of Him about whom we shall speak, I shall try, with whatever words I can command, to reveal my belief about this topic, not leaning upon my own ability but following in the footsteps of the holy fathers.

5. Your majesty inquires whether that which in the church is received into the mouth of the faithful becomes the body and blood of Christ in a mystery or in truth. That is, whether it contains some hidden element which becomes patent only to the eyes of faith, or whether without concealment of any mystery the appearance of the body is seen outwardly in what the mind's eyes see inwardly, so that everything which takes place becomes clearly visible; and whether it is that body which was born of Mary, suffered, died, and was buried, and which, rising again and ascending into heaven, sits on the right hand of the Father.

6. Let us examine the first of these two questions, and, to prevent our being stopped by ambiguity of language, let us define what we mean by "figure," what by "truth," so that keeping our gaze fixed on something quite certain, we may know in what path of reasoning we ought to direct our steps.

7. "Figure" means a kind of overshadowing that reveals its intent under some sort of veil. For example, when we wish to speak of the Word, we say "bread," as when in the Lord's Prayer we ask that daily bread be given us,[37] or when Christ speaking in the Gospel says, "I am the living bread who came down from heaven";[38] or when he calls himself the vine and his disciples the branches.[39] For all these passages say one thing and hint at another.

[37] Luke 11:3.   [38] John 6:41.   [39] John 15:5.

8. "Truth," on the other hand, is representation of clear fact, not obscured by any shadowy images, but uttered in pure and open, and to say it more plainly, in natural meanings, as, for example, when Christ is said to have been born of the Virgin, suffered, been crucified, died, and been buried. For nothing is here adumbrated by concealing metaphors, but the reality of the fact is represented in the ordinary senses of the words. Nothing else may be understood than what is said. In the instances mentioned above this was not the case. From the point of view of substance, the bread is not Christ, the vine is not Christ, the branches are not apostles. Therefore in this latter instance the figure, but in the former the truth, is represented by the statement, that is, the bare and obvious meaning.

9. Now let us go back to the matter which is the cause of what has been said, namely, the body and blood of Christ. For if that mystery is not performed in any figurative sense, then it is not rightly given the name of mystery. Since that cannot be called a mystery in which there is nothing hidden, nothing removed from the physical senses, nothing covered over with any veil. But that bread which through the ministry of the priest comes to be Christ's body exhibits one thing outwardly to human sense, and it proclaims another thing inwardly to the minds of the faithful. Outwardly it has the shape of bread which it had before, the color is exhibited, the flavor is received, but inwardly something far different, much more precious, much more excellent, becomes known, because something heavenly, something divine, that is, Christ's body, is revealed, which is not beheld, or received, or consumed by the fleshly senses but in the gaze of the believing soul.

10. The wine also, which through priestly consecration becomes the sacrament of Christ's blood, shows, so far as the surface goes, one thing; inwardly it contains something else. What else is to be seen on the surface than the substance of wine? Taste it,[40] and it has the flavor of wine; smell it, and it has the aroma of wine; look at it, and the wine color is visible. But if you think of it inwardly, it is now to the minds of believers not the liquid of Christ's blood, and when tasted, it has flavor; when looked at, it has appearance; and when smelled, it is proved to be such. Since no one can deny that this is so, it is clear that that bread and wine are Christ's body and blood in a figurative sense. For as to outward appearance, the aspect of flesh is not recognized in that bread, nor in that wine is the

---

[40] Cyril of Jerusalem, *Catech.* 4.

liquid blood shown, when, however, they are, after the mystical consecration, no longer called bread or wine, but Christ's body and blood.

11. For if, as some would have it, nothing is here received figuratively, but everything is visible in truth, faith does not operate here, since nothing spiritual takes place, but whatever it is, it is wholly received according to its bodily sense. And since faith, according to the apostle, is "the evidence of things not appearing," [41] that is, not of substances, visible but invisible, we shall here receive nothing according to faith since we distinguish what it is according to the senses of the body. Nothing is more absurd than to take bread as flesh and to say that wine is blood, and there will be no mystery in anything which contains nothing secret, nothing concealed.

12. How, then, shall that be called Christ's body and blood in which no change is recognized to have taken place? For every change [42] is brought either from that which it is not to that which it is, or from that which it is to that which it is not, or from that which it is to that which it is. In that sacrament, however, if it only be considered from the point of view of simple truth, and is believed not otherwise than it appears, no change is recognized to have been made. For it has not passed over from what it was not to something which it is, in the manner in which transition takes place when things are given birth, since, indeed, they formerly did not exist, but, in order that they might exist, they made the transition from not being to that which is being. But here the bread and wine existed before they made the transition into the sacrament of Christ's body and blood, but not the transition which takes place, however, from what is being to what is not being, the transition which takes place in things which experience destruction through disappearance. For what perishes, formerly existed and what never existed, cannot undergo perishing. Here also that kind of transition is recognized not to have occurred, since according to the truth the appearance of the creature which formerly existed is recognized to have remained. [43]

13. Likewise, that change which takes place from what is in what is, which is observed in things that undergo variableness of quality—for example, when what was formerly black is

[41] Heb. 11:1.
[42] Cf. Ps.-Augustine, *Categoriae decem ex Aristotele decerptae* 21 (MPL 32. 1439A).
[43] Ambrose, *De sacram.* 2.5, p. 66 Botte: ⟨*Spiritus Sanctus*⟩ *quasi columba.*

changed into white—even this type of change is recognized not to have taken place, for nothing is apprehended to have been changed either in touch or color or smell. If therefore there is nothing here changed, then it is nothing but what it was before. It is, however, another thing because the bread is made the body, the wine the blood, of Christ. For so he himself says: "Take and eat: this is my body." [44] Likewise, speaking of the cup, he says: "Take and drink: this is the blood of the New Testament which shall be shed for you." [45]

14. Those who are here willing to take nothing in a figurative sense, but insist that everything exists in simple truth, must be asked in reference to what a change has been produced, so that the elements now are not what they previously were, that is, bread and wine, but are Christ's body and blood; whether so far as appearance and their real nature, and the shape of things visible, go—that is, the bread and wine—they have undergone no change in themselves. And if they have suffered no change, they exist no different than they were before.

15. Your highness, glorious prince, sees in what direction the understanding of those who believe these things comes out. They deny what they are supposed to maintain, and what they believe they are demonstrated to be destroying. For they faithfully profess Christ's body and the blood, and when they do this, they certainly maintain that the elements are not what they were before, and if they are otherwise than they were before, they admit of change.[46] Since this cannot be denied, let them say in what respect the elements have been changed, for nothing is really seen to have been changed in them in a bodily sense. Therefore, they will admit it to be necessary, either that the elements have been changed in some respect other than the bodily one, and on account of this seem to be not what they are in truth but appear to be something other which they are not with respect to their own essence, or, if they should be unwilling to admit this, they will be forced to deny that they are Christ's body and blood, a fact not only wrong to state but even to think.

16. But since they confess that they are Christ's body and blood and that they could not be such without some change for the better being made, and this change did not take place

---

[44] Matt. 26:26.   [45] Matt. 26:28; Mark 14:24.
[46] The Magdeburg Centuriators (*Cens.* 9 *de doctrina*): "Ratramnus has the seeds of transubstantiation; for he uses the words 'commutation' and 'conversion.'"

in a corporeal sense but in a spiritual, it must now be said that this was done figuratively, since under cover of the corporeal bread and of the corporeal wine Christ's spiritual body and spiritual blood do exist. Not that they are actually two substances differing in themselves, namely, body and spirit, but one and the same thing from one point of view has the appearance of bread and wine; from another, however, it is Christ's body and blood. For as far as the physical appearances of both are concerned, the appearances are those of things created in a corporeal sense; but as far as their power is concerned, inasmuch as they have been spiritually made, they are the mysteries of Christ's body and blood.

17. Let us consider the font of holy Baptism, which is not undeservedly called the fountain of life, because it refashions in newness of a better life those who descend into it, and to those who are dead from sin it grants the boon of life in righteousness.[47] Does what in one respect is observed to be the element of water acquire that power? Yet unless it acquired that power of sanctification, it would never be able to grant life to the dead—the dead, however, not after the flesh but after the soul. Nevertheless, if in that font one were to take into consideration only what the bodily senses see, it appears that a liquid element, subject to corruption, acquires no power save that of cleansing bodies. But there is added the power of the Holy Spirit through consecration of a priest, and it becomes capable of purifying not only bodies but also souls, and it removes spiritual filth by means of spiritual power.

18. There you have it: in one and the same element we see two contraries, that is, something lying close to corruption confers incorruption and that which does not have life grants life. It is clear that in that font there is something which bodily sense may touch and is therefore changeable and corruptible, and on the other hand there is also what faith alone may see, and therefore cannot run any risk of losing life. If you ask what outwardly washes, it is the element; if, however, you ponder what washes inwardly, it is power of life, power of sanctification, power of immortality. Therefore, in its own properties, water is corruptible; but in the mystery, it is healing power.

19. So also Christ's body and blood, viewed outwardly, are something created and subject to change and corruption. If, however, you weigh the power of the mystery, they are life, granting immortality to those who partake of them. Therefore,

[47] Cf. Rom. 6:11, 13.

what are seen and what are believed are not the same. For with respect to what are seen, they, themselves corruptible, feed a corruptible body; but with respect to what they are believed to be, they, themselves immortal, feed souls which will live forever.

20. The apostle also, writing to the Corinthians, says, "Do you not know that our fathers were all under a cloud, and they all passed over the sea, and all in Moses were baptized in the cloud and in the sea, and all ate the same spiritual food and all drank the same spiritual drink? For they drank from the spiritual rock which followed them, and the rock was Christ."[48] We notice that the sea and the cloud bore the appearance of baptism, and in them, that is, in the cloud or the sea, the fathers of the older covenant were baptized. Could the sea, in so far as it appeared to be an element, have the power of baptism? Or could the cloud, in that it revealed a condensation of air, make the people holy? Yet we dare not say that the apostle did not truly speak in Christ when he said that our fathers were baptized in the cloud and the sea.

21. And although that baptism did not bear the form of the Baptism of Christ which today is practiced in the church, that it really was, nevertheless, a baptism and in it our fathers were baptized, no one in his right mind will dare to deny, unless mad enough to presume to contradict the apostle's words. And therefore the sea and the cloud granted the purification of sanctification not with respect to what they were as body, but they contained the sanctification of the Holy Spirit with respect to what they were invisibly. For in them was a visible form which appeared to the bodily senses, not in a representation but in truth, and from within spiritual power shone forth, which appeared not to the eyes of the flesh but to the lights of the soul.

22. Likewise the manna given the people from heaven, and the water flowing from a rock were really corporeal, and they fed and watered the people in a corporeal sense, yet the apostle calls both that manna and that water spiritual food and spiritual drink. Why does he? Because the power of the spiritual word inhered in these bodily substances which fed and watered the souls rather than the bodies of the believers. And since that food or drink foreshadowed the mystery of Christ's body and blood, which the church celebrates, Saint Paul maintains that our fathers ate that same spiritual food and drank that same spiritual drink.

[48] I Cor. 10:1–4.

23. You ask, perhaps, what is the same? That very thing, surely, which today the believing people in the church eat and drink. For it cannot be thought otherwise than that He is that one and the same Christ who then in the desert fed with his flesh the people who had been baptized in the cloud and in the sea, and gave them to drink of his blood, and now in the church feeds the people who believe with the bread of his body and gives them to drink of the stream of his blood.

24. This is what the apostle wished to suggest, when, after he said that our fathers ate this same spiritual food, and drank this same spiritual drink, then added, "For they drank from the spiritual rock which followed them, and the rock was Christ." [49] He wished us to understand that in the desert Christ stood in the spiritual rock, and gave the people to drink of the stream of his blood, who afterward has showed to our times the body assumed from the Virgin, which for the salvation of believers hung upon the cross, and from it has shed the stream of his blood, by which we might not only be redeemed but even might drink of it.

25. Marvelous, surely, because incomprehensible and inestimable! Not yet had He assumed the form of man, not yet for the salvation of the world had he tasted death, not yet had he redeemed us by his blood, and already in the desert our fathers through spiritual food and invisible drink were eating his body and drinking his blood. So the apostle stands as witness, crying out that our fathers ate the same spiritual food and drank the same spiritual drink. One must not inquire by what method this could be done, but exercise the faith that it was done. For the very One who now in the church, with omnipotent power, spiritually changes the bread and wine into the flesh of his body and the stream of his blood, then also invisibly made the manna given from heaven to be his body and the water which had been poured forth from the rock to be his very blood.

26. This is what David understood when he proclaimed in the Holy Spirit: "Man ate the bread of angels." [50] For foolish it is to suppose that the corporeal manna given to the fathers feeds the heavenly host or that those who feast at the tables of the divine Word are satisfied by that sort of victuals. For the psalmist certainly showed (or rather it was the Holy Spirit speaking in the psalmist) both what our fathers received in that heavenly manna and what the faithful ought to believe in

[49] I Cor. 10:4. [50] Ps. 78:25 (77:25, V).

the mystery of Christ's body. In both is certainly meant Christ, who feeds the souls of believers and is actually the food of the angels, and in both instances this is not the sense of bodily taste, nor corporeal nourishment, but the power of the spiritual Word.

27. And from the words of the Evangelist we learn that our Lord Jesus Christ before he suffered, "having taken bread, gave thanks, gave to his disciples, saying, 'This is my body which is given for you. Do this in remembrance of me.' Likewise also the cup, after he ate, saying, 'This is the cup, the New Testament, in my blood, which shall be shed for you.'" [51] We see that Christ had not yet suffered, but already the mystery of his body and blood was in effect.

28. We do not think that any of the faithful can doubt that that bread was made Christ's body because in giving it to his disciples he says, "This is my body which is given for you." Neither can he doubt that the cup contains Christ's blood, of which he himself says, "This is the cup, the New Testament, in my blood, which shall be shed for you." As, then, a little while before he suffered, he could change the substance of bread and the created wine into his own body which was about to suffer, and into his blood which was later to be shed, so also in the desert he had the power to change the manna and water from the rock into his flesh and blood, and his flesh survived long afterward to be hanged on the cross for us, and his blood to be shed for our cleansing.

29. Here also we must consider the proper interpretation of his words: "Unless you shall eat the flesh of the Son of Man, and drink his blood, you shall not have life in you." [52] For he does not say that his flesh which hung on the cross would have to be cut to bits and eaten by his disciples, or that his blood which was to be shed for the redemption of the world would have to be given to his disciples to drink. This would have been a crime if, in accordance with what men outside the faith then understood,[53] his blood were to be drunk or his flesh to be eaten by his disciples.

30. For this reason a little later in the same passage he says to his disciples who were receiving Christ's words, not as unbelievers but as believers, though hitherto it did not enter into their thoughts how those words would have to be understood: "Do you take offense at this? What if you should see the Son of

---

[51] Luke 22:19 f. (Vulgate of Matt. 26:28); Mark 14:24, used in part.
[52] John 6:53.   [53] John 6:52.

Man ascending where he was before?"[54] This is as if he were to say: "Do not think that you must eat in a bodily sense my flesh or drink my blood, distributed to you in pieces or having to be so distributed, since after the resurrection you will see me ascending into the heavens with the fullness of my entire body and of my blood. Then you will understand that my flesh does not have to be eaten by believers, as men without faith suppose, but the bread and wine, by the mystery truly changed into the substance of my body and blood, must be taken by believers."

31. And he goes on to say: "It is the Spirit which gives life; the flesh is of no avail."[55] He says that the flesh is of no avail in the sense in which those without faith understood. In some other way it bestows life as it is taken through the mystery by those with faith. And this, as he makes it clear by saying: "It is the Spirit which gives life." So in this mystery the effect of the body and blood is spiritual. It gives life, and without its effect the mysteries are of no avail, since they, indeed, feed the body but cannot feed the soul.

32. Here arises that question which many express when they say that these things do not happen in a figure but in truth. When they say this, they are shown to be out of harmony with writings of the holy fathers.

33. Saint Augustine, the great doctor of the church, writes in Book III of his work *On Christian Doctrine*[56] as follows:

> "'Except you shall eat,' says the Saviour, 'the flesh of the Son of Man, and shall drink his blood, you shall not have life in you.' This seems to order a shameful crime. Therefore it is a figure, enjoining that we should have a share in the Lord's suffering, and that we should faithfully[57] remember that for us his flesh was crucified and wounded."

34. We see that that doctor says that the mysteries of Christ's body and blood are celebrated in a figurative sense by the faithful. For he says that to take his flesh and his blood in a fleshly sense involves, not religion, but crime. This was the view held by those who, understanding the Lord's statement in the Gospel not in a spiritual but in a fleshly sense, departed from him, and were already not going with him.[58]

---

[54] John 6:61 f.   [55] John 6:63.
[56] Augustine, *De doctr. Chr.* 3.16.24 (MPL 34.74–75, tr. NPNF, 1st ser., 2.563).
[57] Here Augustine: "sweetly and profitably."
[58] John 6:66.

35. The same man, writing in his letter[59] to Bishop Boniface, says among other things:

"Of course, we often say, as the Pascha is approaching, that tomorrow or the day after is the Lord's Passion, although he suffered many years ago, and his Passion did not occur except once. Likewise, on that Lord's Day we say, 'Today the Lord is risen,' although since the day on which he rose so many years have passed. Why is no one so foolish as to accuse us of lying when we speak in this way because we give these names to such days on account of some resemblance with the events that occurred on them, with the result that the day is called that day although it is not the very day on which the event took place but in the revolution of time it is like it, and the event is said to have occurred on that day on account of its sacramental celebration, although the event took place, not on that day but one long since passed? Was not Christ once for all sacrificed in his person? And yet is he not sacrificed in the sacrament, not only in all the celebrations of the solemnities of the Pascha, but before the congregation daily, so that the man does not lie who says, when asked, that he is sacrificed? For if sacraments did not have some resemblance to the things of which they are sacraments, they would not be sacraments at all. By virtue of this resemblance, however, in most cases they derive their names from those things of which they are the sacraments. So, therefore, as in some manner the sacrament of Christ's body is Christ's body, the sacrament of Christ's blood is Christ's blood, so the sacrament of faith is faith."

36. We see that Saint Augustine says that the sacraments are one thing and that the things of which they are sacraments are another. Moreover, the body in which Christ suffered, and the blood which flowed from his side, are things, but he says that the mysteries of these things are the sacraments of Christ's body and blood which are celebrated for the memory of the Lord's Passion, not only each year in all the solemnities of the Pascha, but even every day in the year.

37. And although the Lord's body, in which he once suffered is one thing, and the blood, which was shed for the salvation of the world, is one thing, yet the sacraments of these

---

[59] Augustine, *Epist.* 98.9 (formerly 23.9) *ad Bonifatium episcopum* (MPL 33.359–364, quotation in coll. 363 f. = CSEL 34.520–533, quotation on pp. 530 f., tr. NPNF, 1st ser., 1.409). Date is 408.

two things have assumed their names, being called Christ's body and blood, since they are so called on account of a resemblance with the things they represent. So also the annual celebrations are called the Pascha and the Lord's resurrection, although he suffered in his own person and rose again once and for all, and those days cannot now be called back since they are past. Yet the days on which the remembrance of the Lord's Passion or of his resurrection is celebrated are called by their name, and for the reason that they have some resemblance to those days on which the Saviour suffered once and for all and rose again once and for all.

38. This is why we say: "Today or tomorrow or the day after is the Lord's Pascha or his resurrection," although those days on which these events occurred are now many years past. So also we say that the Lord is sacrificed when the sacraments of his Passion are celebrated, although he was sacrificed in his own person for the salvation of the world once and for all, as the apostle says, "Christ suffered for you, leaving to you an example for you to follow his footsteps."[60] He does not say that daily he suffers in his own person what he did once and for all. He has left us, however, an example which in the mystery of the Lord's body and blood is daily represented before the believers, so that whosoever draws near to it knows that he ought to associate himself in His sufferings, of which he awaits the image in the sacred mysteries, according to that passage in Wisdom:[61] You have approached "the table of the mighty. Pay careful attention to what is set before you ... knowing that you ought to prepare such things." To approach the table of the mighty is to be made a participant in the divine offering. The consideration of what is set before you is the understanding of the Lord's body and blood. Whoever shares in them knows that he ought to prepare them, so that he may, by dying, be the imitator of Him, the memory of whose death he confesses, not only in believing but even by tasting.

39. Likewise the blessed apostle to the Hebrews:[62]

"For it was fitting that we should have such a high priest, holy, innocent, unstained, separated from sinners, and made higher than the heavens. He has no need, like those priests, daily to offer sacrifices, first for his own sins, and then for

---

[60] I Peter 2:21.
[61] Prov. 23:1 (closer to Septuagint than to Vulgate). Paschasius (MPL 120.1273) also quotes this passage but differently.
[62] Heb. 7:26–28.

those of the people. [The Lord Jesus Christ] [63] did this once and for all, by offering himself."

What he did once and for all, now he repeats daily, since once for all he offered himself for the sins of the people. Yet this same offering is celebrated each day by the faithful but in a mystery, so that what the Lord Jesus Christ once and for all fulfilled by offering himself, this in memory of his Passion is daily enacted through the celebration of the mysteries.

40. Nor is it falsely said that in those mysteries the Lord is both sacrificed and suffers since they bear appearance of his death and Passion, of which they are representations. For this reason they are called the Lord's body and the Lord's blood because they take His name whose sacrament they are. On this account the blessed Isidore in the books of *Etymologies*[64] says:

> "Sacrifice is so called from *sacra* and *fieri*, 'that which is made holy,' because it is consecrated by mystical prayer to commemorate the Lord's suffering in our behalf. For this reason, we, at his bidding, say that the body and blood of Christ is what, though made[65] of the earth's fruits, is consecrated and becomes a sacrament through the invisible action of God's spirit. This sacrament of bread and cup the Greeks call the *Eucharistia*,[66] which in Latin may be rendered *bona gratia*.[67] And what is better than the blood and body of Christ?"

But the bread and wine are likened to the body and blood because, just as the substance of this visible bread and wine nourishes and stimulates the outer man, so the Word of God, who is living bread, refreshes faithful souls that share in it.[68]

41. That catholic doctor also prescribes that this holy mystery of the Lord's Passion should be practiced in memory of the Lord's suffering in our behalf. When he says this, he shows that the Lord's Passion has taken place once and for all, but that His memorial is represented in the sacred rites.

---

[63] Bracketed words are Ratramnus' expansion of a personal ending.
[64] Isidore of Seville, *Etymologiae sive origines* 6.19.48 (Lindsay) = MPL 82. 255 f.
[65] Isidore has, "It is."
[66] See Matt. 26:27; Mark 14:23; Luke 22:17, 19.   [67] "Good grace."
[68] Both Boileau and Bakhuizen attribute this sentence to Isidore, but it is not in the text. Cf. his *De eccl. off.* 1.18.3 (MPL 83.755) for a somewhat similar passage.

42. This is why the bread which is offered, although from the fruits of the earth, is transferred into the body of Christ while it is being consecrated. So also the wine, though it flowed out of the vine, is made the blood of Christ through the consecration of the divine mystery—not visibly, of course, but as this doctor says, working invisibly through the Spirit of God.

43. This is why they are called Christ's blood and body, because they are received, not as what they outwardly seem, but as what inwardly, through the agency of the divine Spirit, they have been made. And because they exist as something far different, through the agency of invisible power, from what they visibly appear to be, he points out the distinction, when he says that the bread and wine are likened to the Lord's body and blood, because,[69] just as the substance of this visible bread and wine nourishes and stimulates the outer man, so the Word of God, who is living Bread, refreshes faithful souls that share in it.

44. By saying this he confesses most plainly that in the sacrament of the Lord's body and blood, whatever is taken outwardly is suited to the repair of the body, but the Word of God, who is the invisible Bread existing invisibly in that sacrament, feeds the minds of the faithful by giving them life when they invisibly share in it.

45. Hence also the same doctor[70] says:

"There is a sacrament in any celebration when what is done takes place in such a way that it is understood to mean something which must be taken in a holy sense."

When he says this, he reveals that every sacrament contains something hidden in the divine, and it is one thing that appears visibly and another which must be taken invisibly.

46. Next, he shows what sacraments the faithful should celebrate and says:

"The sacraments are Baptism and anointing, the body and blood. They are called sacraments because, under cover of corporeal things, the divine power secretly works the salvation of these same sacraments. Hence, they are called sacraments from powers both secret and holy."

And in the following passage he says: "In Greek it is called a *mystērion* because it has a secret and hidden character."[71]

---

[69] The source is §40, not Isidore, from here to the end of the section.
[70] Isidore, *Etym.* 6.19.39 f., immediately following quotation cited in n. 64.
[71] Isidore, *Etym.* 6.19.42, after omission.

47. What are we taught from this except that the Lord's body and blood are called mysteries because they possess a secret and hidden character, that is, in one respect they are what they outwardly signify, and in another they are what they effect inwardly and invisibly?

48. Hence also they are commonly called sacraments because under cover of corporeal objects the divine power secretly dispenses the salvation of those who receive it by faith.

49. From all that has thus far been said it has been shown that Christ's body and blood which are received in the mouth of the faithful in the church are figures according to their visible appearance, but according to their invisible substance, that is, the power of the divine Word, truly exist as Christ's body and blood. Therefore, with respect to visible creation, they feed the body; with reference to the power of a stronger substance, they feed and sanctify the souls of the faithful.

50. Now it is proposed to examine the second question and to see whether that very body which was born of Mary, suffered, died, and was buried, and which sits on the right hand of the Father, is what is daily taken in the church by the mouth of the faithful through the mystery of the sacraments.

51. Let us inquire what Saint Ambrose thinks of this, for he says in the first book of the *Sacraments*,[72]

> "Truly remarkable is it that God rained manna for the fathers and they were fed each day on this food of heaven. Whence it is said that 'man ate the bread of angels.'[50] But nevertheless those who ate that bread all died in the desert. That food, however, which you receive, that living Bread which came down from heaven, provides the substance of life eternal, and whoever shall eat of it shall not die in eternity, and it is Christ's body."

52. See with what respect that doctor says Christ's body is the food which the faithful receive in the church. He says: "That living bread which came down from heaven provides the substance of life eternal." According to this, what appears, what is taken in bodily form, what the teeth press into, what is swallowed by the gullet, what is taken into the cavern of the

---

[72] Ratramnus now begins to use two works of Ambrose, *De sacramentis* (MPL 16.435–482) and *De mysteriis* (*ibid.* 405–426), of which Bernard Botte has recently printed in *Sources Chrétiennes* (Paris, 1949) an excellent edition. The present quotation is from *De myst.* 8.47, p. 123 Botte = MPL 16.421C, not from *De sacram.*, as Ratramnus says.

stomach, does not provide the substance of eternal life, does it? In that way it feeds the flesh that will die, and provides no incorruptibility, and it cannot truly be said of it that "whoever shall eat of it, shall never die."[73] That which the body takes is corruptible and cannot bestow on the body the boon of never dying, since what lies close to corruption has no power to bestow eternity. There is, therefore, life in that bread not apparent to the eyes of the body, but seen by the sight of faith; this is also "the living bread that came down from heaven"[74] and concerning which it is truly said, "Whosoever shall eat of it shall never die," and which is Christ's body.

53. Likewise, in the following passage, when he speaks of the almighty power of Christ, he says:

"Cannot the word[75] of Christ, which was able to make from nothing that which was not, change the things that are into what they were not? Is it not a greater act to give new things than to change their natures?"[76]

54. Saint Ambrose says that in that mystery of Christ's blood and body a change took place, both miraculously because divinely and ineffably because incomprehensibly. Let those who here are willing to receive nothing according to the power inwardly latent, but wish to think that what appears visibly is all there is, say in what respect this change has been made in these elements. For with respect to the substance of things created, what they had been before consecration, that they afterward are. They were bread and wine before; they seem to remain of this same appearance now when consecrated. Therefore, what faith sees, what feeds the soul, what provides the substance of eternal life, has been changed inwardly by the mighty power of the Holy Spirit.

55. Likewise in the following passage:[77]

"Why do you seek here the order of nature in Christ's body when the Lord Jesus himself was given birth by the Virgin contrary to nature?"

56. Here now one of my hearers rises and says that it is Christ's body which is seen and his blood which is drunk, and

[73] John 6:50.   [74] John 6:51.
[75] Ambrose, *De myst.* 9.52, p. 125 Botte = MPL 16.424A, uses *sermo*, not *verbum*.
[76] Ambrose: "For it was not less to give things new natures than to change their natures."
[77] *De myst.* 9.53 f., p. 126 Botte = MPL 16.424B: "*We* seek." Cf. Rabanus Maurus, *De sacris ordinibus* 7.10.

that one ought not to ask how this was made but one ought to hold that it was so made. You seem, indeed, to have the right idea, but if you carefully examine the force of the words, you believe, indeed, by faith that it is Christ's body and blood. But if you were to perceive that what you believe you do not yet see—for if you saw it, you would say, "I see"—you would not say, "I believe that it is Christ's body and blood." Now, however, because faith sees all that is, and the eye of flesh perceives nothing, understand that it is not in appearance but in power that Christ's body and blood are what they appear to be. This is why he says,[78] "Here the order of nature should not be regarded but the power of Christ should be venerated, which, what he wills, how he wills, and into whatever he wills, both creates what was not and changes what has been created into that which it had not been before." The same author adds:[79] "It is the true flesh of Christ which was crucified which was buried. It is truly, therefore, the sacrament of his flesh. The Lord Jesus Christ himself proclaims it: 'This is my body.'"[80]

57. How carefully, how intelligently was the distinction made! About the flesh of Christ which was crucified, which was buried, that is, with respect to which Christ was both crucified and buried, he says, "It is the true flesh of Christ." But about that which is taken in the sacrament, he says, "It is truly, therefore, the sacrament of His flesh," distinguishing the sacrament of the flesh from the truth of the flesh, seeing that he would say that He was crucified and buried in the truth of the flesh which he had assumed from the Virgin, but he would say that the mystery which is now enacted in the church is a sacrament of His true flesh, openly instructing the faithful that that flesh with respect to which Christ was crucified and buried is not a mystery but the truth of nature. This flesh, however, which now contains his likeness in the mystery, is not flesh in appearance but in a sacrament. If, indeed, it is bread in appearance, in the sacrament it is the true body of Christ, even as the Lord Jesus proclaims, "This is my body." [81]

58. Likewise, in the following passage:[82] "What we are to eat, what we are to drink, the Holy Spirit has elsewhere expressed to you by the prophets when he says: 'Taste and see

---

[78] Not found in Ambrose, though printed in MPL 121.150 as his and attributed to him in the Baltimore edition.
[79] Follows quotation cited in n. 78.
[80] Matt. 26:26.   [81] Matt. 26:26; Luke 22:19.
[82] *De myst.* 9.58, p. 127 Botte=MPL 16.426A, inexactly quoted.

that the Lord is good. Blessed is the man who hopes in him.' "[83] That bread, corporeally tasted, or that wine when drunk, did not show how good the Lord is, did it? For whatever affects the taste is corporeal and gives pleasure to the tongue. To taste the Lord—is that to have a sense experience of something corporeal? Therefore he invites us to try the savor of a spiritual taste, and in that drink and bread nothing is thought of corporeally but all is felt spiritually, since God is a Spirit, and "blessed is the man who hopes in him."

59. Likewise he goes on to say: "Christ is in that sacrament because it is the body of Christ. It is therefore not corporeal food but spiritual." [84] What is more obvious, more clear, more divine? For he says, "Christ is in that sacrament." He does not say, "Christ is that bread, that wine." Were he to say this, he would be preaching that Christ is corruptible (which God forbid!) and subject to mortality, for whatever in that food is seen or tasted in a corporeal sense is liable, surely, to be corruptible.

60. He adds, "Because it is the body of Christ." You get up and say: "Look here, he clearly confesses that that bread and that drink is Christ's body. But see how he adds, 'It is therefore not corporeal food but spiritual.' Do not use the sense of the flesh, for here there is no suggestion of that. It is, indeed, Christ's body, though not corporeal but spiritual. It is Christ's blood, though not corporeal but spiritual. Nothing, therefore, is here to be taken in the corporeal but in the spiritual sense. It is the body of Christ but not corporeally; and it is the blood of Christ but not corporeally."

61. Likewise he continues:[85] "The apostle for this reason says of His symbol, 'Our fathers ate a spiritual food and drank a spiritual drink.' [86] For the body of God is spiritual. The body of Christ is the body of the divine Spirit because Christ is spirit as we read:[87] 'The Lord Christ is spirit before our face.' "

---

[83] Ps. 34:8 (33:9, V).   [84] Follows quotation cited in n. 82.
[85] Follows immediately preceding.   [86] I Cor. 10:3, 4.
[87] Both Ambrose and Ratramnus have read Lam. 4:20 in an Old Latin text not consonant with that in any current Protestant Bible. The adjective *christos* alludes to an anointed person, i.e., the last reigning king of Judah, not to the Christ, but Ambrose is merely following the patristic consensus which regularly interprets the word as a prefiguration of Christ: e.g., Justin Martyr, *Apol.* 1.55.5; Irenaeus, *Demonstr. Apost. Teaching* 71 (ACW 16.93, also p. 202, notes 302 f.); *Adv. Haer.* 3.10.3; Tertullian, *Adv. Prax.* 14, *Adv. Marc.* 3.6; Origen, *Hom. in Cant. Cant.* 1.6; *Dial. c. Heracl.* 172 (LCC 2.454), *De princip.* 2.6.7, 4.1.25; Cyril of Jerusalem, *Catech.* 13.7, 17.34; Augustine, *De civ. Dei* 18.33. See also Paschasius Radbertus (MPL 120.1229 f.).

62. Most splendidly he has taught us how we ought to understand the mystery of Christ's blood and body. For having said that our fathers ate spiritual food and drank spiritual drink, and yet no one doubts that that manna which they ate and that water which they drank were corporeal, he adds with reference to the mystery now enacted in the church, defining the sense in which it is Christ's body: "For the body of God," he says, "is a spiritual body." God is surely Christ, and the body which he assumed from Mary, which suffered, which was buried, which rose again, was surely the true body, that is, one which remained visible and could be touched. But the body which is called the mystery of God is not corporeal but spiritual. If it be spiritual, it is now not visible or capable of being touched. Hence blessed Ambrose adds, "The body of Christ is the body of the divine Spirit." For the divine Spirit exists as nothing which is corporeal, nothing corruptible, nothing capable of being touched. But this body which is celebrated in the church with respect to its visible appearance is both corruptible and capable of being touched.

63. How, therefore, is it called the body of the divine Spirit? With respect to the fact that it is surely spiritual, that is, with respect to the fact that it is invisible and not capable of being touched, and on this account incorruptible.

64. Hence he added, "Because Christ is spirit, as we read, 'The Lord Christ is spirit before our face.'" Clearly he shows with respect to what it is held to be Christ's body, namely, with respect to the fact that the Spirit of Christ is in it, that is, the power of the divine Word, which not only feeds the soul but even cleanses it.

65. On this account the same authority himself next says,[85] "Finally, 'that food strengthens' our heart and that drink 'gladdens the heart of man,' as the prophet[88] said." Corporeal food does not strengthen our heart and corporeal drink does not gladden the heart of man, do they? But to show what food and what drink they are of which he is speaking, he expressly adds "*that* food" and "*that* drink." What does he mean by "that"? The body of Christ, of course, the body of the divine Spirit, and that it may be impressed more clearly upon us, Christ is the Spirit of which he is speaking, "The Lord Christ is Spirit before our face." By all this he openly shows that

---

[88] Ps. 104:14 f. (Ps. 103:15, V), a very loose quotation following neither Septuagint nor Vulgate. The psalter was widely quoted with the attribution, "The prophet says," until the end of the Reformation period.

nothing in that food and nothing in that drink must be taken in a corporeal sense but all must be considered spiritually.

66. For the soul, which is here meant in the phrase "heart of man," is not fed upon corporeal food or corporeal drink, but is nourished and quickened on the Word of God. This is openly affirmed by that same doctor in the fifth book of *The Sacraments*:[89] "It is not that bread which enters into the body but that bread of life eternal which supports the substance of our soul."

67. And that Saint Ambrose did not say this about ordinary bread but about the bread of Christ's body, the following words of his discourse make abundantly clear. He is speaking about the daily bread which those who believe ask to be given.

68. And therefore he adds: "If it is daily bread, why do you wait a year to take it again, as the Greeks in the East were accustomed to do? Therefore, take daily what is daily of advantage to you. So live that daily you may deserve to receive it." Therefore it is clear what bread he is speaking about, namely, the bread of Christ's body, which, not from what goes into the body, but from what is the bread of life eternal, supports the substance of our soul.

69. By the authority of this most learned man we teach that a great difference separates the body in which Christ suffered, and the blood which he shed from his side while hanging on the cross, from this body which daily in the mystery of Christ's Passion is celebrated by the faithful, and from that blood also which is taken into the mouth of the faithful to be the mystery of that blood by which the whole world was redeemed. For that bread and that drink are Christ's body or blood, not with respect to what they seem, but with respect to the fact that they spiritually support the substance of life. That body in which Christ suffered once and for all exhibited no different appearance from the one it really had. For it was what it truly seemed, what was touched, what was crucified, what was buried. Likewise, his blood, trickling from his side, did not appear one thing outwardly and conceal another thing inwardly, and so true blood flowed from the true side. But now the blood of Christ which the believers drink, and the body which they eat, are one thing in appearance and another thing in meaning—the one, what feeds the body on corporeal food; and the other, what nourishes the mind on the substance of life eternal.

[89] Ambrose, *De sacram.* 5.24, p. 95 Botte = MPL 16.471B, inexactly quoted.

70. Concerning this the blessed Jerome[90] writes in his commentary on Saint Paul's Epistle to the Ephesians as follows:

"The blood and flesh of Christ are understood in a twofold sense, either that spiritual and divine sense of which he himself speaks, 'My flesh is truly food and my blood is truly drink,' [91] or the flesh which was crucified and the blood which was poured out from the soldier's spear." [92]

71. By no small difference this doctor distinguishes Christ's body and blood. For while he says that the flesh or blood which are daily received by the faithful are spiritual, the flesh which was crucified and the blood which was shed from the soldier's spear are, on the other hand, said to be neither spiritual nor divine. He clearly suggests that they differ between themselves as much as differ things corporeal and things spiritual, things visible and invisible, things divine and human, and because they differ in themselves, they are not identical. Moreover, the spiritual flesh which is received in the mouth by the faithful and the spiritual blood which daily is presented to believers to be drunk differ from the flesh which was crucified and from the blood which was shed from the soldier's spear, as the authority of this man testifies.

72. They are therefore not the same. For that flesh which was crucified was made from the flesh of the Virgin, of bones and sinews joined together and marked with the lineaments of human parts, quickened to life of its own and harmonious motions by the spirit of a rational soul. But the spiritual flesh which spiritually feeds the people who believe, consists, with respect to the appearance it outwardly bears, of grains of flour molded by the hand of an artisan, joined together without sinews and bones, having no characteristic variation of parts, animated by no rational substance, unable to move of its own accord. For whatever in it furnishes the substance of life is of spiritual might, invisible in efficacy, and divine power. With respect to its outward view it is far different in constitution from that which it is believed to be with respect to the mystery. Furthermore, the flesh of Christ which was crucified revealed nothing different outwardly from what it was inwardly, because it existed as true flesh of true man, a body really true having the appearance of a true body.

73. It must be considered that in that bread not only Christ's body but the body also of the people believing on him should

---

[90] Jerome, *In Eph.* 1:7 (MPL 26.481).   [91] John 6:55.   [92] John 19:34.

be symbolized by the many grains of flour of which it is made because the body of the people who believe is increased by many faithful ones through Christ's word.

74. Wherefore, as in the mystery that bread is taken as Christ's body, so also in the mystery the members of the people who believe in Christ are suggested, and as that bread is called the body of the believers, not in a corporeal sense but in a spiritual, so of necessity Christ's body must also be understood not corporeally but spiritually.

75. As also in the wine which is called Christ's blood mixing with water is prescribed,[93] the one element is not allowed to be offered without the other, because the people cannot exist without Christ, nor Christ without the people, so also can the head not exist without the body, nor the body without the head. So then, in that sacrament, the water represents the people. Therefore, if that wine which is consecrated by the liturgy of the ministers is changed into Christ's blood in a corporeal sense, the water, likewise, which is mixed with it, must of necessity be converted corporeally into the blood of the people who believe. For where there is one consecration, of a consequence there is one action, and where there is a like transaction, there is a like mystery. But we see that in the water nothing is changed with respect to the body, so also for this reason in the wine there is nothing corporeally exhibited. Whatever is meant in the water concerning the body of the people is accepted spiritually. Therefore it is necessary that whatever in the wine is suggested concerning Christ's blood should be accepted spiritually.

76. Likewise, things that differ from each other are not the same. Christ's body which died and rose again, and having become immortal "will now not die again, and death will have no further dominion over him," [94] is eternal and no longer capable of suffering. That which is celebrated in the church is temporary, not eternal. It is corruptible, not incorrupted. It is on the road, not in its homeland. They, then, differ from each other, and are, for this reason, not the same.

77. But if they are not the same, how is it called the true body of Christ and the true blood? For if it is Christ's body and the statement that it is Christ's body is true, it is Christ's body in truth; and if it is in truth the body of Christ, the body of

---

[93] On mixing of water with the wine see F. J. Dölger, *Der heilige Tisch in den antiken Religionen und im Christentum* (Münster i. W., 2d ed., 1928), 2.491–496; Ambrose, *De virg.* 3.5.22.

[94] Rom. 6:9.

Christ is both incorruptible and incapable of suffering, and therefore eternal. Therefore, this body of Christ which is enacted in the church must necessarily be incorruptible and eternal. But it cannot be denied that what is divided into bits to be consumed is corrupted, and when ground by the teeth is transferred into body. It is one thing, however, which is outwardly done, but another which through faith is believed. What pertains to the sense of the body is corruptible, but what faith believes is incorruptible. Therefore, what appears outwardly is not the thing itself but the image of the thing, but what is felt and understood in the soul is the truth of the thing.

78. Hence the blessed Augustine in his commentary on John's Gospel, speaking of Christ's body and the blood, says:[95]

> "Moses also ate the manna, Aaron also ate the manna, Phinehas also ate the manna, many there ate the manna who pleased God, and did not[96] die. Why? Because they understood the visible food spiritually, they hungered spiritually, they tasted spiritually, so that they might be satisfied spiritually. We also today receive the visible food, but the sacrament is one thing and the power of the sacrament is another."

Likewise, later on he says:

> "This is the bread which descended from heaven. By this bread he meant manna, by this bread he meant the altar of God. Those were sacraments; in symbols they are different, in the thing meant they are alike. Hear the apostle: 'I do not want you to be ignorant, brethren, that our fathers were all under the cloud . . . and all ate the same spiritual food, and all drank the same spiritual drink.' Spiritual, surely, and the same; not corporeal and different, because they had manna, we something else, but what they had was spiritual, as in our case. And he adds: 'And they all drank the same spiritual drink.' . . . They had one thing, we something else but visible in appearance, yet what this same thing meant was spiritual power. How, then, was it the same drink? 'They drank,' he says, 'from the spiritual rock which followed them.

---

[95] Augustine, *In Ioann. evang. tract.* 26.11 (MPL 35.1611).
[96] Had they not had the manna there in the desert, they would have died before their time, but did not. See, however, the quotation from Ambrose in §51 and the quotation in Paschasius (note 45) above for the statement that they did die.

Moreover, the rock was Christ.'[97] The source of the bread was the same as the source of the water. The rock was Christ for a sign, the Christ true in word and in flesh."[98]

79. Likewise:

"'This is the bread coming down from heaven, so that if anyone ate from it, he would not die.' But what pertains to the power of the sacrament is not what pertains to the visible sacrament; who eats it within, not outside, who eats it in his heart, not who crushes it with his teeth."[99]

80. Likewise, in later passages,[1] he brings in the Saviour's words and says:

"'Do you take offense at this? Because I said I give you my body to eat and my blood to drink? What if you were to see the Son of Man ascending where he was before?' What is this? For this reason he revealed what had moved them; for this reason he laid open why they had taken offense. For they thought that he would destroy his own body. He said, however, that he would ascend into heaven actually whole: 'When you see the Son of Man ascending where he was before.' Certainly, either you will then see that he is destroying the body not in the way you think or you will then understand that his grace is not consumed by bites, and he says: 'The spirit is what quickens, the flesh is of no avail.'"[2]

81. And much later[3] he adds:

"'Yet whoever,' says the same apostle, 'does not have the Spirit of Christ, he is not his.'[4] Therefore, 'it is the spirit which quickens, for the flesh is of no avail. The words which I spoke to you are spirit and life.'[5] What does 'are spirit and life' mean? The words must be spiritually understood. Have you understood them spiritually? They are spirit and life. Have you understood them after the flesh? They are also spirit and life but not for you."[6]

82. We learn clearly from the authority of this doctor, expounding the Lord's words about the sacrament of his body

---

[97] I Cor. 10:4.   [98] Augustine, *loc. cit.* (MPL 25.1612).
[99] *Ibid.*   [1] Augustine, *loc. cit.* (MPL 35.1616).
[2] John 6:63, unintentionally copied by Ratramnus: it is the heading for the next comment by Augustine and has no connection with the thought here.
[3] Augustine, *loc. cit.* (MPL 35.1618). "The same apostle" refers to a quotation from Saint Paul not copied by Ratramnus.
[4] Rom. 8:9.   [5] John 6:63.   [6] John 6:63.

and blood, that those words of the Lord are to be understood in a spiritual and not a carnal sense, even as he himself says: "The words which I speak to you are spirit and life."[7] The reference is to the words concerning his body that must be eaten and his blood that must be drunk. For he was speaking of this when his disciples were offended. Therefore, in order that they be not offended, the divine Master calls them back from the flesh to the spirit, from the bodily sight to the invisible understanding.

83. We therefore see that that food of the Lord's body and that drink of his blood, with respect to which they are truly his body and truly his blood, are so, namely, with respect to spirit and life.

84. Likewise, what are the same are included in a single definition. Of the true body of Christ it is said that it is true God and true man: God, who was born from God the Father before time; man, who at the end of time was begotten from the Virgin Mary. While, however, this cannot be said about the body of Christ which exists in the church through the mystery, in a certain sense it is recognized to be the body of Christ, and that sense is in a figure and an image, so that the truth itself is felt.

85. In the prayers which are said after Christ's body and blood, when the people answer "Amen," so in the voice of the priest it is said: "Receiving the pledge of life eternal, we humbly pray that of what we touch in the image of the sacrament we may have a clear share."[8]

86. For both the pledge and the image are of something other than themselves; that is, they regard not themselves but something else. For the pledge of that thing is that for which it is given, its image that of which it shows the likeness. These things signify the thing of which they are; they show it, in a form not clear. Since this is so, it is apparent that this body and blood are the pledge and image of a thing that is to come, so that what now is shown through the likeness will in the future be revealed through its manifestation. If now they signify it, in the future they will, however, make clearly known that what is

---

[7] John 6:63.
[8] This prayer occurs earliest in the Gelasian Sacramentary (2.36 in oct. apost., prid. non. Iul.: see MPL 74.1174A), and was never in the Gregorian sacramentaries or the Roman missal. See H. A. Wilson, *The Gelasian Sacramentary: Liber Sacramentorum Romanae Ecclesiae* (Oxford, 1894) 186, where the text is slightly different; Bruylants, *Les Oraisons du Missel Romain, texte et histoire* (Louvain, 1952) 1.116.

now involved is one thing, what will be manifested in the future is another.

87. Wherefore, both the body and the blood of Christ are what the church celebrates, but as a pledge, as an image. It will, however, be truth when it is no longer either the pledge or the image, but the truth of this thing will appear.

88. Likewise in another place we read:[9] "Let thy sacraments perfect in us, we ask, O Lord, what they contain, so that what now we have in appearance, we may receive in actual truth." This means that these things are possessed in appearance, not in truth, that is, through the likeness, not through the manifestation of the thing itself. Appearance and truth differ from each other. On this account the body and blood possessed in the church are different from that body and blood which in Christ's body are recognized now to be glorified through the resurrection. This body is both a pledge and an appearance, but that body is truth itself. This shall be practiced until that one is reached; but when it is reached, this one will be taken away.

89. And so it appears that they are separated from each other by as great a difference as exists between the pledge and the thing on behalf of which the pledge is handed down, and as exists between appearance and truth. Thus we see that a great difference separates the mystery of Christ's blood and body which now is taken by the faithful in the church from that which was born of the Virgin Mary, suffered, died, rose again, ascended to the heavens, sits on the right hand of the Father. For what is done on the way must be accepted spiritually, because faith, which does not see, believes and spiritually feeds the soul and gladdens the heart and provides life and incorruption, provided what feeds the body, what is pressed by the teeth, what is broken into bits, is not considered, but what is in faith received spiritually. But that body in which Christ suffered and rose again exists as his own body, assumed from the body of the Virgin Mary, capable of being touched or visible even after the resurrection, as he himself said to his disciples: "Touch and see that a spirit does not have flesh and bones such as you see I have."[10]

---

[9] For the text of this post-Communion prayer (*ad completa*) in the mass for Ember Saturday in September, see H. Lietzmann, *Das Sacramentarium Gregorianum* in *Liturgiegeschichtl. Quellen* 3 (Münster, 1921) p. 95; Wilson, *op. cit.*, 1.63; *Missale Romanum* (New York-Malines, 1906) p. 337.
[10] Luke 24:39.

90. Let us also hear what the blessed Fulgentius says in his little book *On Faith*:[11]

"Hold most firmly and never doubt that the only begotten God himself, the Word made flesh, has offered himself for us as a sacrifice and an offering to God with sweet fragrance, to whom, with the Father and the Holy Spirit, animals were sacrificed by the patriarchs, the prophets, and priests, in Old Testament times, and to whom now, that is, in New Testament times, with the Father and the Holy Spirit, with whom he shares a single divinity, the sacrifice of bread and wine, the holy catholic church throughout the world does not cease to offer in faith and love. In those flesh offerings the symbolism was the flesh of Christ which for our sins he, himself without sin, would offer, and of the blood which he[12] would shed for the remission of our sins. Moreover, in that sacrifice the giving of thanks and the commemoration is of Christ's body which he offered for us and of his blood which the same God shed for us. Concerning this the blessed apostle Paul says in The Acts of the Apostles:[13] 'Take heed for yourselves and for all the flock in which the Holy Spirit has made you overseers[14] to lead[15] the church of God which he has acquired with his blood.' In those sacrifices, therefore, which we were obligated to offer, this was symbolized in a figure; in this sacrifice, which, however, has now been offered for us, it is revealed to sight."

91. Saying that there was indicated in those sacrifices what we were obligated to give, but in that sacrifice what has been given is commemorated, he clearly suggests that as the former sacrifices held a figure of things to come, so the latter sacrifice is a figure of things past.

92. When this is said, he has most clearly shown how much difference there is between the body in which Christ suffered and this body, which is for commemoration of his Passion or his death. For that body was his own and true, possessing nothing in it either mystical or figurative. This, however, is mystical, revealing one thing outwardly through the figure, representing another thing inwardly through the understanding of faith.

93. Let us present here a testimony of Father Augustine, because it supports the validity of what we have said and

---

[11] Fulgentius of Ruspe, *De fide* 1.19.60 (MPL 65.699AB).
[12] Fulgentius, "The same God."   [13] Acts 20:28.   [14] *Episcopoi*.
[15] *Regere* is Greek *poimainein*, to guide and to rule.

provides a limit for our discourse. In a sermon[16] which he delivered before the congregation on the sacrament of the altar he begins as follows:

"What you see now on God's altar you already saw in the night that is past, but what it is, what it means, how great is the sacrament it contains, you have not yet heard. What you see, therefore, is bread and a cup, as your eyes also tell you. What, however, your faith asks to be informed is that the bread is Christ's body and the cup is Christ's blood. This was put briefly because it is altogether enough for faith, but faith requires instruction. The prophet says: 'Unless you believe, you will not understand.'[17] You can say to me, 'You have taught us to believe; expound for us that we may understand.' For such a thought as this can arise in the mind of someone: 'We know whence our Lord Jesus Christ received flesh, namely, from the Virgin Mary. He was nursed as an infant, was fed; grew, was reared to adolescence; suffered persecution from the Jews, was hanged on the cross, slain, taken down from the cross, buried, and on the third day rose again. On the day he willed it he ascended into heaven. Thither he raised his body. From thence he shall come to judge the living and the dead; he is there now, sitting on the right hand of the Father. How is the bread his body and how is the cup, or what the cup holds, his blood?' These things, brothers, are called sacraments because one thing is seen in them and another is understood. What is seen has a corporeal appearance; what is understood has spiritual fruit."

94. With this statement the venerable authority instructs us what we ought to think about the Lord's own body which was born of Mary and now sits on the right hand of the Father, the body in which he will come to judge the living and the dead, and what we should think about the one placed on the altar and partaken by the people. The former is whole, not cut into parts, nor concealed in any figures; the latter, which is contained on the Lord's Table, and is a figure because it is a sacrament, has also, as it outwardly seems, a corporeal appearance which feeds the body, but inwardly understood it has spiritual fruit which quickens the soul.

95. And wishing to say something openly and clearly con-

---

[16] This sermon 272 (MPL 38.1246 f.) is quoted almost *in toto* by Fulgentius of Ruspe, *Epist.* 12 *ad Ferrandum . . . de salute Aethiopis moribundi* (MPL 65.391C–392A). Ratramnus transcribes about three fourths of the text.
[17] Isa. 7:9 (OL).

cerning this mystical body, he says in the passage following:[18] "If, therefore, you wish to understand Christ's body, listen to what the apostle says: 'You are Christ's body and members.'[19] If, therefore, you are Christ's body and members, your mystery has been placed on the Lord's Table; you receive your mystery. To that which you are, you answer, 'Amen,' and in answering, you give assent. You[20] hear, then, 'Christ's body,' and you answer 'Amen.' Be a member of Christ's body, so that the 'Amen' will be true. Why, then, in the bread? Here let us advance nothing on our own. Let us listen to the apostle himself when he speaks concerning that sacrament: 'We who are many, one bread, one body'[21] in Christ," etc.

96. Saint Augustine sufficiently instructs us that as the body of Christ, placed on the altar in the form of bread, is symbolized, so also the body of the people as they receive it, in order that he might clearly show that Christ's own body is that in which he was born of the Virgin, in which he was nursed, in which he suffered, in which he died, in which he was buried, in which he rose again, in which he ascended into the heavens, in which he sits on the right hand of the Father, in which he shall come to the judgment. This, however, which has been placed on the Lord's Table contains his mystery, just as it also contains in the same manner the mystery of the body of the people who believe; in the words of the apostle's witness, "We who are many, one bread, one body" in Christ.

97. May your wisdom take notice, most famous prince, that since the testimonies of the Holy Scriptures and the words of the holy fathers have been cited, it has been most clearly shown that the bread which is called Christ's body, and the cup which is called Christ's blood, is a figure, because it is a mystery, and that there is no small difference between the body which exists through the mystery and that which suffered, was buried, and rose again. Since this body, the Saviour's own, exists, and in it there is neither any figure nor any symbol, but it is recognized as the very manifestation of the thing itself, and those who believe long for sight of it, since it is our Head, and when it is seen our longing will be satisfied; since he himself and the Father are one substance, not with respect to the fact that the Saviour has body but with respect to the fullness of divinity which dwells in Christ and man.

98. But in that which is enacted through the mystery there is a figure not only of Christ's own body, but also of the people who

---

[18] Continuation of quotation in §93. [19] I Cor. 12:27.
[20] The pronoun becomes singular. [21] I Cor. 10:17.

believe in Christ, for it bears the figure of both bodies, that is, the one which suffered and rose again, and the body of the people reborn in Christ through Baptism and quickened from the dead.

99. Let us add also that that bread and cup, which are named and are Christ's body and blood, present a memorial of the Lord's Passion or death, in the manner in which he himself said in the Gospel: "Do this in remembrance of me." [22] The apostle Paul explains this and says: "As often as you eat this bread and drink this cup, you will proclaim the Lord's death until he comes." [23]

100. We are taught by the Saviour, as well as by Saint Paul the apostle, that that bread and that wine which are placed on the altar are placed there as a figure or memorial of the Lord's death, so that what was done in the past may be recalled to memory in the present; that, made mindful of his Passion, we may through it be made partakers of the divine boon, through which we have been freed from death; recognizing that when we have arrived at the point of seeing Christ we shall have no need of such aids by which we are reminded what that measureless goodness bore for us, since, seeing him face to face, we shall not be moved by any outward remembrances of things temporal, but through contemplation of the truth itself we shall see the manner in which we ought to give thanks to the Author of our salvation.

101. Let it not therefore be thought that, since we say this, in the mystery of the sacrament either the Lord's body or his blood is not taken by the faithful when faith receives what the eye does not see but what it believes; for it is spiritual food, spiritually feeding the soul, and bestowing a life of eternal satisfaction. So also the Saviour himself speaks when he commends this mystery: "It is the spirit which quickens, for the flesh is of no avail." [24]

102. Desiring to be obedient to Your Majesty's command, I have presumed, though small in ability, to discuss matters not small, not following the presumption of our own thought but gazing upon the authority of our forebears. Should you approve of these words catholically spoken, attribute it to the merits of your faith which, having laid aside the glory of royal greatness, did not blush to seek a reply of truth from a man of low estate. Should this not, however, please you, attribute it to our lack of wisdom which was not strong enough to expound effectively what it desired.

[22] Luke 22:19 n. (R.S.V.)   [23] I Cor. 11:26.   [24] John 6:63.

A Reply to the Three Letters (Selections)

INTRODUCTION

NOT INFREQUENTLY THE STUDENT ENCOUNTERS A work which is more important than its writer even where the ascription of authorship is certain. But more often than not, in such an instance, the significance of the book has so far outstripped concern with the person who wrote it that precise information about the authorship may be inaccessible. Such is the case of the following treatise which we present in translation.

Entitled *A Reply to the Three Letters*[1] and written in the name of the church of Lyons, it is customarily attributed to Remigius, who was enthroned as bishop of the diocese between March 31, 852 (the date of Bishop Amulo's death) and September 12, 852 (the date of Emperor Lothair's first communication to Remigius as bishop), and who died on October 28, 875.[2] Two other treatises, also written in the name of the church, appear as his works, namely, *On the General Ruin of All Mankind Through Adam and the Special Redemption of the Elect Through Christ*, and *On Steadfastly Holding the Truth of Scripture and Faithfully Following the Authority of the Holy Orthodox Fathers*,[3] a meager output for a man whose public life spanned almost a quarter of a century, particularly as compared with twice that amount published by

---

[1] *Libellus de tribus epistolis*, MPL 121.985A–1068A. The reader will find that predestination figured in the so-called Semi-Pelagian controversy in Vincent's day. See above.

[2] L. Duchesne, *Fastes Épiscopaux de l'Ancienne Gaule* (Paris, Fontemoing et Cie., 1910), 2.173.

[3] *Absolutio cujusdam quaestionis de generali per Adam damnatione omnium et speciali per Christum ex eadem ereptione electorum*, MPL 121.1067B–1084B; *Libellus de tenenda immobiliter Scripturae veritate et sanctorum orthodoxorum patrum auctoritate fideliter sectanda*, MPL 121.1083C–1134D.

his predecessor's predecessor (Agobard) in a similar length of time.[4] We may compare the literary products of Agobard and Remigius still further. The three treatises ascribed to the latter are narrowly theological, while the works of the former are political, polemic, pastoral, even poetic, as well as theological. Moreover, within the sphere of theology the subject of the three books attributed to Remigius is basically the problem of predestination in some of its ramifications, whereas the tractates of Agobard range over a wide variety of theological themes, the use of images, folk paganism, liturgical allegory, ethics, church–state relations, Jewish practices, the inspiration of Scripture. Still further, the three books supposed to be Remigius' are hardly more than compilations of Biblical and patristic texts. While Agobard's treatises also employ that same familiar device, they do display sparks of originality, personal warmth, moments of penetrating imagination, and some stylistic elegance.

It is entirely possible that the three works ascribed to Bishop Remigius are indeed the products of his mind and pen, but some have thought that they were at least edited, if not written, by someone else.[5] Even if basically his own, they were no doubt prepared for publication by scholars in the scriptorium of Lyons. If so, we can hardly resist the inference that they are in some degree the work of the greatest ninth century scholar of Lyons, Deacon Florus. The harsh remarks about the deceased Amalarius are reminiscent of Florus' own bitterly polemic treatises about that man when he was alive.[6] The hostility exhibited toward Eriugena also recalls Florus' lengthy attack on the Irishman's errors.[7] Both the *Reply to the Three Letters* and Florus' critique of Eriugena employ the same method of direct quotation from the offending document followed by refutation of it. The reliance on Saint Augustine was of course characteristic of most medieval theology, but in particular of the school

---

[4] In MPL 121, the three treatises attributed to Remigius fill about 148 columns; in MPL 104, Agobard's writings fill about 319 columns.
[5] H. Schrörs, *Hinkmar Erzbischof von Rheims: sein Leben und seine Schriften* (Freiburg i/B, 1884), 129; Duchesne, *op. cit.*, 2.173, n. 5; M. Manitius, *Geschichte der lateinischen Literatur des Mittelalters* (Munich, Beck, 1911), 1.397; and (inferentially) J. M. Hanssens, *Amalarii episcopi opera liturgica omnia* (Studi e Teste, 138; Città del Vaticano, Biblioteca Apostolica Vaticana, 1948), 1.57, 82.
[6] See his three *Opuscula adversus Amalarium*, MPL 119.71D–96C.
[7] *Adversus Joannis Scoti Erigenae erroneas definitiones liber*, MPL 119.101B–250A.

of Lyons.[8] Even so, it is significant that Deacon Florus, a special student of the great doctor of the church, had compiled from his writings very extensive expositions of all the Pauline epistles (including Hebrews).[9] If he did not compose the *Reply to the Three Letters*, he was a ready source of Augustinian information for the author.

The *Reply* was one of the numerous works evoked by the predestinarian controversy which has plagued Christian history since the days of Saint Paul. The problem has so many ramifications that it is difficult to treat briefly, but we may suggest the extent of its discussion. Latourette states succinctly that "the issue was the freedom of man's will and the manner in which God's grace operates."[10] Perhaps, however, it was not so simple, for the issue has not only been soteriological but has often become metaphysical. It may, for instance, be a question whether God is truly the *almighty* maker of all things visible and invisible, "whose will can know no let nor hindrance," or whether man can in some degree thwart the will of omnipotence. If so, if the creature can, even in the slightest manner, defeat the Creator's purpose, can challenge the power of God, then indeed we have not one omnipotent, but two—a logical absurdity.

The debate has not remained on the level of logic and exegesis; it has become involved with emotion and feeling. Augustine, the greatest exponent of predestination, was certainly influenced in considerable measure by belief that his own conversion was wrought by God beyond his human consent, as was doubtless true also in the case of Saint Paul. Later such theologians as Thomas Bradwardine and Martin Luther had similar experiences. Even so, there have been others—Thomas Aquinas and Calvin, for example—who have unemotionally employed the doctrine as a lever with which to move the pride of man, the overweening vainglory which asserts that man's works are of some value in themselves and apart from God.

The *Reply* was a part of the debate which had as its center the

---

[8] See M. L. W. Laistner, *Thought and Letters in Western Europe A.D. 500 to 900* (London, Methuen and Co., 1931), 184 and *passim*.

[9] *Expositio in epistolas beati Pauli ex operibus sancti Augustini collecta*, MPL 119.279A–420B. The catenae are not given in full in MPL, merely the opening and closing phrases of the Augustinian interpretation of each verse.

[10] K. S. Latourette, *A History of Christianity* (New York, Harper, 1953), 177.

unhappy Saxon monk Gottschalk.[11] Born about 805 of noble parentage, he was given in infancy to the monastery of Fulda. Although he there began a lifelong friendship with the gentle Walafrid Strabo and the scholarly Lupus of Ferrières, he came to hate monastic restrictions, especially since he had been subjected to them through no choice of his own. So about the age of twenty-five he deserted Fulda and went first to Corbie, then to Orbais. In the meanwhile he undertook an intensive study of Augustine as well as composition of those poignant poems which are the best products of ninth century Latin literature. Having secured surreptitious ordination to the priesthood, Gottschalk abandoned monastic life to travel in Italy. Not long thereafter he began to preach the most severe version of Augustinian theology, the dogma of double predestination, the doctrine that God not only designated those to be saved, but also actively decreed the precise number of those to be damned. On his return to Germany he was charged with heresy at Mainz in 848 by Rabanus Maurus. Sent to Hincmar, archbishop of Rheims, he was in the following year at Kierzy divested of priestly office, beaten, and sentenced to imprisonment for the remainder of his life. He died between 866 and 869.

Gottschalk's personality and theological position were such that the leading lights of Frankish thought lined up either in opposition or in defense. Hincmar of Rheims, Pardulus of Laon, and Rabanus Maurus of Mainz were his chief enemies, and Prudentius of Troyes, Ratramnus of Corbie, Deacon Florus, Amulo of Lyons, Remigius of Lyons, and even Lupus of Ferrières (at least in part) were his advocates. So impressive an array for the poor monk constrained Hincmar to appeal for assistance. Hence it was ironical that Amalarius of Metz and John Scotus Eriugena were invited to enter the controversy. Gottschalk was condemned, as noted earlier, but as the furor subsided it came to be realized that the cure proposed by the Irishman was worse than the bite of the Saxon. That, however, is another story.

So severe and merciless was the punishment meted out to Gottschalk at Kierzy that his persecutors apparently felt the need of justifying themselves before the bar of public opinion, as at a much later date Calvin had to vindicate his action against Michael Servetus. That portion of the justification

[11] On Gottschalk, see Manitius, *op. cit.*, 1.568–574; Laistner, *op. cit.*, 243–246, 287–289; H. O. Taylor, *The Mediaeval Mind*, 4th ed. (London, Macmillan, 1930), 1.224 f., 228; 2.226–228.

which concerns us here seems to have taken the form of three letters, two reputed to have been addressed by Hincmar and Pardulus to the church of Lyons and one by Rabanus which, although directed to an episcopal colleague, was in time also transmitted to Lyons. These three letters constitute the occasion for the *Reply* in the name of the church of Lyons. The date would therefore be about 853, after the council of Kierzy (849), also after the accession of Remigius, but before the council of Valence (855).

The *Reply* lends itself readily to outline which could be elaborated in great detail, but a brief one only will be presented here. After an introduction which states the circumstances of its writing, the body is divided into three parts, of which the first is by far the longest:

I. Reply to Hincmar (chs. 1-38)

    A. Statement of Gottschalk's five controverted theses (ch. 1)
    B. The seven "rules of faith" by which the church of Lyons proposed to judge the theses (ch. 2; chs. 3-6 omitted)
    C. Confirmation of four of Gottschalk's theses and rejection of the fifth (chs. 8, 10, 21; chs. 7, 9, 11-20, 22, 23 omitted)
    D. Description of Gottschalk's punishment and criticism of it (chs. 24 f.; chs. 26-38 omitted)

II. Reply to Pardulus (chs. 39 f.)

    Very brief; herein occur the important references to Amalarius and Eriugena.

III. Reply to Rabanus (chs. 41-47)

    A. Proof that the writer refutes what no one denies (ch. 41; chs. 42-46 omitted)
    B. Summary of objections, reply to each, and conclusion (ch. 47)

Not only have we omitted many entire chapters as indicated above, but also a number of briefer passages which contain wearisome patristic commentary which does not advance the argument. There seems to be no previous translation into any vernacular, no edition later than the one incorporated into MPL, and no significant treatment, medieval or modern, of

Bishop Remigius.[12] Florus, however, is slowly but surely receiving his due.[13]

[12] See the indexes of Manitius, *op. cit.*, and Laistner, *op. cit.* As late as 1948, Hanssens, *op. cit.*, 1.57, 82, cites only the edition in MPL.

[13] Two modern students of Florus, Dom Celestin Charlier and Dom André Wilmart, have published a number of scholarly papers, of which the following are particularly pertinent: Wilmart, "Un lecteur ennemi d'Amalaire," *Revue Bénédictine*, 36 (1924), 317-329; "Sommaire de l'Exposition de Florus sur les Epitres," *ibid.*, 38 (1926), 205-214 (immediately followed on pp. 214-216, by his "Note sur Florus et Mannon à propos d'un travail récent"); "Une lettre sans adresse écrite vers le milier du IXe siècle," *ibid.*, 42 (1930), 149-162; Charlier, "La compilation augustinienne de Florus sur l'Apôtre," *ibid.*, 57 (1947), 132-186; "Une œuvre inconnue de Florus de Lyon: la collection 'De Fide' de Montpellier," *Traditio*, 8 (1952), 81-109. See also Hanssens, "Un document 'antiamalarien,'" *Ephemerides Liturgicae*, 41 (1927), 237-244; "De Flori Lugdunensis 'Opusculis Contra Amalarium,'" *ibid.*, 47 (1933), 15-31; and Cabaniss, "Florus of Lyons," to appear in a forthcoming issue of *Classica et Mediaevalia*. It would be going too far afield here to list Florus' forty-five or more works.

A Reply to the Three Letters (Selections)

THE TEXT

In the name of our Lord Jesus Christ. Here begins a short treatise about three letters of venerable bishops and what we should understand about their meaning and their claims in comparison with the canon of catholic faith.

From certain venerable men, namely, from three bishops, letters were brought to our church, that is, to the church of Lyons. Of these the two former ones seem to explain and exhibit what would appear to them simple and sincere answers to a certain profound and obscure problem which has for a number of years been discussed by many persons with varying degrees of debate or argumentation, the truth about divine foreknowledge and foreordination. They inquire and demand very carefully what our aforesaid church (with God's inspiration and help) thinks about the same subject so as to reply to them truthfully and faithfully.

One of them [Hincmar] who is indeed placed first among these three, speaks also of a certain pitiable monk who by his restless and arrogant presumption is said to have stepped forth boldly as the one who raised and stirred up this problem or rather stumbling block. In his letter he aptly and briefly explained fully how in two assemblies of bishops the monk had been heard, judged, and condemned. In separate propositions he in like manner related what had been presented by himself and others at that time as well as what is being presented by them today.

The second [Pardulus] also recalled about six persons who had written against him. Yet he did not complain that any one of them gave satisfaction with reasoning adequate for the matter about which inquiry was made.

The third [Rabanus] is known to have written not especially to our church but to a certain other bishop, and to have set forth and explained what (according to his opinion) should be held or taught by him on this matter.

When we had read all these things and had (as God gave us ability) discussed them carefully and faithfully among ourselves, it seemed quite clear to us that, rebuked by the disturbance of their opinions, which of compelling necessity appear like so many flapping fringes, as well as by the perturbation of simpler and ignorant brethren, who we know are wavering by the uncertainty of such problems, it seemed quite clear to us that we ought to prepare for the interrogators a reply of faith (of such kind as the Lord should vouchsafe to grant), drawn not from our understanding but from the most blessed fathers of the church. For (in so far as the Lord vouchsafes to help) assurance of faith may by a study of such a reply be increased both for ourselves and for others who perchance wish to read them, since the more earnestly and the more clearly it is proclaimed, the more faithfully God's truth must be observed and the more reverently and obediently the authority of the fathers must be followed.

1. The first writer therefore who, as we stated above, describes the activity of that pitiable monk, refutes his teaching, and reports his condemnation, asserted that he had afterward assumed the name of preacher of his own volition and had offered himself as an evangelist to barbarian and pagan peoples. He then related with these words the sequence of his preaching:

"Having initiated his preaching from a point of origin somewhat different from John who said, 'Repent, for the kingdom of heaven has come near,'[14] and from Paul[15] who taught that one comes to know the Creator of things visible and invisible through the mediation of visible things, he has undertaken to proclaim that before all worlds and before whatever God did from the beginning, he foreordained to the Kingdom whom he willed and he foreordained to death whom he willed[16]; that those who have been foreordained to death cannot be saved, and those who have been foreordained

---

[14] Matt. 3:2.   [15] Rom. 1:19 f.
[16] See ch. 8 below for defense of this thesis by the church of Lyons. Incidentally, we may note here that in our translation we have used the words "foreordination" and "predestination," indiscriminately to translate one Latin word. Our standard in this is merely variety.

to the Kingdom cannot perish[17]; that God does not wish all men to be saved, but only those who are saved; and that what the apostle says, 'Who desires all men to be saved,' is said of all those only who are saved[18]; that Christ did not come that all might be saved, nor did he suffer for all, but only for those who are saved by the mystery of his Passion[19]; and that, after the first man fell by free will, no one can employ free will for doing good but only for doing evil." [20]

Other things Hincmar related about Gottschalk's other deeds not derived from the course of doctrine. It seems to us in part incredible that, in preaching to peoples who do not know the Lord, he should neglect to summon them first of all to repentance and to persuade them to make a reasonable distinction between creature and Creator, so that they may not, through the error of idolatry, worship and serve "the creature rather than the Creator, who is blessed forever," [21] but that he should set before them problems exceedingly difficult even for believers and savants, problems about God's judgments and the mystery of foreordination and redemption. Yet passing over the quite absurd and unfitting objection to this matter, we believe that among the faithful or even among priests of those parts one should raise and set forth such things as those by which a new and marvelous preacher of great and new things might be esteemed, rather than that one should be of so great fatuity and stupidity as to be charged with obtruding such things unreasonably and preposterously upon those who are altogether ignorant of every godly matter. If he persists, he should be deemed among them as one not to be listened to, but rather to be utterly laughed at, and to be kept from the ears of everyone.

Of the aforesaid five propositions which Gottschalk is said to have preached or to have proposed in the councils where he was summoned to be heard and adjudged, and which he is supposed to have been willing to defend and confirm, that which by the inspiration of our loyalty to God seems to our insignificant person contrary to the rationale of true faith we believe should be defined, not in fear with precipitate and thoughtless haste, but should, with all care for piety, be faithfully asked, knocked for, and sought[22] with most devout zeal for finding

---

[17] Ch. 10 below for defense.
[19] Chs. 14 f. (omitted) for defense.
[21] Rom. 1:25.
[18] Chs. 11–13 (omitted) for defense.
[20] Ch. 21 below for refutation.
[22] Cf. Matt. 7:7; Luke 11:9.

and preserving the truth. Thus, with all animosity and strife removed, we may pursue with faith and one accord, not what by human error seems true to us, but what truth itself shall make clear. What should be done earnestly and faithfully (in so far as we can with the help of God), we believe must be put in the first place and must be recommended as strongly as it now recurs to our insignificant memory, namely, that there are seven rules of faith deriving authority from sacred Scripture and most earnestly commended by the holy and orthodox fathers concerning God's foreknowledge and foreordination, which each catholic ought to adhere to most loyally. Whoever savors of things contrary to them is to be attested as not thinking in a catholic manner.

2. Of these the *first* is that we most strongly and faithfully hold that Almighty God foreknew and foreordained nothing merely in relation to time, but just as he himself is eternal and unchangeable without any beginning, so also is his foreknowledge and foreordination eternal and unchangeable.

In God there is no new will, no new plan, no new arrangement, no new decision, as though from eternity he was not with himself and in himself but only afterward came into existence. Nothing is accidental to his divinity and in his deity nothing can be increased, diminished, or changed. Therefore whatever he foreknew, he foreknew from all eternity; whatever he foreordained, he doubtless foreordained from all eternity. Unto this belief Holy Scripture directs and informs us, "O eternal God, who art the examiner of secret things, who knowest all things before they come to pass. . .,"[23] as also does Almighty God himself when he testifies of himself, "I the Lord indeed do not change."[24] By the prophets, moreover, he sets forth the eternity of his foreordination in another place: "I the Lord have spoken and I have done it,"[25] that is, "What now through the prophet I have said would be accomplished long afterward

---

[23] Susanna 42 (Dan. 13:42, V). Cited twice more in passages which we omit, this verse was obviously a *crux interpretum* in the predestinarian controversies. See, for example, its use by Florus, *Sermo de praedestinatione, ad init.* (MPL 119.96D); Amulo, *Responsio ad interrogationem cujusdam de praescientia vel praedestinatione divina et de libero arbitrio, ad init.* (MPL 116.97A); Hincmar, *De praedestinatione Dei et libero arbitrio posterior dissertatio*, 6 (MPL 125.90C).

[24] Mal. 3:6.

[25] Ezek. 17:24. Note here and elsewhere the predilection of the church of Lyons for paraphrase. It has been observed also in the works of Agobard and Claudius of Turin (who was trained in Lyons).

in its own time, I have already accomplished by the eternity of foreordination in me, nor is that awaited by me as still future which by my unalterable appointment is already certain to be done."

Almighty God came to say this in the following manner: through the prophet he had narrated in advance a parable of two trees as a figure of two peoples, Jews and Gentiles. One of these he says that he had brought low from loftiness and withered its greenness; the other he had made lofty from scrubbiness and full of leaves from dryness, "All the trees of the region shall know that I the Lord have brought low the high tree and made high the low tree; I have dried up the green tree and made the dry tree flourish." [26] He adds immediately thereafter, "I the Lord have spoken and I have done it." Or, in other words "What I have now spoken by the prophet and what I shall yet do among men I have already accomplished by eternal foreordination," that is, both his mercy and his judgment. As the apostle says, exhibiting his "kindness and severity" [27] by the eternally foreordained rejection or exaltation of each people, he brings one low and dries it up by a just decision; the other, however, by gratuitous mercy he exalts and makes to flourish forever. What can therefore be sought more plainly and more distinctly concerning the foreordination of each part (that is, of the elect as well as of the reprobate), when, through faithlessness, the withering of one and, through faith, the flourishing of the other, both are equally declared to have been foreordained in its eternal predestination by the just decree of God?

Such also is the passage in the same prophet Ezekiel which pertains to the portion of the reprobate, wherein, under the figure of Gog and Magog, the eternal ruin of all wicked peoples and of the enemies of God's people (that is, pagans, Jews, and heretics, and especially Antichrist and those who with him will persecute the church of God) is foretold. The prophet thereupon adds, "Behold, it is coming and it has been brought about, says the Lord God," [28] that is, "What among men will come after so long a time and what will be after so long a time, with me in eternal foreordination is not yet to come but has already come, is not yet to be, but already is." In this way too the psalmist, showing forth the appropriate portion of the elect and of the reprobate, that is, by the eternal decree of God the former predestined to mercy, the latter to perdition, speaks clearly and

[26] Ezek. 17:24.   [27] Rom. 11:22.   [28] Ezek. 39:8.

openly of the elect, "The mercy of the Lord is from everlasting to everlasting upon those who fear him," [29] but of the reprobate, "Those who withdraw themselves far from you shall perish in their wickedness; you have destroyed all those who have gone awhoring from you." [30] In so far as it pertains to them in their own days, "those who withdraw themselves far from you" shall of course perish by an ultimate judgment, but in so far as it pertains to the foreordination of your eternal decree you have already destroyed them.

The apostle teaches us how to understand this unchangeableness of the divine counsel and decree wherein God's oath is interposed, as, for instance, when he explains that he swore to Abraham himself concerning the heirs of Abraham's faith: "Since God, making a promise to Abraham, had no one greater by whom to take an oath, swore by himself, saying, 'Blessing will I not bless you and multiplying will I not multiply you?'" [31] Shortly afterward he states: "God, wishing to show so much the more abundantly to the heirs of the promise the unchangeableness of his decree, interposed an oath, so that by two things in which it is not possible for God to lie, we have a very strong assurance, we who have fled for refuge to hold fast the hope set before us." [32] As therefore in the portion of the elect who are the inheritors of the divine promise and prediction, God wished by an oath to show forth the immutability of his plan (that is, the immutable arrangement of his eternal predestination, according to the explanation of the apostle), so also in the portion of the reprobate, where God's oath is interposed, nothing is exhibited other than the unchangeableness and immutability of his eternal counsel and foreordination of damnation and perdition for them. Almighty God shows that they are reprobate when he asserts of them, "They have not understood my ways." [33] Furthermore he shows that by his unalterable plan (that is, the unchangeable predestination of his decree) they are foreordained to eternal damnation and perdition, when he immediately adds, "To whom I swore in my wrath that they shall not enter my rest." [34] But if anyone thinks that is to be understood only of those reprobates who were led out of Egypt by Moses and who during the forty years in the wilderness were always rebellious and faithless, whose corpses finally lay scattered in that same desert, and not rather as a

---

[29] Ps. 103:17 (102:17, V).
[31] Heb. 6:13 f.; cf. Gen. 22:16 f.
[33] Ps. 95:10 (94:11, V).
[30] Ps. 73:27 (72:27, V).
[32] Heb. 6:17 f.
[34] Ps. 95:11 (94:11, V).

figure of the death of all the reprobate generally with a special damnation and ruin, listen to the apostle as he speaks dreadfully yet truthfully, "All these things affected them for a figure, but they were written for our correction, upon whom the ends of the ages have come." [35] Elsewhere he says, "Let us therefore hasten to enter that rest, so that none may fall through the very same example of unbelief." [36]

This certainty and unchangeableness of divine foreordination whereby God has already made his decrees for the future, the blessed prophet Isaiah has marvelously displayed, as blessed Augustine truthfully but succinctly explains, "He who has indeed foreordained all future things by certain and unalterable causes has already accomplished whatever he will do. For by the prophet it has been said of him, 'He who has accomplished whatever things will be.'" [37] The same teacher also in another place speaks of him: "God does not, as men do, repent of any of his deeds; there is for absolutely all his affairs a fixed decree as well as certain foreknowledge." It is therefore both eternal and immutable with him since of absolutely everything, good as well as evil, which comes to pass in the world eternally before the world, his foreknowledge is certain by his foreknowing and his decree is fixed by his determination.

This continuing unchangeableness of God's foreknowledge and foreordination before time and regulating all things in time, blessed Judith also professed wonderfully and briefly in her prayer to God when she was victorious over those enemies of God's people, the Assyrians: "You have accomplished all former things and you have meditated those which come after, and that has been done which you have willed, and in your providence you have set forth your decrees." [38] She says, "You have accomplished all former things and you have meditated those which come after," not that a restlessness and inconstancy of ebbing and flowing opinions should be believed of God, but that by a single and eternal intuition he discerns in an immutable manner, he comprehends in an incomprehensible manner, all that goes before and all that comes afterward in created things. She says, "In your providence you have set forth your decrees," that is, "Your decrees which you administer in the world you have in your providence set forth before the

---

[35] I Cor. 10:11. [36] Heb. 4:11.
[37] Augustine, *On Rebuke and Grace*, 23 (NPNF, 1st ser., 5.481). The Scriptural quotation is Isa. 45:11, according to LXX.
[38] Judith 9:4 f.

world; and whatever you have willed to be done in time you have in your counsel determined outside of time."

For Almighty God knows how to create new things without any novelty of will. He knows how to be at work although resting and how to be at rest although working. He can apply to a new work, not a new, but an eternal plan. When therefore he says that he has considered first one thing then another, he is not (heaven forbid!) varying with some inconstancy, but contrary to our mutability he, the unchangeable one, is merely operating in differing ways, not by a variable plan. Wherefore the blessed apostle James says of him, "With whom there is no changeableness or shadow of alteration." [39] The book of Ecclesiasticus says of his glories: "Everything that has been recognized was created by God beforehand. Likewise also after its completion he still regards everything." [40] Again: "From everlasting to everlasting he supervises, and nothing is marvelous in his sight." [41]

[Chapters 3–7 omitted.]

8. That we should most firmly and loyally hold this canon of faith, blessed Augustine carefully and briefly commends thus in his book on *The City of God*:

"We divide the human race into two kinds: one, those who lived according to man; the other, according to God. These also we mystically call two cities, that is, two societies of men, one of which is predestined to reign forever with God; the other, to undergo eternal punishment with the devil." [42]

Later, carefully discussing the rise of these two cities, that is, of the city of God and the city of the devil, he says:

"Therefore the former, Cain, was born of those two parents of the human race and he belongs to the city of men; the latter, Abel, to the city of God. The former was born a citizen of this world; but the latter, a pilgrim in this world, belongs to the city of God. Foreordained by grace, elect by grace, he is by grace a pilgrim here below, by grace a citizen there above. So far as he belongs to himself he arises from the same lump, but God is like a potter. The apostle maintains this figure not foolishly but intelligently, 'Out of the same lump' he made 'one vessel for honor, the other for

---

[39] James 1:17. [40] Ecclesiasticus 23:30 (23:29, V).
[41] Ecclesiasticus 39:20 (39:25, V).
[42] Augustine, *The City of God*, 15.1; cf. M. Dods' translation, NPNF, 1st ser., 2.284.

ignominy.'[43] He first made the vessel for ignominy, but afterward the other for honor. Since in one and the same man, as the apostle says, 'it is not the spiritual which is first but the physical, and then the spiritual.'"[44]

Similarly, in the *Manual* which he wrote for Laurentius, archdeacon of the Roman church, he speaks of the same matter:

"When the angelic and human creation had sinned, that is, had done not what God had desired but what it had itself wished, it was also by the selfsame will of the creature, by which that was done which God did not desire, that he himself accomplished what he wished, employing evil as well as good things for the damnation of those whom he justly foreordained to punishment and for the salvation of those whom he benevolently foreordained to grace."[45]

We have set forth these few things from two books of the aforesaid most blessed teacher which he not only wrote in a catholic and truthful manner but also reworked in a careful and faithful manner. For anyone who has perused his books of *Retractations* clearly knows that his authority on this matter (that is, on divine predestination to both ends, of the elect to glory, of the reprobate to punishment) is openly scorned and despised by some. Because he himself piously and humbly reproves and corrects himself, they suppose that wherever it might seem proper to them they could also reprove him. Although he set them an example of humility, they do not blush to aspire to overweening presumption. Let them recognize at least from these books that this word of divine predestination is fixed on the part of the reprobate, because they are said most truthfully and rightly to be predestined by divine judgment not to guilt but to punishment, not to an evil work which they do voluntarily but to evil itself which they will reluctantly suffer in eternal tortures. He would not censure such a belief in his writings, nor would it be censured by anyone who thinks in a catholic and sober manner. In modern times,[46] therefore, it would in vain be deemed worthy only of censure and rejection

---

[43] Rom. 9:21.   [44] Augustine, *op. cit.*, 15.1 (NPNF, 2.284 f.).
[45] Augustine, *Enchiridion*, 100; cf. translation by L. A. Arand, ACW, 3:94 f., and by A. C. Outler, LCC, 7.337–412.
[46] Boethius is supposed to have been the first writer to use the word *modern*. Here the comparison of "modernity" vs. "antiquity" is with the synod of Orange (529).

by us who are of such great inexperience and frailty, but rather it should be examined and understood with careful and humble affection. If there are those who seem to be offended by this (as though by the word, "predestination," a necessity of doing evil is intended to be imposed on anyone), they should rather be instructed and taught briefly and plainly that God has foreordained no one to sin but only to pay the penalty for sin. By that foreordination he compels no one to do evil, but rather declares the judge to be just who preferred that no sins be committed, yet foreknew that he would justly punish such deeds and hence foreordained that he would justly punish. For by this predestination he did not foreordain man's evil deed but man's just punishment.

[Remainder of this chapter and chapter 9 omitted.]

10. With one meaning, one mouth, one spirit, the most blessed fathers of the church proclaim and commend the immovable truth of divine foreknowledge and foreordination in both instances, namely, of the elect and of the reprobate; of the elect to glory, of the reprobate not to guilt but to punishment. Herein they boldly state that there is demonstrated for us an immutable order, not of temporal arrangements, nor of those beginning at a particular time, but of the everlasting designs of God. They affirm, moreover, that none of the elect can perish and that, because of the hardness and impenitence of their heart, none of the reprobate can be saved. The truth of Holy Scripture and the authority of the holy and orthodox fathers proclaim this with complete agreement and they inculcate it upon us to be believed and held without any doubting. Wherefore, if the shallowness of that wretched monk is condemned, his temerity disapproved, his insolent talkativeness blamed, divine truth should not for that reason be denied. For according to the catholic faith Almighty God, even before the establishment of the world, before he made anything, did from the beginning by his own free benevolence predestine certain ones to the kingdom by the sure, just, and unchangeable motives of his own eternal counsel. Of these none will perish since his mercy defends them. He predestined others by his own just judgment to death because of the desert of their impiety which he foresaw. Of these none can be saved, not because of any ferocity of divine power, but because of the untameable and constant villainy of their own wickedness. What, then, remains but for us humbly to renounce (in accordance with God's revelation to us) whatever we have otherwise tasted and for us faithfully to embrace the

truth which is becoming clearer to us. "For," as the apostle teaches, "we cannot do anything against the truth, but only for the truth." [47]

[Chapters 11–20 omitted.]

21. In the aforementioned letter that poor monk is said further to have declared that after the first man fell by free will, no one of us can exercise free will for doing good but only for doing evil. It is not only astonishing and unheard of but, as far as we can discover, incredible that a man reared by believers among believers and trained in the writings of the church fathers could be aroused to think, much less to say, that after the Fall of the first man none of the faithful could exercise free will to do good but only to do evil, as though in us the will is not free for anything but evil, as though the grace of God alone works in us for good apart from free will. If, however, he had made the general statement, "None of mankind," and had added, "Without God's grace," and had further added, "Cannot rightly exercise free will," it would have been an absolutely catholic statement with the catholic meaning. But since he insists on saying that none of us (that is, of the faithful) can exercise free will except for doing evil, what else is claimed by such an assertion, by such presumptuous novelty, than that the volition of the human mind (which before sin entered was free to love, desire, and enjoy the true good) has been so vitiated by the first man when he sinned, and has indeed perished, that free volition has remained in man solely and only for evil. But to do good man has no free volition, only the good derived from divine grace. We recall having found or heard of this type of error among no other heretics and certainly among no catholics. Hence, as we have said, this information about that monk seems incredible to us.

As one and the same man can be healthy, can from health become ill by some want of moderation, and can by a salutary medicine be made well again, so the free volition of the human mind, which aforetime was sound, became feeble when the first man sinned. What was sound has been corrupted, and what was alive is now dead. Before sin entered, it was truly sound, vitiated by no sinful frailty, but through sin itself it has been so weakened that one may truthfully cry out to God, "I said, O Lord, be merciful to me; heal my soul, for I have sinned against thee." [48] When by the right physician it is healed, a rejoicing and favored people exclaims, "O Lord our God, I cried to thee,

---

[47] II Cor. 13:8. [48] Ps. 41:4 (40:5, V).

and thou hast healed me." [49] Truly that was saved which had been distorted or corrupted by no evil will within or evil activity without. Truly it became corrupt when by evil will it deserted God, and by desertion lost the good which it had. Wherefore realizing this corruption within itself and earnestly longing to be free of it one groans and says, "I have gone astray like a lost sheep; seek thy servant, for I do not forget thy commandments." [50] Daily he finds need for the one seeking and saving him: "For the Son of man came to seek and to save that which was lost." [51] That one was alive so long as he clung to Him to whom we say, "With thee is the fountain of life; and in thy life we shall see light," [52] living in him and through him of whom it is written in the Gospel, "The life was the light of men." [53] But by deserting this life and this fountain of life one became alienated from the life of God and died, "because the soul that sins shall die." [54] One does not have in himself or of himself any vital feeling endeavoring toward true life unless he be raised up and made alive through Him who says, "This my son was dead and is alive again; he was lost, and is found," [55] and unless he be animated by that Spirit of whom the apostle speaks, "The letter kills, but the Spirit gives life." [56] So they are dead and are daily brought to life, of whom the Lord speaks in the Gospel, "The hour is coming, and now is, when the dead will hear the voice of the Son of God, and those who hear will live." [57] To them the apostle cries, "Awake, you who sleep, and arise from the dead, and Christ will enlighten you." [58]

Let no deceiver and caviler venture to charge that we say that free will is lost and dead through the sin of the first man as though he should be understood to have lost his proper nature in which he has by nature the inherent volition of free will. For he did not lose his nature, but the goodness of his nature; he did not lose the ability to will, but the ability to will the good. When his soul died, he did not lose his proper nature, in which as he has always existed so also he always continues to live according to a certain manner. Yet he truly dies, not of course by the dissolution of matter but by the loss of his own true life, which for him is God. For that reason the free will of man needs one who will seek and find, so that it may be saved from its lost estate; it needs one who will raise up and make alive, so that it may be alive again from the dead; it needs, moreover, one who

[49] Ps. 30:2 (29:3, V). [50] Ps. 119:176 (118:176, V). [51] Luke 19:10.
[52] Ps. 36:9 (35:10, V). [53] John 1:4. [54] Ezek. 18:4.
[55] Luke 15:24. [56] II Cor. 3:6. [57] John 5:25. [58] Eph. 5:14.

will ransom, so that what was in abject slavery can be set free. It was in abject slavery because it was subdued by sin, and "everyone who commits sin is a slave of sin."[59] From that slavery it was set free by Him who said, "If the Son will make you free, then you will be free indeed,"[60] as well as by the gift of the Holy Spirit, of whom the apostle says, "Where the Spirit of the Lord is, there is freedom."[61] Through the fault of the primal lie, man (and in him all mortal kind) had ruined true freedom of volition, which before was free to strive for and possess the true, divine, eternal good. Nor is there any way to recover that happy and true freedom of good volition unless through Christ's redemption it become free and through the grace of the Holy Spirit it be translated from the slavery of sin into the liberty of righteousness.

[Chapters 22 and 23 omitted.]

24. After these matters a certain narrative was introduced which does not seem to require refutation in our present reply. The author of the letter then adds more concerning the meeting of the council of bishops to consider and determine the questions or charges which that wretched monk is reported to have set forth or taught. (It seems to me that enough has already been displayed about them above.) How the aforesaid monk was condemned by decree of the bishops because he refused to acquiesce in their sentence is described as follows.

"Wherefore," Hincmar relates, "in the presence of the bishops who had been summoned to Kierzy on royal business by royal command, in the presence also of Lord Wenilo, who had come thither, I strove to restrain him as soon as he either said or (when questioned) replied nothing worthy of consideration by the many listeners. But, with the slipperiness of a snake, he leveled personal insults against each member of the council when he had no reasonable answer. So because of his most shameful insolence he was, according to the Rule of Saint Benedict, adjudged by the abbots and other monks as deserving of a beating. Since, contrary to canonical precept, he strove ceaselessly to stir up civil and ecclesiastical difficulties, and refused to examine himself or in any manner to humble himself, he was then cast out by the bishops and condemned in accordance with church laws."

In this statement it seems especially nonsensical that the abbots of monasteries who were present were first allowed to

[59] John 8:34. [60] John 8:36. [61] II Cor. 3:17.

sentence to murderous scourgings the aforesaid pitiable monk, who had been brought thither for the verdict of bishops; and that only then were the bishops allowed to condemn him according to church laws. For a man who has already been adjudged a heretic in accordance with ancient practice and the authority of the church should belong solely to the decision of bishops either for condemnation or for absolution. He should not be sentenced first by men of lower rank and then afterward by bishops. Of the murderous floggings to which he is said to have been sentenced according to the Rule of Saint Benedict [62] and by which he is said to have been cut almost to death in a most bitterly savage manner without any mercy, let them rather judge among themselves what moderation and measure ought to have been observed in accordance with ecclesiastical and priestly pity or even monastic modesty. That he is reported to have hurled insults at the bishops is, of course, truly wicked and mad, and he should be utterly condemned to a just vengeance. Even so, however, it should be done not by themselves but by others.

But of those opinions which he is proved to have preached first, then to have set forth at the council, and in no wise to have been willing to change, let each reader forgive us, let also the reverend author of that letter forgive us, for as we have already sufficiently demonstrated above on divine and patristic authority it seems to us that without any hesitation those things which he has said on the subject of divine foreordination are true according to the canon of the catholic faith. They have been quite manifestly proved from the fathers who have spoken the word of truth; and they must never be rejected or spurned by any one of us who wishes to be deemed a catholic.

In this matter therefore we grieve that ecclesiastical truth has been condemned, not a wretched monk. In that statement of the apostle wherein he speaks of God "who desires all men to be saved and to come to the knowledge of truth," [63] we believe that the interpretation of the most blessed Augustine (always devoutly accepted by the whole church and to be so accepted to the end of the world) has been followed. Treating of so great a problem with the twofold testimony of apostles

---

[62] The Rule of St. Benedict, 27. There are many editions and translations. A quaint version is the Latin and Anglo-Saxon interlinear version edited for the Early English Text Society series by H. Logeman, *The Rule of S. Benet* (London: Trübner, 1888), 59 f. A new translation is planned for *Library of Christian Classics*, vol. 12.   [63] I Tim. 2:4.

and prophets being brought together, he explained in many passages of his books, especially in the treatise called the *Manual*, how each truth must be received according to a sound understanding of the faith, and he makes clear what seems to him the more probable interpretation of so great a matter. It would not be proper for his absolutely truthful interpretation to be condemned on the part of any man by the catholic priests of God, lest he whose authority is followed be adjudged the heretic rather than the one who is supposed to be in error. Although certain other holy and venerable fathers may be found who have received these words of the apostle more simply, yet the opinion of both should be held in honor, and (as we explained above) no one should be spurned for the other, because one is proved to be true by divine authority, the other is believed by a certain kindly judgment not to deviate from the truth.

The treatment concerning the value of the Lord's blood which was given for those only who wished to believe is manifestly (as we have satisfactorily shown above) the opinion of the same blessed fathers, the same indeed which that one, we think, learned by reading and which he was afraid to disapprove. Wherefore, even if other fathers of equal standing are found who claim that the glorious value was given as well for those who will never believe and who will perish in their own wickedness, we believe it better that both be honored and one not be condemned for the other, because one is plainly confirmed by divine authority, while the other, if it is religiously perceived, should not be rejected. But what he is supposed to have said, namely, that we have free will only to do evil but not to do good, if he really does think so and has spoken so, that is certainly not derived from divine authority nor drawn from the teachings of the holy fathers but patently derived from his own error. For our free will, which was conquered by sin but not destroyed, has been set free by the grace of God in us and is aroused to do good so that even we ourselves may be co-workers of the same grace. Wherefore, if that one has erred so absurdly and foolishly, there is a clear statement of the apostle who says, "Brethren, if a man is overtaken in any trespass, you who are spiritual restore him in a spirit of gentleness, looking to yourself, lest you too be tempted." [64] Indeed, by reason of insolence, rudeness, and no check on his tongue, as well as by the restless inconstancy of his instability, that has perhaps rightly happened to him of which one reads in Solomon, "He

---

[64] Gal. 6:1.

who is thoughtless in speech will suffer evils."[65] Again, "He who imposes silence on a fool assuages wrath."[66] In another place, "Drive out a scoffer and strife will go out with him, and quarrelings and abuses will cease."[67]

25. Nonetheless we ought not to be so provoked by the wickedness and impudence of any man, that we despise, assail, or even dare condemn divine truth and the venerable authority of our fathers. We should ever be mindful of the apostle, who says, "We cannot do anything against the truth, but for the truth."[68] It should rather come to pass that fathers be honored in their sons and sons in their fathers, as Solomon says, "Sons' sons are the crown of the aged, and the glory of sons' is their fathers."[69] Of them this command is given elsewhere: "Stand in the assembly of wise elders and be joined to their wisdom from the heart, that you may be able to hear every record about God."[70] Again: "Do not despise the record of wise elders; be conversant with their proverbs. . . . Let not the record of the older men pass by you, for they themselves learned from their fathers. From them you will learn understanding and in time of need you will give an answer."[71] Of these this command is elsewhere written: "Ask your father, and he will show you; your elders, and they will tell you."[72] Again, "Do not cross over the ancient boundaries which your fathers have established."[73]

Absolutely everyone therefore not only deplores but also shudders at the unheard of and conscienceless brutality by which the wretched man was slashed to ribbons with murderous floggings. So pitiless was the treatment (as those who were present have informed us) that when a fire had been lighted in front of him he was compelled almost in dying condition to cast into the flame with his own hands and burn to ashes a little book in which he had assembled passages of Scripture and the holy fathers to exhibit at the council. Formerly all heretics were overcome and vanquished by words and debates. In that way the perversity which the man seemed to possess would have been bridled and no offense would have been brought upon religious matters, especially since those sentiments contained in

---

[65] Prov. 13:3.
[66] Prov. 26:10. There is an important textual note on this verse in R. Knox, trans., *The Old Testament* (New York: Sheed and Ward, 1952), 2.943 n.
[67] Prov. 22:10.   [68] II Cor. 13:8.   [69] Prov. 17:6.
[70] Ecclesiasticus 6:35.   [71] Ecclesiasticus 8:9, 11 f.
[72] Deut. 32:7.   [73] Prov. 22:28.

the little book (except the very last one) were not his own but those of the church. They should not have been consigned to the flames, but should have been handled in a kind and peaceful investigation. Moreover, that condemnation of the pitiable man to prison, so long, so inhuman, and for so many years, should (so we believe) have been tempered with some compassionate mildness and comfort, or indeed should have been remitted so that a brother for whom Christ died might be gained through charity and the spirit of gentleness rather than be enveloped in more abundant melancholy. Wherefore, as God knows (in so far as he vouchsafes to observe), we add with the charity which blessed apostle John commends to us, "By this we know the love of God, that he laid down his life for us; and we ought to lay down our lives for the brethren." [74]

[Chapters 26–38 omitted.]

39. In the second letter there are a few points of which it may be appropriate to speak, but others which must be passed over in silence. When, therefore, concerning the aforesaid problems, Pardulus, who wrote this second letter, wanted briefly to explain the zeal for the investigation, as well as the diversity of opinions and the eagerness with which it was desired that something certain and unambiguous should be found and shown about these matters, he speaks thus: "Many of us have written." And when he named five of them (among whom he mentioned that even Amalarius had written), he added, "But because there was such strong disagreement among them, we constrained that Irishman named John, who is at the king's palace, to write." A little later, he continues, "But what very great contention there was among us I will intimate to you."

[Remainder of chapter 39 omitted.]

40. Among those who are mentioned as having written for them about so great a problem as divine foreknowledge and foreordination, Amalarius is cited and John Scotus is said to have been urged by them to write. We take with great offense and pain the fact that discreet churchmen have done themselves so great a wrong as to consult on the system of faith that Amalarius who by his words, books of lies, and prolonged, fanciful, and heretical debates has (in so far as he could) infected and seduced almost all the churches of Frankland and some also in other regions. It is not so much that he should have been questioned about the faith as that all his writings should have

[74] I John 3:16.

been destroyed by fire immediately after his death, lest simpler ones, who are reputed to esteem them very highly and read them zealously, be uselessly occupied in reading them and be thereby dangerously deceived and beguiled.

It is an even greater shame and reproach that they urged that Irishman to write, who, as we have most truthfully ascertained from his writings, does not adhere to the very words of the Scripture as hitherto understood. He is so filled with fanciful imaginations and errors that not only should he never be consulted about the verity of the faith, but also those books of his should be deemed deserving of every ridicule and scorn, unless he hastens to correct and amend them. Otherwise he should either be pitied as a madman or be accursed as a heretic.

41. The third letter, which was not written to our church but to a certain friend of the venerable bishop, takes up a discussion which (it seems to us) is both unnecessary and irrelevant to the matter about which the inquiry is made. For in the current dispute, as we have already stated often enough and in different ways above, inquiry is not made whether God has foreordained the wicked and unrighteous to their wickedness and unrighteousness or has foreordained them to be wicked and unrighteous so that they cannot be otherwise. Absolutely no one in modern times is known to say that or to have thought it. That is in any case a monstrous and abominable blasphemy, as though God were by his foreordination the author of wickedness and unrighteousness, as though he compelled some men to be wicked and unrighteous. The question is rather whether by his own just decree he foreordained to suffer eternal punishment those whom he utterly and truthfully foreknew would be wicked and unrighteous by their own fault and would persist in wickedness and unrighteousness until death.

The author of this letter [Rabanus], ignoring the second question which is at present agitated among many people, strives rather against the former impious opinion and directs the entire body of his disputation to the fact that a good and just God could never be for anyone the cause, source, or author of sin and wickedness. But as we have said, all believers acknowledge that with faith and without hesitation. Employing the words of a little book entitled *Remembrancer*, he exerts himself to affirm that there is no divine foreordination to the just condemnation of the same wicked and unrighteous ones, and that divine predestination is to be believed only of the lot of the elect. Wherefore, since he indeed wrote before all those who in modern times are reported to have written on this matter, they who declare and affirm in like manner about divine foreordination seem to pursue his authority for themselves.

At the very beginning of his letter, he says, "It has been agreed among us that I compile from divine Scripture and the statements of the orthodox fathers some little work about the heresy which wicked and mistaken persons are erecting concerning God's foreordination, inducing others into that error. The purpose of such a work would be to vanquish completely the error of those who speak so badly of the good and just God as to claim that his foreordination makes it impossible for a man predestined to life to fall into death or for one predestined to death in any manner to recover himself unto life. Although the author of all things, God, the Creator of the world, is not the cause of any downfall or ruin, he is the source of the salvation of many."

In these words Rabanus mentions first the heresy and the heretics who savor divine predestination so that according to the Scriptures and the holy fathers they believe faithfully that it applies to both lots, the elect and the reprobate. They believe that Almighty God out of his great goodness has eternally foreordained the former to glory, and out of the vast equity of his decree has foreordained the latter to punishment. For that reason he should be admonished and recalled to a reflection on religion lest in the character of those whom he so easily calls heretics he be found to condemn the holy and venerable fathers.

[Chapters 42–46 omitted.]

47. After all these things the letter concludes thus: "He is therefore constrained by a sevenfold guilt who dares commit such blasphemy, twisting the good meaning of predestination by impious words into a perverse meaning.

"First, because he presumed to say that his creator, the greatest God, is malevolent in that he decrees his work to perish in vain and without reason.

"Secondly, because he endeavored to claim that Truth himself is deceptive who through Holy Scripture promises the reward of eternal life for those who believe rightly and do good, and who foretells the penalty of death for those who sin and do not repent.

"Thirdly, because, when he asserts that God does not assign rewards to those who do good and torments to those who do evil, he proclaims as unjust that just judge who will judge with equity the living and dead.

"Fourthly, because he does not fear through error to pretend that the Redeemer of the world poured out his blood in vain, since He cannot because of the compulsion of foreordination come to the aid of those who believe and hope in him.

"Fifthly, because he envies the good angels that our Saviour through the creation of men filled up their number, which the devil had diminished, breaking it by pride.

"Sixthly, because by his own opinion he favors the devil rather than God, when he consigns them to the lot of his perdition whom divine grace has decreed to attain salvation.

"Seventhly, because it is obvious that he is hostile to the whole human race when he asserts that it cannot be rescued from the Fall of the first parent, from the guilt of its own enormities, or even from the power of the enemy through faith in Christ and the sacrament of Baptism, but is obliged by the criminal foreordination of its own creator to be plunged into Tartarus." [75]

In these words Rabanus presents seven theses or propositions in which he charges with falsehood and error, not (as he claims) those who are blaspheming against God, but those who are faithful believers in God, those who truly acknowledge and commend God's mercy and judgment in the deliverance of the elect and in the damnation of the reprobate. Yet he cannot show to be true or reasonable any of those things which he charges in his seven propositions.

First, no one says that his creator, the highest God, is malevolent (heaven forbid!) as though He were ill-willed toward his creation, for his will is ever good to the good. If it seems evil to the evil, it is nonetheless always just and therefore cannot be evil. Scripture speaks to this point: "With the holy thou shalt be holy; and with the blameless thou shalt be blameless; with the chosen one thou shalt be chosen; and with the perverse thou shalt be perverse." [76] Of these words blessed Augustine says: "There is a hidden depth by which you will be known as holy with the holy, because you are the one who makes holy. With the blameless man you appear blameless, because you bring harm to no one, but each is rather constrained by the toils of his own sins. By the one whom you choose you will be chosen, but with the perverse you will appear perverse, since they declare, 'The way of the Lord is not

---

[75] For the Biblical use of the word "Tartarus," see both Greek and Latin of II Peter 2:4.
[76] Ps. 18:25 f. (17:26 f., V).

straight, for their way is not straight.'" [77] He does not decree in vain and without cause that his own work perish, but as for those whom he most truly foreknew would be evil and unrighteous and would continue in their evil and unrighteousness, he decreed, appointed, and foreordained that they would perish for just and most proper reasons, as he says, "Whoever shall have sinned against me, him will I blot out of my book." [78]

Secondly, no one who faithfully believes and acknowledges divine predestination to each lot, that is, of the elect and of the reprobate, endeavors to prove that Truth himself is deceptive, but rather is absolutely true and trustworthy in all his words and holy in all his works, because to the elect, as he has foreordained, he promises and assigns the rewards of everlasting life. On the other hand, to sinful and impenitent reprobates he repays everlasting punishments by his own just decree as he has foreordained.

Thirdly, the truth of divine predestination does not proclaim the just judge to be unjust, since according to it rewards are returned to those who do good and continue in good, and torments are inflicted upon those who do evil and remain in evil.

Fourthly, no necessity of his own predestination renders the Redeemer of the world unable through the glorious worth of his own blood to come to the aid of those who believe and hope in him, for by that price he forever comes to the aid of all his elect. Because he does not come to the aid of the reprobate, they through their own evil and unrighteousness spurn his price. Even if he can save them, he nevertheless wishes by a just vengeance to condemn some for the purpose of showing forth the terror of his sternness.

Fifthly, that same sternness of divine predestination does not envy the good angels, lest, because of the multitude of the reprobates dying daily, their number (which was diminished through the fall of the devil and his angels) should not be filled up and restored. For faith knows most assuredly that as many elect of the human race will agree thereto as it is certain that so many elect angels remained there. Such is the testimony of Scripture which says, "He fixed the bounds of the peoples according to the number of the angels of God." [79]

---

[77] Augustine, *Exposition of Psalm 17* [R.S.V., 18] (NPNF, 1st ser., 8.52). The Biblical citation, Ezek. 18:25, is not according to the Vulgate, but some Old Latin version employed by Augustine.
[78] Ex. 32:33.   [79] Deut. 32:8, LXX.

Sixthly, this foreordination does not favor the devil rather than God, since it daily compels the devil to lose those whom divine grace by the same foreordination has decreed to attain everlasting salvation. Moreover, it confirms that absolutely none of God's elect can belong to the lot of the devil himself.

Seventhly, faith in this predestination does not drive anyone into the supposition that he cannot be rescued from the fall of the first parent, from the guilt of his own enormities, and from the power of the enemy through faith in Christ and the sacrament of Baptism. Most truthfully it brings to pass in all the elect "that they may be always giving thanks to God, even the Father, who has qualified them to share in the inheritance of the saints in light. He has delivered them from the dominion of darkness and transferred them to the kingdom of the Son of his love." [80] The predestination of their creator (namely, God) is not harmful to the reprobate, that is, the predestination which most justly punishes their persistent and untameable wickedness. Crushed by the use of that wickedness and by its very grievous burden, they are plunged into Tartarus, falling into the abyss like a stone, drowning in the raging waters like lead. The Apocalypse, speaking in frightful accents of the whole city of this world (that is, the entire multitude of the damned), prophesies and threatens what will come to pass at the Last Judgment, "A mighty angel took up a stone like a great millstone and threw it into the sea, saying, 'With this violence shall Babylon the great city be thrown down, and shall be found no more.'" [81]

[Conclusion] Since these things are so, with all animosity of strife and overweening confidence in novelties laid aside, let us faithfully acknowledge divine truth, let us obediently pursue the authority of the fathers, let us vigilantly beware of the most deceitful vanity of error and falsehood; with God's help keeping inviolate the treasury of true faith once for all entrusted to us, avoiding the godless novelties of speech and contradictions of science falsely so called, by professing which certain ones have forgotten about the faith.[82]

---

[80] Col. 1:12 f.   [81] Rev. 18:21.   [82] Cf. I Tim. 6:20 f.

GOD'S WORD IN HOLY SCRIPTURE

Gregory the Great: The Commentary on Job (Selections)

INTRODUCTION

GREGORY THE GREAT, BISHOP OF ROME FROM 590 to 604, is more remarkable in the history of the church for his achievements as an ecclesiastical statesman than for the number and brilliance of his writings. Even in the case of that one work of his which did win him greatest fame as author, the celebrated *Book of Pastoral Rule*,[1] he owed its popularity in the Middle Ages to the practical values found in it by the parish priest or diocesan administrator rather than to originality. It has been said of Gregory that he knew how to express the truths which he found in Augustine in language simple enough for the people of his day to understand. Gregory would himself have been the first to deny any claim for his works as great literature.

The main facts of his life are well known. He was born at Rome about 540, of a patrician family, perhaps the Anicii. His father Gordianus was some sort of official and his mother Silvia has also been canonized, as were two paternal aunts, Tarsilla and Aemiliana, so that an early biographer has said that Gregory was "brought up a saint among saints."[2] After an

[1] *Liber regulae pastoralis* (often "Pastoral Care"), MPL 77.12–128, tr. by J. Barmby (NPNF, 2d ser., vol. 12–13); H. Davis (ACW 11). Gregory also wrote *Libri iv dialogorum de vita et miraculis patrum Italicorum et de aternitate animarum* (MPL 77.149–430); *Homiliae xl in Ezechielem* (MPL 76.781–1076); *Homiliae xl in evangelia* (MPL 76.1075–1314), and the Commentary on Job, of which below.

[2] The life of Gregory by Paul the Deacon (Warnefrid) is in MPL 75.41–86; see H. Grisar's edition in *Zeitschr. f. kath. Theol.* 11 (1887) 166–172; that by John the Deacon is in MPL 75.87–242, while the Benedictine life appears, *ibid.* 241–262. P. Ewald discovered in Saint Gallen MS. 567 (s. viii–ix) a still earlier life of Gregory by a monk of Whitby, portions of which he printed in *Historische Aufsätze dem Andenken an Georg Waitz*

education of which we know nothing except that it was probably excellent for its day, Gregory became prefect of Rome under the emperor Justin II, in 573 or even earlier. In the next year, however, he decided to become a monk and himself founded six monasteries on family estates in Sicily and a seventh in Rome, this dedicated to Saint Andrew, on the site of and perhaps even in the family residence on the Caelian Hill.[3] Later this foundation was rededicated to the memory of Gregory himself by Pope Gregory II (715–731),[4] Saint Andrew being then relegated to a chapel.

In 578 the monk was ordained one of the seven regionary deacons,[5] and in the spring of 579 was sent by Pelagius II (578–590) on an embassy to the emperor Tiberius II in Constantinople. Here he was to remain until 585, acting as representative of Pelagius at the imperial court. The purpose of the mission may have been, as claimed, to get approval for the consecration of Pelagius before imperial confirmation had arrived, or to gain aid against the Lombards, then menacing Rome, or perhaps to attend a council.

While in Constantinople, Gregory engaged in a doctrinal controversy on the resurrection with the local patriarch Eutychius (552–582), but from Gregory's point of view, no doubt, the most permanent results of the mission were the opportunity to see the ineffectiveness of the Byzantine government's administration, and the lasting friendship he made with Leander of Seville, of whom more later.

About 585 he was recalled to Rome and soon afterward was made abbot of the monastery of St. Andrew, only to be once more called to larger service by the disastrous flood and plague which afflicted Rome in 589,[6] in which the first of many victims was Pope Pelagius II, who died in February, 590. Almost immediately the people chose the deacon Gregory to be his successor, and after an attempt to reject the responsibility thrust upon him, Gregory was consecrated on September 3, 590.

gewidmet (1886) 17–54. The full text was printed by Francis Aidan Gasquet, *A Life of Pope St. Gregory the Great* (Westminster, 1904), tr. by Charles W. Jones, *Saints' Lives and Chronicles in Early England* (Ithaca, Cornell Press, 1947), pp. 97–121.

[3] On the Clivus Scauri, just north of the modern church of S. Gregorio Magno.
[4] The present structure dates from 1633.
[5] In medieval times the diaconate was more important than now and this was a special sort of diaconate, at that.
[6] See Gregory of Tours, *Hist. of the Franks* 10.1 (ed. Dalton 2.425).

Meanwhile, it is said, he organized a penitential procession around the city, at the end of which, so the story goes, the people saw the angel Michael on the top of Hadrian's mausoleum, sheathing his sword as a sign of the end of the pestilence.

Among the first works of the new pope was completion of his *Moralia* or commentary on The Book of Job,[7] from which our selection is taken. This had been begun as lectures at Constantinople, but was finished in the first year of the pontificate and sent with a dedicatory letter (here translated) to his old friend Leander, now bishop of Seville. Elsewhere[8] Gregory says of this work that since it was "weak both in sense and language as I had delivered it in homilies, I have tried as I could to put it into the form of a treatise, which is in course of being written out by scribes." In a letter[9] from Licinianus, bishop of Cartagena, Gregory is informed that Leander had spoken to Licinianus of the work and of Gregory's dissatisfaction with it, but Licinianus had not seen it. Again,[10] Gregory sends Leander some of the sheets not previously forwarded. The dedicatory letter and part of the first chapter of the Commentary have been chosen for inclusion because they admirably present the ideal of medieval Biblical exegesis.

Gregory's other activity as pontiff need be mentioned only briefly. As his 853 letters[11] show, he engaged ceaselessly in his effort to insure adherence by ecclesiastical administrators to a high standard of spirituality and to maintain in the temporal field an efficient administration of the *Patrimonium Petri*, the church's extensive lands. As a valiant fighter for the primacy of the See of Peter, he must be regarded as a leading— if not, indeed, the chief—founder of the medieval papacy. He was an ardent promulgator of missionary activity in distant lands, of which the most familiar is, of course, the sending of Saint Augustine to Britain in 597. He has been credited with important contributions in the reform of the liturgy and the

---

[7] *Expositio in beatum Iob seu Moralium libri xxxv*, reprinted in MPL 75.527–1162, from the 1705 edition by the Benedictines of St. Maur. The *Moralia* were translated by J. Bliss and published anonymously in *A Library of Fathers of the Holy Catholic Church*, etc. (Oxford: Parker; London: Rivington, 1844), in three volumes. Our selection appears in this translation in vol. 1, pp. 1–15. The dedicatory letter is in MPL 75.509–516 and also in MGH Epist. 1–2, edited by P. Ewald and L. M. Hartmann (1891–1899), the best edition of the letters.
[8] Gregory to Leander, Epist. 1.43 (NPNF, 2d ser., 12.87 f.): May, 591.
[9] Gregory, Epist. 2.54 (NPNF, 2d ser., 12.121); the date is 591/2.
[10] Gregory, Epist. 5.49 (NPNF, 2d ser., 12.181), the date is 594/5.
[11] MPL 77.431–1352.

development of the plain chant. Finally, he found time to employ the powers of the church to defend and protect Italy from the Lombards and other enemies of the peace, made necessary by the inefficient administration of the governors sent from the Eastern court. All this he carried on, indeed, when hampered by ill health.

For these and other aspects of Gregory's career, see J. Barmby, *Gregory the Great* in "Fathers for English Readers" (London, S.P.C.K., 1892); P. Batiffol, *Saint Grégoire le Grand* (Paris, 3d ed., Gabaldi, 1928), pp. 99–109 on the *Moralia*; E. Clausier, *St. Grégoire le Grand, Pape et Docteur de l'Église* (Paris, 1886–1891); F. Homes Dudden, *Gregory the Great: His Place in History and Thought* (London, Longmans, 1905); H. Grisar, *S. Gregorio Magno*, tr. by A. DeSanctis (Rome, 1928); Sir Henry H. Howorth, *Saint Gregory the Great* (London, Murray, 1912); H. Leclercq, "Grégoire le Grand" (DACL 5.2.1753–1776, portrait, 1761 f.); C. Wolfsgruber, *Gregor der Grosse* (Ravensburg, 1897).

Gregory the Great: The Commentary on Job (Selections)

THE TEXT

DEDICATORY LETTER

Gregory, servant of the servants of God, to the most reverend and most holy Leander,[12] his brother and fellow bishop.

1. Having first made your acquaintance, most blessed brother, long ago at the city of Constantinople, when I was kept there by business of the Apostolic See and you had been sent there on a Visigothic embassy with a mission connected with the faith,[13] I explained to you everything which displeased me about myself: how I postponed for a long period the grace of conversion, and, even after I was inspired by heavenly desire, thought it better still to wear the garments of secular life. For what I should seek from the love of eternity was already revealed to me but ingrown habit had so enshackled me that I did not change my outward habiliments. And since my spirit up to that point compelled me to serve this world, so far as outward appearance goes, many forces out of the care of this same world began to overwhelm me, so that I was held to it now, not only in appearance, but, what is more serious, in my mind also. At last, in flight from all these burdens, I sought the haven of the monastery and, having left everything of the

---

[12] Leander, born at Cartagena c. 550 or earlier, was brother to Fulgentius, bishop of Cartagena and Ecija; to Florentina, a celebrated nun; and to Isidore of Seville, his successor, all four of them canonized. He was active in the conversion of Visigothic Spain from Arianism, presided at the third Council of Toledo in 589, and delivered the closing sermon *De triumpho ecclesiae ob conversionem Gothorum*. His extant works are in MPL 72.873–898; three of Gregory's letters are addressed to Leander. See J. Bolland *et al.*, *Acta Sanctorum*, March, 2.275–280; J. Mabillon, *Acta Sanctorum ord. S. Benedicti* 1.378–385; O. Zöckler (NSH 6.434 f.); Pierre Suau (CE 9.102).

[13] The story is in John the Deacon, *S. Gregorii Magni vita* 1.27 (MPL 75.73).

world behind, as I then believed in vain, I escaped, poor man, from the shipwreck of this life. For as often a ship, carelessly moored, is, when the storm grows strong, drawn out by the billow even from the safest harbor, so suddenly I found myself again, under the cloak of the church's order,[14] on the deep sea of secular affairs, and how tightly I should have held to the quiet of the monastery which, when I had it, I did not hold strongly, this I learned only when I lost it.

For when, as I was on the point of receiving the duty of ministry at the holy altar, my own inclination to decline was opposed by the virtue of obedience, this was undertaken because the church demanded it,[15] a duty which I might, if permitted, with impunity turn aside by fleeing from it again. After this, against my will and though I struggled against it, since the ministry of the altar is heavy, there was also added the weight of pastoral care.[16]

Now I bear this with the greater difficulty since, feeling myself unequal to it, I draw my breath with no consolation of confidence. This because, now that evils are increasing,[17] the end approaching, the temporal affairs of the world are in a state of confusion. We ourselves, who believe we serve the inner mysteries, are involved in cares without.[18] As in that moment when I approached the ministry of the altar, action was taken also about me without my knowledge, that I might receive the weight of the sacred order, so that I might more freely serve in the earthly palace, to which, of course, many of my brethren from the monastery, bound to me by kindred affection, followed me. I see that this was done by divine agency so that following their example, at the calm shore of prayer, I might be safely moored by the anchor's hawser when billowed about by the ceaseless forces of secular affairs. To their fellowship I fled, as to the harbor of the safest port, from the rolling waves of earthly stress, though that duty, when I was drawn out of the monastery from a life of former quiet, had almost slain me with

---

[14] The mission to Constantinople.   [15] *Sub ecclesiae colore.*
[16] Gregory speaks of his unworthiness of the pontificate in Epist. 1.6 (NPNF, 2d ser., 12.74, written soon after the consecration, to John the Faster, bishop of Constantinople 582–595).
[17] On Gregory's actual experience with natural disaster, see Gregory of Tours, *Hist. of the Franks* 10.1 (Dalton's ed., 2.425), and his whole pontificate, even his whole life, was an object lesson in perils caused by failure of the Byzantine emperor to give peace to Italy through appointment of able exarchs.
[18] Political activity made necessary by the same disturbing conditions.

the dagger of its activity. Among them, however, through the encouragement of serious reading, the stimulation of daily devotion roused my spirits. Then these same brethren were pleased, and you yourself, as you remember,[19] brought pressure upon them, that they should force me by their urgent pleas to expound the book of blessed Job, and in proportion as the Truth[20] should infuse me with power, to open to them the mysteries of such great depth. Besides the burden of their own plea they placed this upon me also, that I should make known not only the words of the story in their allegorical senses but should apply the allegorical senses to the practice of moral virtues. To this they added something still more difficult: that I should bolster each truth taught with proof texts, and when the proof texts were presented, if they should appear perhaps involved, I should unravel them by further exegesis.

2. Presently, however, when I learned the character and the magnitude of the task to which I was being dragged in this obscure work not hitherto treated, I was beaten down, I admit, solely by the weight of listening to their exhortations, and through weariness I gave in. But at once suspended between the alternatives of fear and duty, when I lifted up my eyes to the Bestower of the gifts of the soul, every hesitation was laid aside and then I realized with certainty that what the love of my brethren's hearts ordered me to do could not be impossible. I had, of course, no hope that I should be adequate to the task, but strengthened by my very lack of confidence in myself, I forthwith raised my hope to Him by whom "the tongue of the dumb was loosened, who gave eloquence to the tongues of babes"[21]; who converted the meaningless and unintelligible brayings of an ass into the perceptibility of human conversation.[22] What would be remarkable if he who expresses his truth, when he wishes, even through the mouths of beasts of burden, should furnish understanding to a stupid human being? Girt up, then, with the strength of this thought, I roused my own parched soul to search for the fountain of such great depth, and though the life of those to whom I was forced to provide this exegesis far surpassed my own, I nevertheless did not believe it wrong if a leaden pipe should be used to provide flowing water for men's use.

Thus, soon afterward, when these same brothers had taken their places before me, I delivered the first parts of the book,

[19] See *Epist. ad Leandrum* 1.43 (NPNF, 2d ser., 12.88).
[20] Christ.   [21] Wisdom 10:21.   [22] Num. 22:21–30.

and because I found a little free time, I dictated the later parts. And when I had greater hours of leisure, adding much, cutting out a little, leaving a few things as they were found, I put together into books, while I revised, the parts which had been orally delivered by me, and I took care to compose the later parts in the same style as I had spoken the first. Thus, while running through and carefully correcting the parts spoken orally, I succeeded in making them assume the appearance of a written work, and the parts I had first written did not seem far different from spoken language, so that while the one was extended, the other contracted, that which came into being by different method might become something homogeneous. Although I increased by a third the spoken part, I omitted almost as much, because although my brothers drew me on to other subjects, they did not want this to be revised too carefully.

Inasmuch as they kept prescribing numerous items, and I desired to obey them, at times providing expositions, at others lofty contemplation, at still others a tool for teaching morality, the bulk of this work came to thirty-five books, with which I filled six manuscripts. This is why in it I often seem almost to be neglecting the order of exposition and to be devoting myself a bit more to broad reflection and moral instruction. Yet whoever speaks about God must take care to try to instruct the character of his hearers. He must consider it the proper procedure in speaking if, when a chance to edify occurs, he turn aside for personal benefit from the topic on which he began to speak. The expounder of Holy Scripture ought to be like a river, for if the stream flowing along in its bed should on its flanks come into contact with curving valleys, it at once turns into them its powerful current, and when it has filled them full, it suddenly pours back again into its channel. That is how, certainly, the expounder of the divine Word should be, so that when he discusses any topic, if perchance he finds an opportunity presented to him suitable for edification, he may turn the streams of his eloquence into it as if it were a nearby valley, and when he has poured over this adjacent field of instruction, he may fall back into the channel of speech he had originally set before him.

3. You must know, however, that we run over some topics in historical exposition, and in some we search for allegorical meaning in our examination of types; in still others we discuss morality but through the allegorical method; and in several

instances we carefully make an attempt to apply all three methods. In the first instance we lay the historical foundation; in the second, through the typological sense we erect a structure of the mind to be a citadel of faith; finally, through the grace of moral instruction, we clothe the edifice, as it were, with a coat of color. What must one really believe the words of truth to be but food taken for the refreshment[23] of the mind? When we discuss these topics in various methods, changing them often, we set a feast before the mouth, in such a way as to eliminate distaste from our reader who, dining like a banqueter, scrutinizes what is offered him and takes what he sees is more palatable.

But at times we neglect to expound the obvious words of the narrative so as not to reach too late the obscure meanings. At times they cannot be understood literally because, when the obvious meaning is taken, they engender in the readers, not instruction, but error. For see what is said: "Under whom those who carry the world are bowed down."[24] Who would not know that so great a man as Job is not following the empty tales of the poets so as to view the great bulk of the world as borne aloft on the sweat of a giant?[25] Again, struck by calamities, he says: "My soul has chosen hanging and my bones death."[26] Who in his right mind would believe that a man of such great fame, who, of course, as all agree, received from the eternal Judge rewards in proportion to the virtue of his patience, had determined in the midst of his afflictions to end his life by hanging? In some instances, also, the words themselves militate against the possibility of their literal interpretation. For he says, "Let the day perish on which I was born and the night on which it was said, 'A man has been conceived.'"[27] And a little later he adds, "Let the darkness seize it and let it be covered over with bitterness."[28] And as a curse for the same night he adds, "Let that night be unique."[29] Surely this day of his birth, rolling round in the onrush of time itself, could not stand still. How, then, could it have become veiled in darkness? Having passed away, of course, it no longer existed, nor yet if, in the nature of creation, it still were to exist, could it feel bitterness. It is clear, then, that he is not speaking at all of an

---

[23] Cf. John Chrysostom, *Hom. in Ioh.* 4:1 (NPNF, 1st ser., 14.16).
[24] Job 9:13 (Vulgate; R.S.V. different).
[25] The allusion is to the pagan concept of the Titan Atlas as in Hesiod, *Theog.* 517; Aeschylus, *Prom.* 347 ff.
[26] Job 7:15.   [27] Job 3:2.   [28] Job 3:5.   [29] Job 3:7.

insensate day when he wishes it to be struck by a sense of bitterness. And if the night of his conception had passed away like other nights, how could he wish that it be unique? As from the lapse of time, it could not now be fixed, so also it could not be separated from contact with the other nights. Again he says, "How long wilt thou not spare me nor let me go until I swallow my spittle?" [30] And yet a little while before he had said, "My soul was hitherto unwilling to touch them, and now from necessity they are my food." [31] Who does not know that spittle is more easily swallowed than food? Since he says he is taking food, it is absolutely unbelievable that he cannot swallow spittle. Another time he says, "I have sinned; what shall I do to thee, thou guardian of men?" [32] And surely, "Thou wantest me to consume the iniquities of my youth." [33] And in another reply he adds, "My heart shall not reproach me throughout my whole life." [34] How, then, is he not reproached by his heart throughout his whole life when he openly testifies that he has sinned? For never do guilt of deed and irreproachability of heart coincide in the same man. But surely the literal sense of the words, when they are compared, cannot be made to agree, and it shows that something different should be sought in them, as if the words were explicitly to say, "Though you see that we, in so far as our obvious meaning is concerned, are destroyed, nevertheless seek in us something logical and consistent that may be found to reside in us."

4. At times, however, he who fails to take the words of the story in a literal sense hides the light of truth that has been offered to him, and when he labors to find in them some other inner meaning, he loses what he could easily have arrived at on the surface. For the holy man says, "If I have denied to the poor what they desired, or have made the eyes of the widow to wait; if I have eaten my morsel alone, and the orphan has not eaten of it; . . . if I have seen anyone perishing because he had no clothing, or a poor man without covering; if his loins have not blessed me, and if he was not warmed with the fleece of my sheep . . ." [35] If we forcibly twist such a passage into an allegorical sense, we make all these deeds of mercy to be as naught. For as the divine Word stimulates the wise with mysteries, so it often kindles the simple with an obvious statement. It holds in the open the means of feeding children, but keeps in secret the means of causing souls to hang upon the adoration of the

[30] Job 7:19.　　　[31] Job 6:7.　　　[32] Job 7:20.
[33] Job 13:26.　　[34] Job 27:6.　　[35] Job 31:16–20.

sublime. Indeed, it is, as I said, like a river, shallow and deep, in which a lamb may walk and an elephant may swim. As therefore the opportunity of each and every passage demands, so the course of exposition is studiously changed. In order that it may the more truly discover the sense of the divine Word, as each topic demands, it varies according to the case.

5. This exposition, then, I have transmitted to your beatitude for revision, not because I owed it to you as something worthy of you, but because I remember that when you asked for it, I promised it. Whatever in it your holiness may find mediocre or unpolished, may you as quickly grant me your pardon as you do not overlook the fact that I speak poorly. For when the body is worn with trouble, so when the mind is afflicted, eagerness for speaking grows dull. Now many years have rolled round in their courses since I began to be tortured by frequent pains of the flesh, and each hour and each moment I grow faint with lack of good digestion, [36] and I breathe with difficulty under mild yet constant fevers.

Meanwhile, I give serious attention to the saying in the Scripture, "Everyone who is received by God is beaten," [37] and the harder I am pressed by these present evils, so the more certainly do I breathe with anticipation of the eternal. And perhaps it was the design of divine providence that, afflicted thus, I should expound Job who was also thus afflicted, and that I should, under the lash, the better understand the mind of the one who was also lashed. Nevertheless, it is clear to those who rightly think about it that weariness of the flesh is no small obstacle to my enthusiasm for my work, in that when the power of the flesh scarcely is sufficient for the function of speaking, the mind cannot express its feelings in proper fashion. For what is the duty of the body except to serve as the instrument of the heart? And no matter how skilled a man may be in the art of singing, he cannot realize the fulfillment of this art unless for this purpose his external functions are in harmony, because the instruments, when shaken, do not give forth the song in proper tones, nor does the breath produce an artistic sound if the reed rattles when it is split. How much more seriously impaired is the quality of my exposition in which the broken instrument diminishes the grace of rhetoric so that it contains no artistic skill? When you run through the pages of this work, please do

---

[36] Gregory, as well as Leander, suffered much from gout, on which see Epist. 9.121 (NPNF, 2d ser., 13.34) and 11.32 (*ibid.* 13.58).
[37] Heb. 12:6.

not look for literary nosegays, because in expounders of Holy Writ the lightness of fruitless verbosity is carefully repressed, since the planting of a grove in God's temple is forbidden.[38] And we are all clearly aware that as often as the tops of the grain stalks luxuriate into undesirable leafage, the heads of the grain do not fill out so well. This is why I have foreborne to employ the very art of rhetoric which the examples of superficial learning teach. For as the sense of this letter proclaims, I do not flee from the collision of metacism,[39] I do not avoid the confusion of a barbarism, and I disdain to preserve the rules of position and order[40] and the cases of prepositions, because I consider it very unbecoming that I should tie down the words of the heavenly oracles to the rules of Donatus.[41] No precedent of the translators of sacred Scripture requires these rules to be observed by any exegetes. Because our exposition takes its origin surely from this authority, it is surely proper for that which issues forth like a shoot to model itself on the appearance of its mother. I am using here, however, the new translation,[42] but as the necessity of proof demands, I take now the new, now the old, so that, because the Apostolic See, over which, with God's design, I preside, uses both, the labor of my study may be supported by both.

The Preface, Chapter Two

The Author Is the Holy Spirit

Who wrote the work it is completely superfluous to ask since by faith its author is believed to have been the Holy Spirit.[43]

[38] Deut. 16:21.
[39] Metacism is the juxtaposition of one *m* before another or of final *m* before a word beginning with a vowel, which in the classical poets is called elision; its avoidance, hiatus.
[40] Doubtless he means the *clausulae*, patterns of prose rhythm much used by certain stylists, on which see W. H. Shewring, *Oxford Classical Dictionary* (Oxford, 1949) 738–740.
[41] On Aelius Donatus, fourth century grammarian, of whom Jerome had been a pupil, and who was influential in late antiquity and the Middle Ages, see H. Keil, *Grammatici latini* 4.355–402. Gregory's disdain for the rules of grammar is in sharp contrast with what his contemporary Gregory of Tours says of him (*Hist. of the Franks* 10.1), that so "accomplished was he in grammar, dialectic, rhetoric, that he was held second to none in all the city." He doubtless supposes that the pope possessed these qualities without having genuine knowledge that he did.
[42] That is, Jerome's translation, now called the Vulgate, nearly two centuries old, but the *Vetus Latinum* which preceded was not yet superseded.
[43] Cf. Thomas Aquinas, *Summa Theol.* Qu. 1, Art. 10: "I answer it is to be

The One who dictated that it be written wrote it himself. He himself wrote it who was the inspirer of the scribe's work, and through his voice handed down to us Job's acts for imitation. If we were reading the words of any great man whose letters we have received, but asked with what pen the words were written, it would certainly be silly, knowing the author of the letters and understanding his meaning, yet to investigate the sort of pen used to set down their words. Since, then, we understand the subject matter and hold its author to be the Holy Spirit, what else are we doing when we search for the writer except to make inquiry about the pen as we read the letter?

> said that God is the Author of Holy Scripture, who has the power not only to adapt words to convey a meaning, which even man may do, but even things themselves, and so whereas in all sciences words have a signification, this particular science has this property, that the very things which are signified by words do also signify somewhat further." See Oxford translation of the *Moralia*, 1.11 f., Note A.

Alcuin of York: Commentary on the Epistle to Titus (Selections)

INTRODUCTION

ALCUIN[1] WAS BORN IN THE NEIGHBORHOOD OF York about 735 and died at the abbey of St. Martin of Tours in France, on May 19, 804. His place in history is based primarily on personal influence upon the lives of the men and women with whom he came into intimate contact at the court of Charlemagne, including the great king himself, and on his distinguished achievement as the schoolmaster par excellence, not only of the students in the palace school, but also of the whole Frankish empire.

He was fortunate in his birth of good family, a relative of Saint Willibrord, whose life he afterward wrote[2]; fortunate, also, in being placed at an early age in what must then have been the best school available, the Cathedral School of York, established by Egbert (d. 766), first archbishop of York, where he came under the personal tutelage of Ælbert, first a teacher in the school and then its head, builder of the famous library. Under such a master Alcuin was thoroughly grounded in learning both ecclesiastical and classical, and as a result was soon promoted to the post of teacher and, when Ælbert in turn became archbishop, to that of head.

At about the age of thirty Alcuin was ordained deacon and he may never have advanced beyond that rank, for he was fond

---

[1] His name, Alchvine, was Latinized to *Alcuinus* (Alcuin) but the man was fond of pseudonyms and was often called Albinus or Flaccus, whence the Abbé Migne calls him Flaccus Albinus (MPL 100, title page).

[2] English translations by A. Grieve, *Willibrord, Missionary in the Netherlands* in "Lives of Early and Medieval Missionaries" (London, S.P.C.K., 1923); by C. H. Talbot, *The Anglo-Saxon Missionaries in Germany* in "The Makers of Christendom" (New York, Sheed and Ward, 1954), 1–22.

of calling himself "Albinus, a humble Levite." It has also been thought that he never became a professed monk according to any rule, even though afterward an abbot.

In March, 781, while on the way back from a trip to Rome, whence he had gone to obtain the pallium for Eanbald, he encountered Charlemagne at Parma, and shortly after his return to England was invited by the Frankish king to head his palace school. Though he made later several visits to his native land, he thenceforth resided on the continent, the first scholar at Charlemagne's court, the friend of all the great and near great, a valiant fighter for orthodoxy against the Adoptionists[3] and their most vigorous antagonist at the Synod of Frankfort in 794.

In 796 he was made abbot of the monastery of St. Martin at Tours and of other establishments, where he numbered among distinguished pupils Theodulph, afterward bishop of Orléans; Rabanus Maurus, later archbishop of Mainz; Adalhard, first abbot of New Corbie in Saxony; and the liturgist Amalarius of Metz. Throughout this last period of his life he remained in close contact with Charlemagne and the court.

Mention should be made of his activity in the reform of the Frankish liturgy to make it conform to the standard of the Roman rite; in the compilation of a *homiliarium* or collection of sermons to be used by the clergy, and of a sacramentary.[4]

As was natural, a considerable portion of his literary output was in the field of secular learning—works on grammar, spelling, astronomy, and the like.[5]

The selection here translated will thus serve the twofold purpose of being representative of the literary work of a great figure of the Carolingian age, and also will provide a fair sample of the type of Biblical exegesis which was characteristic of the period.

A contemporary life of Alcuin says that he wrote commentaries on four epistles of Saint Paul, namely, Ephesians, Philemon, Titus, and Hebrews, and various early writers[6] claim that he wrote commentaries on all fourteen epistles. If so, all are lost except those on Philemon, Titus, and Hebrews, these three preserved in Codex Einsiedlensis B 9 (saec. ix), which was transcribed by P. Meinrad-Prenzer, printed by

---

[3] See MPL 101.9–438.   [4] MPL 101.439–645.
[5] MPL 101.847–1000. The poems are *ibid.*, 723–846, the hagiographical works, *ibid.*, 665–722.
[6] See MPL 1107—they were Sixtus Senensis, Joannes Trithemius, Joannes Baleus, and Antonius Possevinus.

Froben Forster (Ratisbon, 1777), and reprinted in Migne's *Patrologia latina* 100.1025–1084. The commentary on Titus appears there in columns 1107–1126.

Like most writers of his time, Alcuin makes free use of material copied from his predecessors, especially from the church fathers. Thus, the commentary on the Epistle to the Hebrews was largely derived from that of John Chrysostom,[7] while those on Philemon and Titus are hardly more than revisions, with additions, of the corresponding commentaries of Jerome.[8] To show the limits of Alcuin's indebtedness to Jerome, Migne's edition prints the new material within brackets and indicates divergences. We have not thought it desirable in a series such as this to retain these brackets, but we offer the following paragraph as a sample to show how much is Jerome and how much Alcuin, words added by Alcuin being italicized:

" 'And that you should appoint presbyters in the cities as I directed you': *There are, however, bishops who do not consider the merits of individuals but are cajoled by their entourage or are related to them by ties of kinship.* From this it is clear that they who, having despised the law of the apostle, have been willing that ecclesiastical rank be conferred on anyone, not according to merit but out of favoritism, are acting against Christ, who has prescribed what sort of person should be appointed presbyter in the church through the words of his apostle in the following passages: *Beyond all these the greatest evil is those who obtain clerical office through bribery: the blessed Peter, prince of apostles at the beginning of the church, strikes out terribly against these in the person of Simon Magus.*"

We do not think it necessary either here or in the notes to enter into discussion of the thorny questions of the authorship of this Epistle to Titus or of its bearing on the development of the early church. Those who desire illumination on such topics will do well to seek it in modern commentaries on the Pastoral Epistles. Sufficient is it to say that neither Jerome nor Alcuin had the slightest doubt that the true and sole author of the Pastoral Epistles and the Epistle to the Hebrews was Saint Paul.

Consult: Eleanor S. Duckett, *Alcuin, Friend of Charlemagne* (New York, Macmillan, 1951); C. J. B. Gaskoin, *Alcuin, His Life and Work* (Cambridge, 1904); W. Wattenbach and E. Dummler, *Monumenta Alcuiniana* in *Bibliotheca Rerum Germanicarum* (Berlin, 1873), vol. 6; A. F. West, *Alcuin and the Rise of the Christian Schools* (New York, 1893).

[7] MPG 63.9–236, tr. by F. Gardiner (NPNF, 1st ser., 14.335–522).
[8] Jerome on Titus is in MPL 26.589–636.

Alcuin of York: Commentary on the Epistle to Titus (Selections)

THE TEXT

Preface

This letter the apostle wrote[9] from the city of Nicopolis, which is situated on the coast of Actium, to Titus, his pupil and son in Christ, whom he had left in the island of Crete to instruct the churches. For he did not wish the Cretans, from whom[10] the seeds of idolatry first grew, to remain in his absence in ancient error. And though he asked Titus to come to him on account of the necessity of preaching, he directs Artemas and Tychicus to come there, so that by their teaching and support the Cretans might be encouraged.

CHAPTER 1

1. "Paul, a servant of God, yet an apostle of Christ Jesus": In the letter to the Romans he began thus: "Paul, a servant of Christ Jesus, called an apostle."[11] In this one, however, he says that he is a servant of God, but an apostle of Christ Jesus. If the Father and the Son are one, and he who has believed in the Son believes in the Father, the status of servant in the case of the apostle Paul and of all saints must be referred without distinction to the Father or to the Son because one God is the Father and the Son, and is to be worshiped in one condition of servant. For this is the servitude of love, not of the letter of the law which kills but of the spirit which quickens. A servant of God is one who is not a slave of sin, because "everyone who does a sin is a servant of sin."[12]

---

[9] The error originates in Jerome or his source: the apostle did not write from Nicopolis (see Titus 3:12).
[10] The allusion may be to the pagan tradition that Zeus was born in Crete.
[11] Rom. 1:1.   [12] John 8:34.

"Yet an apostle of Jesus Christ": Paul claims great authority for himself among Christians. He uses as title the phrase "apostle of Christ," so that from the very authority of the name he may strike terror into his readers, and arouse them to respect for his preaching, indicating that all who believe in Christ should be subordinated to himself.

"According to the faith of God's chosen and their knowledge of truth": This must be taken in reference to what is said above, "Paul, a servant of God, yet an apostle of Christ Jesus."

"According to the faith of God's chosen": That is, of those who are not only called but chosen. Of the chosen themselves there is great diversity in works, opinions, and words. Therefore, he added, "according to their knowledge," that is, those who possess a knowledge of truth according to faith. That both the true faith and the knowledge of truth may agree, he added, "which is in accordance with godliness," because some truth is not in accordance with godliness, like grammar, dialectic, geometry, and arithmetic,[13] for these arts have to do with a true knowledge of proper discourse, but it is not a knowledge of godliness. A knowledge of godliness is to be acquainted with God's law, to understand the prophets, to believe the gospel, not to be ignorant of the words of the apostles, and, the greatest good, to love God with the whole heart, with the whole mind, and with all strength.[14] This is the truth, the understanding of which is according to godliness, and is based

2. "On hope of eternal life," because whoever understands it, to him it grants the reward of immortality, and though without godliness a knowledge of truth gives pleasure for the present, yet it does not have the eternity of rewards, "which God who does not lie has promised ages ago," and

3. "Has manifested in his time" in Christ Jesus. Yet to whom has he long ago promised it and later made it clear, except to his wisdom which was always with the Father, since he rejoiced when the world was completed and was joyful over the sons of men, and again promised to those, whoever they were, who would believe in it that they would have eternal life? Before he laid the foundations of the world, before he poured forth the seas, raised up the mountains, hung aloft the sky, established the earth beneath, this was promised by God, in whom there is

---

[13] Neither *trivium* nor *quadrivium* but two arts from each.
[14] Matt. 22:37, Luke 10:27.

no deceit—not that he can lie, if he were unwilling[15] to break forth into words of falsity, but that he who is the Father of truth and himself truthful can have no deceit in him.

Does it seem inappropriate to discuss briefly why God is alone truthful, and every man is, in the apostle's word, called a liar? And, if I make no mistake, as He alone is said to possess immortality, though he has made the angels and many reasoning creatures to whom he has given immortality, so he alone is said to be truthful, not because the other immortals are not lovers of the truth, but because he alone is immortal and true by nature. But let the others acquire immortality and truth from his gift: it is one thing to be true and to have it by nature and of oneself, another thing to be subject to the power of the one who gives you what you possess. But we must not pass over in silence how God who does not lie has promised eternal life endless ages ago. By him, according to the story in Genesis, the world was made, and through the changes of nights and days, likewise of months and years, seasons were established, in this journey and rotation of the earth the seasons pass away and come again—and either will be or have been. Thus it is that certain of the philosophers[16] do not think that time is present but that it is either past or future; that everything we speak, do, think, either while it takes place passes away, or if it has not yet been done is still awaited. Therefore, before these times of the world, one must believe there was an eternity of ages in which the Father with the Son and the Holy Spirit always existed, and, as I say, all eternity is a single time of God; indeed, there are countless times, since he himself is infinite who before the times exceeds all times. Not yet has our world existed six thousand years, and how many eternities and how many times before the beginnings of the centuries must one think there were in which angels, thrones, powers, and other forces served the Creator and existed, by God's order, without change and measurements of times. Before all these times which neither does speech dare to utter, nor the mind to comprehend, nor thought to touch upon in silence, God the Father promised his Word to his Wisdom that that very Wisdom of his, and the life of those who would

---

[15] *Nollet*, where *vellet* ("were willing") would seem better and keep the sense, if not the syntax, of Jerome's *et nolit* ("not that he can lie and does not wish to").

[16] The source may be Aristotle, *Physics* 4.10, p. 218a (see English version by R. P. Hardie and R. K. Gaye in W. D. Ross's Oxford translation (Oxford, Clarendon Press, 1930) 2.218a.

believe, should come into the world. Pay careful attention to the text and the order of the reading, how life eternal, which God who does not lie promised eternal ages ago, is not different from God's Word.

"He manifested, in his own times, his own Word": that is, this eternal life he promised is itself his Word which in the beginning was with the Father, and God was the Word, and the Word was made flesh and dwelt among us.[17] That this Word of God, that is, Christ himself, is life, is witnessed in another passage which says, "I am life."[18] But life that is not short, not limited by any times, but everlasting, eternal, which has been made manifest in most recent ages through the preaching which was entrusted to Paul, the doctor and teacher of the Gentiles, that it should be proclaimed in the world and became known to men, in accordance with the command of God the Saviour, who has willed us to be saved by fulfilling what had been promised.

"In the preaching which was entrusted to me according to the command of God our Saviour": We read in The Acts of the Apostles[19] how Paul, while hastening to Damascus, was suddenly called and how Ananias said of him, "This is my chosen vessel."[20] And again, "Separate for me Paul and Barnabas."[21] That they should preach Christ to the Gentiles was the command of the Saviour. The word, wisdom, and teaching in which Titus was instructing the churches of Christ, made him, of course, the apostle's own son, and separated from anything shared in by others. Let us see what follows after that:

"According to a common faith": Did he mean a faith shared by all who believed in Christ or shared only by himself and Titus? It appears to me better to take this as meaning the faith shared in by Paul and Titus than as the faith of all believers among whom, on account of the diversity of minds, faith could not be common but different.

Finally, the preface of the letter and the preface's greeting of the apostle to Titus are ended in this way:

4. "Grace and peace from God the Father and Christ Jesus our Saviour": This can be taken to mean either that grace and peace are from God the Father as well as from Christ Jesus, both being given by both, or grace may be taken with reference to the Father and peace with reference to the Son.

---

[17] John 1:1–14. [18] John 14:6. [19] Acts 9:1–9.
[20] Acts 9:15. [21] Acts 13:2.

5. "This is why I left you in Crete, that you might correct what was lacking": It was an apostolic prerogative to lay the foundation like a wise architect, but it was the task of Titus and his other disciples to build on it. After Paul had softened the hard hearts of the Cretans by leading them to faith in Christ and had tamed them both by speech and by signs,[22] with the result that they believed in God the Father and in Christ, he left his disciple Titus in Crete to strengthen the knowledge of the growing church, and if anything seemed to be lacking, to amend it, and he himself hastened on to other nations that again he might lay the foundation of Christ in them. They[23] had, of course, been corrected by the apostle, yet they still needed corrections, for everything which is corrected is uncompleted.

"And that you should appoint presbyters in the cities as I directed you": There are, however, bishops who do not consider the merits of individuals but are cajoled by their entourage or are related to them by ties of kinship. From this it is clear that they who, having despised the law of the apostle, have been willing that ecclesiastical rank be conferred on anyone, not according to merit but out of favoritism, are acting against Christ, who has prescribed what sort of person should be appointed presbyter in the church through the words of his apostle in the following passages. Beyond all these the greatest evil is those who obtain clerical office through bribery: the blessed Peter, prince of apostles at the beginning of the church, strikes out terribly against these in the person of Simon Magus.[24]

"For a bishop ought to be blameless, as a steward of God": The same man is, therefore, a presbyter who is also a bishop[25]; and before, at the devil's instigation, there arose partisan differences of religion in the church, and among the people it was said, "I am of Paul, I am of Apollos, or I am of Cephas,"[26] churches were governed by the common counsel of the elders.[27] But after each one thought that those whom he had baptized were his own and not Christ's, it was decided over the whole earth that one of the elders should be chosen to be placed over the others and to him the whole care of the church should belong and the seeds of schisms be destroyed. This can be proved from other letters[28] of the same apostle, and also from

[22] Demonstration of supernatural powers.   [23] The Cretans.
[24] Acts 8:9–24.   [25] Cf. Jerome, *Epist.* 146 *ad Evangelum.*
[26] I Cor. 1:12.
[27] It is Jerome who is speaking. This is a *locus classicus* in discussions of the history of the ministry.
[28] The authoritarian tone of the letters rather than any particular passage.

The Acts of the Apostles, in which it is said that Paul called the presbyters from Ephesus,[29] to whom afterward he said among other things, "Take heed to yourselves and to all the flock in which the Holy Spirit has made you bishops to feed the church of the Lord which he obtained with his blood."[30] Those he called presbyters before he now calls bishops. And Peter, who got his name from the steadfastness of his faith,[31] in his letter says, "So I exhort the presbyters among you as a fellow presbyter and witness of Christ's sufferings: feed the Lord's flock which is in your charge."[32] Formerly every presbyter was rightly called a bishop, but now every bishop can be called a presbyter, not every presbyter a bishop, because in order to exclude the hotbeds of dissension, the whole care of the churches has been entrusted to one, as to a father who loves his children and governs those who are subject to him, not with the imperial power[33] but with paternal piety. Let them, like sons, of each rank in the churches, show respect to their bishops. Let us see, then, what sort of presbyter or bishop should be ordained.

6, 7. "If any man is blameless, the husband of one wife, having children who are believers and not open to the charge of profligacy or not slaves to sin.[34] For a bishop ought to be blameless, as a steward of God": First, let him be a blameless steward of Christ's church of the sort which in Timothy he calls "above reproach."[35] For how can anyone be in charge of the church and ward off evil from its midst who has rushed into a like fault? Or with what freedom can he correct a sinner when he knows that he has admitted into himself what he reproves in another. We must understand the phrase "husband of one wife" to mean that he who must be chosen to the episcopate

---

[29] Acts 20:17.
[30] Acts 20:28.
[31] Allusion to the word play in Matt. 16:18.
[32] I Peter 5:1, 2.
[33] *Tribunicia potestas*: in earlier republican times the authority of the *tribunus plebis* was initially confined to veto of acts and legislation oppressive to plebeians. Later, ambitious and able tribunes sometimes applied the *quid pro quo* principle to enact their own legislative program. Under Augustus and his successors the *tribunicia potestas* was, together with *proconsulare imperium*, the basis of the emperor's power by which earlier constitutional forms were made to continue the republic in appearance, if not really.
[34] Both here and in the heading below, the words "to sin" (*peccato*) represent an addition not corresponding to anything in the Greek or Vulgate. The children are to be subordinate to their father, but our commentators make it "not subordinate to sin."
[35] I Tim. 3:2.

should have a respectable marriage, that one befouled with wandering lust should not dare to take his place at God's altar. Not that we think, however, that every man who has had but one wife is better than a man who has had two,[36] but that he can in his teaching exhort others to observe monogamy and continence who displays his own example. There are those who understand this commandment of the apostle ("husband of one wife," that is) to mean "teacher of the catholic church," not to be carried abroad through heretical errors through the brothels of the different sects. But certain people also think that this apostolic decree forbids bishops to go out from the church or from the city[37] to a church in quest of gain. Because it is a rare man who wants to pass from a greater and a richer to a lesser and a poorer status.[38]

"Having children who are believers and not open to the charge of profligacy or not slaves to sin"[34]: The righteous man is not thereby defiled from the faults of his children but freedom of reproving others is reserved by the apostle for the ruler[39] of the church. How can one remove another's particle of dust from another's house if one has in the sins of one's children a beam in one's own house? For a bishop ought to be such a man as not to be afraid to reprove other people on account of his own children's faults, lest by chance some brother may quietly answer, "Why don't you take the trouble to reprove your own children?" For if the sins of his children disqualify the righteous man from the episcopate, how much more ought they to disqualify him from removing his own sins from Christ's altar? Finally, it should be said that in the Scriptures sons should be thought of as *logismos*, that is, as thoughts, but daughters as *praxeis*, that is, as works, and he now is commanding that that man should be made bishop who is keeping his thoughts and works under his own control and truly believes in Christ and is spotted by no stain of secret faults.

"A bishop, therefore, ought to be blameless, as a steward of God": Among the stewards, then, one is sought for who is found faithful and, not eating and drinking with the drunken,

---

[36] On deuterogamy see W. P. LeSaint's translation of Tertullian's *Treatises on Marriage and Remarriage* in ACW 13 (Westminster, Newman Press, 1951).
[37] Or, perhaps, from life as secular priests to a monastic retirement.
[38] Hosius of Cordova (MPL 8.1317C): *Nullus enim episcopus adhuc inveniri potuit, qui a maiori civitate in minorem transire studuerit.* This is from Canon 1 of the Council of Sardica (see C. J. Hefele, *History of the Councils*, 2:110).
[39] *Princeps*.

may strike at the servants and handmaidens of his Lord; but let him wisely await the unknown day of the Lord's coming and give meanwhile to his fellow servants the food of catholic doctrine. Let the bishop and the presbyter know that the people are not his servants but his fellow servants. For this reason let him not dominate them as common slaves but let him teach them with all love as sons.

"Not arrogant": That is, not puffed up or pleased with himself at being a bishop, but one embracing good works and seeking that which contributes to the good of most.

"Not wrathful": That is, as a leaf hanging on a branch is moved by a light wind. And nothing is really more disgraceful than a wrathful teacher; for he who at times is angry is not full of anger, but he really is called full of anger who is frequently conquered by this passion.

"Not a drunkard": But now it is enough to have said that, according to the apostle, there is profligacy in wine, and wherever there is gluttony and drunkenness, there lust rules. We are surprised that the apostle condemned drunkenness among bishops and presbyters, since in the old law there was also a commandment that priests[40] when entering the Temple to minister to God should drink no wine at all.[41] The Nazarites are also to abstain from all wine and strong drink, while they let their holy hair grow long.[42]

"Not violent": This may be taken in a simple sense that he may edify the mind of his hearer to keep him from quickly stretching forth his hand to slaughter or to rush to arms; or, more subtly and better, that the bishop may do nothing to offend the minds of those who understand and see, but that he may be calm of speech, pure of character, and not destroy the one whom the moderation of his life and his words could teach.

"Not greedy for gain": Seeking for such is to think more about things present than things to come. A bishop who is desirous of being an imitator of the apostle should be content, when he has food and clothing, with only these.[43] Let those who serve the altar live from the altar.[44] "Let them live," he says, not "let them become rich." Up to this point the apostle's words have been prescribing what a bishop or presbyter ought not to have; now, on the contrary, what he ought to have is explained.

---

[40] *Sacerdotes*: the word often meant in Jerome's day, bishops, and something of this flavor may be present here. See above, Vincent, p. 38.
[41] Lev. 10:8. [42] Num. 6:2–5.
[43] I Tim. 6:8. [44] I Cor. 9:13.

8. "But, hospitable, kind": Above everything, hospitality is prescribed for one who is to be a bishop, for if everybody wants to hear from the Gospel this: "I was a stranger and you took me in,"[45] how much more should a bishop, whose house ought to be a common guesthouse and in it those pilgrims who come should be kindly received, so that even their feet should be washed in humble duty?

"Chaste, just, holy": If laymen are ordered on account of prayer to refrain from intercourse with their wives, what should be thought of the bishop who is to offer spotless sacrifices of holy prayers daily for his own sins and those of the people? For Abimelech[46] the priest refused to give to David and his boys[47] the display[48] bread unless he should hear that the boys were clean from women—not only from other men's women but their own. There is as much difference between the display bread and Christ's body as between shadow and bodies, between a picture and its reality, between foreshadowings of future events and the events of which they are the foreshadowings. As, then, the virtue of hospitality, kindness, ought peculiarly to be in a bishop, so, also, chastity and, as I said, modesty are the proper marks of a priest,[49] so that he not only should abstain from unclean acts but also [see] that the mind that is to make[50] the body of Christ be free from unlawful touch and thought of error. A bishop ought to be just and holy, and to practice justice among the people over whom he is placed, and not to show any respect of persons in his judgment but decide justly for every person; and holy with respect to his life, so as not only to teach with words, but also to instruct the people entrusted to him by his example.

9. "Self-controlled, holding firm to that faithful word which is according to doctrine": It befits a bishop to be abstinent, not only in carnal desire but even in the moderation of his speech, and in particular in his thought, that he keep under control what he thinks, what he speaks, and what he does. Finally, let him acquire that "faithful word which is according to doctrine," [that] as he is in some sense the faithful word of God and worthy of every acceptance, he may also display him-

[45] Matt. 25:35.
[46] I Sam. 21:1–6 has "Ahimelech" and the corresponding Vulgate (I Reges 21:1–6) has "Achimelech."
[47] Not sons but followers.
[48] The Vulgate *propositionis panis* is here *panis sanctus* and *panis propositionis* in verse 6 below.
[49] *Sacerdotalis*.   [50] By consecration.

self in such a manner so that everything he says may be thought worthy of belief and that his words may be the rule of truth.

"So that he may be able to give instruction in sound doctrine and confute those who contradict it": That is, he may be able to comfort those who are tossed about in the tempests of this life, and through sound doctrine, that is, catholic doctrine, destroy heretical wickedness. Doctrine is called sound in opposition to doctrine that is weak and feeble. It is of such a character that it can confute freely those heretics who speak against it, whether Jews or the wise ones of this world. The higher matters, which he places on the virtues of a bishop, involve a life that is honorable, but when he says "so that he may be able to give instruction in sound doctrine and confute those who contradict it," this must be taken with reference to perfect knowledge, because if only the life of the bishop is holy, living so, he can be of profit to himself, but if he be instructed in doctrine and the word, he can also teach others, and not only teach and instruct his own, but even strike at his opponents.

10, 11. "There are also many insubordinate men, empty talkers and deceivers, especially those who are of the circumcision, who ought to be confuted, who are upsetting whole houses, teaching what they ought not, for the sake of base gain": He who is to be first in the church, let him have eloquence accompanied by integrity of life, lest his works without speech be silent, and his sayings blush at his wicked deeds. There are many and not a few who corrupt the good seed of God's Word with empty argumentation. They also strive to support their wicked doctrine with quotations of the Holy Scriptures twisted about. So it befits the teacher of the church diligently to learn the Holy Scriptures, so that if struck on the right cheek, he may at once turn[51] the other toward the striker. These are the Jews of the circumcision[52] who then tried to overthrow the nascent church of Christ and to bring in the teaching of the law, namely, circumcision and the Sabbath and other teachings from the law. Such men the teacher of the church, to whom the souls of the people have been entrusted, ought to master by means of the Scriptures and to silence them by weight of witnesses. They are upsetting, not one or a few homes, but all the families with their masters, teaching about differences of foods, when all foods are clean to the clean. But since their "god is their belly," [53] for the sake of base gain they

---

[51] Luke 6:29.   [52] Judaizing Christians.   [53] Phil. 3:19.

wish to make their own disciples, so that, as if they were schoolteachers, let them be received and honored by their followers. So every heretic who deceives men by any tricks, and is deceived, speaks what he should not for the sake of base gain. The gainer is perverse to the death of souls, not to their life. On the other hand, the one who rebukes, in accordance with the gospel, his wandering brother, and corrects him, has gained him. What can be greater gain or what can be more precious than if anyone gains a human soul for God?

12. "A certain one of them, a prophet of their own, has said, 'Cretans are always liars, evil beasts, lazy bellies'": Notice that this must be said twice: what he says here: "A certain one of them, a prophet[54] of their own, has said," is coupled with the passage above, "This is why I left you in Crete, that you might correct what was lacking," and to it refers the phrase, "A certain one of them, a prophet of their own, has said," that is, of the Cretans. Or it must be joined to the passage just preceding, "There are also many insubordinate men, empty talkers and deceivers, especially those who are of the circumcision." These many insubordinate men, empty talkers and deceivers of minds, together with those who are of the circumcision, ought to be bridled, these upsetters of whole houses, teaching what they ought not, for the sake of base gain. Of such people, that is, of those who teach for the sake of base gain, a certain one of them, a prophet of their own, has said—the phrase "a prophet of their own" should be referred, not especially to the Jews and to those particularly who are of the circumcision, but to the many who are insubordinate, empty talkers and deceivers of minds, who, of course, because they were in Crete, must be believed to be Cretans. For this verse is said to be found in the *Oracles*[55] of the Cretan poet Epimenides, whom in the present passage, by a pun, he called a prophet. Such Christians,[56] of course, deserve to have such prophets in the same way as there were prophets of Baal and of idols, as one reads in the books of Kings.[57] Finally, that book from which the apostle took this bears the title of *Oracles*. Because it seems to imply some sort of divination is what, I think, the apostle looked at to see what pagan divination it should promise, and he misapplied the

[54] Epimenides of Crete (6th century B.C.), usually referred to as a poet, was also a wonder worker.
[55] For the Χρησμοί, see Clement of Alex. *Strom.* 1.14.59; J. Rendel Harris, *The Expositor* 1906, 305; 1907, 332; 1912, 348.
[56] See MPL 100.1083.   [57] I Kings 18:22, 25, 40.

verse when he was writing to Titus, who was in Crete, so that he might refute the false teachers of the Cretans on the authority of one from their own island. The apostle is found to have done this same thing in other places, as in The Acts of the Apostles,[58] finding an inscription "To an unknown God," he took from this something serviceable for his preaching.

13. "The testimony is true": Not the whole poem from which the testimony is taken, not the whole work, but only this testimony.

13, 14. "Therefore, rebuke them harshly, that they be sound in faith, not paying attention to Jewish myths or the commands of men who turn from the truth": He says, Rebuke them harshly since they are liars and evil beasts and lazy bellies, who argue for what is untrue, who like wild animals thirst for the blood of people they have deceived, and not working in silence eat their bread, "whose god is their belly and whose glory is their shame."[59] Such as these "rebuke that they be sound in faith," concerning which soundness of faith he speaks in the following passages: The old men are to be temperate, serious, modest, sound in faith and love and patience. Concerning this soundness of faith he writes also to Timothy, "If any man teaches otherwise and does not agree that the words of our Lord Jesus Christ are sound"[60]: He calls them sound words, and [says] that in those who keep them soundness works.

"Not paying attention to Jewish myths or the commands of men who turn from the truth": Concerning them he discusses at great length to the Galatians,[61] and the Romans,[62] who thought that there was a difference between foods, since some seem to be clean, some unclean. Therefore, now he continues:

15. "All things are clean to the clean": That is, to those who believe in Christ, and know that every creature is good and that nothing should be rejected which is received with thanksgiving.

"To the defiled, however, and to the unclean nothing is clean, but unclean is their mind and conscience": Therefore, what is unclean by nature becomes unclean to them through fault, not because something is clean or unclean, but on account of the character of the eaters. Food that is lawful and customary in the catholic church is clean to the clean, unclean to the

---

[58] Acts 17:23.   [59] Phil. 3:19.   [60] I Tim. 6:3.
[61] Gal. 2:12 contains the only reference to food in this epistle (Peter ate with Gentiles), but the circumcision party is discussed at length.
[62] Rom. 14:14–23.

defiled whose mind and conscience are unclean; so any unfaithful and defiled persons are not helped even by the bread of benediction or the Lord's cup, but are made even more defiled, because anyone who eats unworthily of that bread or drinks from the cup, eats and drinks to his own condemnation.[63] So it is in us to eat either clean or unclean things, for if we are clean, the creature is clean for us; if we are unclean and unfaithful, everything becomes common for us, whether by the heresy dwelling in our hearts or by consciousness of sins.

16. "They profess to know God but deny it by their deeds for they are detestable, unreliable, unsound with respect to every good deed": According to what is said in Isaiah, "This people honors me with their lips, but their heart is far from me."[64] In the way that anyone honors with lips and goes far away in his heart, so anyone who professes God in speech denies him in works. One denying God in works, having pretended to profess him, is properly detestable and profane, and one who has been persuaded without true reason, and is disobedient, is properly called unreliable. The corrupt of mind will deny Christ, not only in witnessing, but as often as we are conquered by vices and sins, and act contrary to God's commandments, so often we deny God, and, conversely, as often as we do well, we profess God and praise him.

CHAPTER 2

[Verses 1-6 omitted.]

7. "Show yourself a model of good deeds": There is no use for anyone to be practiced in oratory and to have his tongue worn out in speaking, unless he teaches more by example than by word.

"In doctrine, in integrity": In "doctrine," he says, so that you may fulfill with work what you teach with your mouth. But "integrity" pertains more properly to virginity, whence another translation has "in incorruption,"[65] for virgins are called uncorrupted.

8. "In gravity, sound speech that cannot be censured": It is befitting that a teacher of the church have gravity, that is,

---

[63] I Cor. 11:27.   [64] Isa. 29:13.
[65] No trace of a codex with this reading is given in Wordsworth and White's *Novum Testamentum Latine, editio minor* (Oxford, 1911), though they do cite this passage of Jerome.

good character. Reference has been made above to sound speech.

"That cannot be censured": We speak in this instance, not of anyone so eloquent or wise as to be beyond censure by anyone, but of one who has done nothing or said nothing worthy of censure, though his opponents stand ready to censure.

"So that a man from the opposite party may be afraid, having nothing bad to say against us": Let the man from the opposite party, that is, the adversary, have nothing true or resembling the truth to object to, however ready he may be to censure. This man from the opposite party can be taken to be the devil, who is the accuser of our brothers, as the Evangelist John says,[66] who, when he has nothing evil to object to in us, blushes, and the accuser cannot accuse. For in Greek "devil" is the same as "accuser."[67]

9, 10. "Slaves to be subject to their masters, pleasing them in every respect, not contradictory, not cheating, but exhibiting good faith in every respect": Since the Lord our Saviour, who in the Gospel says, "Come to me, all of you who labor and are heavily laden and I will give you rest,"[68] thinks no condition, age, or sex foreign to blessedness, for this reason, now, the apostle establishes directions even for slaves, that is to say, when they are made a member of the church, which is Christ's body, and they pursue eternal salvation itself. And what Titus ought to teach, did teach, the old men, old women, young women, young men, above, so now he has established as directions for the slaves. First, that they be obedient to their masters in all things; in all things, however, which are not contrary to God; so that if a master gives orders which are not opposed to holy Scripture, let them be subject to their master in servitude, but if he commands what is contrary, let them obey the spirit rather than the body.

"Pleasing": This is to be taken in two senses, that is, pleasing themselves in their slavery, and also pleasing their masters, completing faithfully and in humility everything which they are ordered to do.

"Not contradictory": He says this because the worst fault in slaves is to contradict their masters and to grumble when they order anything. For if a slave must of necessity fulfill what a master orders, why should he not do this agreeably?

---

[66] Perhaps allusion to John 8:3–11.
[67] The Greek word διάβολος, from which Latin *diabolus*, English *devil*, and cognates, means "slanderer."   [68] Matt. 11:28.

"Not stealing":[69] This is another fault of slaves which Christian teaching corrects, but a thief is condemned, not only in major matters but also in lesser. In a theft, it is not what is carried off that receives the attention but the mind of the one who does the stealing. So let the slaves be subject to their masters in all things. Let them be satisfied with their state so as to bear their servitude with equanimity, not to contradict their masters, not to steal, and after that "to show good faith in all things that in all things they may adorn the doctrine of God our Saviour." For if under the masters of their flesh they are faithful in a very small matter, they will begin under the Lord to have greater matters entrusted to them. He adorns the Lord's doctrine who does those things which are products of his condition. How can anyone be faithful in God's property and in churchly duty who cannot display reliability toward a master after the flesh?

11-14. "For the grace of God our Saviour has appeared for all men, training us to renounce irreligion and worldly passions, to live soberly, uprightly, and piously in this life, awaiting our blessed hope and the coming of the glory of our great God and Saviour Jesus Christ, who gave himself for us, to redeem us from all iniquity, and to purify a people acceptable to himself who are zealous for all good deeds": After the list of teachings for Titus, what training he ought to give the old men, the old women, the young women and the young men, finally, even the slaves, he rightly now continues: "For the grace of God the Saviour has appeared for all men." There is no other difference of free or slave, Greek or barbarian, circumcised or uncircumcised, woman or man, but with Christ, we are all one, we are all called to God's Kingdom. When we have sinned, we must be reconciled to our Father, not through our own merits but through the Saviour's grace, either because Christ himself is the living and existing grace[70] of God the Father, and we have not been saved by our own merit, as is said in another passage, "You will save them for nothing,"[71] This grace has therefore shown forth upon all men, to "train them to renounce irreligion, worldly passions, to live soberly, uprightly, and piously in this life." What to renounce irreligion, worldly passions, is, I am sure can be understood from our explanation given above: "They profess to know God but they deny him by

---

[69] In the heading above, the Latin is *fraudantes* ("cheating"), the Vulgate reading, here *furantes* ("stealing").

[70] Alcuin reads unintelligibly *gratiae* for Jerome's *gratia*.

[71] Ps. 55:8 (Septuagint). The Vulgate and Protestant Bibles differ greatly.

their deeds." Worldly passions, therefore, are what are piled up from the beginning of this life, and since they are lovers of this world, they pass away completely with the cloud of this world. Since we, however, shall live in Christ modestly and uprightly, sinning, of course, neither in body or mind, let us live piously also in this life. This piety awaits "the blessed hope and coming of the glory of the great God and our Saviour Jesus Christ." For as irreligion avoids in fear the coming of the great God, so confidently from its own work and faith piety awaits him. Where is that serpent Arius, where that sinewy snake Eunomius?[72] The great God is called Christ the Saviour, not the firstborn or every creature,[73] not God's Word and Wisdom, but Jesus Christ, which are the names of the One who assumed humanity. Nor are we speaking of another Jesus Christ, another Word, as the Nestorian[74] heresy falsely alleges, but the same one both before the ages and in the ages and before the world, and through Mary—no, from Mary—we call the great God, our Saviour Jesus Christ, who gave himself for us, that by his precious blood he might redeem us from all iniquity, and purify a people acceptable to himself who are zealous for good works, that is, who imitate them.

15. "Speak these things and exhort": It appears that the word "speak" should be referred to doctrine, and the added word "exhort" refers to comforting, but he continues further with, "Reprove with all authority," that is, whoever does not listen to doctrine and comforting is worthy of reproof and deserves to hear, "You have forgotten the comforting which God speaks to you as sons."[75]

"Let no one disregard you": The sense is: Let no one of those who are in the church live, through your slothful action, so that he thinks himself better. What sort of edification will there be in a disciple if he takes himself to be greater than his teacher? For this reason bishops, elders, and deacons ought to be very vigilant to excel in character and speech all the people over whom they preside.

CHAPTER 3

[Omitted.]

[72] Arius (c. 256–336), the well-known opponent of Athanasius. Eunomius was an Anomoean of the fourth century.
[73] This phrase was contained in the creed presented by Eusebius of Caesarea to the Council of Nicaea, but was omitted in the Creed as adopted.
[74] See Vincent of Lérins, pp. 50, 53.   [75] Heb. 12:5.

Claudius of Turin

INTRODUCTION

"IT IS WELL KNOWN THAT SPAIN HAS PRODUCED some learned and very eloquent men as indeed some invincible defenders of the catholic apostolic faith." So wrote Jonas, bishop of Orléans (d. 843). He did not cite any examples but he was correct, for Spain was the homeland of Seneca, Martial, and Lucan, as well as of Paulus Orosius, Isidore, Martin of Braga, Theodulph of Orléans, and Agobard of Lyons, the last two being contemporaries of Jonas. "But," he continued, "all believers must grieve sorely that Spain has, alas, frequently spawned, and still spawns, archheretics who with perverse doctrines try to besmirch the simplicity of the catholic faith and who with many superstitions oppose the authority of God's holy church."[1] Since this fact is, in part, the burden of his book, Bishop Jonas provided the names of the erring ones, Bishop Elipandus of Toledo and Bishop Felix of Urgel, both of them leading adoptionists, the former in Moorish Spain, the latter in Carolingian Spain. The mischievous opinion, classified as Nestorianism, had been finally checked by church and state in the Frankish empire by the year 800, and Felix, having spent the last years of his life in confinement in Lyons, had died in 818, the year in which Jonas had been invested with the see of Orléans.[2]

Since even his enemies had conceded that Felix was a man of exemplary life, he had a following that remained loyal to his memory for the next few years. Not long after the death of Felix the teaching and especially the activities of Claudius,

[1] Jonas, *De cultu imaginum*, I, *ad init.* (MPL 106.307CD).
[2] Allen Cabaniss, "The Heresiarch Felix" (*Catholic Historical Review*, 39 [1953], 129–141).

bishop of Turin, evoked from Jonas the dramatic accusation that "Felix himself was reincarnated in his disciple Claudius as Euphorbus was in Pythagoras" and that "he was endeavoring through that selfsame disciple to hurl poisoned darts at the traditions of the church, if not indeed at the canon of catholic faith."[3] We have nothing on Claudius' early life other than the statement of his enemies that he came from Spain.[4] Precisely when he was born and when he came to Frankland, as well as his relation to Felix, are likewise unknown. Apparently his first residence in Frankland was at Lyons, where under the direction of Bishop Leidrad (d. December 28, 815) he pursued the study of Scripture in the school which was already challenging the pre-eminence of Tours. It is therefore possible that he may have come to Frankland when Felix was tried at Aix in 799, and to Lyons when (perhaps even because) Felix was assigned to that diocese for detention. His learning and probably his personality so appealed to Leidrad that, in retirement at Soissons, the bishop complained when Claudius neglected to correspond with him and begged the younger man to visit him or at least send a letter.[5]

From Lyons, Claudius was summoned to serve as a Biblical scholar at the court of King Louis in Aquitaine, chiefly at the palace of Chasseneuil but also at the palace of Ebreuil in Auvergne. At the death of Charles the Great (814) and the accession of Louis the Pious to imperial prerogatives, Claudius accompanied his master to Aix-la-Chapelle, continuing to produce many commentaries on Genesis, Matthew, Galatians, Ephesians, and Philippians.[6] His work, unoriginal and uninspired, with a heavy reliance on allegory, was (as he himself states) derived mainly from Origen, Hilary, Ambrose, Jerome, Augustine, Rufinus, John Chrysostom, Fulgentius, Pope Leo I, Maximus of Turin, Gregory the Great, and the Venerable Bede, Saint Augustine, of course, being the predominant source.[7]

---

[3] Jonas, *op. cit.*, I, *ad init.* (MPL 106.309C).
[4] *Ibid.* (MPL 106.310C).
[5] Theodemir, letter to Claudius, *ad init.* (MGH:EpKA, 2.605; MPL 104.623A).
[6] See Bibliography of Claudius' works.
[7] Claudius, *Catena super sanctum Matthaeum, praefatio, ad init.* (MPL 104.835C). The note on the mention of Rufinus, cited in MPL 104.835D, is as follows: "I think it is a scribal error for 'Rabanus.' In the *Catena* where the letter *R* is written I am certain that 'Rabanus' and not 'Rufinus' should be understood, for that entire passage which begins, 'If anyone shall divorce his wife for any reason other than fornication,' belongs to Rabanus. This

The reputation of Claudius for learning was widespread. Abbots Dructeramnus and Justus and Emperor Louis the Pious had early recognized his ability, had asked him for commentaries, and had by 816 received from him the required works together with appropriate dedications.[8] As noted above, his former bishop, Leidrad, was longing for a visit or a letter. And Nibridius, bishop of Narbonne (d. c. 827), added his plea a little later.[9] There is no cause for wonder that about the year 816, when the see of Turin fell vacant, Louis designated his palatine scholar as the ordinary of that diocese. Claudius was accordingly consecrated and invested with the office of bishop.

During the remaining years of his life he tried to fulfill the functions both of scholar and of pastor. The latter work was unusually heavy and exacting, but Claudius refused to remain in the ivory tower of his study, although his inclination may have been to do so. Once he stated the case very aptly to his friend, Abbot Theodemir, who was continually begging Claudius for commentaries to be used by his monks. "Thus far I have been unable to comply with your wish," wrote Claudius, "not because of indolence or negligence, but because of brutal attacks against our commonwealth and because of the extravagant perversity of evil men. These two matters have been torturing me so much that life itself has already become irksome to me. Yet, although my strength is failing I refuse to run away by myself to take a little rest."[10] Of the two troubles which he mentions, one was external attack on his neighborhood by marauding bands of Muslim pirates. Much of his energy was consumed in leading resistance against the raiders. Again let him tell the story: "Never did I realize," he complained to Theodemir, "that pastoral care of a diocese brings with it so many affairs which create ever larger anxieties. I spend the winters going to and fro over the imperial highways so that not much time remains for study. By the middle of spring I find myself in company with our armed forces on the way to our fortifications near the seacoast, where in constant dread we keep

---

I consider quite remarkable because Claudius and Rabanus were contemporaries, but Claudius was, to be sure, slightly older." On the contrary, we do not positively know that Claudius was older or younger, since we do not know the date of his birth. Manitius, *op cit.*, 1.390, note 4, 394, note 3, accepts the reading "Rufinus" instead of "Rabanus," and cites evidence that the borrowing was made by Rabanus, not by Claudius. It seems more likely.

[8] See Bibliography of Claudius' works.   [9] See note 5 above.
[10] Claudius, commentary on Leviticus, *praefatio, ad init.* (MPL 104.615D).

watch against those Ishmaelites, the Moors. Of course, I carry along my parchment, for although I bear a sword both day and night, I try with books and pen to complete the exposition which I undertook at your request."[11]

That statement gives us a glimpse into the life of a warrior-bishop, but with this difference: he was a man who could not only wield the sword as well as perform his spiritual ministrations, but one who could also stubbornly maintain the life of the mind in the midst of so many distractions. He reminds us, not so much of Pope Julius II, as of another man named Julius, Gaius Julius Caesar. It is probable that the trouble which he called "the extravagant perversity of evil men" provoked ever greater expenditure of Claudius' time and vitality. Hardly had he been installed in the see of Turin when he entered a long-range struggle to suppress certain superstitious practices in his diocese. "As soon as I came to Italy," he tells us, "I found all the basilicas filled, in defiance of God's law, with those sluttish abominations, images. Since everyone was worshiping them, I undertook single-handed to destroy them."[12] To him, reared during the impressionable years of childhood in Moorish and adoptionist Spain, the veneration of human craftsmanship was heathenish, idolatrous, unchristian. So, the warrior-bishop still, he launched an all-out offensive: "As much as I have been able, I have suppressed, crushed, fought, and assaulted sects, schisms, superstitions, and heresies. And as much as I am still able, I do not cease to do battle against them."[13]

Needless to say, our vigorous and independent bishop made enemies. He states indeed that he was openly cursed in the streets and that his very life was often in danger.[14] In spite of all difficulties, however, he continued to write and publish. Within a few years after his accession to the diocese of Turin, he prepared studies of Romans, I and II Corinthians, and Philemon, chiefly at the instigation of Abbot Theodemir. In the meanwhile, the latter had, as others may have, heard disturbing reports from Turin, and even Pope Paschal I was making ready to express disapproval. While remaining ostensibly friendly toward Claudius, Theodemir nevertheless delivered the Corinthian commentary to a council of bishops and magnates in the imperial city of Aix for their consideration.

[11] Claudius, commentary on I and II Corinthians, *praefatio, ad med.* (MPL 104.839A).
[12] Claudius, *Apologeticum, ad init.* (MPL 105.460D).
[13] *Ibid.* (MPL 105.459D–460D).   [14] *Ibid.* (MPL 105.460D).

Without informing Claudius of his action, he asked him for a treatise on Leviticus and an interpretation of certain passages in I and II Samuel and I and II Kings. The former was completed about 823; the latter, about 824. But while Claudius was at work on the latter, a message came from Aix relaying information about Theodemir's double-dealing. Immediately the prelate of Turin accused Theodemir of lying against him and creating a scandal.[15] The abbot explained that a rumor was rampant throughout the Carolingian empire that Claudius was spreading a novel sect in opposition to the catholic faith, largely a negative heresy compounded of aversion to the veneration of images and the cross, to papal supremacy and penitential pilgrimages to Rome, and to intercession of the saints.[16] Somewhat later, Dungal, the celebrated Irish recluse and astronomer, added insinuation to gossip: "The Jews praise Claudius above all others in this realm and constantly quote him. Because he differs from their religion at no point, they call him the wisest of Christians. Other Christians, however, they deride and insult as ignorant, awkward louts who should learn from Claudius and become his disciples. He in turn exalts them and, even more, their kinsmen the Saracens, with excessive eulogies."[17] Dungal added that Claudius had even deleted the names of the saints from the litany and other offices of the church and had repudiated commemoration of the anniversaries of saints as "a vain observance and a useless custom."[18]

The prelates and magnates at Aix summoned Claudius to appear before them to defend himself, but the daring bishop obstinately refused and declared the assembly to be a "synod of asses."[19] Yet the militant prince of the church did not hesitate to enter the fray. Skillfully employing a *reductio ad absurdum*, he transmitted to Theodemir a sarcastic "apology" which one of his enemies (Jonas of Orléans) said was "of such prolixity that it surpassed in size the psalter of David with fifty more psalms added."[20] Claudius readily admitted all the charges made by the abbot except the one about Roman pilgrimages. Concerning them he hedged by stating that he neither approved nor

[15] Claudius letter to Theodemir, *ad fin.* (MGH:EpKA, 2.608 f.).
[16] Claudius, *Apologeticum, passim.*
[17] Dungal, *Responsa contra perversas Claudii Taurinensis episcopi sententias, ad fin.* (MPL 105.528A). The phrase, "*Et maxime suos affines Saracenos,*" is ambiguous and may mean, "his kinsmen" (or, "neighbors"), as well as "their kinsmen."
[18] *Ibid.* (MPL 105.528D).   [19] *Ibid.* (MPL 105.529A).
[20] Jonas, *op. cit.*, I, *ad init.* (MPL 106.312C).

disapproved them because they neither injured nor benefited anyone.[21] But for all his frankness and independence nothing was done to the bishop of Turin, probably because Frankish opinion itself was divided on the question of images. In any event, the imperial diet of 825 steered a middle course between the extremes of iconoclasm and iconodulism, as we note in relation to the work of Bishop Agobard of Lyons.

Probably to conciliate the iconodules of his realm, Louis the Pious submitted Claudius' apology to Jonas of Orléans and Dungal for study and rebuttal. Dungal was quick to answer Claudius, certainly before 829[22]; Jonas was slower and more detailed. Indeed, for one reason or another, Jonas' three books on the veneration of images did not appear until fifteen years later (c. 840), when both Claudius and Emperor Louis were dead.[23] It has been suggested that the reason for the delay was that as Claudius grew older he mellowed and became moderate.[24] Another reason seems more likely. An eremitic recluse can speak his mind without let or hindrance, but a bishop, a man of the world, must to some degree temper his expression to public opinion—and iconodulism did not overwhelm Carolingian Gaul until after the middle of the ninth century. Jonas associated Claudius unjustly with the Arian and Spanish adoptionist heresies; charged him with grammatical errors, plagiarism, dishonesty[25]; and with devastating urbanity

---

[21] Claudius, *Apologeticum, ad med.* (MPL 105.463AB).

[22] Dungal addressed his *Responsa* to both Louis the Pious and his elder son, Lothair, as corulers. Louis, however, deposed Lothair from coemperorship in 829, which therefore becomes a *terminus ante quem* for Dungal's reply. Moreover, Dungal, near the beginning of his work (MPL 105. 468B), says: "A very careful inquiry concerning the matter of painted representations was held at the palace by our most glorious and religious princes two years ago as I recall (*ante ut reor biennium*)." This could be a reference to the council of Paris in 825, but it may refer to the smaller council of prelates and magnates which met in Aix in 824 to study the case of Claudius. It seems therefore that Dungal's *Responsa* must have appeared c. 827 or 828.

[23] Jonas, *op. cit.*, being addressed to Charles the Bald, is therefore dated after the death of Louis the Pious, June 20, 840.

[24] Poole, *Illustrations of the History of Medieval Thought and Learning*, 33.

[25] Arianism, Jonas, *op. cit.*, I, *praefatio* (MPL 106.307-308); adoptionism ("Felicianism"), *ibid.*, I, *ad init.* (MPL 106.309C); defective grammar, *ibid.*, I, *ad init.* (MPL 106.315B), *ad med.* (MPL 106.325A; see especially MPL 106.316C-317A, where Jonas taxes Claudius mercilessly for using the passive voice in a place requiring the active voice); Pelagianism, *ibid.*, I, *ad med.* (MPL 106.330CD); dishonesty, *ibid.*, III, *praefatio* (MPL 106.363D). The quite real charge of plagiarism is of unusual interest,

answered him point by point, citing Scripture, the fathers, and Christian and pagan poets.

But even with such weighty opinion ranged against him, Claudius ended his days in relative security. He continued his Biblical expositions with commentaries on Joshua and Judges and perhaps other books.[26] The date of his death is not known: he died presumably about 827.[27] His position was sufficiently strong and appealing so that a faction lingered for a decade or two,[28] and copies of his works were multiplied, studied, and used by such men as Rabanus Maurus, Haimo of Chalon-sur-Saône, and Agobard of Lyons,[29] but ultimately his type of thought came to be deemed heretical.

The samples of Claudius' works which we have chosen for translation are the introductions and part of chapter 3 of his commentary on Galatians. They will serve as an illustration of his major literary activity, the exposition of Scripture. Except for a few sentences, they have not hitherto appeared in a modern translation and the bulk of his writings still remains inedited. What has been published is indicated in the bibliography below.

> since the practice was general among ancient and medieval writers. After quoting a passage from Claudius, Jonas continues: "These are not your words, Claudius; they belong to the blessed martyr Cyprian. You have omitted some and altered others and put them forward as your very own. But that illustrious teacher wrote those words to Demetrianus, a man devoted to the worship of idols. ... I cannot be more amazed that you have been willing so secretly to steal the words of someone else than that you have supposed you could hide the theft from others." He then shows how Claudius has subtly changed some of the words to make them suit his purpose.
>
> [26] See Bibliography of Claudius' works.
> [27] About 841 Walafrid Strabo, *Libellus de exordiis et incrementis quarundam in rebus ecclesiasticis rerum*, 8 (MPL 114.928D–929A), states: "In addition to his other vainglorious ineptitudes, a certain Claudius, bishop of Turin, but a waverer along the path of truth, as his name suggests, attempted to renew the Greek quarrel about images in the days of Emperor Louis (God rest his soul!), but he died condemned by his own verdict before he was pierced by the darts of various men who wrote against him."
> [28] A deduction from the publication of Dungal's and Jonas' replies. There was evidently a need for rebuttal of Claudius' views.
> [29] For Rabanus and Haimo, see reference in Manitius in note 7 above. For Agobard, cf. Claudius in Jonas, *op. cit.*, I (MPL 106.325D) and Agobard, *Liber contra eorum superstitionem qui picturis et imaginibus sanctorum adorationis obsequium deferendum putant*, 19 (MPL 104.215A). Since Agobard wrote a year or two later than Claudius, he was probably quoting Claudius, unless both were using a common source.

BIBLIOGRAPHY

1. Commentary on Genesis, 811, dedicated to Abbot Dructeramnus; second ed., some years later, to Abbot Theodemir; and another recension, still later, to Emperor Louis. MGH:EpKA, 2.590–593, contains the letter of dedication to Dructeramnus; the rest is inedited.

2. Catena on St. Matthew, 815, dedicated to Abbot Justus. MGH:EpKA, 2.593–596, and MPL 104.835B–838B, the letter to Justus; the rest inedited.

3. Commentary on Galatians, c. 815 or 816, dedicated to Dructeramnus. MPL 104.842C–912A, entire; only the letter of dedication appears in MGH:EpKA, 2.596 f.

4. Commentary on Ephesians and Philippians, c. 816, dedicated to Louis the Pious. MGH:EpKA, 2.597–599, and MPL 104.839C–842B, letter of dedication only; remainder inedited.

5. Commentary on Romans, c. 816–820. Inedited; MGH:EpKA, 2.599 f., and MPL 104.927A–928A contain a paragraph from it in praise of Saint Augustine as an interpreter.

6. Commentary on I and II Corinthians, c. 820, dedicated to Theodemir. Inedited; MGH:EpKA, 2.600–602, and MPL 104.837C–840B contain the letter of dedication.

7. Commentary on Philemon, c. 820 or 821. MPL 104.911C–918B.

8. Commentary of Leviticus, 823, for Theodemir. MGH:EpKA, 2.602–605, and MPL 104.615C–617B, the letter of dedication; MPL 104.617C–620B, brief selections; the remainder inedited. The letter of dedication is dated March 9, 823, two years after a commentary (in four books) on Exodus (i.e., c. 821?) now lost, and eight years after the second edition of the commentary on Genesis (i.e., c. 815?); see MPL 104.615C. The commentary on Exodus is also referred to by Abbot Theodemir; see his letter in MGH:EpKA, 2.605–607, and MPL 104.623A–626D.

9. Commentaries on I and II Samuel, I and II Kings, and Ruth, c. 824, for Theodemir. MGH:EpKA, 2.605–607, and MPL 104.623A–626D contain an inquiry from Theodemir to Claudius asking for an interpretation of thirty places in the books of Samuel and Kings; MPL 104.627A–634B, another inquiry about seventy-two places. MGH:EpKA, 2.607 f., and MPL 104.633B–635C are Claudius' reply to Theodemir's query. Claudius refers to his exposition of the Pentateuch and

the books of Samuel and Kings, to which he says he has added "a brief little commentary" on Ruth. Thereupon follows, MPL 104.635C–834C (excluding 809D–811B), the commentary on Samuel and Kings, based on Theodemir's series of questions. The "little" exposition of Ruth is inedited.

10. Letter to Theodemir complaining that he had presented Claudius' commentaries on Corinthians to a council of bishops and magnates at Aix-la-Chapelle for condemnation, c. 824. MGH:EpKA, 2.608 f.; MPL 104.809D–811B.

11. A treatise attacking the veneration of images, 824 or 825, addressed to Theodemir in answer to his aspersions. Only fragments remain of a total work which was said by Bishop Jonas of Orléans to have been more than one and one third times the length of The Psalms of David (MPL 106.312C) and which was entitled *Apologeticum atque rescriptum Claudii episcopi adversus Theodemirum abbatem*. Most of the excerpts appear in Jonas, *De cultu imaginum, libri III*, MPL 106.305B–388A, *passim*; and many of them also in Dungal, *Responsa contra perversas Claudii Taurinensis episcopi sententias*, MPL 105.465A–530A. Fragments have also been transmitted as a single work and appear in MGH:EpKA, 2.610–613, and MPL 105.459D–464D. A sentence at the conclusion of the work, "You said this of Paschal, bishop of the Roman church, who is already absent from the present life," suggests 824 (the year Pope Paschal I died) or 825 as the date of composition.

12. Commentaries on Joshua and Judges, c. 825 or 826. MGH:EpKA, 2.609 f., contains the introduction or preface; the rest is inedited.

13. There may have been other commentaries now lost: (a) Exodus (see No. 8 above); (b) Numbers and Deuteronomy (see reference to *Pentateuch* under No. 9 above; also MPL 104.840A, as under No. 6 above); (c) Hebrews (see *Retractio Claudii episcopi de auctoribus explanationum super epistolam ad Hebraeos*, MPL 104.926D–927A.

Manitius, *Geschichte der lateinischen Literatur des Mittelalters*, 1.395, lists some of the MSS. of the works mentioned in Nos. 1–12 above. MPL 104.615C–918B, 925B–928A, and 105.459D–464D contains all the works of Claudius thus far edited except two. MGH:EpKA, 2.586–589, contains excerpts edited by E. Dümmler, all of which appeared earlier in MPL except Nos. 1 and 12 above.

The most recent lengthy studies of Claudius seem to be the books by L. Laville, *Claude de Turin* (Montauban, 1889), and

E. Comba, *Claudio di Torino, ossia la protesta di un vescovo* (Florence, 1895). More briefly there are articles by E. Dümmler in *Sitzungsbericht der klassischen preussischen Akademie der Wissenschaften* (1895), 301–319, 427–443, and G. Boffito in *Atti della Reale Accademia delle scienze di Torino*, 33 (1898), 250–285. R. L. Poole, *Illustrations of the History of Medieval Thought and Learning*, 2d ed., revised (London: S.P.C.K., 1920), 24–33, is an interesting interpretative essay, but Manitius, *op. cit.*, 1.390–396, is probably the best treatment to date. Other articles are quite old and out-of-date. In the nature of the case there have been several essays attempting to portray Claudius as a pre-Reformation Protestant, but most of them are negligible.

Claudius of Turin: Commentary on Galatians (Selections)

THE TEXT

LETTER OF DEDICATION

Claudius, sinner, to the most pious abbot, Dructeramnus, master singularly cherished by me in Christ with highest honor.

Unless I am deceived, already three years and more have elapsed since the time when you undertook by your vehement love to arouse me—still in the land of Auvergne in the palace of that pious prince, Lord Louis, then king,[30] now emperor—to arouse me, still restrained by indolence of mind, to take up some fruitful labor in the epistles of Saint Paul, teacher of the Gentiles. Depressed by the toils and whirlwinds of the world, I have thus far been unable to comply with your command. But now in this Lenten season I have, by God's favor, essayed to arrange the epistle of blessed Paul (also called apostle) to the Galatians with intermingled sentences drawn from the treatises of the blessed fathers Augustine and Jerome. When I discerned in these tractates that many things failed to serve as suitable explanation, I had recourse to other books of the aforesaid father Augustine and thence I endeavored to complete the exposition wherein it failed in those works. I have endeavored also, as I saw fit, to add within their treatment my own words which might connect both expositions without harsh breaks, and which might appeal to the mind of the reader and tend to prevent squeamishness. Meanwhile I am eager and happy to dedicate this to your holiness as though it were some booty, so that as often as you take it and read you will deign to remember

---

[30] "Lord Louis, then king [of Aquitaine], now emperor..." Charlemagne died on January 28, 814; Louis entered Aix-la-Chapelle late in February, 814, and was crowned by the pope in July or August, 816. Hence the date of Claudius' exposition could be c. 814–816. "More than three years ago" would therefore be c. 811–813, when he was *in Alverni cespitis arvo* (which we may translate, "on the soil of Auvergne").

me. May the measureless and omnipresent love of Christ unite into one those whom the distances of earth keep apart.

Of the other epistles also many selections are already at hand to the explanation of which, if the Lord wills and grants me life and health and if you will pray for me, I shall try to turn as quickly as I can. May the holy and merciful God vouchsafe, for the progress and adornment of his church, to increase your reverend beatitude with years and merits. Farewell in the Lord, O man of God, and remember me.

Summary of Galatians

The Galatians are Greeks. Galatia is so called from the ancient nations of Gauls by whom it was occupied. For the Gauls, summoned to aid the king of Bithynia, divided the realm with him after victory was achieved. Mingled thereafter with the Greeks, they were at first called Gallo-Greeks, but now Galatians, from the ancient name of the Gauls. Their country is designated as Galatia. Initially they received the word of truth from the apostle; but after his departure they were tempted by false apostles to return to the law and circumcision. The apostle, writing to them from Ephesus, recalls them to belief in the truth. The Galatians were especially persuaded and seduced by false apostles with this argument, namely, that they heard that Paul (through whom they believed the true gospel) was not an apostle because he had not been chosen by the Twelve, nor had he ever followed Christ as Peter and the others had. He considered it needful to refute this calumny by true reasons and by the authority of the Holy Spirit, proving in turn that he was commissioned neither by men nor through men, but through Him who chose both him and the others for the apostolate.

Another Summary

This is the reason why the apostle writes to the Galatians: that they may understand how God's grace acts so that they may be no longer under law. Although the grace of the gospel was preached to them, there were certain ones of the circumcision, Christians in name only, not yet possessing the favor of grace itself, but wishing to remain under the burdens of the law which the Lord God had imposed, not upon those who are subject to righteousness but upon those who are subject to sin, that is, by giving a just law to unjust men to make their sins manifest, not to take them away. (For he does not remove sins except by the grace of faith which works through love.) These Judaizers, therefore, were seeking to put under the burdens of the law the Galatians who were already under that grace, earnestly assuring them that the gospel availed nothing if they were not circumcised and if they did not undertake other carnal observances of the Jewish rite. So they began to deem Paul (by whom the gospel had been preached to them) as an apostle suspect, as one not maintaining the custom of the other apostles who compelled the Gentiles to become Jews first. The apostle Peter had indeed yielded to the pressure of such men and had been drawn into their deception, as though he too thought that the gospel was of no avail to the Gentiles unless they fulfilled the burdens of the law. From this deception, however, the apostle Paul rescued him, as he relates in this particular epistle.[31]

The same issue appears also in the epistle to the Romans, but it seems that something different provoked the dispute there and stirred up the quarrel which had arisen between those Jews who had become believers and those Gentiles who had also become believers. The former felt that the gospel came to them as reward for the merits of the works of the law, and they were unwilling for that reward to be granted to the uncircumcised as though to men without merit. The latter, on the other hand, boasted that they were preferred to Jews, murderers of the Lord.[32] But in this present letter he writes to them who had already been disturbed by the authority of those who were from the Jews and who were urging observance of the law. For they had begun to believe them, as though the apostle Paul had not preached the truth because he did not wish them to be circumcised. Hence he began thus: "I am astonished that you are so quickly being brought away from Him who called you into the glory of Christ, unto another gospel."[33] With that brief introduction, therefore, he pressed to an investigation of the issue, although indeed by the very salutation (when he says that he is an apostle "not from men nor through man,"[34] a phrase which he is found to have uttered in no other epistle) he gives sufficient indication that those who use such persuasion are not of God but of men, and that so far as pertains to authority of gospel testimony he should be held superior to

---

[31] Gal. 2:11–14. [32] Cf. Rom., chs. 2 to 4 and 11.
[33] Gal. 1:6. Both Greek and Vulgate have "grace of Christ" for Claudius' "glory of Christ."
[34] Gal. 1:1.

other apostles, since he had come to know that he was an apostle, not of men or through man, but through Jesus Christ and God the Father. Therefore, if God permits and aids our endeavor, we have undertaken for consideration and study special topics from the very beginning of the epistle.

Exposition of Galatians, Ch. 3

"O senseless Galatians, who has bewitched you not to give ear to the truth?" [35] This passage can be understood in two ways. Either the Galatians are called senseless as moving away from more important things to minor matters, in that they began in a spiritual manner but now approach the end in a fleshly manner; or, on the other hand, each province has its own characteristics, that is, each nation is presumed to possess a good or bad quality which another nation does not have. Turning aside from those depths, we shall strive after the higher things, stating that they can either be accused of a stupidity by which they cannot distinguish the spirit of the law and the letter of the law, or else be misled by the defect of their nation so that they are unteachable, mad, and quite sluggish in respect of wisdom. Moreover, the next phrase, "who has bewitched you," speaks of an enchantment which is peculiarly harmful to babies, children, and those who do not yet walk with firm footing. A certain pagan poet says, "I know not what eye bewitches my gentle lambs." [36]

Whether this be true or not, God knows (as the reader will discover), because it can happen that demons also may be subject to this sin and may steal from good works those whom they know to have begun or to be making progress in God's work. In this case we think that the example derived from common opinion is true, namely, that tender age is injured by enchantment. Thus the Galatians, only recently born in the faith of Christ, nourished on milk, not on solid food, have been bewitched as it were with a certain poison and are vomiting forth the food of the Holy Spirit, but not from a stomach nauseated with faith. For these are the words of a man angered by the marvel that they have been so corrupted as to be unaware that they have been entangled. Everyone who is bewitched turns from good to evil, just as these have turned from freedom and serenity to slavery and anxiety.

"Before whose eyes Jesus Christ was outlawed and crucified

---

[35] Gal. 3:1.   [36] Vergil, *Eclogues* 3.103.

for you."[37] Well was Christ outlawed for us, whose cross and passion, buffetings and scourgings, the whole chorus of prophets foretell, that we may come to know his cross not from the gospel only (in which he is recorded as the crucified), but even long before the crucified vouchsafed to come down to earth and become man. It is no little praise of the Galatians that they so believed on the crucified that he was present with them as the proscribed one, that is, that frequently reading the prophets and understanding all the sacraments of the old law they came to the faith in an orderly way.

"This only I want to learn from you: did you receive the Spirit by works of the law, or by hearing with faith?"[38] Surely the reply is, By hearing with faith. For faith was preached to them by the apostle, by which preaching they truly experienced the coming and the presence of the Holy Spirit. At that time, when the invitation to faith was new, the presence of the Holy Spirit was manifested with sensible miracles, as we read in The Acts of the Apostles.[39] This had been done among the Galatians before the infamous ones came to subvert and circumcise them. The meaning therefore is this: if your salvation were in those works of the law, the Holy Spirit would not be granted to you unless you had been circumcised.

His next attack was, "Are you so stupid that although you began with the Spirit, you are now ending in the flesh?"[40] That is, as he said above in the introduction, there may be some who are perplexing you and wishing to reverse the gospel of Christ. Perplexity is opposed to order. It is true order to rise from carnal things to spiritual, not to lapse from spiritual things to carnal, as befell them. Although Jews receive the Spirit not otherwise than through faith, you think that the Spirit does not suffice unless you are also placed under the law. But this is a reversal of the gospel, which, since it is not good, is not the gospel although it is set forth as such.

"Did you undergo so many things without reason, if indeed without reason?"[41] They had already endured many things for the faith, not fearfully as though placed under the law, but

---

[37] Gal. 3:1. One of the most intriguing verses in the New Testament. The Greek suggests that the Galatians may have seen some kind of representation of Christ crucified, either dramatic or painted. But that is probably pressing etymology too far. Note that Claudius' text reads "*proscriptus*" (outlawed) instead of "*praescriptus*" (portrayed), as do some MSS. of the Vulgate.

[38] Gal. 3:2.   [39] Cf. Acts 2:4; 10:44-46; 13:9-11; 19:1-6; etc.
[40] Gal. 3:3.   [41] Gal. 3:4.

rather in their sufferings they had conquered fear by love, since "God's love had been diffused in their hearts through the Holy Spirit" [42] whom they had received. Therefore without reason, he says, have you suffered so many things, you who wish to fall back into fear from the love which has sustained so many things in you, if indeed you have suffered so many things without reason. The words "if indeed" are not the words of one doubting but of one affirming. As also is that verse, "If it is nonetheless just with God to repay with affliction those who afflict you, and to grant rest with us to you who are afflicted." [43] For what is said to have been done with reason is superfluous, yet the superfluous is neither beneficial nor harmful. But attention must be given that it may not tend to destruction. For that is not to rise but to fall, and albeit they have not yet fallen, they are already inclining to fall.

Certainly the Holy Spirit was still working in them, as he says in the following: "Does he therefore who bestows the Spirit on you and works mighty works in you do so by works of the law or by hearing with faith?" [44] "He bestows" (that is, he administers) must be read in the present tense, to show that the Holy Spirit is supplied to worthy ones at all times every hour and every moment. And in so far as one progresses in God's work and love, by so much the more will he have in himself the mighty works of the Holy Spirit which hearing with faith, not works of the law, brings to completion. Not that works of the law should be despised and simple faith be grasped apart from them, but that the works themselves are adorned by faith in Christ. That statement of the wise man is well known, not that the faithful live by justice, but that the just live by faith. [45] At the same time it is shown that the Galatians, the Holy Spirit having been received after faith, had the gifts of mighty works, namely, prophecy, diversities of tongues, healings of diseases, and others, which are listed among the gifts of the Spirit in the epistle to the Corinthians. [46] Yet after so many things they were ensnared by false teachers, perhaps because they did not possess the grace of discerning the spirits.

"As Abraham believed God and it was reckoned to him for righteousness." [47] That was especially triumphant in him, because the faith of the Gentiles was accounted for righteousness before he was circumcised. Hence what was said to him is of

---

[42] Rom. 5:5. [43] II Thess. 1:6, 7. [44] Gal. 3:5.
[45] Hab. 2:4; cf. Rom. 1:17; Gal. 3:11; Heb. 10:33 f.
[46] I Cor. 12:7–11. [47] Gal. 3:6; cf. Gen. 15:6; Rom. 4:3; James 2:23.

unusual importance, that "in you shall all nations be blessed" [48] by imitation of his faith wherein he was justified even before the sacrament of circumcision and before the servitude of the law which was given at a much later time. Properly is such faith accounted as righteousness for one who, having surpassed the works of the law, has deserved well of God by reason of love, not of fear.

"You realize therefore that they who are of faith are the sons of Abraham." [49] It is true that believers are Abraham's sons, for if Abraham was first justified by faith, as many as believe after him are his sons, whether Jews or Gentiles. In the epistle to the Romans he discussed at greater length the fact that faith was reckoned to Abraham as also to others who believed with this intention, because even while uncircumcised Abraham believed and boasted that he would see the day of the Lord.[50] He did see and he did rejoice, wherefore also it is said to the unbelieving Jews, "If you were Abraham's children, you would do Abraham's works." [51]

"Scripture, moreover, foreseeing that God justifies the Gentiles by faith, foretold to Abraham, 'In you shall all the Gentiles be blessed.' Those therefore who are of faith will be blessed with faithful Abraham." [52] Not, of course, that the actual writing, the ink and the parchment which are inanimate, can foreknow future events, but that the Holy Spirit and the meaning which lies hidden in the letters predicted things to come after many centuries. There is an example taken from Genesis (but therein quite uninterpreted): "And in your seed shall all the nations of earth be blessed." [53] The apostle, interpreting this of Christ, says, "It is not written 'in seeds' as though many, but as one only, 'in your seed,' namely, Christ." [54] Sometimes, therefore, they either took away or added words. No one indeed supposes that all nations have been blessed in Isaac or in Jacob, in the twelve patriarchs or in other descendants of the stock of Abraham. In Christ Jesus alone they praise God throughout all nations and a new name is hallowed over the earth.

"For all who are of the works of the law are under a curse; for it is written, 'Cursed be everyone who shall not abide in all things which have been written in the book of this law to do them.'" [55] It will be understood that as a result of fear, not

[48] Gen. 22:18; cf. Gal. 3:16. [49] Gal. 3:7.
[50] Rom., ch. 4. [51] John 8:39. [52] Gal. 3:8 f.; cf. Gen. 12:3; 18:18.
[53] Gen. 22:18. [54] Gal. 3:16. [55] Gal. 3:10.

of freedom (that is, with corporal and prompt vengeance), punishment will be executed upon those who would not abide in all things which have been written in the book of the law. It would also happen that in the very punishment of the bodies the accursed ones would, moreover, dread the disgrace. That one, however, is justified before God who worships him freely, not with desire to grasp nor with fear of losing anything from him except himself. For in him alone is our true bliss and perfection. Since he is invisible to carnal eyes, he is worshiped in faith as long as we live in this flesh, as the apostle said above, "The life I now live in the flesh I live by faith in the Son of God," [56] and that is the very righteousness to which pertains the assertion that the just lives by faith. Herein he wished to show that no one is justified by the law, since it is written that the just lives by faith. Therefore what he now says to have been promised in the works of the law must be understood of the law itself. Thus he who lives by such practices as circumcision of the flesh and other observances is so involved in the law that he must live under the law, although he has now put the so-called law for the very works of the law, as will be manifest later. He says, "The law, however, is not of faith, but he who has done them shall live in them." [57] He does not say, "He who has done it shall live in it," so that in this place you may understand the law as put for the very works of the law, but those who were living in these works certainly feared that if they did not do them they would suffer stoning or crucifixion or some such punishment. He therefore who does them, he says, shall live in them; that is, he shall have a reward so that he will not be punished by that death.

If anyone shall live in this life not of faith toward God, he shall, when he departs hence, have that quite immediate reward. Surely he does not live of faith who either desires or fears immediate things which are seen, since faith in God pertains to invisible things which shall be given hereafter. There is this particular justice in the works of the law, when it is not left without its own reward, that he who does them shall live in them. Hence he says to the Romans, "If Abraham was justified by works, he has renown, but not before God." [58] It is one thing not to be justified, another not to be justified before God. He who is not entirely justified pays attention neither to

---

[56] Gal. 2:20.   [57] Gal. 3:12; cf. Lev. 18:5.
[58] Rom. 4:2. The negative does not appear in MPL, but the omission is doubtless a printer's error, since the context requires it.

those things which have a temporal reward nor to those things which have an eternal reward. He, however, who is justified by the works of the law is not justified before God, because he expects therefrom temporal and visible advantage. Yet, as I have said, there is indeed a certain earthly and carnal justice so-called. The apostle himself calls it justice when he says elsewhere, "As to the justice which is under the law," I who was engaged in it was "blameless." [59] For that reason our Lord Jesus Christ, who was to grant freedom to those believing, did not keep to the letter certain of those observances. When his hungry disciples plucked ears of grain on the Sabbath, he replied to those who were displeased that "the Son of man is Lord even of the sabbath." [60]

His anger did not blaze carnally for a carnal observance and sustain the penalty set for those who did not keep it, but that believers might be in themselves entirely free from fear of such penalty, to which applies what he now added as follows: "Christ redeemed us from the curse of the law, having been made a curse for us, since it is written, 'Cursed is everyone who hangs on a tree.'" [61] A man's death belongs to the nature of penalty for sin; wherefore it is also called sin. Not that a man sins when he dies, but that it is because of sin that he dies. In other words, the tongue properly so designated is that fleshly part which moves between the teeth and under the palate, yet that also is called a tongue which results because of the tongue, as the Greek tongue or the Latin tongue. Moreover, that member of the body which we use for work is designated the hand, but in Scripture that is called a hand which is brought about by the hand. We say, "His hand is stretched forth ... His hand is observed by him ... I hold your hand," [62] all referring to the hand as a part of a human being. Now I do not deem writing a part of a human being, yet it also is called a hand because it is done by the hand. So not only is that great evil which is worthy of punishment, sin itself, called sin, but also death, which comes because of sins. Christ did not commit that sin which renders one liable to death, but for us he underwent that other, namely, death itself, which was inflicted upon human nature by sin. That which hung on the tree was cursed by Moses. There death was condemned to reign no longer and was cursed to die. Wherefore by such "sin" of Christ our sin

---

[59] Phil. 3:6.
[60] Matt. 12:8; Mark 2:28.
[61] Gal. 3:13; cf. Deut. 21:23.
[62] Cf. Isa. 14:27, and similar passages.

was condemned that we might be set free, that we might remain no longer condemned by the rule of sin.

Why, therefore, does Faustus [of Riez] marvel that sin was accursed, that death was accursed, that mortality of the flesh was accursed apart from any sin in Christ? Yet because of man's sin it was inflicted upon Christ, because he assumed a body from Adam, since from Adam descended the Virgin Mary who gave birth to Christ. God had said in paradise, "On the day you shall touch it, you will surely die."[63] This is the curse which hung on the tree. Let him deny that Jesus was accursed who denies also that Jesus died, for he who confesses that he died cannot deny that death occurs because of sin, for which reason it is itself called sin. Let him hear the apostle as he speaks. Since our old man was crucified at the same time with him (one will understand that it was he whom Moses called accursed), the daring apostle speaks of Christ, "He was made a curse for us," as he was not afraid to say that he died for all. Hence he died because he was accursed, for death itself occurs, by virtue of the curse, and every sin is accursed, whether actual sin which evokes punishment or the punishment which is also called sin because it is evoked by sin.

Christ bore our punishment, yet apart from guilt, in order to free us from our guilt and to bring to an end our punishment. I might have said these things out of my own capacity, but the apostle inculcates it many times to arouse those who are asleep and to confound those who are caviling. "God sent his own Son," he says, "in the likeness of sinful flesh,"[64] not because He came of the stock of mortal kind in Mary through a man, but because death occurs as a result of sin. That flesh, although of a Virgin, was nonetheless mortal; thus, in so far as He was mortal, He had the likeness of sinful flesh. This he also calls sin, as he says later, "that for sin He might condemn sin in the flesh."[65] Similarly in another place he says, "Him who knew no sin, He made to be sin for us, that we might be the justice of God in him."[66] Why, therefore, should Moses be afraid to call accursed that which Paul was not afraid to call sin? The prophet should have clearly foreseen and proclaimed this, being ready with the apostle to be reproved by heretics. For whoever reproves the prophet for having identified the curse is compelled to reprove the apostle for having identified the sin, since the curse is by all means a companion of sin. Nor is it a

---

[63] Gen. 2:17 conflated with Gen. 3:3.
[65] *Ibid.*
[64] Rom. 8:3.
[66] II Cor. 5:21.

greater malice that he should add the phrase "of God" so as to say, "Cursed of God is everyone who is hanged on a tree." For if God did not hate sin and our death, he would not have sent his own Son to undertake it and destroy it.

Why should it be a marvel if what God hates is accursed of God? The more mercifully he hates our death which hung on the tree while Christ was dying, the more cheerfully he grants us the immortality which will happen when Christ comes again. As for another word, "everyone," that is, "Cursed is everyone who is hanged on a tree," it is not so certain that Moses foresaw less that the just ones would be on the cross as that he foresaw very well that heretics would deny the reality of Christ's death, and that, wishing to separate Christ from this curse, they would separate him even from the reality of death. But if that was not a true death, then no curse was hanged on the tree with the crucified Christ if he was not truly crucified. Against such heretics of the distant future Moses long before cried out, "O you to whom the reality of Christ's death is displeasing, you are turning your backs without reason, for cursed is everyone who is hanged on a tree, not this one or that one but everyone, everyone, even God's Son, absolutely everyone. That is precisely what you do not wish, hence on the one hand you overdo, on the other you lead astray. The one who is accursed for us is displeasing to you, because the one who died for us is displeasing to you." For then is Adam outside the curse of that one if he is outside His death.

When He suffered death because of man and on man's behalf, he did not disdain also because of man and on man's behalf to suffer the curse which accompanies death, even that one, even that Son of God, always living by his own justice, but because of our faults dying in the flesh assumed by reason of our penalty. Wherefore the word "all" was added, lest Christ be said not to attain to real death, if by an unwise and false sense of honor he is separated from the curse which is inextricably joined to death. But he who is faithful to gospel truth already understands that no insult to Christ comes from the mouth of Moses. When he called him accursed because he was hanged on a tree, it did not affect the divine quality of his majesty but the condition of our punishment. It is therefore no praise of Christ from the mouth of Manichees when they deny that he had mortal flesh in which to suffer a real death. For by that prophetic curse is understood the praise of humility; but by that heretical quasi honor is charged the reproach of falsehood.

If then you deny the curse, you also deny the death. If you indeed deny the death, you fight not only against Moses, but also against the apostles.

If, on the other hand, you acknowledge the death, you also acknowledge that He underwent the penalty of our sin without our sin. But when you hear about the penalty of sin, believe that it comes either from a blessing or from a curse. If the penalty of sin comes from a blessing, wish always to be in the punishment of sin. But if you wish to be freed from it, believe that it has through the justice of the divine decree come from a curse. Acknowledge, therefore, that He whom you confess to have died for us also underwent the curse for the good. When Moses said, "Cursed is everyone who is hanged on a tree," he wished to signify nothing other than every mortal and dying person who is hanged on a tree. He could have said, "Cursed is everyone who is mortal," or, "Cursed is everyone who is dying." But that is what the prophet does assert, since he knew that Christ's death would be a hanging on the cross and that there would be heretics who would say, "He did indeed hang on the tree but in semblance only, so that he would not really die." Therefore by insisting on "accursed," he insisted on nothing other than "really dead," knowing that the death of sinful men (which He underwent apart from sin) came from that curse, according to the statement, "If you touch it, you will die the death." [67]

"That we might receive through faith the adoption of the Spirit." [68] That is, that what is not feared in the flesh but loved in the Spirit may be announced to those who are to believe. "Brethren, I speak after the manner of mankind: no one scorns or overrules a person's confirmed will." [69] Although a testator may alter his will, he does not alter the confirmed will, for it is confirmed only by the testator's death. As a testator's death tends to confirm his will since he can no longer change his plan, so the immutability of God's promise tends to confirm the inheritance of Abraham whose faith was accounted for justice.

"The promises were declared to Abraham and to his offspring. It does not say, 'And to offsprings,' as though to many, but, 'And to offspring,' as though to one, who is Christ." [70] The apostle says that the offspring of Abraham to whom the

---

[67] Gen. 3:3.
[68] Gal. 3:14. The Greek and the Vulgate have "promise of the Spirit" instead of "adoption of the Spirit."
[69] Gal. 3:15.   [70] Gal. 3:16.

promises were declared, that is, all Christians imitating the faith of Abraham, whom he reduces to a single unit by commenting that it was not said, "And to offsprings," but, "To your offspring." Because faith is one, those who live carnally by works cannot be justified with those who live spiritually by faith. But that statement is easily overcome: the law had not been received, nor after so many years could it have been so given as to make the ancient promises to Abraham of no effect. If the law justifies, then Abraham who lived long before the law was not justified. Since that cannot be admitted, one is compelled to acknowledge that man is not justified by works of the law but by faith. At the same time we are compelled also to realize that all the ancient fathers who were justified were justified by faith alone. For since we are saved in part by believing the Lord's past or rather first coming, in part by believing his future or rather second coming, this is the whole story, namely, they in order to be saved believed both advents as yet future, the Holy Spirit making revelation to them. Wherefore that statement is made, "Abraham longed to see my day; and he saw it and was glad." [71]

Although four hundred and thirty years earlier the promises had been made to Abraham that in him all nations would be blessed, yet observance of the law would live therein because of Him who made it when after four hundred and thirty years it was given to Moses on Mount Sinai. This, however, could be asked: Why was it therefore needful for the law to be given so long a time after the promise, when after the law was given there could arise a suspicion that the promises had been of no use, or if the promise still held, the law, even when given, would be of no benefit?

Foreseeing such a question, the apostle himself, in the following verses, raises it and explains it: "Why then the law? It was appointed because of transgressions, till the seed came to whom the promise had been made. It was ordained through angels by the hand of an intermediary. Now an intermediary does not belong to one only; yet God is one." [72] Since the promise made to Abraham still stood, since the law afterward given by Moses seemed to have been produced in vain, he explains why it was given: "Because of transgressions," he says. For after the

---

[71] John 8:56. The Greek and the Vulgate have "rejoiced to see" instead of "longed to see." Several paragraphs following this quotation have been omitted in this translation.
[72] Gal. 3:19 f.

people's offense in the wilderness, after the worship of the calf and the murmuring against the Lord, the law followed to prevent transgressions. The law was therefore appointed for the people who were haughty so that they could not receive the grace of charity unless they were humbled. Since without this grace they could in no way fulfill the precepts of the law, they were humbled by transgression to seek grace and to realize that because they were proud they would not be saved by their own merits; one is not just by his own authority and power but only by the hand of an intermediary who justifies the unrighteous. The entire dispensation of the Old Testament was administered by angels, the Holy Spirit working in them and the Word of truth himself, not as yet incarnate but never withdrawing from any truthful administration. Although that dispensation of the law was distributed by angels, they acted sometimes in their own character, sometimes in God's character, as also is the custom of the prophets.

Pride is humbled by that law which shows up those who are ill, which does not destroy even by scandal of lying. It was indeed distributed through angels, but by the power of an intermediary, that he himself might free from sins those who through transgression of the law have been compelled to confess that they needed the grace and mercy of God for their sins to be remitted and for them to be reconciled to God in a new life through Him who poured out his blood for them. By transgression of the law pride had to be shattered in those who, glorying in Abraham as their father, were boasting as though they possessed righteousness by birth and were the more arrogantly, the more disastrously, vaunting the superiority of their own merits over other nations because of circumcision. But the Gentiles might be humbled very easily apart from transgression of this kind of law. As for men who saw clearly that they derived no source of righteousness from their ancestors, the grace of the gospel found them slaves to idols. As it could not be said of them that the righteousness of their parents was not in worship of idols as they thought it was, so also could it be said of the Jews that the righteousness of their father Abraham was false. The latter were for that reason told, "Bear therefore fruit worthy of penitence, that you may not say to yourselves, 'We have Abraham as father.' For God is able from these stones to raise up sons for Abraham."[73]

The former, however, were told, "Therefore be mindful that

---

[73] Luke 3:8.

formerly you, Gentiles in the flesh who are called the uncircumcision by that which is called the circumcision made in the flesh by hand, were at that time without Christ, were alienated from the society of Israel, and were strangers to the covenants, not having hope of the promise and without God in this world."[74] The Jews are shown to have been unfaithful ones severed from their own olive tree; the Gentiles, faithful ones grafted from the wild olive upon the olive tree of the Jews. The pride of the former ones should have been worn away by transgression of the law, as when in the epistle to the Romans the apostle would have exaggerated their sins. "Now you know," he states in the words of Scripture, "that whatever the law says it speaks to those who are within the law, so that every mouth may be stopped, and the whole world may be accountable to God,"[75] Jews indeed by transgression of the law and Gentiles by wickedness apart from the law. He also says again, "God has shut up all things in unbelief, that he may have mercy upon all."[76]

"Is the law then against the promises of God? Certainly not."[77] The law was not given to remove sin, but to consign all things under sin. The law showed to be sin that which those blinded by custom might think to be righteousness, so that in this way those who have been humbled may know that their salvation is not in their own hand but in the hand of an intermediary. "Certainly not," because the law is not hostile to the promise, indeed rather confirms it, as Moses once said, "God has raised up for you a prophet from your brethren."[78] This statement the apostle Peter applies to Christ in The Acts of the Apostles.[79]

"For if a law had been given which could make alive, righteousness would truly have been by the law. But Scripture has enclosed all things under sin, that the promise based on faith in Jesus Christ might be given to those who believe. Now before faith came, we were confined under the law, shut up unto that faith which would be revealed."[80] As the intermediary between God and man was in the middle between the one giving and the one receiving the law, so the law itself,

---

[74] Eph. 2:11 f. The Greek seems to require the translation, "Strangers to the covenants of promise," while the Vulgate seems to require the translation here given.

[75] Rom. 3:19.

[76] Rom. 11:32. MPL has *"in credulitate,"* an obvious error for *"in incredulitate."*

[77] Gal. 3:21. [78] Deut. 18:15. [79] Acts 3:22. [80] Gal. 3:21–23.

which was given after the promise, crept in the middle between the promise and its fulfillment. It must not for that reason be thought to shut off the promise merely because that which follows later seems to abolish what was before, but, because it could not give life, nor bestow what the promise had first assured, it is obvious that it was given to protect the promise, not to overthrow it. For if a law had been given which could assure life and offer what the promise had assured, the promise would certainly be deemed removed by the law. But now appointed because of transgressions (as we said above), it rather censures those sinners to whom it was given after the promise to serve as a restraint and, if I may so speak, as a prison, that since through freedom of will they were unwilling innocently to await fulfillment of the promise, now shackled by legal bonds and reduced to the servitude of commandments, they might be preserved until the coming of a future faith in Christ which will cause the consummation of the promise.

That is called righteousness which is considered as righteousness before God, namely, the righteousness of faith, for although the law had a righteousness, it was for the present world only; it would not justify one before God because it could not remit sins, nor make righteous men out of sinners. It was rather given for this purpose: by terror to provoke men to the good life and to punish the disrespectful. Therefore a law was not delivered which could give life but one which could condemn. One should not suppose, however, that Scripture is the author of sin because it is said to have concluded all under sin, since it sets forth the commandment which is taught by the mouth, and thus proves sin but does not cause sin. In the same manner a judge is not an author of crime when he fetters evil men, but he restrains them and by the authority of his decision pronounces them guilty, that later, if he wishes, princely kindness may release those who owe the penalty. As it is said, "Before faith came, we were confined under the law, shut up unto that faith which would be revealed." That is to say more clearly, "The guilt of the law no longer binds us who have been set free by grace." For before we who have been humbled could receive spiritual grace, we could receive nothing at all unless the letter commanding what we could not fulfill had slain us. Hence the statement, "The letter kills, but the Spirit gives life." [81] Only the fear of one God was their constraint, and what offenders against the law itself discovered tended not toward ruin but

---

[81] II Cor. 3:6.

toward advantage for those who believed. Awareness of a serious illness causes one to desire a physician more strongly and to love him more eagerly. He loves most to whom most has been forgiven.[82]

"The law therefore was our custodian in Christ Jesus, that we might be justified by faith. But when faith has come, we are no longer under a custodian; for you are all sons of God through the faith which is in Christ Jesus." [83] *Paidagōgos*[84] is a Greek word which means "lackey." Sometimes we use it to mean the instructor or nurse of children. He who is assigned to children is called by this term because of his relation to them, that is, he guides and curbs their youthful playfulness that their hearts inclined to faults may be subdued while tender childhood is polished with studies and coerced by fear of punishment and is thus prepared for the greater disciplines of philosophy and government. Nevertheless the one of whom this word is used is not the teacher or father; nor does the one who is taught expect either inheritance or learning from such a person. The latter attends to another person's child and he will withdraw from him after the child has reached the lawful age for receiving an inheritance. Finally, this word *"paidagōgos"* also suggests that it is derived from what he does for the children, namely, teach them. Therefore the law of Moses was appointed for an insolent people after the likeness of a sterner *paidagōgos* to restrain them and prepare them for a future faith. After it came, and we believed in Christ, we are no longer under him.

The guardian and the trustee depart from us and we, entering upon the lawful age of maturity, are truly denominated sons of God for whom we are brought to birth, not by the abrogated law but by our mother, faith,[85] which is in Christ Jesus. But after the age of maturity has been reached, when the heir is called a free man and a son, if anyone should wish to be under a *paidagōgos*, let him understand that he cannot live by the laws of a child. For where now can that be fulfilled, "Three times in the year shall every male of yours appear in the presence of the Lord your God," [86] with Jerusalem fallen and

[82] Cf. Luke 7:47. [83] Gal. 3:24–26.
[84] The R.S.V. translation of the Greek word ("custodian") hardly fits the contexts found here. The word "lackey" intends to imply the fact that the *paidagōgos* was a slave. The literal meaning is really "child-guide."
[85] The phrase, "our mother, faith," is an interesting and somewhat unusual expression. The customary "mother" is "holy church" or similar language.
[86] Ex. 34:23.

the Temple reduced to ashes? Where also the salutary sacrifices for sin? And with the altar entirely demolished, where the baking of the cereal offerings, the oblation of the whole burnt offerings, the everlasting fire? What punishment indeed could be distinguished for the criminal ones, when Scripture says, "You shall purge the evil from the midst of you," [87] while Jews are the servants and Romans the rulers? So it comes to pass that they live neither under father nor under *"paidagōgos"* as long as the law cannot be fulfilled after the coming of faith, and faith cannot be held fast as long as the law is revealed as the *"paidagōgos."*

"For all of you who have been baptized in Christ have put on Christ." [88] That Christ is the clothing of believers is proved not only from this particular passage but also from another one where the same Paul exhorts, "Put on the Lord Jesus Christ." [89] While they are changed, they put on Christ when they are called that which they believe. If therefore those who have been baptized in Christ have put on Christ, it is obvious that they who have not put on Christ have not been baptized in Christ. The fact that he says that they are all sons of God through the faith by which they who have been baptized have put on Christ has this significance: that the Gentiles might not despair of themselves because they were not held in guard under a *"paidagōgos,"* that they might not for that reason think themselves not to be sons of God, but rather by putting on Christ through faith all become sons. Not sons indeed by nature, as was the only Son who is also the Wisdom of God; nor indeed by power and singleness of undertaking to hold and to play the part of Wisdom, as the Mediator himself did alone with his own Wisdom acknowledged apart from the intervention of any intermediary. They become sons by participation in Wisdom, that is, by the provision and superiority of faith in the Mediator, which grace of faith is now called clothing, since they who have believed in Christ have put him on, and have thereby become sons of God and brethren of the Mediator.

"There is neither Jew nor Greek, there is neither slave nor free, there is neither male nor female, for you are all one in Christ Jesus." [90] The Jew is not better because he has been circumcised, nor is the Gentile worse because he still has his foreskin, but Jew or Greek is better or worse because of the quality of faith. Moreover, a slave and a free man are not separated by their condition, but by faith, because a slave can

[87] Deut. 13:5.   [88] Gal. 3:27.   [89] Rom. 13:14.   [90] Gal. 3:28.

be better than a free man, and a free man can outstrip a slave, by the quality of faith. Similarly, male and female are distinguished by strength and weakness of body, but faith is reckoned by devotion of mind. It often comes to pass therefore that a woman may be esteemed a man in the matter of salvation, and a man surpass a woman in piety. Since, however, such circumstances may exist, the total disparity of kind, condition, and body may be destroyed by baptism into and clothing with Christ. We are all one in Christ Jesus, that as Father and Son together are one, so also we are one together.

If faith by which one walks uprightly in the present life accomplishes this, how much more completely and how much more amply will the splendor do so when we shall see face to face? For now because of the righteousness of faith[91] we have ever so many first fruits of the Spirit who is life (although the body is still dead by reason of sin), that diversity of nation, condition, or sex, has already by the unity of faith been removed, yet, alas, it remains in everyday affairs and its order must be preserved along the journey of this life. Even the apostles who pass along to us most healthful rules learn how they may live together in accordance with the difference of nation, Jew and Greek; with the difference of condition, master and slave; with the difference of sex, husband and wife; indeed, with any other difference which arises. It was our Lord who first said, "Render to Caesar the things that are Caesar's, and to God the things that are God's." [92] For there are some things which we keep in unity of faith without any distinction, and others in the order of this life along the way, lest God's name and our Saviour's teaching be blasphemed, and this not only for the sake of conscience, that we may do so, not feignedly, as in the eyes of men, but with undefiled awareness of love toward God, who wishes all men to be saved and come to knowledge of the truth. To his statement, "You are all one in Christ Jesus," he added, "but if you are one in Christ, you are therefore Abraham's seed." This shows that the one seed, Christ, is to be understood not only as the Mediator but also as the church of which body he is the head, so that all may be one in Christ and may according to promise receive the inheritance through faith for which one had been shut up; that is, until the coming of faith the people were kept in restraint under a *"paidagōgos"*

---

[91] For "righteousness of faith" MPL has *injustitiam*; it should of course read *justitiam*.
[92] Matt. 22:21.

until a suitable age when those would be called into liberty who have been called among the same people according to plan, that is, those who have found grain in that granary.

"But if you are Christ's, you are therefore Abraham's seed, heirs according to promise." [93] For that reason the promises were made to Abraham and his seed (that is, Christ Jesus). Consequently those who are Christ's sons (his seed) are also said to be the seed of Abraham, of whose seed they are the offspring. But whenever our Lord Jesus is designated as Abraham's seed, it should be understood in a carnal manner that he was begotten of his stock. As often, however, as we, who have taken the Saviour's word seriously and have believed in him, have assumed the nobility of Abraham's family to whom the promise was made, we ought to receive the seed of faith and of preaching in a spiritual manner. Finally, this too should be pondered, that when it is said of the Lord that the promises were made to Abraham and to his seed (namely, to Christ Jesus), one must employ the word "promises" in the plural; but when of those who through Christ are the seed of Abraham, the word "promise" is used in the singular, as in the present passage, "You are therefore Abraham's seed, heirs according to the promise." It is indeed fitting that what is said of the one Christ in the plural should be used of many men in the singular.

[93] Gal. 3:29.

Defense and Reply to Abbot Theodemir[94]

THE TEXT

Your letter of chatter and dullness, together with the essay subjoined to it, I have received from the hands of the bumpkin who brought it to me. You declare that you have been troubled because a rumor about me has spread from Italy throughout all the regions of Gaul even to the frontiers of Spain, as though I were announcing a new sect in opposition to the standard of catholic faith—an intolerable lie.[95] It is not surprising, however, that they have spoken against me, those notorious members of the devil[96] who proclaimed our Head himself to be a diabolical seducer.[97] It is not I who teach a sect, I who really hold the unity and preach the truth. On the contrary, as much as I have been able, I have suppressed, crushed, fought, and assaulted sects, schisms, superstitions, and heresies, and, as

---

[94] This work by Claudius, *Apologeticum atque rescriptum adversus Theutmirum abbatem*, was originally one and one third times the length of the book of The Psalms (Jonas, *De cultu imaginum*, I, MPL 106.312C), but it has not been preserved in its entirety. Extracts of it were submitted to Jonas of Orléans and Dungal for rebuttal. Excerpts only have therefore been transmitted; most of them are cited by Jonas, some by Dungal. There seem to be MSS. of the excerpts from the eleventh or twelfth century. Whether they were prepared from the replies of Jonas and Dungal or from an original exemplar of the extracts alone is not known; probably the latter, since there is at least one sentence noted below which does not appear in the rebuttals and since both Dungal (MPL 105.467C) and Jonas (MPL 106.312C) seem to imply as much. The *Apologeticum* as printed in MPL 105.459D–464D gives a deceptive illusion of being a unified whole. We have therefore resorted to the following device in our translation: we have given an indication of each passage as it is incorporated in Jonas' work. The reader is thus left to decide for himself whether the various passages are really continuous.

[95] Jonas, *op. cit.*, I (MPL 106.312D).   [96] Note the doctrine of *corpus diaboli*.
[97] Jonas, *op. cit.*, I (MPL 106.313B).

much as I am still able, I do not cease to do battle against them, relying wholeheartedly on the help of God.⁹⁸ For which reason, of course, it came to pass that as soon as I was constrained to assume the burden of pastoral duty and to come to Italy to the city of Turin, sent thither by our pious prince Louis, the son of the Lord's holy catholic church, I found all the churches filled, in defiance of the precept of Truth, with those sluttish abominations—images.⁹⁹ Since everyone was worshiping them, I undertook singlehanded to destroy them.¹ Everyone thereupon opened his mouth to curse me, and had not God come to my aid, they would no doubt have swallowed me alive.²

Since it is clearly enjoined that no representation should be made of anything in heaven, on earth, or under the earth,³ the commandment is to be understood, not only of likenesses of other gods, but also of heavenly creatures,⁴ and of those things which human conceit contrives in honor of the Creator.⁵ To adore is to praise, revere, ask, entreat, implore, invoke, offer prayer. But to worship is to direct respect, be submissive, celebrate, venerate, love, esteem highly.⁶

Those against whom we have undertaken to defend God's church say,⁷ "We do not suppose that there is anything divine in the image which we adore. We adore it only to honor him whose likeness it is." ⁸ To whom we reply⁹ that if those who have abandoned the cult of demons now venerate the images of the saints, they have not deserted their idols but have merely changed the name.¹⁰ For if you portray or depict on a wall representations of Peter and Paul, of Jupiter, Saturn, or Mercury, the latter representations are not gods and the former are not apostles, and neither the latter nor the former are men, although the word is used for that purpose. Nonetheless the selfsame error always persists both then and now.¹¹ Surely if

---

⁹⁸ *Ibid.* (MPL 106.314AB).   ⁹⁹ *Ibid.* (MPL 106.315AB).
¹ *Ibid.* (MPL 106.316B).   ² *Ibid.* (MPL 106.317C).
³ Ex. 20:4 f.   ⁴ Jonas, *op. cit.*, I (MPL 106.318A).
⁵ *Ibid.* (MPL 106.318D).
⁶ Dungal, *Responsa contra perversas Claudii Taurinensis episcopi sententias* (MPL 105.471D).   ⁷ Jonas, *op. cit.*, I (MPL 106.325A).
⁸ *Ibid.* (MPL 106.325C).   ⁹ *Ibid.* (MPL 106.325A).
¹⁰ *Ibid.* (MPL 106.325D); cf. Agobard, *Liber contra eorum superstitionem qui picturis et imaginibus sanctorum adorationis obsequium deferendum putant*, 19 (MPL 104.215A). Cf. the well-known pun: "they kept the *nomen* and changed the *numen.*"
¹¹ Jonas, *op. cit.*, I (MPL 106.325D–326A). The passage beginning, "that if those who have abandoned," and ending, "persists both then and now," appears also in Dungal, *op. cit.* (MPL 105.472A).

men may be venerated, it is the living rather than the dead who should be so esteemed,[12] that is, where God's likeness is present,[13] not where there is the likeness of cattle or (even worse) of stone or wood, all of which lack life, feeling, and reason.[14] But if the works of God's hands must not be adored and worshiped, one should ponder carefully how much less are the works of men's hands to be adored and worshiped or held in honor of those whose likenesses they are.[15] For if the image which one adores is not God, then in vain should it be venerated for honor of the saints who in vain arrogate to themselves divine dignities.[16]

Above all, therefore, it should be perceived that not only he who worships visible figures and images, but also he who worships any creature, heavenly or earthly, spiritual or corporeal, in place of God's name, and who looks for the salvation of his soul from them (that salvation which is the prerogative of God alone), that it is he of whom the apostle speaks, "They worshiped and served the creature rather than the Creator." [17]

Why do you humiliate yourselves and bow down to false images? Why do you bend your body like a captive before foolish likenesses and earthly structures? God made you upright, and although other animals face downward toward the earth, there is for you an upward posture and a countenance erect to heaven and to God. Look thither, lift your eyes thither, seek God in the heights, so that you can avoid those things which are below. Exalt your wavering heart to heavenly heights.

Why do you hurl yourself into the pit of death along with the insensate image which you worship? Why do you fall into the devil's ruin through it and with it? Preserve the eminence which is yours by faith, continue to be what you were made by God.[18]

But those adherents of false religion and superstition declare, "It is to recall our Saviour that we worship, venerate, and adore a cross painted in his honor, bearing his likeness." [19] To them nothing seems good in our Saviour except what also seemed good to the uprighteous, namely, the reproach of suffering and

[12] Jonas, *op. cit.*, I (MPL 106.326B).   [13] *Ibid.*
[14] *Ibid.* (MPL 106.326C); cf. Agobard, *op. cit.*, 18 (MPL 104.222D).
[15] *Ibid.* (MPL 106.329BC).   [16] *Ibid.* (MPL 106.329C).
[17] *Ibid.* (MPL 106.329D). The quotation is Rom. 1:25.
[18] *Ibid.* (MPL 106.330D). This is the passage attributed by Jonas to Cyprian's letter to Demetrianus.
[19] *Ibid.* (MPL 106.331C).

the mockery of death. They believe of him what even impious men, whether Jews or pagans, also believe who doubt that he rose again. They have not learned to think anything of him except that they believe and hold him in their heart as tortured and dead and always twisted in agony. They neither heed nor understand what the apostle says: "Even though we once regarded Christ according to the flesh, we now regard him thus no longer." [20]

Against them we must reply that if they wish to adore all wood fashioned in the shape of a cross because Christ hung on a cross, then it is fitting for them to adore many other things which Christ did in the flesh. He hung on the cross scarcely six hours, but he was in the Virgin's womb nine lunar months and more than eleven days, a total of two hundred and seventy-six solar days, that is, nine months and more than six days. Let virgin girls therefore be adored, because a Virgin gave birth to Christ. Let mangers be adored, because as soon as he was born he was laid in a manger. Let old rags be adored, because immediately after he was born he was wrapped in old rags.[21] Let boats be adored, because he often sailed in boats, taught the throngs from a small boat, slept in a boat, from a boat commanded the winds, and to the right of a fishing boat ordered them to cast the net when that great prophetic draught of fish was made. Let asses be adored, because he came to Jerusalem sitting on an ass. Let lambs be adored, because it was written of him, "Behold, the Lamb of God, who takes away the sins of the world."[22] (But those infamous devotees of perverse doctrines prefer to eat the living lambs and adore only the ones painted on the wall!)

Still further, let lions be adored, because it was written of him, "The Lion of the tribe of Judah, the Root of David, has conquered." [23] Let stones be adored, because when He was taken down from the cross he was placed in a rock-hewn sepulcher, and because the apostle says of him, "The Rock was Christ." [24] Yet Christ was called a rock, lamb, and lion tropologically, not literally; in signification, not in substance. Let thorns of bramble-bushes be adored, because a crown of thorns was pressed upon his head at the time of his Passion. Let reeds

---

[20] *Ibid.* (MPL 106.334C). The Biblical quotation is II Cor. 5:16, a favorite passage of Berengar of Tours.
[21] "Old rags" is a literal translation. Perhaps "swaddling clothes" would be more satisfactory.
[22] John 1:29.   [23] Rev. 5:5.   [24] I Cor. 10:4.

be adored, because with blows from them his head was struck by the soldiers. Finally, let lances be adored, because one of the soldiers at the cross with a lance opened his side, whence flowed blood and water, the sacraments by which the church is formed.[25]

All those things, of course, are facetious and should be lamented rather than recorded. But against fools we are compelled to propose foolish things, and against stony hearts to hurl, not verbal arrows and sentiments, but stony blows.[26] "Return to judgment, you liars," you who have departed from the truth, who love vanity, and who have become vain[27]; you who crucify the Son of God anew and hold him up for display[28] and thereby cause the souls of wretched ones in disordered masses to become partners of demons. Estranging them through the impious sacrilege of idols, you cause them to be cast away by their own Creator and thrown into eternal damnation.[29]

God commanded one thing; they do otherwise.[30] God commanded them to bear the cross, not to adore it; they wish to adore what they are spiritually or corporally unwilling to bear.[31] Yet thus to worship God is to depart from him, for he said,[32] "He who wishes to come after me, let him deny himself and take up his cross and follow me."[33] Unless one forsake himself, he does not approach the One who is above him; nor is he able to apprehend what is beyond himself if he does not know how to sacrifice what he is.[34]

If you say that I forbid men to go to Rome for the sake of penance, you lie.[35] I neither approve nor disapprove that journey,[36] since I know that it does not injure, nor benefit, nor profit, nor harm anyone.[37] If you believe that to go to Rome is to do penance, I ask you why you have lost so many souls in so much time, souls whom you have restrained in your monastery, or whom for the sake of penance you have received into your monastery and have not sent to Rome, but whom you have

---

[25] Jonas, *op. cit.*, I (MPL 106.336BCD).   [26] *Ibid.* (MPL 106.338D).
[27] *Ibid.* (MPL 106.339A). This contains a Biblical phrase from Isa. 46:8.
[28] *Ibid.*, an allusion to Heb. 6:6.   [29] *Ibid.* (MPL 106.339B).
[30] *Ibid.*, II (MPL 106.350C).   [31] *Ibid.* (MPL 106.351B).
[32] *Ibid.* (MPL 106.352B).   [33] *Ibid.* (MPL 106.352D); Matt. 16:24.
[34] *Ibid.* (MPL 106.353C). Jonas charges that Claudius cribbed this passage from Gregory the Great.
[35] *Ibid.*, III (MPL 106.365D). The word "you" here and following is singular, evidently directed to Theodemir personally.
[36] *Ibid.* (MPL 106.366C).   [37] *Ibid.*

rather made to serve you.³⁸ You say that you have a band of one hundred and forty monks who came to you for the sake of penance,³⁹ surrendering themselves to the monastery. You have not permitted one of them to go to Rome.⁴⁰ If these things are so (as you say, "To go to Rome is to do penance"), what will you do about this statement of the Lord: "Whoever causes one of these little ones who believe in me to stumble, it is expedient for him that a millstone be hung around his neck and that he be drowned in the deep, rather than cause one of these little ones who believe in me to stumble"? ⁴¹ There is no greater scandal than to hinder a man from taking the road by which he can come to eternal joys.⁴²

We know, indeed, that the Evangelist's account of the Lord Saviour's words are not understood, where he says to the blessed apostle Peter, "You are Peter, and on this rock I will build my church, and I will give you the keys of the Kingdom of Heaven." ⁴³ Because of these words of the Lord, the ignorant race of men, all spiritual understanding having been disregarded, wishes to go to Rome to secure eternal life.⁴⁴ He who understands the keys of the Kingdom in the manner stated above does not require the intercession of blessed Peter in a particular location,⁴⁵ for if we consider carefully the proper meaning of the Lord's words, we find that he did not say to him, "Whatever you shall loose in heaven shall be loosed on earth and whatever you shall bind in heaven shall be bound on earth." ⁴⁶ One must know hereby that that ministry has been granted to bishops of the church just so long as they are pilgrims here in this mortal body. But when they have paid the debt of death, others who succeed in their place gain the same judicial authority, as it is written, "Instead of your fathers, sons are born to you; you will appoint them princes over all the earth." ⁴⁷

Return, O you blind, to the true light that enlightens every man who comes into this world,⁴⁸ because the light shines in darkness, and the darkness does not envelop it.⁴⁹ By not

---

³⁸ *Ibid.* (MPL 106.369C).   ³⁹ *Ibid.* (MPL 106.371A).
⁴⁰ This passage occurs neither in Jonas nor in Dungal, but see MPL 105.463B.
⁴¹ Jonas, *op. cit.*, III (MPL 106.373D–374A); Matt. 18:6.
⁴² *Ibid.* (MPL 106.375A).   ⁴³ Matt. 16:18 f.
⁴⁴ Jonas, *op. cit.*, III (MPL 106.375BC).   ⁴⁵ *Ibid.* (MPL 106.376D).
⁴⁶ *Ibid.* (MPL 106.378B).
⁴⁷ *Ibid.* (MPL 106.379C); Ps. 45:16 (44:17, V).
⁴⁸ Cf. John 1:9.   ⁴⁹ Cf. John 1:5.

looking at that light you are in the darkness. You walk in darkness and you do not know whither you are going, because the darkness has blinded your eyes.[50]

Hear this also and be wise, you fools among the people, you who were formerly stupid, who seek the apostle's intercession by going to Rome; hear what the same oft-mentioned most blessed Augustine utters against you.[51] In *On the Trinity*, Book VIII, he says, among other things,[52] "Come with me and let us consider why we should love the apostle. Is it because of the human form, which we hold to be quite ordinary, that we believe him to have been a man? By no means. Besides, does not he whom we love still live although that man no longer exists? His soul is indeed separated from the body, but we believe that even now there still lives what we love in him."[53]

Whoever is faithful ought to believe in God when he makes a promise, and by how much the more when he makes an oath.[54] Why is it necessary to say, "O that Noah, Daniel, and Job were present here." Even if there were so much holiness, so much righteousness, so much merit, they, as great as they were, will not absolve son or daughter.[55] He therefore says these things that no one may rely on the merit or intercession of the saints,[56] for one cannot be saved unless he possess the same faith, righteousness, and truth which they possessed and by which they were pleasing to God.[57]

Your fifth objection against me is that the apostolic lord was displeased with me (you state that I displease you as well).[58] You said this of Paschal, bishop of the Roman church, who has departed from the present life.[59] An apostolic man is one who is guardian of the apostle[60] or who exercises the office of an apostle.[61] Surely that one should not be called an apostolic man who merely sits on an apostle's throne but the one who

---

[50] Jonas, *op. cit.*, III (MPL 106.380BC).
[51] *Ibid.* (MPL 106.383C).
[52] Augustine, *De Trinitate*, VIII, 5, par. 8, in NPNF, 1st ser., III, 119.
[53] This entire paragraph appears in Dungal, *op. cit.* (MPL 105.498C); the latter part does not occur in Jonas.
[54] Jonas, *op. cit.*, III (MPL 106.381B).
[55] *Ibid.* (MPL 106.381D).   [56] *Ibid.* (MPL 106.382A).
[57] *Ibid.* (MPL 106.383A).   [58] *Ibid.* (MPL 106.385A).
[59] *Ibid.* The reference is to Pope Paschal I, who died in 824.
[60] *Ibid.* (MPL 106.385B). Dungal, *op. cit.* (MPL 105.486AB), does not quote this statement, but he does note the absurd etymology and rightly holds it up to ridicule.
[61] Jonas, *op. cit.*, III (MPL 106.385C).

fulfills the apostolic function.⁶² Of those who hold the place but do not fulfill the function, the Lord once said, "The scribes and Pharisees sit on Moses' seat; so keep and perform whatever things they tell you. But be unwilling to act according to their works, for they talk but they do not practice."⁶³

⁶² *Ibid.* Jonas continues, "We too do not hold that anyone on the apostolic throne has been elevated to the dignity of the apostles unless he fulfills the apostolic function." But Jonas' zeal had brought him to the brink of heresy! Cardinal Angelo Mai, editor of the *Bibliotheca veterum patrum* (reproduced in MPL 106), therefore hurriedly adds the warning, "*Caute lege.*"

⁶³ Jonas, *op. cit.*, III (MPL 106.386A); Matt. 23:2 f.

Rupert of Deutz

INTRODUCTION

ONE DAY IN THE EARLY YEARS OF THE TWELFTH century, Cuno, abbot of Siegburg, and Rupert, abbot of Deutz (now part of Cologne), were engaged in a spiritual conversation concerning the authority of Holy Scripture. The particular topic chanced to be the well-known vision in the seventh chapter of The Book of Daniel. Since the abbots identified the third beast, the leopard, with the Greeks of Alexander and his successors, the discussion shifted slightly to include mention of the patriotic Maccabees. At that point Cuno rather unexpectedly interposed this thoughtful query, "I would like to know more precisely why we in holy church commemorate with lessons and hymns their warlike defense with as much solemnity as we celebrate the patient endurance of holy martyrs who made no defense."[1] The troubled question is peculiarly apt. If "God's Kingdom is truly one of peace, of charity, and of brotherhood, an empire of devotion, and the dominion of truth, justice, and meekness," why, indeed, should they, who "in many battles resisted bloodthirsty barbarity with material weapons . . ., have secured for themselves an illustrious remembrance in God's church?"

But the abbot of Deutz had a keen and ready answer: "Their struggle and their military might have, with God's help, been of inestimable profit to us and to the whole world. For the devil was working through Antiochus Epiphanes to destroy all memory of and all hope and faith in the promise of God to Abraham that in his seed all nations would be blessed.[2] What was it that Antiochus did? 'He erected on God's altar the detestable idol of abomination; throughout the cities of Judea his

[1] The feast of the Maccabees is August 1.   [2] Gen. 22:18.

men erected sanctuaries; at the doors of homes and in the streets they burned incense and offered sacrifice; the books of God's law they tore up and cast into the flames. And if anyone was found with the books of God's covenant or if anyone was found observing God's law, him they put to death according to the royal edict.'[3] All this was done in an effort to annihilate the Jewish people, so that in Abraham's seed, that is, in Christ, all nations should not be blessed and so that God's purpose and promise might be of no effect. But, thanks be to God, good Cuno, the foundation was successfully defended and from it have come great results. God's truth has been mightily fulfilled and the Maccabees were the ones who accomplished that feat. For that reason they can rightfully claim an illustrious renown in God's church."

When Rupert had thus spoken and had added more "about other ancient saints through whose labors and wars it was necessary for God's Word to protect that people through whom he intended to become incarnate for the salvation of the human race," Abbot Cuno was so delighted with the explanation that he exclaimed, "Write me a book about the victory of God's Word!" So insistent was he that Rupert ultimately yielded to persuasion and wrote the treatise which he has summarized in these sentences: "Great and powerful is God's Word, who has prevailed, but great also is the enemy who was conquered. It was a mighty struggle and mighty were its events."[4] (Of this book we present some characteristic selections below.)

From the incident just related one can conjure up the quiet of the cloister garth broken only by the two monks in their earnest, learned conversation, and one might long for such tranquillity. But the momentary vision is quite deceptive. Both men were constantly embroiled in bitter controversies, political as well as theological. And, above all, both men lived in exciting times: the rancorous strife of investitures had not yet subsided in uneasy compromise, the first crusade was in the very recent past, the noise of the schools (realism and nominalism) was strident; more simply, the "renaissance of the twelfth century" was in full swing. Mere mention of some contemporaries, Peter Abelard, Suger of Saint-Denis, Bernard of Clairvaux, and Peter the Venerable, will suggest the vitality of the era in which Rupert lived.

[3] I Maccabees 1:54–57.
[4] This entire incident is recounted by Rupert in a letter to Cuno which serves as preface to the treatise, *On the Victory of God's Word*; see MPL 169.1215–1218.

Rupert was presented in childhood as an oblate to the Benedictine abbey of Saint Lawrence at Liége. He may have been born of Germanic origin near that city. His date of birth is not known but it must have been near the last quarter of the eleventh century. Reared in the monastery of Saint Lawrence under Abbots Berengar (1076–1115) and Heribrand (1115–1130),[5] he was ordained priest in the early years of the twelfth century, possibly about 1106. In 1113 he was transferred to the abbey of Siegburg, where he became an intimate of Abbot Cuno. Through the influence of Archbishop Frederick of Cologne, he was elected abbot of Deutz in 1119 or 1120, where (except for occasional visits elsewhere) he remained in canonical residence until his death which occurred about 1130.[6]

From his earliest days he was a prolific writer. Before he left Liége he had written several long poems: one in praise of the Holy Spirit, another in heroic verse concerning the incarnation, and still another in Sapphics on the history of his monastery; and hymns in honor of Saints Theodard, Goar, and Severus; as well as a prose chronicle of the cloister, lives of Saints Augustine and Odilia, a commentary on Job, and a lengthy work on liturgy. He had also begun his quite extensive treatise on the works of the Trinity (see below, bibliography, No. 4).

Already, however, his life was disturbed by controversy. First, there were those who, envious of his literary productivity, complained that the writings of the holy fathers should be sufficient without all the books of new, unknown, and unauthoritative persons. Next, the followers of William of Champeaux (bishop of Châlons-sur-Marne, 1113–1121) challenged his doctrine of the Eucharist, accusing him of being either an adherent of Berengar of Tours or perhaps of the doctrine of impanation.[7] It is true that Rupert's language is ambiguous enough for eminent exponents of the Tridentine

[5] Rupert's letter to Cuno which serves in part as introduction to *De sancta Trinitate et operibus ejus*; see MPL 167.196A. The works of Rupert are full of such biographical details.
[6] Some, however, place his death as late as 1135.
[7] The doctrine of impanation is an attempt to explain the Eucharistic Presence by asserting that as in the incarnation Christ as God entered into a hypostatic union with flesh, so in the Eucharist he similarly enters into a hypostatic union with bread and wine. The word is of sixteenth century origin; the doctrine clearly expressed is of fourteenth century origin. It is not (and has never been) an authoritative doctrine of any Christian body. Rupert's language, although ambiguous and unguarded, has been explained in a Tridentine manner by Gerberon (see *Bibliographical Note*).

faith, such as Cardinal Bellarmine, Vasquez, and others, to take offense, and for antipapal theologians, for example Wyclif, Salmasius, and others, to claim him for their own. Yet Rupert has received an elaborate and possibly definitive *apologia* from the celebrated Maurist (and erstwhile Jansenist) of the early eighteenth century, Gabriel Gerberon.[8]

A third issue was raised by both William of Champeaux and Anselm of Laon (d. 1117) involving the doctrine of predestination. These champions (or their followers) taught that in some manner God had actively willed sin and hence the Fall of Adam. Rupert denied that teaching.[9] Thereupon they charged him with denying also God's omnipotence. His defense[10] reminds us of the arguments attributed to Remigius of Lyons. Not content with a literary prosecution of his position, Rupert mounted his mule and rode off to meet his antagonists. Anselm died on the very day Rupert entered Laon. The latter proceeded immediately to Châlons where he engaged in a lively debate with Bishop William.[11] Fortunately Rupert had powerful advocates in addition to his pen, namely, Cuno of Siegburg (later bishop of Ratisbon), Frederick of Cologne, and William of Palestrina, a papal legate. We have already noted that he was held in such esteem as ultimately to become abbot of the monastery of Saint Héribert at Deutz.

A list of his extant writings follows:

1. *Carmina de s. Laurentio*, ed. E. Dümmler, *Neues Archiv*, 11.175–194; thirteen religious poems written before 1113.

2. *Chronicon s. Laurentii Leodensis*, ed. Wattenbach, MGH: Scriptores, 8.262–279; from the foundation of the monastery in 959 to 1095.

3. *De divinis officiis per anni circulum libri XII*, MPL 170.13A–332D. This great study of the liturgy, completed by 1111, dedicated to Cuno, is quite similar to the *Liber officialis* of the ninth century Amalarius of Metz. It puts Rupert in the category of competent liturgiologists.

4. *De Trinitate et operibus ejus libri XLII*, MPL 167. 199D–1828B. Addressed to Cuno, this work was begun before 1113 but completed in 1117. It is a series of theological commentaries on Scripture. The first section, Books 1–3, deals with the proper

---

[8] See *Bibliographical Note* at the end of this Introduction.
[9] Rupert, *De voluntate Dei* (see list of his writings in this Introduction).
[10] Rupert, *De omnipotentia Dei* (see list of his writings in this Introduction).
[11] Rupert, *Super quaedam capitula regulae divi Benedicti*, I, ad init. (MPL 170. 482D–483A).

work of God the Father from the beginning of the world to the Fall of Adam; the second, Books 4–33, with the proper work of God the Son from the Fall of Adam to the incarnation of Christ; and the third, Books 34–42, with the work of God the Holy Spirit from the incarnation until the end of the world (chiefly a discussion of the seven works of the Holy Spirit). Herein there seems to be an anticipation of the three ages of Abbot Joachim of Fiore (d. 1202).

5. *Super Iob commentarius*, MPL 168.963A–1196C; probably an early work.

6. *In Cantica canticorum de incarnatione Domini libri VII*, MPL 168.839A–962B; written at the request of Cuno about the same time as the preceding work. Rupert says that it was inspired by a vision. Although he applies most of this Scriptural text to the excellences and prerogatives of the blessed Virgin, Rupert nonetheless denies that she was conceived without sin. Herein there is a certain comparison with his younger contemporary, Bernard of Clairvaux.

7. *De voluntate Dei*, MPL 170.437A–454C; written between 1113 and 1115.

8. *De omnipotentia Dei*, MPL 170.453D–478C. This and the preceding, written about the same time, were part of the controversy with William of Champeaux and Anselm of Laon.

9. *In evangelium s. Joannis libri XIV*, MPL 169.203A–826A. Dedicated to Cuno, this contains, in part, an attack on the Eucharistic teachings of Berengar of Tours. It was written before 1117.

10. *In Apocalypsim Joannis apostoli libri XXII*, MPL 169.827A–1214C. Dedicated to Frederick of Cologne, it was written perhaps about the same time as No. 12 below, that is, 1117–1126.

11. *In duodecim prophetas minores libri XXXII*, MPL 168.11C–826D; written over a period of years ending c. 1126 and dedicated to Frederick of Cologne.

12. *De victoria Verbi Dei*, MPL 169.1215A–1502B; written before 1126 and dedicated to Cuno. Manitius, *Geschichte der lateinischen Literatur des Mittelalters*, 3.129, calls this Rupert's theological masterpiece. Rupert himself refers to this treatise in his preface to the last six prophets mentioned above, indicating that he interrupted his work on the minor prophets to write this. He also cites this book in his *De glorificatione Trinitatis et processione sancti Spiritus*, III, 21; VII, 14; and in *De gloria et honore Filii hominis*, XII; see below.

13. *Vita s. Heriberti archiepiscopi Coloniensis*, MPL 170.389D–428A; written before 1126 for Abbot Markward, Rupert's predecessor at Deutz.

14. *Passio b. Eliphii martyris*, MPL 170.427B–436D; for Abbot Alban of Saint Martin.

15. *Anulus sive dialogus inter Christianum et Judaeum libri III*, MPL 170.561A–610C; written for Cuno before 1126. The title is derived from the parable of the Prodigal Son, Luke 15:22; see the very interesting paragraphs at the end of Books II and III (MPL 170.578C and 610C). On such dialogues in the Middle Ages, consult A. Lukyn Williams, *Adversus Judaeos* (Cambridge: Cambridge University Press, 1935). Shortly before the time when Rupert flourished, a Hispano-Arab, Abu Muhammad Ali ibn Hazm al-Andalusi (994–1064), had written a book known as *The Dove's Neck-Ring* about love and lovers. One cannot but wonder if there is some tenuous connection between the works of Rupert and Ibn Hazm. See A. R. Nykl, *A Book Containing the Risala Known as The Dove's Neck-Ring* (Paris: Geuthner, 1931), translated from the unique manuscript in the University of Leiden which was edited in 1914 by D. K. Pétrof.

16. *De laesione virginitatis et an possit consecrari corrupta*, MPL 170.545B–560B; before 1126. To a monk of Stavelot who made the inquiry, Rupert reluctantly says that such a nun can be professed if the violation did not have her consent.

17. *Super quaedam capitula regulae divi Benedicti abbatis libri IV*, MPL 170.477D–538B; written for Cuno after a visit to Monte Cassino. This is the most autobiographical of Rupert's writings.

18. *Altercatio monachi et clerici quod liceat monacho praedicare*, MPL 170.537C–542C.

19. *De eodem epistola ad Everardum abbatem Brunwillarensem*, MPL 170.541D–544C.

20. *De gloria et honore Filii hominis: super Matthaeum libri XIII*, MPL 168.1307A–1634C. Dedicated to Cuno in 1126 when he had just become bishop of Ratisbon, this is the most allegorical of Rupert's works.

21. *De glorioso rege David ex libris Regum*; written in 1126, but still unpublished.

22. *De glorificatione Trinitatis et processione sancti Spiritus libri IX*, MPL 169.13D–202A; written about 1127–1128 for Pope Honorius II (1124–1130).

23. *De incendio oppidi Tuitii sua aetate viso liber aureus*, MPL 170.333A–358A. Composed of exhortations to his monks con-

cerning the burning of Deutz on the night of August 28, 1128, this contains an account of the miraculous escape of the Sacred Host.

24. *De meditatione mortis libri II*, MPL 170.357B–390C; further reflections (incomplete) evoked by the burning of Deutz.

Doubtfully attributed to Rupert are a commentary on Ecclesiastes (*In librum Ecclesiastis commentarius*, MPL 168.1197A–1306D) and five books on the apostolic life (*De vita vere apostolica dialogorum libri V*, MPL 170.611A–664A).

Rupert's works show his extensive learning in the classical, Biblical, and patristic fields.[12] Although in common with most scholars, he has a penchant for the citation of authorities, he demonstrates nonetheless a high degree of independence in his thought. His *Victory of God's Word*, for instance, has some of the vast sweep of Augustine's *City of God*, but with a different and quite interesting point of view. Rupert recounts, not a tale of two cities, but a mighty warfare between the Second Person of the Trinity and the proud old serpent, a tale of incredibly powerful foes locked in an age-long struggle. The line of battle stretches from the fall of Lucifer to the final victory of the Word at the end of historical time. "All Holy Scripture," says Rupert, "is a book of the wars of the Lord. . . . For what else is contained therein but the strife of God's Word against sin and death?"[13] As the Maurists have said, "The style of writing is lofty and the religious ideas are noble and magnificent. A study of the book is, therefore, a delightful occupation. Although Rupert employs authorities, he does it in a manner that gives his work a charming novelty."[14] Our selections give only a bare intimation of the quality of the work. The few passages from his commentary on Saint John are included chiefly because they too have something to say about the Word.

The treatise *On the Victory of God's Word* was first published at Nuremberg in 1525 with annotations by the Lutheran Osiander. Negotiations were already in process for securing the other works of Rupert when the Roman Catholic Cochlaeus edited them and had them published in Cologne in 1526–1528 at the firm of Francis and Arnold Birckmann. Later editions appeared there in 1540 and 1577; at Mainz in 1602 and 1631; at Paris in 1638; and at Venice in 1748–1751. The last-mentioned, printed

[12] Manitius, *op. cit.*, assembles many of Rupert's classical citations.
[13] Rupert, *De victoria Verbi Dei*, II, 18 (MPL 169.1257 f.).
[14] Quoted in MPL 170.778D.

by Michael Pleunich, is the one incorporated in MPL. The interest which the works of Rupert have attracted is illustrated by the zeal of Wessel Gansvoort (c. 1420–1489) for them.[15] Apart from profound knowledge of and devotion to Scripture, and perhaps a trace of mystical immediacy in religion, the two men had little in common. Wessel's type of thought led directly to Luther and even more to Zwingli, while Rupert's more lasting fame lay in liturgiology and sacramentalism.

Biographical Note

The works of Rupert contain a great amount of autobiographical material, after which a primary source is Reiner von Lüttich (1157–c. 1182), *De ineptiis cujusdam idiotae* (MGH: Scriptores, 20). The fundamental studies are: Gabriel Gerberon, *Apologia pro R. D. D. Ruperto abbate Tuitiensi in qua de Eucharistiae veritate eum catholice sensisse et scripsisse demonstrat vindex* (Paris, 1669), conveniently reprinted in MPL 167. 23C–194C; and the Maurist treatment of Rupert's life and works in their *Histoire littéraire de la France*, 11 (1759), 422–587, also reprinted in MPL 170. 703B–804A. Remarkably few historians have had an interest in Rupert, chiefly some nineteenth century students with specialized concerns: N. C. Kist, "Rupertus Tuitiensis," in *Archief Kerk. Gesch. Nederl.* (1850); J. Daris, "La Vierge de Dom Rupert," in *Bull. Inst. Archéol. Liégeois* (1886); R. Rocholl, *Rupert von Deutz* (Gütersloh, 1886); and J. Müller, *Über Rupert von Deutz und dessen Vita s. Heriberti* (Cologne, 1888). The latest treatment seems to be O. Wolff, *Mein Meister Rupertus* (Freiburg i/B, 1920). Above all, of course, there is Manitius, *Geschichte der lateinischen Literatur des Mittelalters*, 3.127–135.

[15] See E. W. Miller and J. W. Scudder, *Wessel Gansfort: Life and Writings*, 2 vols. (New York, Putnam's, 1917), 1.55 f.; 2.320 f.

Rupert of Deutz: Commentary on Saint John[16] (Selections)

THE TEXT

PREFACE

The disciple "whom Jesus loved, who had lain close to his breast at the supper,"[17] in his own Gospel exhibits a true testimony that his lover is indeed the Christ, God's Son; that is, that He is not only man, born at the end of the ages, of the Virgin's womb, but also God, begotten of God the Father, before all ages. All sacred Scripture, being divinely inspired, bears witness to this truth, but the original motivation as well as the text of this book by John defends that proposition in particular and in an especially lucid manner. The original motivation was derived from the fact that, when the author was sent into exile by Domitian (the second persecutor of Christians as Nero was the first), heretics invaded the church like wolves in a sheepfold deprived of its shepherd: Marcion, Cerinthus, Ebion, and other antichrists, who denied that Christ existed before Mary and who stained the simplicity of evangelical faith with perverse teaching. For that reason, urged by almost all the bishops then in Asia, having prayed earnestly to the Lord after a fast undertaken by all of them together, and having drunk the grace of the Holy Spirit, John wrote this Gospel, which dispelled all the obscurity of the heretics with the light of truth thus suddenly exposed.

The text of the work is wholly of such sort as the requirement of lawful testimony demands. In order that there might be two witnesses, another witness no less able, John the Baptist, was associated with him. For "out of the mouth of" no fewer than

---

[16] Rupert, *In evangelium s. Joannis commentariorum libri XIV*, MPL 169.203A–826A. Our brief selections are his preface (MPL 169.203A–206C) and his remarks on John 1:1–3, 14 (MPL 169.205D–209B, 220C–223C).
[17] John 21:20.

"two witnesses shall every word stand." [18] Since John therefore was added who "came for testimony, to bear witness of the light," [19] the author often appeals for testimony to the statement of the Baptist as well as his own. Of himself he asserts at the end of the book, "This is the disciple who is bearing witness to the things, and who has written these things; and we know that his testimony is true." [20] John is therefore a matchless and unique witness of the Son of God. When he was aroused, not so much concerning the limits and laws of the Kingdom as concerning the very birth of our king, when other witnesses had grown weary or had been crushed by the violent clamor of contradictory voices, he leaped unexpectedly into the midst, in the public hearing of heaven and earth, and with the mighty thunder of his Gospel's voice and the lightning of his flashing word he terrified and put to flight the entire company of evildoers,[21] clearly affirming that Christ is the only consubstantial Son, and therefore the lawful heir of the eternal Father.

Moreover, this testimony ennobles us, all the orphans whom Christ has by eternal testament enrolled as his heirs through his own blood; it favors our hope, which was imperilled by adversaries who sought zealously to diminish it. But why? How could the testament be ratified by which he bequeathed to us a heavenly heritage, if he himself were not the lawful owner of heaven? Or how indeed was heaven his possession, if he himself did not come from heaven and if he had his origin only from Mary? This faithful witness therefore, as we have already observed, comes at the right moment to aid our hope; and while reaffirming the ancient laws of the generous testator he declares with finality that not only heaven but also everything that exists belongs to him; even more, that "all things were made through him, and without him was not anything made." [22] All we who bear witness to the Son of God also bear witness to the Scriptures, and in the way of its testimonies we have delighted as much as in all riches.[23]

We must, above all, explore this testimony and inquire with all our heart; we must covet it with all our soul and love it more than gold and topaz. For if we are merchants of the gospel and are looking for fine pearls, lo, one pearl of great value has been

---

[18] Deut. 19:15. [19] John 1:7. [20] John 21:24.
[21] Ps. 26:5 (25:5, V). The phrase "assembly of evildoers" (*ecclesia malignantium*) was applied by some of the Reformers to the Roman church, as in the First Scots Confession, where it is rendered, "the kirk malignant."
[22] John 1:3. [23] Cf. Ps. 119:14 (118:14, V).

RUPERT OF DEUTZ: COMMENTARY ON SAINT JOHN 259

found.[24] Where can be found another pearl which is of greater value? This one, God, the true lover of souls, fastened on the breast of John's beloved soul as a monument to His peculiar love for him, that he whose virginity was pre-eminent among all the saints and paralleled the virginity of Mary might with living voice disclose to mortals the Word whom the Virgin Mary alone brought forth in the flesh. As all things must therefore be so disposed of that this one pearl may be purchased, so too must all the filth of carnal affections be cleansed from the eyes of the heart by those who study the venerable writings in the school of Christ.[25] Thus only may they be able in some measure to follow that eagle[26] who delights in purity of heart; thus only may they be able with undazzled sharpness of mind to contemplate longer than other creatures the splendor of the everlasting sun, the vision of God himself.

Of him who by the path of purity attains true wisdom, the Lord speaks through Isaiah, "He will dwell on the heights; his eyrie will be the fastnesses of the rocks; bread has been given to him, and his waters are unfailing. His eyes will see the king in his comeliness; they will behold a land of far frontiers."[27] Indeed, what pertains even more clearly to the present matter has been said here as to blessed Job, with different words but with the same meaning: "At the command of the Lord the eagle soars upward and makes its nest on high places; it stays on the rocks and dwells among the steep crags and inaccessible fastnesses. Thence it spies out the prey; its eyes behold it afar off."[28] All these things John, the sublime observer of that Word and His eternal beginnings, has so eloquently pursued, soaring upward as the eagle, gazing with eyes wide open at the rays of the Godhead. On the heights he made his nest, that is, the fortress of his everlasting Gospel.[29] He dwelt among the rocks,

[24] Cf. Matt. 13:45 f. Probably arising from this parable there was an elaborate "pearl cult" in the later Middle Ages, of which the anonymous Middle English poem, "The Pearl," is the most outstanding illustration.
[25] On the *topos*, "the school of Christ," see the references in E. R. Curtius, *Europäische Literatur und lateinisches Mittelalter* (Bern: Francke, 1948), 26, 217, n. 3, and especially 370, n. 3.
[26] The eagle is a traditional art symbol of Saint John the Evangelist. Much of Rupert's comment on the eagle is folklore derived from the bestiaries. Consult T. H. White, trans. and ed., *The Book of Beasts*, translated from a Latin bestiary of the twelfth century (New York: Putnam's, 1954), 105–107.
[27] Isa. 33:16 f.   [28] Job 39:27–29.
[29] One inevitably recalls that, not long after Rupert, the Abbot Joachim of Fiore (d. 1202) wrote about the "eternal gospel." The phrase, of course,

that is, on the stability of truth. And from there he spied out his prey, that is, the glory of that eternal Word whom he alone deserved to grasp. Yet, as was said in the Isaiah passage, "They will behold a land of far frontiers," so also says the verse from Job, "Its eyes behold it afar off," for even this eagle, however sublime, does not see God in his splendor but through a mirror and as in a riddle.[30] As he says, "We are God's children, but it has not yet appeared what we shall be."[31]

Although "its young ones lick up blood,"[32] that is, his hearers are satisfied only with the attested blood of the crucified Lord, since they cannot pierce the mysteries of the Godhead, yet it is not entirely and rightly censurable that we try in some measure to discern the flight of so great an eagle. For the young ones are nourished in their nest so that they may sometime later fly out after their mother in search of food. The great teacher Augustine, like a mighty eagle, has flown through the lofty mysteries which exist in the brilliance of the gospel; we strive, it is true, to follow in the same path but not altogether in the same footsteps. He flew above the distant peaks of the mountains; we meanwhile shall occupy ourselves around the lowest foothills. He hastens to gather all the uppermost fruit of the highest tree; we shall endeavor to reach the little boughs of the letter of the gospel, the little boughs nearest the earth, which Augustine left for little children, that, since greater ones have been satisfied by a lofty explanation of the mysteries, perseverance in the letter may aid the little ones, that is, people like us.

Commentary

"In the beginning was the Word."[33] Behold, Truth, sprung up from the ground,[34] assuming flesh from the Virgin to free us from the devil, was begotten of the virginal soul of John and was clothed with his bodily voice to fight for us against all heretical perversity. He who out of His heart gave utterance to a good word[35] became in the womb of the Virgin a visible and true man although he was the invisible Word. With chaste embrace he himself by the same Word impregnated the beloved John's soul, which He had made His own, in order to go forward through his voice and writing as an audible and

---

is Biblical, Rev. 14:6. In his commentary on Revelation, Rupert, as here, identifies the "eternal gospel" and the gospel written by Saint John (MPL 169.1095A).

[30] I Cor. 13:12. [31] I John 3:2. [32] Job 39:30.
[33] John 1:1. [34] Ps. 85:11 (84:12, V). [35] Ps. 45:1 (44:2, V).

intelligible Word, although he was the unutterable Word. He therefore says, "In the beginning was the Word."

We do not worship as Lord one lately appearing, as Cerinthus, Marcion, Ebion,[36] and other antichrists feign, for what they have claimed, that Christ did not exist before Mary, is a lie. Christ, who is now and forever a man, was the Word in the beginning and before all ages. He was not then all that he now is, namely, flesh and the Word; He was the Word only. Now he is a giant of dual substance and of double will, although one person; in the beginning, however, he was the Word of one substance and of one will. So Christ was before Mary since "in the beginning was the Word."

The Word must not be treated here in an academic fashion, that is, according to its etymology alone. When we were schoolboys studying Donatus [the ancient grammarian], we were taught that a "word" was anything formed by beating the air with the tongue. A "word" of that sort passes through the air in speech. But the Word, who was in the beginning before the very air and before all things that were made, "remains forever."[37] For truly that Word is eternal reason, is everlasting wisdom, is inexpressible understanding, is unalterable truth. Furthermore, since the noun "word" is employed among us equally for an articulate expression and for the unspoken thought of the mind, why may not that eternal reason be quite rightly called the Word, from whom we have our rationality, namely, the general capacity which serves us in forming words. "Therefore do not be children in your thinking," says the apostle.[38] Even if the Word is not of the air, that is, shaped by the beating of the air; even if the Word, to be sure, is not framed as our words are, the Word is nonetheless substantial, is the very Christ who was the Word in the beginning.

But where was this Word? What was his locality? No man knows his worth, as was intimated by blessed Job,[39] but by revelation of the Spirit He is gradually perceived through these statements which follow, first of all through that which is presented as though it were his locality or where he then was in the beginning: "And the Word was with God."[40] Behold, the former words are God's arrows by the light of which we go; this latter statement is his glittering spear by the flash of which we walk, as was foretold by the prophet: "At the light of thine arrows they will go, at the flash of thy glittering spear."[41]

[36] Well-known heresiarchs. [37] Isa. 40:8. [38] I Cor. 14:20.
[39] Cf. Job, ch. 38. [40] John 1:1. [41] Hab. 3:11.

The arrow of the earlier phrase which John hurled first transfixed all those heretics who, with differing blasphemies but with an equal spirit of malice, denied that Christ existed before Mary. With the second affirmation, however, he felled the Patripassians who, denying the Trinity, claim that Father, Son, and Holy Spirit are only one person, not three. But John clearly states, "And the Word was with God," so that you may not doubt concerning the persons when you hear that one is or was with the other. He also suggests the noble divinity of that Word by saying, "He was with God," for what does that sentence mean if not that he was held in grand honor, in highest merit, in great love? "He was with God," but not as gold is with a rich man. With a rich man gold is in his chest, not in his very substance, which may be pitiable and defective, even leprous. But He was with God as wisdom is with a wise man, as might is with a mighty man, as it is observed in blessed Job, "With him are wisdom and might." [42] The rich man's gold is in his pouch, but God's Word is in his heart.

The Word therefore was truly with God. But, as John has already distinguished the persons by saying, "And the Word was with God," so now he connects the substance by saying, "And the Word was God." [43] In those few words he has borne witness to one substance in the two persons of God and His Word. That article of faith the Sabellians endure reluctantly, the Arians receive with difficulty. The Sabellians wish that he had said that there was only one substance of God and his Word, so that there is only one and the same person. The Arians wish that, as he expressed the two persons, so he had no less expressed two differing substances. For they say that the Father alone is God and Creator, but that the Son is a creature, albeit mighty and surpassing. The truth of the present testimony, however, like the voice of a booming thunderclap, reverberates throughout the ends of the earth; that is, it bewilders equally the seared conscience of all parts.[44] So the Homoousians rejoice, confessors of consubstantiality, neither confusing the persons nor dividing the substance, acknowledging with the suffrage of this great witness two persons but one substance of the Father and the Word. For, as John says, "the Word was God."

Thereafter one sentence very beautifully embraces everything that John has expressed in the three propositions already cited: he says, "He was in the beginning with God." [45] How

---

[42] Job 12:13. [43] John 1:1. [44] Cf. I Tim. 4:2. [45] John 1:2.

does this improve upon the fact that "the Word was with God"? Why did the Evangelist not prefer to say, "The Word was in God," but rather reiterates, "He was with God"? This little distinction suggests that he intended some greater matter. For if we wish to signify that some particular matter is of importance, there is a certain propriety in saying that one person is with another. What agreement therefore exists between the two persons? What is the love mediating between them? The question is answered by the next statement, "All things were made through him."[46] That was clearly accomplished because of the love of each for the other, that love which is the Holy Spirit. If you ask, "Who has made all things?" the reply is, "God." If you ask, "How?" lo, you have the answer, "Through him," that is, the Word. If you inquire, "Why?" the response is, "Because he is good." And that is the full Trinity: "All things were made through him."

Worthy of what great praise, of what great adoration is that Word through whom all things were made! Favorable observers lift the eyes of both heart and body to the beauty of the things which have been made, whether visible or invisible.[47] Contemplating carefully, they exult together with heart and voice, "Mighty and beautiful is the talent of God's artist, who is none other than the Word, through whom such mighty and beautiful things were made, for all things were indeed made through him!" Another Scripture testifies, "He spoke and they were made; he commanded and they were created,"[48] namely, those things which summon one to praise the Creator: all his angels, all his hosts, sun and moon, stars and light, highest heavens and all things in them, sea and the things that are therein.[49] Or, as still another Scripture is witness, he said, "Let there be light," and there was light.[50] He said, "Let there be a firmament," and it came into being.[51] Of each of the other things, He said, "Let it be made," and they were made. They were made through the Word, for they were made by speaking, but not by speaking with elemental sound or corporeal voice (for God is a Spirit[52]), but by that kind of speaking with which your soul, O man, which he made in his own image, frames noiseless language whenever it will. . . .

"And the Word became flesh."[53] That Cerinthus and other antichrists may hear what the conjunction "and" signifies, one

[46] John 1:3.
[47] Cf. Rom. 1:19 f.; Wisdom, chs. 12 to 14.
[48] Ps. 33:9 (32:9, V).
[49] Ps. 148:2–4.
[50] Cf. Gen. 1:3.
[51] Cf. Gen. 1:6 f.
[52] Cf. John 4:24.
[53] John 1:14.

should paraphrase thus: "Above I stated, 'In the beginning was the Word, and the Word was with God, and the Word was God.... All things were made through him.' Returning now to that theme, after the interpolation of other testimony, I add, 'And the Word became flesh.'" Let orphans and posthumous children hear about the noble antiquity of their Father. Let them hear and know that through Christ "all things were made," and that through him, who was said to be so much younger than the beginning of the world, the world itself was made, although by heretics and Jews who envy the noble birth of the children he is said not to have existed before Mary. When we hear, "The Word became flesh," we must not consider it the same as if it were said, "The Word changed into flesh." That interpretation is heretical; that explanation is alien to the faith. The Word was not changed into flesh, but by assuming flesh he condescended to fleshly things. Hence, the Word which was with God became flesh just as when you speak you can correctly say, "The word which was in my soul has become vocal."

As when your voice issues from your mouth into the air outside, your "word" still remains in your heart although it has by the sense of hearing entered also into the mind of another person, just so too when the visible flesh of the Word comes forth into public view, the entire Word himself still remains in the Father's heart, although the whole is by the same flesh no less transmitted to us. So the same Word is completely in the Father and completely in the flesh, "reaching from one end to another," [54] from the heart of the Father (beyond and above whom there is nothing), "like a conduit from the overflowing water of a river," [55] across all the orders of angels [56] and down to our flesh, beyond and below which, rotting in the grave because of sin, there is nothing meaner.

We must also not neglect the fact that along with the name and substance of flesh we ought here also to understand the rational soul. The Word of God did not assume flesh with the

---

[54] This phrase from Wisdom 8:1 appears also in the Great Advent antiphon, "O Sapientia," on which see Allen Cabaniss, "A Note on the Date of the Great Advent Antiphons" (*Speculum*, 23 [1947], 440–442).
[55] Ecclesiasticus 24:30 (24:41, V).
[56] The conception of a ninefold order of seraphim, cherubim, thrones, dominions, principalities, powers, virtues, archangels, and angels, popularized by pseudo-Dionysius, was conveyed to the Middle Ages by Eriugena's translation of *The Celestial Hierarchy*. It is, of course, a Biblical idea; cf. Rom. 8:38; Eph. 1:21, 3:10, 6:12; Col. 1:16, 2:10, 15; etc.

soul as the Apollinarian heretics suppose. "For he came indeed to save what was lost," [57] and the whole man was lost, the entire man, both in body and in soul. In his body man was moribund, in his soul already dead, and in both eternally damned. Therefore, to save the whole man, the Word became a complete man of flesh and rational soul. If God the Word took flesh only and not the soul, where did he plant his foundation? Only the rational spirit is spacious enough for that. Although that remark is somewhat rhetorical, it is nonetheless wise. Only as individual men are acquainted with it do they see with the mind, do they perceive with the soul. So much the more therefore did the Word, when he assumed flesh, omit nothing as a special exception to himself, that is, he did not omit the rational soul. Far be such a supposition from the heart and mouth of those who hope in the incarnate Word! For it is especially in the soul that the Scripture is fulfilled by God the Father when he gave utterance to the good Word, "My tongue is the pen of a ready scribe." [58] The true and perfect nature of the Word is clothed with the true and integral nature of man, joined in unity of person without confusion of either substance.

Thus was brought to pass that excellent alloy, that priceless ornament of the human race, in which the gold of divinity has lost none of its refulgence, while the silver of humanity has gained increase of its luster. For that reason was it said, "The Word became flesh." It is as if John had said, "God became man in the manner in which man is customarily described in the Scriptures." Scripture constantly employs the word "flesh" when the whole man is intended, as, "All flesh shall see the salvation of God." [59] On the other hand, the whole man is also signified by the word "soul," as, "Jacob went down into Egypt with seventy-five souls." [60] God therefore became man.

"And dwelt among us." [61] Through all things, from his own invisible ones to our visible ones, he made his way to us. In the reality of our flesh, in all the laws of human nature, he dwelt among us. With a single exception—his mother gave birth to a man not conceived by the seed of man in accordance with the custom of all flesh; she was not defiled by the birth, but, a virgin before bringing forth, she remained a virgin even after bringing forth [62]—with this single exception the true nature of

---

[57] Luke 19:10.   [58] Ps. 45:1 (44:2, V).   [59] Luke 3:6; cf. Isa. 40:5.
[60] A conflation of Acts 7:15 and v. 14.   [61] John 1:14.
[62] Although from Biblical times to the present there have been serious attacks from several angles on the virginity of Christ's mother, the

man ran its entire course. But should a Jew or an accursed Manichee say, "If a virgin gave birth, it was to a wraith," then they should consider the first parents of mankind, Adam and Eve, to have been phantom beings, not real ones, since they had no carnal parents. It is much farther from nature as we know it for a human being to be formed out of the earth than to be conceived of a woman only. It is more marvelous for a man to be created of inanimate and insensate matter than to be begotten without male activity. The former is more miraculous, but the latter is more worshipful; the former is an act of God's might, while the latter is a work equally of his might and his grace. Certain ones, of course, are utterly averse to the belief that the most holy God could endure to be enclosed in a woman's womb. But do they know, I ask, the quality of their aversion? On one hand, there is an aversion which shrinks from reason; on the other, from perception. For example, on the basis of reason we tremble at vice in contrast to virtue (even though according to perception we still enjoy vice more than virtue). On the basis of perception, however, we shrink from touching a snake more than from touching a stone, although according to reason we undoubtedly value more highly the living, sensate body of a snake than the inanimate body of a stone. How, then, are they averse to a woman's womb: on the basis of perception or on the basis of reason? Surely it is perception, not reason, for reason cannot shrink from any substance or nature, indeed from anything that God has made.

God or his Word, since he is reason itself, is not influenced by any of our feelings and does not avoid or hate any creature or any nature which certainly he made and not another; he avoids and hates only the corruption of nature. It is therefore even more appropriate faithfully and devoutly to believe that he did not abhor the inviolate womb of the Virgin.[63] Thus God the Word dwelt among us and sojourned for nine months without taint of sin in the privacy of female nature from which no one of us has emerged without sin. From that place "like a bridegroom leaving his chamber and setting his tent in the

doctrine here stated by Rupert, the perpetual virginity of Saint Mary continues to be upheld. Even many of the sixteenth century Reformers adhered to it. For example, one of the most authoritative and most widely adopted Reformed statements of faith in that era, the Second Helvetic Confession, expressly acknowledges "Mary ever Virgin"; see Allen Cabaniss, "Some Neglected Features in the Early Reformed Confessions" (*Union Seminary Review*, 54 [1943] 291–321).

[63] Here is apparently a reminiscence of the hymn *Te Deum*.

sun,"⁶⁴ He dwelt among us, enveloped in tender flesh as a child and uttering the cries of infancy, made under the law, subordinate to Joseph and Mary, circumcised and purified with sacrifice according to the law like any sinner, enduring hunger and undergoing the artifices of the tempter, suffering also persecution at the hands of men, saddened unto death, fleeing from place to place, and at the very last made obedient even to death.

To what end did this humiliation and weakness at length arrive? John answers, "And we beheld his glory, glory as of the only-begotten from the Father."⁶⁵ He says: "We beheld his glory, and since we have seen it we can bear positive witness to it. We really began to see it by virtue of that sign whereby he changed water into wine when he was invited to a wedding. That was the beginning of signs in the presence of his disciples when he manifested his glory.⁶⁶ Thereafter we saw him opening blind eyes, putting leprosy to flight by his touch, expelling fevers, raising the decomposing dead, loosing the dumb tongue and deaf ear, walking on the waters, calming the winds, stanching the flow of blood, and filling many thousands with a few loaves. We saw also the glory of his transfigured face which should be revealed only to the choirs of angels. At his last but greatest and most glorious moment we saw him rising from the dead. We saw in his hands and feet the scars of the nails; we saw, I say, we stared at, we felt, our very hands touched his side where it was pierced by the lance. We ate and drank with him, and we saw him as he ascended in glory to heaven. We received the Holy Spirit, the Paraclete promised by him. This glory we have seen, glory as of the only-begotten from the Father, that is, so great a glory as no other of all the sons of God is deemed worthy to receive. For all of God's other sons are adoptive children. This one, however, was begotten or rather only-begotten. All the others are sons by grace. This one alone is Son by nature. Rightfully therefore this one, 'fairest in form of the sons of men,' ⁶⁷ has the glory which we have seen, a glory differing from that of all the other sons."

Finally, let us hear the ultimate conclusion of this Gospel prologue. How glorious was the Word which you saw, O John? "Full of grace and truth," he replies.⁶⁸ O noble proclamation, O noble and faithful witness! Are you seeking what kind of

---

⁶⁴ Ps. 19:4 f. (18:6, V), inverted.   ⁶⁵ John 1:14.
⁶⁶ Cf. John 2:1–11.   ⁶⁷ Ps. 45:2 (44:3, V).
⁶⁸ John 1:14.

glory belonged to the only-begotten? It was gold, pure gold, a price worthy of our captivity. That man, rich and noble, came forth from the treasury of the Most High; his body, insignificant though it was, was a chest of precious gold. Lay hold of him, therefore, as he is cut off by the blow of death and seize the talent of grace and truth which is therein.

Rupert of Deutz: On the Victory of God's Word [69] (Selections)

THE TEXT

XII, 9. When the charge was made before Pilate concerning use of the royal title as though it were a great crime, our king, gracious and humble of heart, absolved himself with these words: "My kingship is not of this world; if my kingship were of this world, my servants would surely fight, that I might not be handed over to the Jews; but my kingship is not from here."[70] With the same gracious lips he could have said: "If my kingship were of this world, a horse or chariot would have been brought for me, not the ass upon which I sat three days ago. Those who acclaimed me as king would have displayed accouterments of warlike weapons, not branches of olive trees. And if they should not suffice, I would have asked my Father and he would have offered just now more than twelve legions of angels." He could have said also, "After the distribution of the five loaves among five thousand men, when I became alarmed that they might seize me because of the miracle and force me to be king over them, I would not have fled from them, if it were not true that my kingship is not of this world." In reply to Pilate he could have declared these things, I say, and many others like them as arguments for his innocence who wished no harm to Caesar. He could have done so if Pilate had not been deaf and if it had not been foretold of him, "Do not pour out your words where there is no hearing."[71] He reserved these things to be understood by us, and it is our duty to rebuke his adversaries even though they are dead, because he did not destroy human kingdoms, because he gives heavenly kingdoms,

---

[69] Our selections from Rupert's treatise *De victoria Verbi Dei* are from book XII, chs. 9-17, 27-29 (MPL 169.1470B-1477B, 1484D-1486D).
[70] John 18:36.   [71] Ecclesiasticus 32:4 (32:6, V).

and because their own craftiness deceived them who wished to be deceived, and wickedness lied to them when they said, "We found this man forbidding tribute to be given to Caesar."⁷² He did not make himself such a king, nor did he so gainsay Caesar. Quite the contrary, he says, "Render to Caesar the things that are Caesar's, and to God the things that are God's."⁷³

10. What more shall we say? It was necessary for him to die, and the dragon so often mentioned was standing there, was dwelling there, was waiting there for him to die, because he thought that he was His doom.⁷⁴ He thought, I say, that through death he could devour Him, could annihilate the counsel and purpose of God, so that what had been foretold might not come to pass ("He shall be the long-awaited hope of the Gentiles,"⁷⁵ and, "In him shall all nations be blessed"⁷⁶), which, however, he already fears, since Christ says to the Jews, "You will seek me and you will not find me; and where I am you cannot come."⁷⁷ (He was speaking in answer to the question they were whispering to each other, "Where does this man intend to go that we shall not find him? Does he intend to go to the dispersion among the nations and teach the nations?"⁷⁸) The psalmist sang the truth: "That dragon which thou didst form to sport in it,"⁷⁹ and the Lord himself spoke of it to blessed Job: "Will you play with him as with a bird?"⁸⁰ Again: "Behold, his hope will disappoint him."⁸¹ Truly he was played with or mocked, his hope did disappoint him, since in dying Christ was devoured in vain; rather, when he was devoured, it came to pass by that death, and except through that death it could not have come to pass, for him to go to the dispersion of the nations and teach them.

Let us examine the sacraments, through which according to the promise all nations have been and shall be blessed in

---

[72] Luke 23:2.   [73] Matt. 22:21.
[74] Here and below the implicit reference is to Rev., ch. 12, the account of the apocalyptic woman giving birth while a dragon lies in wait to destroy her offspring. Rupert does not here or at the appropriate place in his commentary on Revelation (MPL 169.1039B–1064B) make a positive identification of the woman as the blessed Virgin. On this subject, consult the brilliant treatment by B. J. LeFrois, *The Woman Clothed with the Sun* (Rome, Orbis Catholicus, 1954); see also Allen Cabaniss, *Our Lady of the Apocalypse*, Oxford Essays, No. 1 (Oxford, Miss., 1954), which appeared shortly before LeFrois' book.
[75] Gen. 49:10 (Vulgate reading).   [76] Gen. 22:18.
[77] John 7:34.   [78] John 7:35.   [79] Ps. 104:26 (103:26, V).
[80] Job 41:5 (40:24, V).   [81] Job 41:9 (40:28, V).

him. Against that dragon we shall marvel at the magnitude of the mockery for the praise of God who formed him to jeer at Him, for when the dragon wishes to oppose, he is enslaved by God's purpose, and when he thinks that he will devour so great a Son of the blessed woman, he fulfills a very effective compliance with His plan.

11. What and how many are the chief sacraments of our salvation? Holy Baptism, the holy Eucharist of His body and blood, and the twofold gift of the Holy Spirit, one for the remission of sins, the other for the bestowal of differing and multiple graces.[82] These *three* sacraments are the necessary means of our salvation;[83] yet these were not to be found or were not found except through his death and resurrection. First, concerning the sacrament of Baptism we believe and know that it flowed from his death when he was presumed to have been devoured, that is, when he was already dead. For, says the Evangelist, "when they came to Jesus and saw that he was already dead, they did not break his legs. But one of the soldiers pierced his side with a spear, and at once there came out blood and water."[84] Redeemed by that blood, we, Jews as well as Gentiles, are washed by that water, the Jews first, then the Gentiles—or rather, the dead first, then the living. For all believers who had died since the beginning of the world and who among the dead were awaiting the blessed hope were the first to receive the fruit of this salvation. They were like catechumens who had not yet participated at the heavenly altar (that is, in the vision of the Godhead), because the wall of hostility had not yet been removed. "And so," they say, "we too were once by nature children of wrath, like the others,"[85] and, "All our righteous deeds are like a polluted garment."[86] Then, however, washed and made clean by that torrent, they entered God's sanctuary, God's Kingdom, which is entirely holy. Since the whole church of all past ages together was baptized at that time, this sacrament has been appointed as though at the door of the same church, so that whoever thereafter wishes to be incorporated in the church may be baptized on his own behalf, since the church was at once completely baptized in Christ's death. For the sacrament of Christ's death

---

[82] The "twofold gift of the Holy Spirit" (on which see ch. 13 below), here considered as one sacrament, is in reality two, penance and ordination.
[83] Four centuries later Luther similarly considered the sacraments as three: Baptism, Eucharist, and penance.
[84] John 19:33 f.   [85] Eph. 2:3.   [86] Isa. 64:6.

is present and effectual when water has been used and the word of the cross spoken, together with invocation of the Holy Spirit. Wherefore the apostle says, "All of us who have been baptized in Christ Jesus were baptized in his death," etc.[87]

There was a long-lasting dispute of the holy Roman church against the practice of the Greeks who wish to require the solemn celebration of the sacrament of Baptism to take place on the feast of Epiphany on the ground that the Lord himself was baptized by John in the waters of the Jordan on that day. The Roman church, through Leo the Great who wrote against that, demonstrates with reason that the baptism of John did not relate to the same virtue, that it was not for remission of sins but for repentance; that the baptism instituted by Christ took its origin in His death, when (as we have already observed) his side was pierced by the lance and when blood and water came forth. This sacrament, therefore, should be celebrated on the anniversary of His death and resurrection.[88]

12. Concerning the sacrament of the Lord's body and blood, it is certain—our statement is really unnecessary—that it is indeed the special and unique commemoration of his suffering and death, and that it had and properly should have had its origin in his suffering and death. This sacrament, indeed, was established as near his death as possible, when he had already been given up to death, on the night on which he was betrayed. For us who now live and still remain, that sacrament has been preserved and transmitted wherein the advantage of his death and resurrection lies hidden under the species of bread and wine. But for those believers who have died, the food has been prepared and bestowed in a marvelous way in that very species wherein he hung on the cross, even as his soul went down to their souls in Hades and his body to their bodies, and was for three days and three nights in the heart of the earth, in the same womb of earth where their bodies had been admitted and received.

[87] Rom. 6:3.
[88] See the service of Holy Saturday in *Missale Romanum* and (in abbreviated form) in G. L. Diekmann, ed., *The Easter Vigil Arranged for Use in Parishes* (Collegeville, Minn.: The Liturgical Press, 1953). Allen Cabaniss, "*Beowulf* and the Liturgy" (*Journal of English and Germanic Philology*, 54 [1955], 195–201), suggests that the ceremonies of baptism may underlie a portion of the Anglo-Saxon epic. Rupert's reference to Greek practice recalls his amusing (to us) statement in *De divinis officiis*, II, 22 (MPL 170.48D): "The arrogance of the see of Constantinople is the mother of many heresies."

Of this very great mystery we do not now propose to treat any longer, yet that it may not be left entirely untouched it is appropriate to say something about the reason why it is necessary to us. This was the reason: The first humans were unfaithful to God and, far more wickedly, were believers in the devil. When they did not see anything except the apple, so pleasantly sweet, fragrant, and beautiful, they believed that from it they would secure the quality of divinity; they believed the devil when he said, "It will not indeed be as God said, 'If you shall eat, you shall die the death.' But it will be as I say, 'If you shall eat, you shall be as gods.'" [89] Over against that food, the food of death, as reason insists, it was necessary for righteousness that another food be provided, the food of life. In like manner it was necessary so that the mind might believe to be present what the eye could not see, might believe it to be truly the food and drink of participation in divinity, might believe it to be effectually the flesh and blood of Christ, although they cannot perceive the appearance of flesh and blood. By this faith, God deems that he has been satisfied by man when he believes in him not less than he formerly believed in the devil.

13. Who does not know that all we who believe receive or have received, through the death of Christ and his blood, the gift of the Holy Spirit, first for the remission of sins? For that reason, on the day when he arose from the dead, late on that same day, he, standing in the midst of his disciples, "breathed on them, and said, 'Receive the Holy Spirit.'" [90] Then he added immediately, "Whose sins you remit, they are remitted to them." [91] Later, on the fiftieth day, they received the second gift of the Holy Spirit for the distribution of graces, which the apostle recalled when he wrote to the Corinthians, "To one is given through the Spirit the utterance of wisdom, to another the utterance of knowledge," etc.[92] The gifts are the kind of which it is written, "When he ascended on high he led captivity captive, he gave gifts to men." [93] Of them the better ones are these: "He appointed some to be apostles, some prophets, some evangelists, some pastors and teachers." [94]

---

[89] Paraphrased from Gen. 3:3 f. [90] John 20:22.
[91] John 20:23. This would be Rupert's "sacrament 3a," that is, penance.
[92] I Cor. 12:8.
[93] Eph. 4:8; cf. Ps. 68:18 (67:19, V). This and the preceding reference in note 92 would be the basis for Rupert's "sacrament 3b," namely, holy orders.
[94] Eph. 4:11.

These are the consolations of the Paraclete, of which He told them when he was about to go away: "Because I have said these things to you, sorrow has filled your heart. Nevertheless I tell you the truth: it is to your advantage that I go away, for if I shall not go away, the Paraclete will not come to you; but if I shall go away, I will send him to you." [95] The phrase, "If I shall go away," is of course rightly understood as though he might have said, "If I shall ascend into heaven," or, "If I shall remove my bodily presence from you." Although they did not have to be sad about his ascension—quite the contrary, they rejoiced with great delight, as Luke recalled when he wrote, "Worshiping him they returned to Jerusalem with great joy," [96] yet they were very sorrowful about his suffering. For "because I have said these things to you," he states, "sorrow has filled your heart." [97] It is therefore more accurately understood that he spoke of his suffering and death when he spoke of going away, for so the Evangelist sought to make clear when he remarked: "Before the festal day of the Passover, when Jesus knew that his hour had come to depart out of this world to the Father. . . ." [98] For did he not then first depart from this world rather than when dead and risen again he ceased to walk with men and endure earthly labors?

14. These three things had to be, and because of these his death was necessary for the nations, since these are the blessings by which all nations are to be blessed in that seed which is Christ. This the great dragon did not know who thought that through death he could devour that Son, that man. He did not know, I say—that is, they over whom he presided did not know—of whom Wisdom speaks, "These things they imagined, yet erred; their own iniquity blinded them, and they knew not the mysteries of God." [99] The apostle says, "Had they understood this (that is, the wisdom which is from God, which we impart among the mature[1]), they would never have crucified the Lord of glory." [2] It is absolutely true that if leviathan, the great whale which is in the sea, had known that under the flesh an iron hook was hidden, he would never have bitten that flesh with which the iron is concealed.[3] He knew that Jesus was

---

[95] John 16:6 f.   [96] Luke 24:52.   [97] John 16:6.
[98] John 13:1.   [99] Wisdom 2:21 f.   [1] I Cor. 2:6.
[2] I Cor. 2:8. The significance of this verse is considered, *inter alia*, by Allen Cabaniss, "The Harrowing of Hell, Psalm 24, and Pliny the Younger: A Note" (*Vigiliae Christianae*, 7 [1953], 65–74).
[3] A crude statement reflecting an early doctrine of atonement enunciated, for instance, by Gregory the Great.

indeed the Christ, the Son of God, and that he had come to save the human race, but he did not know the secret hidden from the world, the plan of God's wisdom, that by the death of one the life of all should be renewed. Christ knew his own plan, but it was hidden from all the ages and indeed so inconceivable to the minds of men that the very apostles comprehended none of these things, although he discussed them privately with them (as the holy Gospels declare in a great many places), since it was not yet time for them to understand before he was glorified in the splendor of the resurrection.[4]

15. Who, then, does understand? Who feels with deepest love what disposition was in the mind of that Son of Man when the woman so often mentioned gave birth to him, while the dragon waited so long to devour him (that is, while evil men waited to destroy his body), to blot out his name? If you can count rightly, he [the dragon] waited seven times with mouth yawning wide, he opened his savage jaws seven times. Disappointed six times, at length the seventh he seized His flesh in his jaw, but to his own hurt, for as we have said above he felt the very offensive iron in that flesh. The *first* attempt of the dragon was when, according to Matthew, cruel Herod sought the life of the new-born babe and because of him slew the infants, as already mentioned above.[5] The *second* was when, according to Luke, he came to Nazareth, where he had grown up, and taught in the synagogue: "They rose up and put him out of the city; they led him to the brow of the hill on which their city was built, that they might hurl him down headlong, but passing through the midst of them he went away."[6]

The *third* was when, according to John, he fled from the presence of the Jews who mocked his statement, "Unless you shall eat the flesh of the Son of man and drink his blood, you will not have everlasting life."[7] For truly, by saying those things, he did flee and hide himself from them, according to the title of the Thirty-third [8] Psalm, which reads thus: "A Psalm of David, when he changed his appearance before Abimelech, who sent him away, and he departed and drummed on the doors of the city gate and spittle ran down on his beard and he was borne away in his own hands."[9] Abimelech is the one who

---

[4] Cf. Luke 18:34.
[5] Matt. 2:16; cf. Rev., ch. 12.
[6] Luke 4:29 f.
[7] Cf. John 6:53.
[8] Ps. 33 in the Vulgate; 34 in R.S.V.
[9] A very curious jumble. The words, "A Psalm of David, when he changed his appearance before Abimelech, who sent him away, and he departed,"

was earlier called Achish. Abimelech means "My Father's kingdom"; but Achish, "How is it?" What "Abimelech" therefore means signifies the Jews, whom Christ at first rightly called his Father's Kingdom. But now they are called "Achish," because they said, "How can this be?"[10]

Wherein did He change his appearance before them? It was herein: he changed the rite of the old sacrifice into a new one. Herein also the spittle ran down his beard: when he said, "Unless you shall eat the flesh of the Son of man and drink his blood," etc., he seemed to them to be babbling childish words, and it is the habit of babies to drool. He drummed on the city gate when he preached the mystery of his Passion to a people reluctant and unwilling to listen to him, because he knew that the time would come when some would believe and open the gate. He was borne away in his own hands when, holding in his hands bread and wine, he said, "Take and eat; this is my body.... This is my blood of the new covenant," etc.[11] According to "Hebrew truth," however, we read, "And he fell in a swoon in their hands."[12]

The *fourth* persecution was when the chief Pharisees sent their servants to seize him. When the servants returned and were asked, "Why did you not bring him?" they replied, "Never did a man speak as this man speaks."[13] Persisting in their effort to accuse him, they then brought forward a woman taken in adultery.[14] The *fifth* persecution was when he said, "Truly, truly, I say to you, before Abraham was, I am," and they took up stones to stone him.[15] The *sixth* was when he said, "I and the Father are one," and again they took up stones to

---

are indeed the title of Ps. 34 (33, V), except that for "Abimelech" the Vulgate actually reads "Achimelech" (or, "Ahimelech") in agreement with the reference in I Sam., ch. 21 (I Kings, ch. 21, V). The R.S.V. and the new Latin version of the Pontifical Biblical Institute (1945) have "Abimelech." The words, "And drummed on the doors of the city gate and spittle ran down on his beard," are from I Sam. 21:13 (I Kings 21:13, V); while the passage, "And he was borne away in his own hands" (the first part of the verse just mentioned), reads in the Vulgate, "And he fell in a swoon in their hands" (see a few lines below in the text and also note 12).

[10] John 6:52.   [11] Matt. 26:26, 28.
[12] I Sam. 21:13 (I Kings 21:13, V). The words "Hebrew truth" refer to the Vulgate version of Scripture; see Beryl Smalley, *The Study of the Bible in the Middle Ages*, 2d ed. (New York: Philosophical Library, 1952), 329–355.
[13] Cf. John 7:32, 45 f.
[14] John 8:1–11 (relegated to a footnote in R.S.V.).
[15] John 8:58 f.

stone him.¹⁶ The *seventh* and last was when they gathered the council against him and did not leave off until they had crucified him.¹⁷

16. Who, I ask, understands his mild and humble spirit in such prolonged struggle with death? The psalmist says, "Blessed is the man who takes thought for the poor and destitute,"¹⁸ whom (according to another psalm) the dragon pursued to death in Judah, in the Jewish people, as "a poor, needy, brokenhearted man."¹⁹ We are almost unteachable or at least slow to learn from Him who says, "Learn from me; for I am gentle and lowly in heart."²⁰ We understand far less than we ought about him, poor, gentle, humble, grieving for us, wounded for us. "Look how the righteous man dies," says the prophet, "but no one lays it to heart."²¹ He also states in the psalm, "I patiently nourished one to be sorrowful with me, but there was no one."²²

But did not blessed Mary take it to heart, was she not at the same time afflicted, when she stood beside his cross watching him die? Yes, she took it deeply to heart, she was grievously afflicted, and (as Simeon had foretold) a sword pierced her soul.²³ With sensitive perception and sorrow the beloved disciple also watched him dying. Although the other disciples had abandoned him and fled, they too grieved with him and sorrow filled their heart. The statements, "No one lays it to heart," and, "There was no one to be sorrowful with me," were made, not according to judgment based on reason, but according to abundance of grief, which sometimes does not allow reason. Quite properly you notice that they were expressed when those who sorrowed with him were so exceedingly few in quantity and number compared with the great crowd of those who jeered and mocked. Yet, when he says elsewhere, "I looked about, but there was no helper; I sought, but there was no one to give aid; so my own arm saved me, and my wrath helped me,"²⁴ that is not a similar complaint; it is simply the affirmation of a fact that absolutely no one, even had one wished to do so, could come to his aid and help him in the battle or encounter when the prince of the world, the ancient sinner, the lord of death, came against him. For there was no

¹⁶ John 10:30 f. ¹⁷ John 11:47, 53. ¹⁸ Ps. 41:1 (40:1, V).
¹⁹ Ps. 109:16 (108:17, V). ²⁰ Matt. 11:29. ²¹ Isa. 57:1.
²² Ps. 69:20 (68:21, V).
²³ Cf. Luke 2:35 and the later hymn "Stabat Mater."
²⁴ Isa. 63:5.

one else who could say of the evil one, "He has no power over me."[25] Nor was there anyone but him in whom there was the arm and wrath (that is, the zeal and courage) of divine nature coupled with human innocence.

17. What then? By looking for a helper was he seeking not to die, he who had come for that very purpose? As he was both God and man, so also he had two wills, one of divinity, the other of humanity, in that very moment of his Passion. Humanity, of course, was naturally frightened at the taste of death and recoiled from it; the soul was possessed by natural love of the body and wished to continue in the flesh. Divinity nonetheless, by a reasonable decision, intended something else, namely, that which was necessary for the salvation of the human race; and humanity preferred the will of that nature to its own will, as in its prayer, "My Father, if it is possible, let this cup pass away from me," yet it added immediately, "nevertheless, not as I will, but as thou wilt."[26] Or: "Nevertheless not my will, but thine, be done."[27] It was therefore according to the decision of divinity that he looked about searching for someone to help him, but it was according to the natural sense of the flesh that he wished this very thing which holy men choose when with the apostle they say, "Not that we would be unclothed, but that we would be further clothed, that what is mortal may be swallowed up by life."[28]

Why did he not only look about and, looking about, seek someone to aid him, but also cry with a loud voice, "Eli, Eli, lama sabachthani?" that is, "My God, my God, why hast thou forsaken me?"[29] We interpret that cry most accurately as if he had said: "O entire fullness of divinity dwelling in me,[30] why do you keep yourself deeply hidden, why are you silent when I am dying? Only a short time ago, when they came to arrest me, you did for a moment utter one statement, 'I am the one whom you seek,' and immediately they drew back and fell to the ground.[31] Lately you also terrified a huge multitude by a flashing from those eyes which now grow dim in death, and what an enormous army could not do, you have done with a whip made of cords, cleansing the Temple, reminding them of that word of the prophet, 'My house shall be called a house of prayer; but you have made it a den of robbers.'[32] Why, then, O most mighty, most powerful divinity of the Word, why have

[25] John 14:30.
[26] Matt. 26:39.
[27] Luke 22:42.
[28] II Cor. 5:4.
[29] Matt. 27:46.
[30] Cf. Col. 2:9.
[31] Cf. John 18:6.
[32] Matt. 21:13; cf. Jer. 7:11.

you forsaken me, your own flesh, hiding yourself within as a sword which is unwilling to leave its scabbard?"[33]

[18–26 omitted.]

27. The hour has come of which he had spoken in a certain passage to the Jews, "The hour has come for the Son of man to be manifested."[34] That hour, I say, has come with the proclamation of a word from the mouth of the Father, speaking thus by the voice of David: "Awake, O my glory! Awake, O psaltery and lute!"[35] What was that psaltery and what was that lute? The very body resting in the grave was both psaltery and lute. It was the lute which the Jews broke in pieces while it was playing the sweet notes of preaching, sounding them forth on the taut string of charity. But the shattering of that lute became for it an occasion of growth, an occasion of greatest advance, for it permitted the ten-stringed psaltery, the sweet-sounding psaltery, to rise up, never to be broken, destined forever to give voice to praise among the peoples, to psalmody among the nations, whose strings no hand may hereafter snap, whose wooden frame no violence may henceforth be strong enough to crush. For, as the apostle says, "Christ rising from the dead dies no more; death no longer has dominion over him."[36] This is the glory of God the Father that in his own work he boasts a great abundance of charity. "Awake, therefore, O my glory!" he exclaims. "Awake, O psaltery and lute!" Does not that soul hear this utterance of the Father, does it not discern this endeavor of the Word, is it not joined to the same Word as bride to bridegroom with an unending kiss, bound with an unrelaxing embrace? Yes, it obviously heard, it fully discerned.

All these things, indeed, of the selfsame Word it knew, it seized upon by more than wifely intuition. It therefore responded with joy, "I will awake at dawn."[37] What is more

[33] Note the almost "Franciscan" pathos of this entire paragraph.
[34] John 12:23.
[35] Ps. 108:1 f. (107:3, V); cf. Ps. 57:8 (56:9, V). Here the words "my glory" and the corresponding words in the Vulgate and LXX are literal translations of the Hebrew. The R.S.V. consistently paraphrases as "my soul," as also does the new Latin version of the Pontifical Biblical Institute. Cf. also Ps. 16:9 and 30:12 (P.B.I. Latin, 15:9 and 29:13). It would seem, however, that if a literal translation is not to be employed (although it is entirely appropriate in these four places) some such paraphrase as "my tongue" would be more suitable than "my soul"; in one instance, Ps. 16:9 (15:9, V), the Vulgate does use "*mea lingua*." The Knox version has "my skill."
[36] Rom. 6:9.   [37] Ps. 108:2 (107:3, V); cf. Ps. 57:8 (56:9, V).

joyful than this reply? What is readier than the heart of the one making this response? The reason is not hidden from us, since at the beginning[38] of the psalm the psalmist spoke in his own name: "My heart is ready, O God, my heart is ready." O heart so agreeably ready, so willingly roused to undertake the command of divinity, the sweet command of the One who says, "Awake!" When the heart is ready to receive this, it thus replies, "I will awake at dawn." But was the heart prepared for this alone? No, indeed, the heart had been prepared to obey, even to die. The heart was utterly ready to give its body to those who were to beat it, its cheeks to those who were to smite them, and not to turn away its face from those who were to scorn it and spit upon it, but to endure all things unto death, even death on a cross.[39] "Yet I did not gainsay them nor did I turn back."[40] It was appropriate for that heart to be ready to respond, "I will awake at dawn," because it had been prepared to obey His Father, who for our sake did not spare him. Therefore, I say, the reason is not hidden from us why the beginning of the psalm thundered forth, "My heart is ready," and why he was not content to say it only once, but repeated it again and again: "My heart is ready, O God, my heart is ready."[41]

28. Who now is that man of whom Wisdom says, "The obedient man speaks of victories"?[42] Even if many men are or have been sons of obedience, there is only one man, one unique man, to whom there was, is, and will be no one similar or as obedient in like or equal manner. This one man alone was obedient in that, having absolutely no sin, he humbled himself unto death, even death on a cross.[43] It is henceforth appropriate that this obedient man always speak of victories. And, behold, he does so with ceaseless, unending speech. His speech is of such a manner, very clear and loud, because it is the very evidence of his wounds to which he submitted by that obedi-

---

[38] Ps. 108:1 (107:2, V). The phrase, "At the beginning of that psalm," proves that Rupert is citing Ps. 108 (107, V), rather than Ps. 57:7 (56:8, V), which is the same—unless by some strange chance, quite unlikely, he was recognizing the division caused by the Hebrew *selāh* or the LXX *diapsalma* at the end of Ps. 57:6 (56:7, LXX).
[39] Phil. 2:8.
[40] Although probably not a quotation of Scripture at all, it may be a conflation of Titus 2:9 and John 18:6.
[41] Ps. 108:1 (107:2, V); cf. Ps. 57:7 (56:8, V). Is Rupert's language here a preparation for the cult of the Sacred Heart?
[42] Prov. 21:28. Here the Vulgate differs from LXX and both differ from the Hebrew.
[43] Cf. Phil. 2:8.

ence. His five wounds are like five tongues. For that reason he preserved in his body the scars of his wounds, that he may always speak of his victories through them as though they were tongues. To whom does he speak? First, of course, to God the Father, then to angels and to men, to all the saints, to all the elect. God the Father looks, and is pleased with those noble testimonies of victories. Angels look, and are aroused to acclamations of praise and glory. Redeemed men look, and unremittingly multiply thanksgivings.

29. We affirm with the apostle and we understand his meaning when he says that father Abraham received and transmitted to his posterity the token of circumcision, the seal of the righteousness of faith. For as a believer Abraham trusted in God who said, "By your offspring all nations shall be blessed," [44] although he had no son, although he himself was already an elderly man, and although his wife was a sterile old woman. Circumcision was the testimony of a great deed, a great seal of faith. It proclaimed to him and his descendants the victory of a great righteousness before God, reminding him of God's promise, lest, sometime, somewhere, being displeased, he avoid offering his posterity "by which all nations shall be blessed." So long as he saw the seal of that promise, so long he declared himself to be faithful and true.

But here at the cross, behold many seals, many seals of righteousness and faith, namely, the five wounds [45] which that obedient Man, that just and faithful Man, suffered as a condition of human salvation. The prophet himself was surely not aware of such a proposed condition: "If he shall offer his own soul for sin, he shall see a long posterity; the will of God shall prosper in his hand; he shall see that for which his soul travailed and be satisfied; by his knowledge shall the righteous one, my servant, justify many; and he shall bear their iniquities." [46] Therefore does not just divinity rightfully award us, his offspring, the palm of justification and salvation when he sees not merely one seal or merely one wound as the seal of righteousness (as was the wound of circumcision), but five wounds of the just Man beating down whatever wrong our flesh has com-

---

[44] Gen. 22:18.
[45] During the Middle Ages there was a cult of the Five Wounds with a proper Mass. That Mass has fallen into desuetude, but the cult still appears occasionally in an attenuated form. Consult A. Franz, *Die Messe im Deutschen Mittelalter* (Freiburg i/B: Herder, 1902), 155–177.
[46] Isa. 53:10 f.

mitted by its five senses? For in Baptism we have pleasantly endured those seals of righteousness and faith which he endured painfully. As by the testimony of one seal, circumcision, he was once expected to come and redeem men, so now by the seal of the five wounds, that is, by the seal of the cross imprinted upon our brows, he is expected to return to judge the living and the dead.

THE VOICE OF THE PREACHER

Guibert of Nogent: How to Make a Sermon

INTRODUCTION

G UIBERT OF NOGENT WAS BORN AT CLERMONT near Beauvais in 1053 and died at Nogent-sous-Coucy near Laon in 1124. At the age of twelve he entered the monastery of St. Germain at Flay, diocese of Beauvais, where he was given the usual classical and theological education of the day, and came, it is said, under the influence of Anselm, then prior of Bec. In 1104 he became abbot of the monastery of St. Mary at Nogent-sous-Coucy, where he remained the rest of his life.

Besides the work which we here translate, he wrote many others. To Bishop Bartholomaeus of Laon he dedicated ten books of his *Moralia on Genesis*,[1] a commentary after the manner of the similar work by Gregory the Great. Mention should also be made of the "Tropologies" on *Hosea*, *Amos*, and *Lamentations*,[2] a treatise *On the Incarnation against the Jews*,[3] a book *On Praise of the Blessed Mary*,[4] a small work *On Virginity*,[5] a *Letter on the Bread Given Judas, and On the Truth of the Lord's Body*,[6] and three works of somewhat greater interest.

The first of these, four books *On Saints' Relics*,[7] was occasioned by the pretense of the monks of St. Médard that they possessed a tooth of Christ. Guibert does not attack the worship of relics in general, but insists that their genuineness be established and that it be proved that the persons from whom they are supposed to come were, indeed, holy. He disapproves of the exhumation and dismemberment of saints' bodies, and denies the existence of the physical parts of the Lord's body except in heaven. He

[1] MPL 156.31–338.   [2] *Ibid.*, 337–488.   [3] *Ibid.*, 489–529.
[4] *Ibid.*, 537–578.   [5] *Ibid.*, 579–608.   [6] *Ibid.*, 527–538.
[7] *Ibid.*, 607–680.

defends, as is to be expected from his date, the doctrine of transubstantiation and lays emphasis upon the intention of the priest as a necessary part of the Mass.

The second is the earliest extant history of the first crusade, called the *Histories of God's Deeds through the Franks* or the *Jerusalem History*,[8] which covers the events of the years 1095–1099 and was written about 1108.

Finally, there are three books of *Monodies, or On His Own Life*,[9] which has been called the most original autobiography of the Middle Ages. Only the first is really autobiographical and carries the account to Guibert's election as abbot; the second is devoted to the monastery of Nogent; while the third is on Bishop Galderich of Laon.

The work which we here translate in large part, for the first time into English, so far as we are aware, bears the Latin title of *Quomodo sermo fieri debeat* (How a Sermon Should Be Made), but is less a book of directions on homiletical method than an exhortation on the necessity of preaching. Our version is based on Lucas d'Achery's edition (Paris, 1651), reprinted in Migne's *Patrologia latina* 156:21–32. The notes by d'Achery (*ibid.* 1017–1202) do not concern this work. Not much has been written on Guibert, but see J. Beckmann, "Guibert von Nogent, OSB" (LTK 4.736); L. d'Achery, "Synopsis Venerabilis Guiberti vitae" (MPL 156.17 f., with *testimonia, ibid.* 17–20); S. M. Deutsch, "Guibert of Nogent" (NSH 5.94); and A. Piolanti, "Guiberto di Nogent" (EC 6.1278 f.).

[8] *Ibid.*, 679–838.   [9] *Ibid.*, 837–1018.

Guibert of Nogent: How to Make a Sermon

THE TEXT

He to whom the duty of teaching belongs runs greatest danger when he departs from doctrine, for, as it is reprehensible to display a wicked example, so also it is surely true that one unwilling to cure sinners by his teaching stands very near to condemnation.

Men differ, however, with respect to their opinions on this matter. Some are unwilling to do this because they are overcome by pride, others by disinclination, others by envy. They refuse, I say, to preach on account of pride, and because many are eager to do it to further their career and for ostentation alone. They do this so as not to get dubbed as sermonizers, a tribe usually notorious for speaking through their belly, which is why they are called ventriloquists by Gregory of Nazianzus[10] and for excessive arrogance are despised.

If a choice is to be made among them, the preacher who harms only himself by his ostentations, and provides instruction for others, is found to be much more useful than the one who conceitedly hides under his conceit something of value which he understands, and produces neither good for himself nor help for others.

Some through envy insincerely neglect holy preaching because, begrudging the good character of others, they are unwilling to tell them how to be made still better, and even feign not to have the knowledge of the Scriptures which they do have, and take no care to expound them to eager and understanding listeners, afraid that their teaching may raise the hearers to their own or even higher level.

---

[10] Gregory of Nazianzus, *Orat.* 2:46 (MPG 35.453–454, tr. NPNF, 2d ser., 7.214).

There is also a third kind of envy which, when someone begins to envy others who follow eagerly good preaching, kindles in itself a desire to speak more passionately, explains obscure passages of Scripture, expounds other less familiar passages, and strives to utter solemn pronouncements in a prepared discourse, not for the purpose of edifying his listeners to do well but so that, desirous of petty glory, the preacher may display his own erudition as greater than that of others. One may, however, distribute good things in a bad way and destroy himself by seeking after others. Yet we ought to rejoice at whatever "way Christ is proclaimed,"[11] and no one, of course, who discusses the word of faith should be rejected because in many there is useful gain.

There are also some disinclined to speak the good, and when their hand shrinks from every pious act, it is no wonder if their tongue grows languid in zeal for sacred preaching. For if he does not propose to do a good deed, how, please tell me, can he for very long entertain good thoughts? Finally, there are those who live a good and chaste life but, because they do not hold a pastoral office in the church, suppose that they do not owe their brothers the word of holy preaching. This is completely absurd, for if through the dumb beast of burden, that is, "through a donkey," according to blessed Peter,[12] God was willing to rebuke the prophet's folly, how much more worthy and almost beyond comparison is human nature to teach and impart learning to one's fellows!

We who have acquired knowledge of the sacred page speak as from God, that is, with God as origin of our entire discourse, and in God's presence seeking to please none but God alone by the preparation of our sermon. For if everything pertaining to exhortation of souls ought to utter nothing but God and to advance nothing of itself as if from itself as its own source, what a sacrilege does he commit who presumes to seek praise for himself out of those divine acts in which praise for God alone should be sought? If theft is humanly a most reprehensible act, what a crime do we think it is to filch from God what belongs to him and to appropriate it to oneself?

Let us also flee from being numbered among those two very bad and disorderly orders, if I may call them such, whom we do not hold in the church as brothers, but tolerate as enemies, of whom the one is composed of those who do wrong and the other of those who are unwilling to do right. Let them be

---

[11] Phil. 1:18.   [12] II Peter 2:16.

designated by the names of the two sons of Judah, Er and Onan,[13] of whom the first was wicked in the sight of the Lord and struck down by him—let him stand for the wicked who are punished by God for their crimes; the second, who was unwilling to raise up seed in the name of his brother, and deserved to be slain by God's agency—let him signify those who refuse to procreate to Christ's honor the fruit of good works by the seed of God's Word in the hearts of the faithful, they who fall under condemnation no less than those who do the evil deeds themselves.

For if, in accordance with the blessed Ambrose,[14] he who does not repel injury from a friend if he can is as much at fault as he who does the injury, what objection is there to saying that he who notices a man sinning and refuses to correct him straightway falls under a like accusation? In the words of the apostle,[15] of course, not only those who do but those who approve the doers are called worthy of death.

Therefore, though he be not bishop or abbot or hold any office of distinction, yet let him act, as the blessed Augustine says,[16] the part of the mask he wears. He is a Christian, if he wishes to live in Christian fashion: then let him make the name of Christian plain in others, as he does in himself....

Let us be members, therefore, of holy church, not dead ones, but rendering our duty befitting the Lord's body so that, as in the outward performance of the most holy mysteries we are most like to the good, we may also, inwardly, be their equals in affection and the effect of the whole piety. Let our book from which the text of our sermon derives be a pure conscience, lest while the tongue is preaching good things to others, the memory of sin gnaw at us inwardly and shackle the force of our words by hidden condemnation. Let prayer precede the sermon so that the soul, brightly burning with divine love, may proclaim what it feels from God, so that as it burns inwardly in oneself, it may kindle with the hearts of hearers. For when a sermon is so lukewarm and dull that it does not please the one who produces it, it would be highly surprising if it were to please anybody, and if a sermon spoken by one who is cast down in a prone position were able to raise others to their feet, then we have certainly discovered that a word of this kind habitually fails to soothe the souls of hearers but crushes them

[13] Gen. 38:6–10; 46:12.
[14] Ambrose, *De officiis* 1:36 (MPL 16:81 =NPNF, 2d ser., 10.30).
[15] Rom. 1:32.   [16] Passage not identified.

with loathing and seriously rouses them to anger. And when we feel that the keenness of our reason is thus less vigorous in us and our eloquence is dulled, and that what ought to be said does not pour forth, and the mind restricted to a narrow compass suffers a failing, under such circumstances, I think a sermon is offered for no use to anybody.

If when there is a rich abundance of the spoken word, and the tongue produces pleasure in the heart, a sermon should not be made too long, how much less so when the memory of what should be said is insufficient and speech itself is hampered, and the spirit grows sleepy? One reads in the blessed Ambrose[17] that a boring sermon awakens anger, and when the same things are said over and over, and are stretched out beyond measure by saying them differently, it usually happens for this reason that those who are worn out with boredom all see the same value in the beginning, the middle, and the end, and those few items which could have been profitable are, when stretched out to an undiscerning extreme, converted into dislike or sometimes almost into hatred.

As food when taken in moderation for the body's nourishment remains in the body but, gulped down in great quantities, turns harmful and causes vomiting, and sexual acts which are licit and not excessive produce offspring, whereas immoderate indulgence accomplishes nothing useful but pollutes the flesh, so verbosity cancels what had already been implanted in the hearts of the listeners and what could have been profitable. When a preacher has great fervor in his soul and his memory does not lack varied matter to be touched upon, and he also possesses power to speak eloquently and elegantly, sufficient for his needs, let him consider the weak ability of those who silently listen and that it would be better for them to receive a few points with pleasure than a great many of which none will be retained, and let him not postpone his conclusion, so that when he is about to preach another sermon, he may find them eager, not reluctant.

In addition, one thing more must be mentioned, namely, that when he is preaching easy and clear truths to the uneducated, he should also take pains to mix in with them some loftier truths which are proper even for the educated, and when he approaches those points which are pleasing to their abilities, he may so explain, and may so expound, as if by grinding, as it were, in a mill, and what formerly seemed hard and difficult

---

[17] Ambrose, *De off.* 1:22 (MPL 16.58=NPNF, 2d ser., 10.18).

even to the learned he may render so clearly and so plainly that what is said can be intelligible to the unlearned and the simple. For as milk is nourishment familiar to infants and very necessary, so that we may even believe infants cannot live without it, yet not only do infants use it, but with pieces of bread broken in it, it even furnishes food to any adults, so, in the majority of instances, when a simple doctrine is placed before the people, and yet something is included on behalf of those with greater understanding on which they may exercise their intelligence, it usually feeds the dull of comprehension in such a way that even the addition of more solid food, that is, the weightier opinion that is inserted, usually pleases the wise. For, in sermons on the Gospels, passages from the Old Testament are customarily used to arouse the attention of the audience, because, something new striking upon their hearing, their spirits are renewed, as it were, from the pleasure of the sound. This happens frequently to those who freely search for the hidden meanings of Scripture and are ever seeking to learn. We have also discovered that simple stories please some people, and use in our sermons deeds of men of old, and adorn with all these devices as one paints a picture with different colors.

We must also speak about what sermon must be delivered particularly for the teacher. There are four rules[18] of Scripture on which every sacred page revolves as if on wheels; that is, the historical, which relates deeds that have happened; the allegorical, in which one thing is understood from another; the tropological, that is, moral discourse in which the establishment and regulating of morals is discussed; the anagogical, namely, spiritual understanding through which as we are about to deal with the highest and heavenly things we are led to still higher. For example, Jerusalem is a certain city, historically speaking; allegorically, it represents holy church; tropologically that is, morally, it is the faithful soul of anyone who sighs for a vision of eternal peace; anagogically, it means the life of the heavenly citizens who see the God of gods when his face is revealed in Zion. Therefore, though out of these four modes

[18] Scripture may be expounded in two senses, the literal or historical and the spiritual, but these were expanded by John Cassian in his *Conferences* 14.8 (CSEL 13.2.404 ff.) into four, the allegorical, tropological, anagogical, historical, which Guibert is here obviously following in what is one of the clearest expositions of the four senses. See John T. McNeill in *The Interpreter's Bible* (New York, Abingdon-Cokesbury, 1952), 1.115–123; also Beryl Smalley, *The Study of the Bible in the Middle Ages* (New York, Philosophical Library, 2d ed., 1952).

everything can be made, or certainly from them individually, nevertheless, if one considers what is more useful for the care of the inner man, the moral mode appears to be of greater value and intelligibility in sermons.

While allegory, of course, is sought for in the prophetic and apostolic books, it edifies almost nothing else but faith, because, to be sure, while we read carefully in the prophets that in olden times God spoke variously in various ways, we learn that the sacraments of the Christian Era were undubitably declared therein. But by God's grace the faith has become known to the hearts of all, and even if we ought to have laid emphasis on it by often discussing it before our hearers, yet it is fitting nonetheless to say, much more frequently, the things which can instruct their character. For it is easier and safer to discuss the nature of virtues than to argue about the sacraments of faith concerning which one ought to speak very moderately to some people. For error can be produced out of too subtle preaching less in those who understand: out of moral instruction, however, the advantage of discretion can be gained most often.

The allegorical sense, if it be sometimes put in the sermon, most often has a pleasing effect. Although if something is said, and it ought to be said several times a day, which may lead us to the faith and to understanding of sacred Scriptures, yet every vigilance in our speech must be kept concerning the movements of the inner man. That is to say, of his thoughts, the experience of which is so common to all men, that no preaching of this sort can be, to my way of thinking, obscure, especially when each man considers within himself, as if written in a book, whatever the tongue of the preacher says about different temptations.

Warning, however, should be given not more about instilling and guarding virtues than about shackling and banishment of vices. There the teacher, when he carefully and clearly teaches what vices are natural and what are beyond nature, what vices grow out of others, and how wicked they are in themselves and because of those which grow from them, brings forth fruit of great value. For when subtleties in the Scriptures are expounded to the simple and uneducated, they quickly slip away in forgetfulness because they are used to dealing only with things corporeal. No wonder that this is so in the case of things spiritual, which they do not see, since even in the case of things corporeal, which they can feel and see, they have no power to remember. Some are so like animals that they understand scarcely anything except things material and such as are visible also to beasts, and they are even completely ignorant of their impulses as well as of vices of their bodies and souls, which they unceasingly suffer in themselves, until they hear from others what, when they have heard, they should hold most firmly. . . .

God grants us the means of rising again when we have been sunk in the struggle of temptation or in the sleepiness of the mind: when he either suggests to our reason a spirit of remorse, that is, makes us to examine the miserable state of our own will, or when, by God's own disposing, we hear ourselves praised by somebody, or are compelled to make a sermon of exhortation to others, and, induced by these means to examine ourselves to see who we are, where we are lying, we utter a groan; or certainly when we are aroused from spiritual torpor through the high eloquence of another's sermon or through the reading of the divine page, or by any one of countless other means, completely unhoped for, we are called back to a life of good deeds.

Therefore, confession must be made to the Lord, especially by those who go "down to the sea,"[19] that is, those who are humbled in the storm of temptation but nevertheless are in ships, that is, are motivated by holy intention, because, even though they are tossed about, they are not sunk, "doing business in many waters."[20] That is to say, in the midst of conflicts and struggles which carnal and spiritual forces make very bitter against them, in this they are submissive to good work, because they do not leave off struggling zealously, nor when burdened by evils do they fall into the pit of despair, but with the gaze of their reason held upon God, they hurl themselves forth. "They saw the deeds of the Lord and his wonderful works in the deep,"[21] that is, in dejection of spirit, in the darkness of the storm, in the fear of sinning they saw—that is, they experienced. For when their trial was great, their rescue was greater, and they owe the greatest thanks.

When, therefore, having escaped these perils, they take into consideration the good state in which they were placed; or that through great security they can, without fear or caution, keep their religion pure; or through foolish joy they rejoice more than is right concerning their good possessions and the continuance of their good fortune; or through contempt are angry with others as if they lie far below themselves on account of their slothful life; or have deserved to sink into temptation or into inactivity and slothfulness, and at times surrendering to, at

[19] Ps. 107:23 (106:23, V). [20] *Ibid.* [21] *Ibid.*, v. 24.

times rising above their passions, that is, they have escaped the fiery furnace of their desires. Very marvelous and exceedingly useful are those things which can be, in situations adverse to him, understood by the one who bears them, which also give mightily instruction to the spirit that understands, even without writing or a book.

Whoever has the duty of teaching can first of all within himself be instructed profoundly, if he wishes, in these and matters like them, and because the experience of inner conflict teaches much more completely than we can say, he can also give wholesome instruction to others in accordance with what the advantages and disadvantages of his own experience have impressed upon him as necessary to remember. Any lazy man, even one who never made any attempt to engage in warfare, can, because he has seen men in combat or heard people tell about wars, say many things about wars, but the man who has actually fought in combat and been fought against, who has served and suffered, remembers wars in a far different fashion.

So it happens also in spiritual matters, when we hear some people speaking eloquently what they have read in books or heard from others. With far different authority does a man preach about spiritual contexts and point out, as it were, what he says, with his finger, whose knowledge stands as witness of the things he orally declares. And indeed it is very profitable to the educated, if even what they themselves know is said to them in eloquent form. If this is uttered with less rhetorical care, however, it produces in them aversion and contempt. This is why when we admonish both the educated and the uneducated at the same time, we ought to set before each group something out of the ordinary, yet intelligible, by which we can remove boredom from those who are well aware of what we are saying. This takes place when, in expounding the readings of the holy gospel, we bring in the moral type of exegesis, expressed in some manner different from the customary commentaries, as we sometimes make an old wall new by smearing it over with plaster.

There are clearly in the gospel certain passages, discussed by the fathers only in the allegorical sense, and expounded as referring to Jews and Gentiles, which, however, if any acute student of the Scriptures will examine them in accordance with the rules of other interpretations, nowhere or almost nowhere will understanding be lacking, but wherever the spirit and will of the reader goes, there also will be a vehicle, that is, Holy Scripture, ready at hand. On the other hand, though for those who have a competent knowledge of the sacred page, this type of practice is of the highest effectiveness, no one should presume, unless he has fully learned by long practice, in the various modes of speaking, that under one and the same thing, with differences of meaning, allegories are frequently composed.

No one should presume, I say, except those learnedly instructed in literature, to understand in his teaching a variety of meanings under the same things and names, as I have said. For example: rock and foundation, water and sky, grass and wood, sun and moon, and countless others; since they mean many things in the Scriptures, the one who is handling some obscure passage should notice, when he meets one of these words, in how many senses it is usually taken in the Scriptures. For instance the word "gold" means divinity, "gold" means wisdom, "gold" means brightness of life and when all things are considered, he may with safety use what he sees fits better the context involved. So, having daily gained confidence, when he has seen through recognition of the meanings that Holy Scripture smiles upon him, moving on now to matters of greater import, which formerly he never could have presumed to attempt, stimulated always by the hope of better things, he advances, is strengthened to no small degree for penetrating those testimonies of sacred speech which come upon him in great droves. This takes place, however, in two ways, that is, by example and by reason: by example, as I have said, of the Scriptural precedent, and by reason when, of course, examples are lacking, and through consideration of the nature of the thing in question, something in accordance with allegory or morality is found, as of precious stones, of birds, of beasts, of which something figurative is said; nothing is offered except on account of the meaning of their natures. In these instances even though no page attests the meaning elsewhere, nevertheless by examining nature the sense is determined.

Gregory of Nazianzus, a marvelously learned man, witnesses in a certain book[22] of his that he had made a habit of attempting for the edification of the soul to allegorize whatever he saw. If anyone grows accustomed to do this with keen reason, not only in divine books but even in almost all which come under one's eyes, he finds an abundance of comparisons very suitable for

[22] Gregory of Nazianzus, *Orat.* 26.9 (MPG 35.1237D–1240A), is probably the passage referred to.

examples and useful meanings of those things which from constant familiarity we make nothing. These are useful in thought in proportion as they are said with greater kindness to hearers, and they are the more pleasing as they are less familiar to them.

A great many of those things which are discovered through reason could be used in sermons, but I fear that if I should begin to speak of this topic, I should lengthen my discourse beyond measure, and I do not know whether I could explain it as clearly as I should like.

Besides, the man who speaks sincerely and whose purpose is far from any desire for praise is usually of especial aid to his hearers, when the only thing understood to be sought is the listener's knowledge of divine subjects and their salvation; when he does not draw them away to his own glory, and great eloquence and conceit cannot be noted. For nothing has usually offended the hearer more than that he knows or thinks his preacher is preaching for the sake of money or display.

He who is recognized as such angers rather than preaches because as he tries to decorate his words the more with lovelier speech, so much the more bitterly does he disgust the hearts of those standing before him—alas—to despise even those things which have been said well by him, and especially himself. Nevertheless, what is pronounced with any eloquence ought to be received as divine in humble spirit.

How you ought to treat these topics in a sermon, I have, my most beloved sir, said so far as my incompetence permits. Now, with God helping, I shall begin to say something about sources from which you can get the material for your sermon.

For every man who is sunk in the confusion of his vices it is, indeed, useful to tell how terrible are the punishments of hell and to relate to him how endless they are with that unspeakable horror they have. Just as for those placed in the heavenly Kingdom no blessedness will be lacking, so, on the contrary, for those eternally damned no misery, nothing which can pertain to punishment, can be absent. And since they will be tortured without any even momentary relief, this particularly and in an incomprehensible manner tortures the souls of the lost because after a thousand thousands of years they have no hope of escaping the torments but know that they must suffer a never dying death forever and ever. For, of course, false hope often refreshes souls sunk in adversity, but there shall be there neither true nor false hope which can console them. But "the animal man," [23] that is, one living like the beasts, whose senses all cling to the things which he sees corporeally, because "he does not take the things which are God's," [24] is so blinded by the habit of earthly lust that nothing which is said to him about the future age can deter him, and, if sometimes it does deter him, because what is said he has not hitherto believed, quickly he removes it from his mind.

Therefore, there must be thrown up in front of him those torments of anxieties and fears which he suffers in this life in the midst of wrongdoing and because of wrongdoing, and which lead to nothing except pain and most shameful grief. For example, the chronic thief, induced by the desire of some object —not terrified, I say, by fear of the night, which would frighten me out of my wits, but not even by loss of his limbs, nor even by fear of being hanged, which he knows he will not escape if caught—goes out to commit theft; he is afraid, of course, and he shakes with fierce trembling, but he is overcome by the force of his desire. And so, such a man, when convicted, is hanged on the gibbet.

I shall speak also about incest, but I shall say it better in the words of that noble Boethius,[25] who says: "What should I say about pleasures, the seeking of which, indeed, is full of anxiety, but the satiety full of repentance?" What is more truly said than this? Placed in the concupiscence of his crime, he is tormented on the rack, feverishly thinking how wicked affection leads to worthless effect; and while he is afraid to recognize what he is doing, he burns with a terrible and unbearable torment: and while he feverishly with impatience struggles to free himself, willy-nilly he is overcome by his own doing. While he is hot with desires, he fiercely complains against himself for the conflict which he bears, and he cries out against his pitiful self, so that he is disgusted with himself and is weary of living. And when what he desires is fulfilled, what torment, what groaning, how late does repentance pursue the unhappy man!

Concerning this I should doubtless say that if he who has so much genuine regret and fruitful repentance after the commission of sin as after he has realized his lust or committed any crime, and in that very reflection of its difficulty, before he first commits the act, how, of course, to accomplish it, then of the regret which comes from the abundance of sin, lasting for but

---

[23] Cf. I Cor. 2:14: *animalis homo* (V). [24] *Ibid.*
[25] Boethius, *De consol. phil.* 3.7 (prose). MPL 156.31 (the text of Guibert) makes the rest of the paragraph appear as quotation from Boethius.

an hour until, to be sure, the accustomed passion returns, he would offer to God the very great fruit of his contrition, worthy of all acceptance. But it is true, certainly, "that the sons of this world are wiser," and, as I say, more lively, "in their own generation than the sons of light." [26] For it is said by the apostles, "Or you will not see Judas how he does not sleep," [27] not because the watchfulness of the apostles would not be better than the sleep of Judas but that the wisdom which he had in evil ought to be present with the apostles in good. And Paul, speaking in human terms, on account of the weakness of our flesh, as we have yielded our bodies to serve iniquity, if not worse than that, so now at any rate he wants us to yield them to serve sanctity.[28]

They[29] knew the bitterness and wisdom of the human soul for evil, who if only they were zealous for good things would be worthy of a title of great praise.

Therefore, let it be thrown up before such men under what darts and tortures they may endure their poor pleasures; let the disgraceful thought be thrown up in which alone the repute of these unhappy men is defiled by open or veiled accusations. If hitherto they do not deign to fear future evils because they do not have them before their eyes or at their sides, let them at any rate fear being subjected to such maddening torments on account of such little pleasures, from which nothing may happen to them except danger and loss of their repute. I speak of this pleasure under the metaphor of the bee, as the aforesaid author says,[30] which carries honey in its mouth, that is, in a bit of some trifling pleasure, but has a sting in its tail, because after it has drained something of sweetness at the bottom, it rewards it with the bitterness of fierce mistrust.

Saint Gregory says[31] that nothing is more blessed than a simple mind. On the other hand somebody[32] says that the mind which suffers from a bad conscience is agitated by its own stings while, continuing to do evil or fearing the evil that has been done, it burns with most piercing inner fires. If, therefore, he takes thought of eternal perdition, let him take thought also of a

---

[26] Luke 16:8.
[27] This has every appearance of a Biblical quotation, but it has been found in neither the canon nor the Apocrypha. So far as the Latin goes, *Judas* may rather be *Judah*.
[28] Rom. 6:19.
[29] MPL 156.32: *noverat* is error for *noverant*.
[30] Boethius, *loc. cit.* (verse).   [31] Gregory the Great, *Moralia* 12.21.
[32] The "somebody" is Lucretius 3.1018 f.

present sense of shame; and, having repented in his heart, let him learn to resist bad habits, carefully searching out, that is, the difference between flesh and spirit, rather, what is flesh and spirit. For a soldier receives instruction in arms to no purpose unless he have a stout heart with which he may fight against the enemy. And what good does it do to recognize the virtues that are the opposites of the carnal pleasures, if the reason, lazy and sluggish, is unwilling to rise up to fight them?

Let us therefore take a bit of true history for an example, while we discuss the hidden meanings of which, we lay open to ourselves the means of a great deal of teaching. Let nobody think that in this we are doing anything revolutionary, knowing that, if, according to the poet,[33] "It was and always shall be right to bring forth the name marked with the present note," it is much more right for all who are learned in the knowledge of the sacred page, preserving the faith and proceeding in accordance with the rules of ancient expositors, to seek out the richness of the Scriptures through the various senses. Therefore, let us speak.

[33] Horace, *Ars Poet.* 58 f. Guibert misquotes *nummum* (coin) as *nomen* (name).

Rabanus Maurus of Mainz: Five Sermons

INTRODUCTION

THE VERSATILE CHURCHMAN[1] WHOM WE HERE present as a preacher bore the sonorous name of Rabanus Maurus Magnentius. The first, sometimes spelled Hrabanus, is his Teutonic name, cognate with English "raven," while the second was given him by Alcuin himself and recalls Maurus, the friend of Saint Benedict. The third means nothing more than "of Mainz."

He was born in that city about 776 and died at the neighboring village of Winkel on February 4, 868. He has not been canonized but enjoys the subordinate rank of "blessed."

For his education Rabanus was sent first to the school in the Benedictine monastery at Fulda in 801, but must very soon have gone to Tours to study theology and the liberal arts under Alcuin, who died in 804. Rabanus then returned to Fulda and was ordained presbyter in 814. By 817 he was director of the school at Fulda but became abbot in 822. In this capacity he completed the rebuilding of the abbey, erected a number of churches and oratories, developed the artistic talents of the monks, increased the properties and immunities of the monastery, but also gave much attention to preaching and instruction in the Scriptures.

In the spring of 842, however, he resigned the abbacy and retired to a church in the neighboring Petersberg to devote himself to spiritual exercises and literary activity. This period of

---

[1] For the early life by Rudolph, see MPL 107.40–68; see also *ibid.*, Jean Mabillon's *B*[*eati*] *Rabani Mauri elogium historicum*. A Vatican codex of Rabanus' early work, the *De laude sanctae crucis* (cod. Reg. lat. 124, fol. 2v., saec. ix) contains a miniature showing the abbot Albinus [=Alcuin] presenting Rabanus Maurus to Saint Martin of Tours.

release from administrative responsibility was ended when on June 26, 847, he was elected in succession to Orgar as archbishop of Mainz. He held his first provincial synod in October of that year, others in 848 and 852. As archbishop, he was noted for his acts of charity, and in the famine of 850 is said to have fed three hundred persons daily.

During the Eucharistic controversy associated with the names of Paschasius Radbertus and Ratramnus, Rabanus took the conservative side, as he did also in condemnation of Gottschalk. The leading Frankish authority in his day on Scripture, the fathers, and canon law, he gave his greatest services to the cause of education, with the result that he was called the *praeceptor Germaniae*.

Among his works are commentaries on most of the books of the Old Testament and Apocrypha, as well as on two Gospels (Matthew, John) and the Pauline Epistles. Rabanus also wrote a considerable variety of doctrinal works, some of which show great indebtedness to Cassiodorus and to Augustine. There are also works on the liturgy, on vestments, on magic, on various problems confronting the pastor, as well as some verse.[2]

In the homiletical field he composed two collections of sermons, one addressed to Haistulf before 826, the other to Lothair. We here translate five of the sermons: (I) Sermon before Our Lord's Nativity[3]; (VII) Sermon on the Lord's Epiphany[4]; (XXII) Sermon on the Day of Pentecost[5]; (XLV) Sermon on Faith, Hope, and Love[6]; and (LVII) Sermon on Contempt for the World and on Future Reward.[7] The text used is that of J. Pamelius, A. de Henin, and G. Colvenerius in six volumes (Cologne 1626–1627), reprinted in Migne's *Patrologia latina*, vol. 110. See A. Hauck (NSH 9.376 f.); Max Manitius, *Geschichte der lateinischen im Mittelalter* (Munich, Beck, 1925) 1.288–302; G. Mollat (EC 10.439); and Michael Otto (CE 12.617). John Mason Neale, *Mediaeval Preachers and Mediaeval Preaching* (London, Mozley, 1856) 29–43, has translations of two other sermons.

[2] MGH PLAC, 2.154–244; the letters in MGH Epist. 5.379 ff., 517 ff.
[3] MPL 110.10–12. [4] MPL 110.18 f. [5] MPL 110.43–45.
[6] MPL 110.83–85. [7] MPL 110.106–108.

Rabanus Maurus of Mainz: Five Sermons

THE TEXT

I. Sermon Before Our Lord's Nativity[8]

As that most holy festival is now approaching on which our Saviour mercifully deigned to be born among men, take care, brothers most dear, to note how we ought to be prepared at the advent of such great power, so as joyfully and gladly to deserve to receive our King and Lord with glory and praise, and in his sight amid the happy throngs of the saints to rejoice with thanksgiving rather than, rejected by him on account of our uncleanness, to deserve eternal damnation among sinners. Therefore, I beg and advise that, as far as we are able, we labor with God's help, so that on that day with sincere and pure conscience, clean of heart and chaste of body, we can approach the Lord's altar and receive his body and blood, not to our judgment but for the cure of our souls.

For in Christ's body does our life consist. The Lord himself has said, "Unless you eat the flesh of the Son of Man, and drink his blood, you will not have life in you." [9] Let him who wishes to have life change his life, then; for if he does not change his life of sin, so as to live righteously, he will receive the true life which is Christ's body to his judgment, and he is made from it more corrupt than whole, is put to death rather than restored to life.

For so said the apostle: "He who eats the Lord's body and drinks His blood unworthily, eats and drinks judgment for himself." [10] And though it behooves us always to be gloriously clad in good works, nevertheless, on the Lord's birthday particularly, there is this obligation, as he himself says in the Gospel[11] that our good works ought to shine before men so that in all things

[8] MPL 110:10–12.
[9] John 6:53.
[10] I Cor. 11:27.
[11] Matt. 5:16 paraphrased.

God may be glorified. Consider this, brothers: If an earthly king or the head of some great family should invite you to his birthday party, what kind of dress would you be anxious to wear when you go, how new, how neat, how elegant, so that the eye of your host would take no offense from its age, its shabbiness, or its dirtiness. Therefore, in this same way, strive zealously, as far as you can, Christ being your helper, that your souls may be decorated by the various ornaments of virtues, decked out with the gems of simplicity and the flowers of sobriety, with clear conscience, when they go to the birthday celebrations of the Eternal, that is, of the Lord our Saviour. Let them gleam with purity, shine in love, be bright with acts of charity, glow with righteousness and humility, dazzle, before all else, with love of God.

For the Lord Christ, should he see you so dressed celebrating his birthday, will himself deign to come himself, and not only to visit your souls but even to remain there and to dwell in them, as it is written: "Because, see, I will come and I shall live and move among them and they shall be my people,[12] and I shall be their God,"[13] says the Lord God. O how happy is that soul which is brought by good works to receive Christ as guest and indweller, ever happy, ever joyful, ever glad, and free from every dread of vices! Conversely, how unhappy is that conscience which stains itself with evil deeds so that Christ does not begin to rest in it but the devil begins to rule in it! Such a soul, if the healing of penitence does not come quickly, is abandoned by the light and seized by shadows; emptied of sweetness, filled with bitterness, invaded by death, separated from life.

Nevertheless, let not such a soul despair of the Lord's goodness, nor be broken by deadly hopelessness, but let it quickly return to penitence, and while the wounds of its sins are fresh and still inflamed, may it make use of the wholesome ointment of its tears, because our Physician is omnipotent, and is used to healing our stripes so that no trace of scars remains.

Only let us have faith in him, and let us continue in good works as far as we are able, and never despair of his mercy. Therefore, my dearest brothers, ever thinking this, let those who are good strive to continue with God's grace in good works, because, not he who begins, but "he who continues to the end, shall be safe."[14] But those who know themselves slow to give alms, ready to give way to wrath, prone to the practice of lust, let them, with the Lord's aid, hasten to rescue themselves from

---

[12] II Cor. 6:16.   [13] Gen. 17:8.   [14] Matt. 10:22.

evils, so that they may merit fulfilling what is good, so that, when the Day of Judgment comes, they may not be punished with the wicked and sinners, but may deserve to arrive at the rewards that are eternal with the righteous and the merciful, under the protection of our Lord Jesus Christ, who with the Father and the Holy Spirit lives and reigns for ever and ever. Amen.

VII. Sermon on the Lord's Epiphany[15]

Recently, my dearest brothers, we have celebrated the festival on which God put on man with his infirmities, and a little later the one on which he was willing to be circumcised according to the law. Now, however, we observe and commemorate in divine praise the one on which God revealed himself in man through his powers.[16] This festival is called, from the Greek, "Epiphany," which we can translate as "manifestation," because on this day the rising of the star showed forth the divine message from heaven, and brought the Magi, diligently searching for it, to the cradle. Or because in Jordan's waters the Saviour consecrated the natural waters for the regeneration of mankind in his baptism, and the true God was marked by the coming of the Holy Spirit and the pronouncement of his Father's voice. Or because in Cana of Galilee at the marriage feast, he turned water into wine, and, as the Gospel witnesses, the beginning of his signs made manifest his glory, and his disciples believed on him; or because with five loaves he satisfied five thousand people, and was proclaimed by the confession of the crowd: "He is truly the prophet who is to come into the world." [17]

All these sacraments being then heard, as the holy fathers have handed down to us, this day is to be venerated because by such signs today the God Christ is manifested in man.

All these events have, indeed, mysteries to be worshiped, but then they do nothing else with us than to commend the catholic faith to us, the one, that is, that works through love, and they teach us so to live that in all things we may please our Creator. But I want, brothers, to say something to you about the three gifts which the Magi offered today to our Redeemer. They offered, of course, as you have just heard when the Gospel was read, gold, frankincense, and myrrh. In those threefold gifts a threefold meaning is contained. In frankincense, they offered

---

[15] MPL 110:18 f.   [16] *Virtutibus*: virtues, good deeds, miracles.
[17] John 6:14.

honor to God's Christ; in gold, royal prestige; in myrrh, the burial of the body. Let us also offer, most beloved brothers, sincere and holy gifts to our God, that is, faith, hope, and love. Let us offer the gold of wisdom, the frankincense of devoted prayer, the myrrh for mortification of the flesh. Let us offer consecration of the flesh, purity of speech, honesty of work. Let us offer purity of mind, chastity of body, and watchfulness of humility. Let us offer sympathy, patience, and continence. Let us offer kindness, sobriety, and mercy. For these are gifts pleasing to God, these are presents that are welcomed which are offered to him but bring advantage also to those who offer them. He needs nothing, lacks no gift, but for him this gift is best which gives him causes for returning gifts. From us he demands no more, asks no more, except our salvation. He regards everything as offered by us to himself, if we have so acted that all things may be offered to us by himself.

But we must seek from him the efficacy of this thing so that his mercy may come upon us, and his mercy may pursue us all the days of our life, so that we may dwell in the Lord's house for the length of our days. May he deign to grant this, who lives and reigns forever and ever. Amen.

XXII. Sermon on the Day of Pentecost[18]

Most beloved brothers, the more we receive the joys of today's celebration, the more we seek for it, and the more eagerly we drink its cooling draught, the more we burn with thirst for it. Today, therefore, we are celebrating Pentecost, that is, the fiftieth day after the Lord's resurrection, on which the Spirit, called the "Paraclete," from the Greek word that means "Comforter," came down upon the apostles[19] according to Christ's promise, and set their hearts afire with his love, and, lighting them with the light of all knowledge, made them steadfast amid the persecutions of the Jews, abounding in heavenly joy.

In the first place, be it known to you not only that this feast was hallowed with the graces of the gospel, but also that it was long before foreshadowed by the mysteries of the law and, by the Lord's command, has been observed through all the years in holy ceremonial. For on this day, as we know, when the disciples were sitting in the dining room, suddenly there was a

[18] MPL 110:42–45.   [19] Acts 2:1–4.
20—E.M.T.

sound from heaven, and the Holy Spirit, appearing in the likeness of fire, bestowed on them a knowledge of all tongues. Moreover, when this sound was heard, there assembled together religious men who had from various nations flocked to Jerusalem for the feast of the Passover, and they were amazed in wonder, since each man heard them speaking the great things of God in his own tongue. And when the disciples explained that the Holy Spirit was the grace which they beheld, long ago promised by the voice of the prophets, and now sent through Christ's bounty, three thousand of them believed, and, when baptized, they themselves also received the gift of the Holy Spirit.

This is the anniversary of that day, this the ever blessed feast of that heavenly blessing. Because its memory ought to be firmly imprinted in faithful hearts, the most beautiful custom of holy church has been implanted, that each year the sacrament of Baptism should be celebrated on it; that when the believers have been washed in the fount of salvation, the holy temple should be made ready for the arrival of the Holy Spirit, and through this not only the memory of what happened of old but also a new coming of the Holy Spirit to new sons of adoption should be celebrated in it.

How, then, the type and figure of the feast of the law agrees with this our feast, let your love note. The sons of Israel, freed from their Egyptian bondage, after the sacrifice of the paschal lamb, went out through the desert to come to the land of promise, and came to Mount[20] Sinai. The Lord descending in fire on the mountain, to the sound of the trumpet, in thunder and lightning, on the fiftieth day from the Passover revealed to them clearly the Decalogue[21] of the law, and as a memorial for the granting of the law he established on that day, each year, a new sacrifice for himself of the fruits of that year, that is, two loaves of the first fruits to be carried to the altar.

So also, after the sacrifice of the true Lamb, that is, Christ, because "Christ was sacrificed for our Passover,"[22] likewise on the fiftieth day, that is, today, the grace of the Holy Spirit was given to the disciples, established in the banquet, that is, in the loftiness of the heavenly teachers, because, outwardly appearing as visible fire, he illuminated their hearts invisibly with the light of knowledge, and set them aflame with the inextinguishable fire of love. The apostles also, at once, when

[20] MPL 110:44 reads *mortem*, error for *montem*.
[21] Ex. 20:3–17.   [22] I Cor. 5:7.

soon the gift of the Holy Spirit was received, offered a new sacrifice in two loaves of bread, that is, in two peoples, when, preaching the gospel to those who had come together, they converted many to faith, and these, reborn from the fount of Baptism and hallowed by the grace of the Spirit, they offered as living first fruits of the New Testament, at the communion of the Lord's altar.

Let us, then, my brothers, thinking about this, and going over it in purity of heart and simplicity of faith, cleanse ourselves from every defilement of the flesh, so that we may merit and receive the Holy Spirit. If, therefore, we leave this world, let us, like the apostles, receive a like Paraclete, that is, the Spirit of truth, which the Father will send us, since there is no esteeming of persons with God the Father, but the promises of the apostles are profitable to us, if we yield the works and desires and deeds which the apostles did.

If, however, we preserve the law of the Lord which is spotless and converts our souls, by fulfilling his commandments, we entrust ourselves, with Christ's grace, as heirs of the Lord and coheirs of Christ, to an everlasting inheritance and to the habitation of the angels.

For this reason I beg of you, my very beloved brothers, that, with faith unimpaired, you believe the Father and the Son and the Holy Spirit, one God in the Trinity and the Trinity in unity, lest the feet of your senses grow lame, or your eyes see poorly, or your hands become dry. For every man who does not well follow the catholic faith, has weak feet, and is dried up from the dryness of his hands.

Do this, then, most beloved, work this out, so that no part of your bodies be corrupted by this weakness, lest carnal desire in you terrify, or greed displease, or unfaithfulness languish, so that, thoroughly purified and cleansed, you may be made the habitation of God, and the Holy Spirit which is said to have descended today upon the apostles may deign to dwell forever in you, under the protection of our Lord Jesus Christ, who also promised this same Holy Spirit, reigning with the Father in the unity of the Holy Spirit forever and ever. Amen.

XLV. Sermon on Faith, Hope, and Love[23]

Every man bearing the name of Christian and every man inspired by the divine sacraments must, most dear brothers,

[23] MPL 110:83–85.

know the plan of the Christian religion and must recognize the love of the faith—that faith, of course, which, as the apostle says, "works through love," [24] which in the present life comforts and strengthens the believers, and in the future leads to the contemplation of God. For that blessed and extraordinary teacher of the Gentiles laid down these three as necessary to our soul when he says, "Now, however, faith, hope, love, these three abide, but the greater of these is love." [25]

First, then, catholic faith is necessary to the Christian, because in it the sons of God are distinguished from the sons of the devil, the sons of light from the sons of darkness. Through it we are reborn in Baptism and obtain eternal life, as it is written, "He who believes and is baptized shall be saved." [26] This is the gate of life, this the door of the Kingdom. Through it knowledge of truth is learned and understanding of the divine is perceived. Through it we find God's grace, but otherwise we cannot please God, because "without faith it is impossible to please God." [27]

For he is truly blessed who by rightly believing lives well and by living well guards right faith. Therefore, as faith is idle without good works, so good works are not profitable without right faith. For which reason blessed James the apostle says: "What profit will there be, my brothers, if any man says he has faith, but does not have works? Faith will never be able to save him: faith without works is idle. For as the body without breath is dead, so faith without works is dead." [28]

Strive, my brothers, before all else to have faith that is right and spotless, and according to the standard of apostolic teaching. Remember the creed established by the holy fathers, and, living religiously, show zeal for its observance. Avoid the deadly opinions of heretics; fear the fatal poisons of sorcerers and magicians; reject completely the unspeakable trappings of soothsayers and fortune-tellers and magicians who have association with demons, and hold in your mind in confession or reveal openly by your acts nothing else than what the catholic faith praises, loves, preaches.

After this faith, then, learn to have firm hope which draws our spirit to things invisible and ingrafts our attention upon the heavenly and eternal and binds it together, as if by indissoluble bonds; which does not deceive but faithfully preserving it leads on to eternal blessedness. No one, then, no matter

---

[24] Gal. 5:6.   [25] I Cor. 13:13.   [26] Mark 16:16.
[27] Heb. 11:6.   [28] James 2:14 f., 17.

how burdened with the huge weight of his sins, ought to give up hope in the goodness of divine piety, but with hope in His sure mercy ought to pray with daily tears for pardon, which he certainly can hope for if he ceases from doing any evil deed. Therefore, we ought not to continue to sin on account of the hope for pardon, nor ought we to despair of pardon because God justly punishes sins, but, with both dangers avoided, let us turn from evil and hope for pardon from God's goodness.

Likewise, also, in every time of deep tribulation, we ought to run with hope to the consolation of the higher piety, because of it alone without a doubt every hope and salvation consist, as in the words of the prophet: "In God is my salvation and my glory; God is my help, and my hope is in God." [29]

For when we advise you, brothers, to have right faith and firm hope, we especially exhort you to take care to have love in you and show it by action in all things. For through it and in it you may know that you will have a true blessedness, because without this no man will see God.

This quality is called by the apostle greater than faith and hope because when the others give way, it alone will remain. For hope follows faith, and blessedness hope, but there is no change for love, but perfection alone endures. This is the citadel[30] of all virtues, this the promise of the Kingdom, this the reward of all the saints in heaven, because in eternal joy the saints have nothing more pleasing, nothing sweeter than the perfect love of God which, because they see it present, they love it more, and enjoy its good more sweetly.

You should know, brothers, that among all of God's teachings love holds the primacy, without the perfection of which the apostle Paul witnesses that nothing can please God, who shows that neither martyrdom, nor contempt for the world, nor the giving of alms, can be of any use without the duty of love.

This is why the Lord answers: "Thou shalt love the Lord thy God from thy whole heart and from thy whole soul and from thy whole mind," [31] and adds also a second like it, "Thou shalt love thy neighbor as thyself. On these two commandments hang all the Law and the Prophets." [32] When he says, "From thy whole heart and thy whole soul and thy whole mind," he means with all understanding and all will and with all memory God ought to be loved. The love of God, however, consists of the complete observance of his commandments, as elsewhere he

---

[29] Ps. 62:5–7 (61:8, V).   [30] Reading *arx* for *ars* of MPL 110:84.
[31] Matt. 22:37–39; see also Luke 10:27.   [32] Matt. 22:40.

says: "If any man love me, let him keep my words." [33] Of this the Truth himself elsewhere says: "In this shall all men know that you are my disciples, if you have love for each other." [34] Likewise the apostle: "The fullness of the law is love." [35] Likewise John the Evangelist says: "We have this commandment from God: let him who loves God, love also his neighbor." [36]

If by any chance anyone asks who is the neighbor, let him know that every Christian is rightly called his neighbor because all of us are sanctified in the baptism of God's son, so that we are brothers spiritually in perfect love. More noble is spiritual descent than carnal, on which the Truth himself says in the Gospel: "Unless anyone be reborn of water and the Holy Spirit, he cannot enter into the kingdom of God." [37]

But he who with this understanding loves his neighbor will surely have in himself true love. Carefully consider this, brothers, and with faith and love ever work out your salvation, having firm hope, because whatever good you do in this life, you will in the future be rewarded by Him in manner beyond imagination, because the author and protector of our salvation is Jesus Christ our Lord, who with the Father and the Holy Spirit lives and reigns as God forever and ever. Amen.

LVII. Sermon on Contempt for the World and on Future Reward[38]

Blessed John the apostle admonishes us, my dearest friends, and summons us to despise things transitory, when he says: "Do not love the world or the things in the world," [39] since "the world and its lust pass away, but he who does the will of God abides forever." [40]

Likewise, also, blessed Paul the apostle, writing to Timothy, gives us instruction. "Teach," he says, "the rich of this world not to be haughty nor to set their hopes on uncertain riches but upon the living God who furnishes us everything in abundance to enjoy. Let them who are rich be generous in their good works, share with those who have not, lay up for themselves a good foundation of treasure for the future, so that they may lay hold of true life." [41]

Pay attention to this, my brothers, and think carefully of what is said, for when the rich are taught to treasure a good

---

[33] John 14:15 loosely. [34] John 13:35. [35] Rom. 13:10.
[36] I John 4:21. [37] John 3:3 loosely. [38] MPL 110:106–108.
[39] I John 2:15. [40] I John 2:17. [41] I Tim. 6:17–19 loosely.

foundation for themselves in the future so that they may lay hold of true life, there is no doubt that there is a false life. This the rich ought especially to hear, who, when the poor see them, grumble, groan, envy their praise, yearn to be made equal, lament their inequality, and when the rich are praised, most of them say, "They are the only ones—they are the only ones who live." On account of these words, then, by which men of slight means flatter the rich, because they live, let them not be puffed up by the words of flattery and think they truly live. "Teach," he says, "the rich of this world not to be haughty nor to set their hopes on uncertain riches but upon the living God who furnishes us everything in abundance to enjoy." They are rich, but where? In their good works, he says. Let them be generous because they do not lose what they give away. Let them share with those who have not and from this lay up for themselves a good foundation of treasure for the future so that they may lay hold of true life, not agreeing with the flatterers who say they live and are the only ones who live. That life is a dream. That wealth flows away as in dreams.

Hear the psalm, you rich men who are very poor: "They slept their dream and all the men of wealth found nothing in their hands."[42] Sometimes a beggar, lying on the ground, shaking with cold, is, however, seized by a dream, dreams of treasures and rejoices, and becomes proud and does not deign to recognize his tattered equal, and while he is asleep, is rich. But when he awakens, he finds he was rejoicing at what was false; when he awakens, he finds that he is truly sorrowful. The rich man dying is like the poor man awaking, who saw treasures in his dreams. For a certain rich man[43] was clothed in purple and linen, a man neither named nor one who should be named, a despiser of the poor man lying before his gate. He was clothed in purple and in linen, as the Gospel witnesses, and each day he dined on fine fare. He died, was buried, awoke, and found himself in flames. Therefore he slept his dream and found no riches in his hands because he did no good with his hands. On account of life, therefore, riches are sought, not life on account of riches. How many have agreed with their enemies to take everything and leave them their life! Whatever they possessed, they bought their life for so much. For what a price must eternal life be acquired, if the life that will perish is so precious!

[42] Ps. 76:6, V, corresponding verse in R.S.V. not comparable.
[43] Luke 16:19–31.

Give something to Christ that you may live in blessedness, if you give all to the enemy that you may live in beggary. From your temporal life, which you redeem at such a price, pay much that your eternal life which you neglect may flourish. You live for a few days, even though you reach old age, for all the days of a man from infancy to old age are few, and if Adam himself were to die today, he would have lived a few days because he had ended them all. A few days, therefore, and these full of labor, in the greatest poverty, among such trials, you redeem, and you are willing to have nothing of all that in order to have yourself. Redeemed today, tomorrow, perhaps, to die; by one man dispatched, perhaps to be slain by another. O man, fragile of body, changeable in time, destructible in death, oppressed by burdens, worn out with worries, hear my advice: Refresh yourself by giving to the poor what you have earned by your labors; give something to the one who has not, because you also do not have anything. For you never have eternal life. Give therefore from what you have that you may receive what you have not. A beggar is knocking at the door of your Lord. God does with his beggar what you do with yours. Give, therefore, and it shall be given to you.

If you are unwilling, you will see, for the poor man cries and says to you: "I ask for bread and you do not give—you ask for life and you do not receive. Let us see which of us works with greater loss, I who am cheated out of a morsel—you who are deprived of life eternal; I who am punished in my belly, you who are punished in your mind; finally, I who burn with hunger or you who have to be consumed in fire, and to be delivered to living flames." I do not know whether the arrogance of the rich man will be able to answer these words of the poor man.

"Give," says the Lord, "to everyone that asks of you." [44] If to everyone, how much more to the needy and wretched, whose thinness and paleness beg, whose tongue is silent, dirtiness and groans ask alms. Hear me, then, O rich man, and may my counsel please you. Redeem your sins with alms; do not depend upon gold. Naked you came from your mother's womb, naked you will return to the earth,[45] and if you will return naked to the earth, for whom are you collecting on the earth? I believe that if you could take anything with you, you would have eaten men alive! Look, naked you will return—why do you bestow the money gathered together by good means or

---

[44] Luke 6:30. [45] Job 1:21 paraphrased.

evil? Send it on ahead of you; transfer the goods that are perishable so that you may arrive at the Kingdom of the heavens. For if to any man you were to give ten coins, in return for which he would later pay you a hundred, how you would rejoice, with much gladness of heart would you exult! If therefore you rejoice at receiving interest, the profit from your Lord, give to your God of his own, for he will return it to you, increased many fold. Do you want to know how many fold he will return it to you? For a morsel, for a penny, for a shirt, you receive eternal life, the Kingdom of the heavens, happiness without end. Pay with your morsel for eternal life, everlasting wealth—it is no purchase, for you give the earth and receive Him who made heaven and earth. For he is himself our reward, without whom a rich man is a beggar and with whom a poor man is abundantly rich. What does a rich man have if he does not have God? What does the poor man not have if he has God?

If, therefore, my brothers, you desire to be rich, love true riches. If you seek the height of true honor, head for the heavenly Kingdom. If you love the glory of offices, hurry to be enrolled in that higher court of the angels. Remember the words of God which you hear with your ears, and strive to fulfill them with deeds. See, everything you do in the world passes away, and to the Last Judgment, with no chance of remaining, you are hastening daily, whether you want to or not. Why, therefore, is what is left loved? Why is that neglected whither it is going? Love the heavenly, reject the earthly, seek the eternal, neglect the temporal, and you can hold the everlasting Kingdom with Him who lives and reigns with God the Father in unity with the Holy Spirit as God forever and ever. Amen.

Ivo of Chartres: Two Sermons

INTRODUCTION

IVO OF CHARTRES, KNOWN TO THE FRENCH AS SAINT Yves, was born of a noble family[1] in the neighborhood of Beauvais about 1040 and died at Chartres, December 23, 1115. He studied philosophy and theology, it is said, at Paris and also at Bec in Normandy as a pupil of Lanfranc and fellow-student of that Anselm who was later of Canterbury. After serving as canon at Nesle in Picardy, he was made prior of the canons regular of St. Quentin at Beauvais about 1080. In this period he made himself one of the ablest teachers in France, so that he was later equipped to infuse new life into the celebrated schools of Chartres, of which diocese he was named bishop in 1090 by Urban II.

This was the time of the investiture struggles, and partisans of his predecessor, Geoffroy, who had been deposed for simony, at first opposed Ivo. Richer, archbishop of Sens, even refused to consecrate him. Ivo went, however, to Rome and was consecrated there by the pope himself, who wrote from Capua on November 25, 1090, to the clergy and people of Chartres.[2] Notwithstanding the papal consecration, Richer dared to summon Ivo to a council at Étampes but nothing came of it.

Early in his pontificate Ivo stood strongly against the

---

[1] He should be carefully distinguished from another St. Yves, son of Haelori, and hence called Yves Hélory, born at the manor of Kermartin in 1253, died there 1303. On this patron saint of the legal profession, see *Larousse du XXe Siècle* (Paris, 1933) 6.1116, and the little book by the lawyer, Alexandre Masseron, *Saint Yves d'après les témoins de sa vie* (Paris, Michel, 1952). Apparently, neither the Cornish nor the Huntingdonshire towns of St. Ives were named for our man: see *Encycl. Brit.*, 11th ed., 24.10; Baedeker's *Great Britain* (Leipzig, 8th ed., 1927), 156, 335.

[2] MPL 151.325.

adulterous marriage of King Philip I of France to Berthade de Montfort, wife of Foulque of Anjou, and boldly wrote a critical letter (no. 15) to the king, for which offense he was imprisoned for a time in the Château de Puiset by Hugues, Vicomte of Chartres, the king's vassal. Released a few months later, Ivo went again to Rome in November, 1093. After Philip I was excommunicated at Clermont in 1095, it was Ivo who in the next year negotiated the first absolution of the king. Throughout his life Ivo displayed the most devoted loyalty to both the papacy and his native land. In the whole of the investiture struggle he constantly belonged to the moderate party and was influential in settling the controversy, though he died before the Concordat of Worms in 1122.[3] He sometimes appeared as a patron of Gallican liberties, and thus won a place in Flacius Illyricus' *Catalogue*[4] as one of the pre-Reformation witnesses to the truth embodied later in the Reformation.

Ivo was often consulted, especially on canonical matters, and he is credited with being the most important canonist in the West before Gratian. His character is well portrayed in his letters and sermons: faithful, high-minded, full of zeal and piety, sound in judgment, and a keen jurist.

The two longest of the works are the *Decretum*[5] and the *Panormia*,[6] both on canon law, completed before 1096. The latter was the more successful and makes an advance over the earlier work of Burchard of Worms (d. 1025), in that it treats a far greater number of canons. The *Prologue*[7] to the *Decretum* furnishes rules for solving discrepancies between passages in the texts of the fathers and councils. A third work on canon law is the *Collectio tripartita*, so called from its threefold arrangement, but it still awaits publication.

A total of 328 letters[8] have been preserved, and there are twenty-five sermons[9] on liturgical, dogmatic, and moral

[3] For his views on this, see Epist. 60, 189, 232, 236, 237.
[4] Matthias Flacius, surnamed Illyricus (1520–1575), *Catalogus testium veritatis qui ante nostram aetatem reclamarunt papae* (Basel, 1556).
[5] MPL 161.59–1022, in fourteen parts.
[6] MPL 161.1037–1344, in eight books.
[7] *Prologus in Decretum a se concinnatum et partibus seu libris septem ac decem digestum* (MPL 161.47–60).
[8] MPL 162.11–290 has 288 letters; Merlet, *Lettres de Saint Yves, évêque de Chartres* (1885), prints forty more. The letters and sermons are in MGH, *Liber imperatorum et pontificum* 2.64–67. Jean Leclercq has begun a new printing of the letters in *Yves de Chartres: Correspondences classiques de l'histoire de France au moyen age* (Paris, Belles Lettres, 1949), vol. 1: years 1090–1098.
[9] Sermons (MPL 162.506–610).

questions, of which we print the twenty-second, *On the Lord's Prayer*, and the twenty-third, *On the Apostles' Creed*.

There is also a commentary on The Psalms which has not yet been printed. The *Micrologus de ecclesiasticis observationibus*[10] is, rather, by Bernold of Constance (d. 1110). Ivo's feast has been kept since 1570 on May 20, but when he was canonized is unknown.

On various phases of Ivo's life and work, consult F. P. Bliemetzrieder, "Zu den Schriften Yves von Chartres" (*Sitzungsberichte d. Akad. Wien* 182 [1918] 6 ff.); J. DeGhellinck, *Le Mouvement Théologique du XIIe Siècle* (Bruges, 2d ed., 1949), 445–459; John Mason Neale, *Mediaeval Preachers and Mediaeval Preaching* (London, Mozley, 1856), 91–101; Leopold Schmidt, "Der heilige Ivo, Bischof von Chartres" (*Studien und Mitteilungen aus dem kirchengeschichtlichen Seminar der theologische Fakultät der k.-k. Universität in Wien* 7 [Wien, Mayer, 1911], 1–129); A. Sieber, *Bischof Ivo von Chartres und seine Stellung zu den kirchenpolitischen Fragen seiner Zeit* (Königsberg, 1885); anonymous articles in *Gallia Christiana* 8.1126 and MPL 161.1–50; and the articles by E. Amann and L. Guizard (DTC 15.3625–3640), K. Guggenheimer (LTK 5.736), and Antonio Rota (EC 7.534 f.).

[10] MPL 162.609 f., 151.974–1022.

Ivo of Chartres: Two Sermons

THE TEXT

XXII. Sermon on the Lord's Prayer

There are two points, dearest friends, to which man ought to give his principal attention, the dignity of his creation and the excellence of his reformation. The dignity of his creation, that he may fear to sin; the excellence of his redemption, that he may not be ungrateful for redeeming grace. For by the will of the Creator alone was man lifted from the low estate of earth and uplifted to God's image by the privilege of reason. This dignity wretched man lost when, persuaded by the devil's seduction, he departed from the teaching of his Creator by his own pride. Thinking of this fall, the psalmist said by way of comfort: "Man when he was in honor, did not understand; he was likened unto beasts that have no intelligence, and was made identical with them."[11] Falling from the highest exaltation, he was, by his own will, condemned to the lowest degradation. He was able to fall of his own act but could not of himself rise again. Man's frailty must bewail this fall in daily lamentation, so that through daily lamentation he may return to the state from which he fell through vain enticements, and what fell by the foot of arrogance must rise by the foot of obedience. Noting this, the psalmist said: "Let not the foot of arrogance come upon me. There those who work iniquity have fallen; they have been pushed down and they could not stand."[12] "They have been pushed down" by inner restlessness; "they could not stand," that is, return of their own action. Of these same people the same psalmist speaks thus: "Because they are flesh, a wind that goes and does not return."[13] For this conversion or resurrection the healing grace of the Redeemer was

---

[11] Ps. 49:12 (48:13, V)—Latin versions differ sharply from the English.
[12] Ps. 36:11 f. (35:12, V).   [13] Ps. 78:39 (77:39, V).

necessary to cure with humility what had been corrupted by the height of pride. Therefore, the Word of God put on the form of a servant[14] in which he could both teach his fellow servants in word and by the example of his life give instruction to them in the discipline of moral living. By word and example he made known humility and obedience when he exhorted his disciples, saying: "Lift my yoke upon you and learn from me because I am gentle and lowly in heart. . . . For my yoke is easy and my burden is light."[15] For the yoke of his obedience is rightly easy, to serve whom is to reign, and the burden of his teaching is light because he does not increase its weight by bearing down but gives assistance for fulfillment through grace. He also spoke of soberness in word when he said, "Let not your hearts be weighted down in gluttony and drunkenness."[16] He who fed the crowd which accompanied him, not on fine food but on barley loaves,[17] taught by example. He taught our zeal, turning it toward inner goods, how to fast, when he said: "When you fast, do not become dismal like hypocrites,"[18] alluding to those who simulate the rigor of fasting by means of filthy wailing, so that they may seem to men to be fasting. How alms should silently be given he was unwilling to pass over, when he said: "When you give alms, let not your left hand know what your right hand is doing,"[19] meaning by this teaching that we should be admonished that when we give alms or do every work of mercy which we do, we should do it, not hunting for the praises of men but with zeal for eternal life, which is meant by the "right hand." He admonished us how also we should pray when he said, "When you pray, however, go into your bedroom,"[20] that is, keep your heart quiet and free of every tumult of activity, "and when the door is shut," that is, the host of fancies shut out, "pray to your Father."

There you have it said how to pray. He also added what should be prayed for, continuing as follows: "Our Father,"[21] etc. This prayer compactly, that is, in seven petitions, comprises all types of prayer which we should address to God, either those referring to good things which we ask for or to evils which should be avoided or our misdeeds which should be destroyed. Of these seven petitions, the three placed first pertain to eternity, the four following to the necessities of this life. For the hallowing of God's name and his coming, by which we under-

---

[14] Phil. 2:5–6. [15] Matt. 11:29 f. [16] Luke 21:34.
[17] Matt. 14:13–21; Mark 6:32–44; Luke 9:10–17; John 6:5–14.
[18] Matt. 6:16. [19] Matt. 6:3. [20] Matt. 6:6. [21] Matt. 6:9–13.

stand his coming in glory and the fulfillment of his will as in heaven, so also on earth, both the righteous and sinners, both soul and body, both Christ and the Church. Although they take their beginning from the lowly coming of Christ, nevertheless, they will be fulfilled only at the end of the world, and all three will remain through eternity. The remaining four, however, appear to pertain to this temporary life because the daily bread, that is, spiritual bread, may be eternal, yet pertains to this life, in so far as it ministers to the soul by certain symbols, that is, spoken or written, and therefore it is so called bread because in work and explanation it is learned, and swallowed, as if it were eaten. Now,[22] also, sins are forgiven us, and we forgive others, which is the second petition[23] of the four, and now[22] temptations infest our life, and the deliverance from evil pertains to this life because we undergo death through God's justice. For this reason we must be delivered by his mercy. Since this is so, the words of the petitions themselves must be handled carefully so that, when understood, they may produce greater affection in the heart and what is asked may be effected more speedily. Let us say, therefore, "Our Father," not submitting to him in fear but in love. No earlier people were told to pray to a father, but the Lord was recommended to those who obeyed him, not in filial love, but subjected to him in the fear of servants. In this word, however, let the rich and noble be admonished, when they have become Christians, not to raise themselves up against the poor and the commonalty, since they say together "*Our* father," something they could not say truthfully and devoutly if they did not recognize themselves as brothers. Therefore, by this name love is stimulated, because sons ought to have nothing dearer than their father, and also humble affection when men say "*Our* Father," and there is also a certain probability that we shall obtain what we ask when even before we ask we have received so great a gift that we can say "*Our* Father." For what now will a Father not give to his sons when they ask him who has already given this very gift of sonship? Finally, how great care touches the mind of one who says "Our Father" that he be not unworthy of so great a Father. Therefore, let the people, a new people called to eternity, use the words of the New Testament, "Our Father." The prayer is brotherly: it does not say "*My* Father," as if praying only for oneself, but

---

[22] That is, in this life.
[23] The text (MPL 162.601) here reads "portion," but *Codex Petavianus* appears to have had the right word.

"*Our* Father," embracing, you see, in a single prayer all who recognize themselves to be brothers in Christ. "Who dwellest[24] in the heavens," that is, among those "whose manner of life is in the heavens."[25] The metaphor is so very appropriate that it may be supposed that there is as much distance between the righteous and the sinner as physically between heaven and earth, for it is said to the sinner, "Earth art thou and into earth shalt thou go,"[26] and in order to symbolize this fact, when we stand for prayer, we turn to the east from which the heaven rises, not because God is there, as if he had left the other parts of the world, but that the soul may be admonished to rise to a more excellent nature, that is, to God. Now let us note what must be asked: "Hallowed be Thy name." This is not asked as if the name of God were not holy, but that it be held holy by men and God may become so known to them that they may think there is nothing more holy to be more feared than to offend him, because to hallow God's name is to fear God, of whom it is said, "The fear of the Lord is the beginning of wisdom,"[27] and elsewhere, "The fear of the Lord remaining holy forever and ever."[28] Next, "Thy kingdom come," that is, be manifested in the world. As the blind do not have this present light, so the Kingdom of God, although it is everywhere, nevertheless is lacking for those who do not know; or so that we may reign through thy gift, thou in us and we in thee. This petition pertains to piety, which is in second[29] place among the Beatitudes, for if piety is that by which the meek are blessed, let us ask that the Kingdom of God may come to us, that is, that we become meek and resist not. Next: "Thy will be done as in heaven, so also on earth," that is, as among the angels, so also among men, or as among the righteous, so also among sinners, or so that the flesh may assent to thy will as the spirit assents.

Does this petition pertain to the knowledge which is placed in third place among the Beatitudes? For if it is the knowledge by which those who mourn are blessed, let us pray that God's will be done as in heaven, so also on earth, that is, that the flesh may assent to the spirit, because from no other source does

[24] The Vulgate agrees with the Greek and has *es* but Ivo has *habitas*.
[25] Phil. 3:20, following Vulgate in which πολίτευμα=*conversatio*, whence the meaningless "conversation" in A.V.
[26] Gen. 3:19. The point would be lost in R.S.V.'s "dust."
[27] Ps. 111:10 (110:10, V).
[28] Perhaps a loose quotation of Prov. 10:23 or 10:27. MPL 162.602 strangely says it is from Matt., ch. 18.
[29] Actually third (Matt. 5:5). See below.

human wretchedness have so much to bewail as that the flesh lusts against the spirit and the spirit against the flesh, so that we are compelled to cry out with the apostle: "Unhappy man that I am! Who shall deliver me from the body of this death?" [30] The fourth petition comes next: "Give us today our daily bread." This can be taken to mean simply corporal food and also spiritually to mean the bread of the divine Word. If the corporal bread is involved, the one who prays does not extend his prayer far into the future: he follows the precept of the Gospel which says: "Do not think about the morrow, for tomorrow will think about itself." [31] So also the blessed apostle warns us, "having food and clothing, to be satisfied with them." [32] But if he receives that bread spiritually, either understand it to be that supersubstantial bread of the soul because he transcends all substance who says of himself: "I am the living bread who came down from heaven," [33] or let it be that very understanding of the divine Word which is necessary for us for the rehabilitation of our damaged souls as long as it is called today. This petition pertains to courage, which is placed in fourth position as one climbs to the highest blessedness, for if courage is that by which those who hunger and thirst after righteousness become blessed, we must pray to be given that daily bread, strengthened[34] by which we may arrive at that perfect state of satisfaction.

Next: "And forgive us our debts." Perhaps someone has sinned against you. Give him pardon when he asks it of you, lest while you deny mercy to your brother, you cut off the forgiveness of your Father, as the apostle James says, "Judgment of God without mercy to him who has done no mercy." [35] This petition is in reference to counsel, which is placed in fifth position among the steps of blessedness, for it is counsel because the merciful are blessed; let us forgive our debtors their debts, and so let us pray that our debts, that is, our sins, be forgiven us, on account of which we are hampered from asking and obtaining pardon unless forgiveness given our brothers hastens it.

Next: "And lead us not into temptation," that is, do not allow us to be led, that is, led astray, by the tempter. This is therefore what we pray, not that God may not permit us to be tempted above what we can withstand, but may give us a

---

[30] Rom. 7:24. [31] Matt. 6:34. [32] I Tim. 6:8.
[33] John 6:41: "living" is added.
[34] *Confortati*, a pun on *fortitudo* rendered above as "courage."
[35] James 2:13.

happy issue with temptation so that we can withstand it. This petition pertains to understanding, which is placed in sixth position in the number of the Beatitudes, for understanding is that by which the pure in heart are blessed, that is, those who have their mind's eye clean of earthly dust. Let us pray not to be led into temptation, that is, not to have a heart of duplicity but one of simplicity, seeking after the good.

Next: "But deliver us from evil," to be sure, not into what we can be led, but from that in which we have been led. In this way there will be nothing left that must be regretted. With this petition that wisdom which has received seventh place among the Beatitudes is in harmony, for if it is wisdom by which the peacemakers are blessed, that is, those who, when all their movements are controlled, force all things to render service to the spirit, we ought to pray to be delivered from evil, for deliverance itself has made us free, that is, sons of God, with the result that in the spirit of adoption we may cry "Abba, Father." [36] Verily, however, in all these petitions, without doubt the meaning is that what is asked for is granted by God, if the covenant of final creation is firmly held.

These three kinds of medicine are especially recommended to us by the heavenly Physician, namely, alms, fasting, and prayer. With these taken as if they were remedies, we may be able to cure evils of long duration, ward off current ones, and, by preserving our health, prevent those in days to come. These three are fitly kinds of cure as they also outdo three kinds of corruption. For every sin either takes place in the soul by consent of a wicked thought to violate God's temple, or takes place in an evil use of the body to wound a neighbor, which is criminal, or takes place in an evil use of the body to corrupt itself, which is shameful. For crimes may take place through the agency of the body, such as homicide, rape, theft, and yet not affect or harm the body of the one who does them, and of them the apostle says: "Every sin, whichever a man does, is outside the body" [37]; but shameful acts are done also through the body and they affect and infect the body, and of them the apostle says: "Who, however, commits fornication, sins against his own body." [38] Properly, therefore, do alms, as if by external medicine, cleanse the crimes which take place outside the body, because as a crime is harmful to a neighbor, so alms, which are outside us, and yet are given through the body, ought to be profitable to a neighbor. But shameful deeds are fitly cleansed

---

[36] Rom. 8:15.   [37] I Cor. 6:18.   [38] *Ibid.*, loosely cited.

by the medicine of fasting, because as the willing flesh has brought us to fault, so, when afflicted, it ought to lead back to pardon. But if there are those with whom these medicines do not agree, so that they cannot give alms on account of extreme poverty or cannot fast on account of weakness of the stomach, they have a third kind of medicine, from which he will be unable to excuse himself unless he refuses to cure the diseases of his soul. This medicine, therefore, which no soul can lack, let us zealously and devotedly often use, fulfilling the precept of the apostle, "Pray without ceasing." [39] For this remedy is available for all diseases, with the result that, diligently used, it may drive away all diseases and restore every corrupted body to health through the aid of our Lord Jesus Christ, to whom are glory and honor forever and ever. Amen.

XXIII. Sermon on the Apostles' Creed

It is known to you, beloved, that soldiers of this life, when about to receive temporal benefices from temporal lords, are first bound by soldiers' oaths, and make profession that they will keep faith with their lords. How much more ought those about to fight for the eternal King and to receive eternal rewards, to be bound by heavenly oaths, and publicly profess the faith through which they are going to please him! For the apostle says, "Without faith it is impossible to please God." [40] He who examines the heart and kidneys recognizes this in our hearts, but on account of preserving the unity of the church, in the dispensation of this present age, an oral confession is necessary along with the faith that is felt in the heart, because "in the heart it is believed unto righteousness but with the mouth confession is made unto salvation," [41] not only of preachers but of hearers also. For not otherwise can a brother be pleased with a brother, nor the peace of the church be preserved, nor can anyone teach another or learn from another the things necessary to salvation except he convey what he has in his heart to the hearts of others by the use of verbal symbols, as if they were his vehicles. Therefore, faith ought both to be preserved in the heart and expressed on the lips, for faith is the foundation of all good things, the beginning of human salvation. Without this no one will be able to reach the number of the sons of God, because without it neither in this world does he acquire the grace of justification nor in the future world will he

[39] I Thess. 5:17.   [40] Heb. 11:6.   [41] Rom. 10:10.

possess life eternal. And if anyone does not walk by faith, he will not reach the place where he can see. Recognizing this, the holy apostles have handed down to us a rule of faith which is expressed in accordance with the number of the apostles, in twelve propositions; and they called it a symbol through which those who believe might hold catholic unity and through which they might confound heretical wickedness. Members of any brotherhood, when they admit a person to their brotherhood, follow the custom of giving him a symbol and thereby strengthen the initial act of faith. Similarly, the holy apostles, establishing among themselves a spiritual brotherhood, have made this symbol by which those desiring to enter their brotherhood might bind themselves together in interchange of the faith and so might become sharers with them of the heavenly table. Therefore, let each man declare the apostolic faith, having confessed it through the lips of his sponsors in Baptism, when he shall have come to years of understanding: "I believe in God," and what he confesses with his lips, let him meditate in his heart. He does not say, "I believe God," [42] although this is necessary to salvation. For it is one thing to believe God because he is God, and a different thing to believe God, that he is truthful, because, as the apostle James witnesses, "even the demons believe and tremble," [43] but they do not believe in God because they are not moved by believing to enter into his will. Therefore, the spirit of fear is of no value to them because there is in them no spirit of love. But let us who through the adoption of grace are sons of God, say: "I believe in God the Father Almighty," that is, let us so believe him that we may cling to him through love. It means the Father who before time began begot the Son coeternal with himself. "Almighty, Creator of heaven and earth," that is, the one who by his omnipotence is creator of things celestial and terrestrial, that is, of things visible and things invisible, so that no one doubts that God can do all things who can, he hears, do all things. These things, however, were said against the Gentiles who through their faithlessness believed that the images which they had made were gods but neglected the true God by whom they were created. "And in Jesus Christ his only Son our Lord." As in the Father, so also must we believe in the Son. And because he is equal in glory with the Father, we owe as much honor to him as

---

[42] Latin *credo Deum* and *credo Deo* are approximate, respectively, to "I believe that [conj.] God . . ." and "I believe God."
[43] James 2:19.

we owe to the Father. "Jesus," however, is interpreted as "Saviour." The word "Christ" is derived from *chrism*,[44] because as ancient kings had holy oil poured on them, so our Lord Jesus Christ was fulfilled by the pouring on of the Holy Spirit. These show that we ought rightly to believe in him who, besides being the equal of the Father, is our Saviour, redeeming us, and Christ, that is, King, ruling us, and our only Lord, receiving us, when the ancient enemy is defeated, to his only Lord.

"Who was conceived of the Holy Spirit," that is, of whose conception the sole author was the Holy Spirit. For as the worm is formed from pure mud under the warming sun, so when the Holy Spirit inspired and hallowed the heart of the Virgin, the flesh of Christ was conceived from the flesh of the Virgin alone, working without any carnal seed. This is why he compares himself to a worm through the psalmist: "I am a worm and not a man,"[45] that is, not conceived in the human manner. "Born of the Virgin Mary," that is, as he did not open the womb of his mother when conceived, so also he did not open it when born. We do not say, as some most wickedly think, that the Holy Spirit had physical contact with the Virgin but that he worked through the might and power of the Creator. "The Word was made flesh,"[46] that is, was made man, conceived by the Virgin through the collaboration of the Father and the Holy Spirit, and born of the Virgin so that by an ineffable kind of procreation he who through the Holy Spirit effected the creation of himself might be in the Virgin the Creator of himself.

"Suffered under Pontius Pilate." The reference to Pilate involves an indication of the time, not an ennoblement of the person.

"Crucified, dead, and buried." The weaknesses of the incarnate Word are here recalled, about which the apostle says: "Because it is the weakness of God, it is stronger than men."[47] For therefore he suffered so that he might re-create us to a state of being incapable of suffering. He was therefore crucified that he might free us from eternal torment. He therefore died a true death, as he was born by a true birth, so that he might free us from eternal death. He was therefore buried that he might bury

---

[44] The real origin is, rather, the Greek adjective χριστός ("anointed" = Hebrew, *Messiah*). The chrism (Latin *chrisma* or *crisma*) was doubtless more familiar to Ivo.

[45] Ps. 22:6 (21:7, V). From the time of Aristotle to the seventeenth century, it was commonly believed that worms and other forms of life were produced by abiogenesis or spontaneous generation.

[46] John 1:14.   [47] I Cor. 1:25.

us with himself, together with our vices and lusts. For this reason the apostle says: "We were buried with Christ by baptism into death, so that in the manner in which Christ rose from the dead by the glory of the Father, we also might walk in newness of life." [48] That is, having laid aside all that is old, we may be formed in the likeness of Christ. For this weakness of Christ has conquered all the strength of the world. "On the third day he rose from the dead." The death of the three-day burial clearly shows that, while the body lay in the tomb, the soul triumphed over the lower world. "He ascended into heaven." Therefore he placed above the heavens at the right hand of the Father the condition of our nature which he had assumed from his human mother. "Sits." That he is said to sit, however, does not mean the position of his members but the power of a judge. "At the right hand of God the Father Almighty." But "at the right hand" must be understood to mean "in highest blessedness," as the goats are put on the left hand,[49] that is, in deepest wretchedness. "Thence he shall come to judge the living and the dead." He will judge the living and the dead, that is, he will raise up those whom his coming will find not yet dead according to our human death and those already dead, or it means by the living and the dead the righteous and sinners. Let those who profess this faith note in this symbol that Christ's humanity, by which they have been reconciled, is commemorated, so that they be not ungrateful for the benefits of their Redeemer, who reconciled them through his humanity, absolved them through his deity, lest by divine law on account of their ingratitude they be deprived of their Father's goods, granted to them.[50]

"I believe in the Holy Spirit," equal and consubstantial with the Father and the Son, proceeding from each equally.[51] For this reason one must also believe in him as in the Father and in the Son. "The holy catholic church," that is, the church throughout the world, not the one of which it is said, "Here it is; there it is," [52] that is, not what is said to be in the bedroom or in the wilderness, but that which is spread throughout the whole world and founded in unity of faith. "The communion of the saints," that is, the truth of the church's sacraments in which

---

[48] Rom. 6:4.   [49] Cf. Matt. 25:33.
[50] That is, as a probate court grants property to the heirs of a decedent.
[51] Here Ivo follows the doctrine of the double procession (the *Filioque* clause in the Niceno-Constantinopolitan creed).
[52] Matt. 24:23: the reference is to Christ, not to the church.

the saints who have departed from this life in the unity of the faith have communicated. "The forgiveness of sins." Not only of those which were forgiven through Baptism but also those which, through humble confession, have been cleansed in worthy satisfaction. "The resurrection of the flesh," which is to be common at the coming of the Lord, but different for the good from the evil, according to which the apostle says, "We shall all rise but we shall all be changed" [53]—for the better, understand. "Life eternal." This is what the same apostle says: "For the corruptible should put on incorruption and the mortal should put on immortality." [54]

These twelve propositions which most firmly pertain to the rule of true faith must be faithfully believed, strongly held, truly, patiently defended, and if we know anyone to lay down as Christian teaching what is contrary to them, we should avoid him like the plague and cast him out as a heretic. For as these propositions are laid down and expressed in brief compass, so they are in harmony with the catholic faith and are opposed to heretical perversity, that those who cling firmly to this rule of faith are not allowed to err or wander from the pathway of right faith. But whoever wishes to think otherwise, let us pray that God may deign to reveal it to him. Let us walk, however, in that which we have received, and in that which is certain for us let us firmly persevere. Teach this symbol to your spiritual children for whom you have made promise in Baptism, whom you have received from the holy fount. Teach this to your children whom you have gotten from your flesh. Teach this to those whom you have admitted to your protection, so that through your instruction they may avoid every error, they may flee from those who are hostile to the Christian faith, and may complete in all virtue those things which are fitting. Through the aid of our Lord Jesus Christ, who lives and is glorified with the Father and the Holy Spirit through undying ages forever. Amen.

[53] I Cor. 15:51. [54] I Cor. 15:53.

Agobard of Lyons

INTRODUCTION

AGOBARD, THE FORTY-FOURTH BISHOP OF LYONS (816–840), was born in 769, presumably in northern Spain. At the age of thirteen he removed to Gallia Narbonensis and in 792 to Lyons. From 804 to mid-816 he served the diocese as suffragan or assistant bishop. His superior, Bishop Leidrad, died December 28, 815, and Agobard was elected to succeed him. His investiture in the see of Lyons took place in August, 816, shortly after the papal coronation of Emperor Louis the Pious.

Agobard's life was one of extensive productivity. Even before he became the ordinary of the diocese, he had combated recrudescences of paganism in the form of weather magic.[1] Hardly had he assumed direction of the church of Lyons when he faced the ethical problem of trials by ordeal and announced his resistance to them.[2] Almost immediately he confronted a short-lived reappearance of the Spanish adoptionist heresy.[3] Throughout the decade 820–830, Bishop Agobard, to the dismay of the court circle, conducted a campaign against what seemed to him to be a dangerous and increasing influence of the Jews in the Carolingian realm.[4] But other matters also attracted

---

[1] *De grandine et tonitruis* (MPL 104.147A–158C), c. 815.
[2] *Adversus legem Gundobadi* (MGH:EpKA, 3.158–164; MPL 104.113B–126B) and *Contra judicium Dei* (MPL 104.249C–286C), c. 817.
[3] *Adversum dogma Felicis Urgellensis* (MPL 104.29C–70A; MGH:EpKA, 3.153, *prooemium* only), c. 819.
[4] *De baptismo Judaeorum mancipiorum* (MGH:EpKA, 3.164–166; MPL 104.99D–106B), c. 823; *Contra praeceptum impium* (MGH:EpKA, 3.179–182; MPL 104.173D–178C), c. 826; *De insolentia Judaeorum* (MGH:EpKA, 3.182–185; MPL 104.69B–76B), c. 827; *De Judaicis superstitionibus* (MGH:EpKA, 3.185–199; MPL 104.77A–100C), c. 827; and *De cavendo convictu et societate Judaica* (MGH:EpKA, 3.199–201; MPL 104.107A–114B), c. 827.

328

his attention: he angered the court by demanding restitution of church lands long ago sequestered by Charles Martel[5]; he belatedly entered the iconoclastic debate on the side of Charlemagne's earlier and unimaginative moderation[6]; he began a handbook of Biblical selections which might serve to restrain human presumption[7]; he prepared an encyclical to his subordinates on clerical worthiness[8]; he urged the summoning of a synod to correct the degraded condition of the clergy[9]; he appealed to political authority to assume greater responsibility for redress of injustice[10]; again he used his prestige to suppress a demonstration of folk paganism in Uzès[11]; and he defended himself against an odious theological attack made by Fredegisus, Alcuin's successor as abbot of Tours.[12]

In the heat of such feverish activity he did not neglect the pastoral obligation to his flock, for from the year 829 or 830 comes his sole extant sermon, *On the Truth of the Faith and the Establishment of All Good*[13] (which we here translate). No doubt there were many others, but this one is probably a fair illustration of Agobard's homiletic style, heavily Scriptural, highly discursive, and seriously theological. It may be outlined in a general manner as follows:

Introduction: a gentle reproof of pilgrimages, I, II.

A. The doctrine of the Trinity, III-V.
B. The doctrine of the incarnation, VI-IX.
C. The union of Christ and the redeemed, X, XI.
D. The tribulation of the redeemed, XII-XV.
E. The community of the damned, XVI-XVIII.
F. The duties of the redeemed, XIX-XXVI.

Conclusion: an exhortation, XXVII, XXVIII.

[5] *De dispensatione ecclesiasticarum rerum* (MGH:EpKA, 3.166-179; MPL 104.227A-250B), c. early 825.
[6] *De imaginibus* (MPL 104.199B-228A), c. 825.
[7] *De spe et timore* (MGH:EpKA, 3.222 f.; MPL 104.323A-326B), c. 826 (?).
[8] *De modo regiminis ecclesiastici* (MPL 104.189A-200A), c. 826.
[9] *De privilegio et jure sacerdotii* (MPL 104.127A-148A; MGH:EpKA, 3.203-206, chs. 11-20 only), c. 826 or early 827.
[10] *De injustitiis* (MGH:EpKA, 3.201-203; MPL 104.185C-190A), c. late 827 or early 828.
[11] *De quorumdam inlusione signorum* (MGH:EpKA, 3.206-210; MPL 104.179A-186A), c. 829.
[12] *Contra objectiones Fredegisi abbatis* (MGH:EpKA, 3.210-221; MPL 104.159A-174C), c. 830.
[13] *Sermo exhortatorius ad plebem de fidei veritate et totius boni institutione* (MPL 104.267C-288A), c. 829 or 830 (?).

During the decade 830–840, the Carolingian empire was rent by civil strife and disorder, and Agobard was in the thick of it although he was then in his sixties. Sensitive to public opinion, he tried in vain to forewarn Emperor Louis of the revolt of 833.[14] In that action he openly espoused the cause of Louis's sons although they were in rebellion against their father,[15] delivered a violent tirade against Empress Judith,[16] and justified the deposition of Louis.[17] As a result, when Louis returned to power Agobard was banished from his see from 834 to 838. His last writings came within the period of exile or immediately thereafter.

While Agobard was away from Lyons, the *locum tenens* of the see was Amalarius of Metz (c. 775 to c. 850), the first liturgical scholar in the Western church. Favoring the Roman standard, yet a daring individualist at heart, Amalarius strove to supplant the old usages of Lyons with his somewhat novel ideas. Led by Deacon Florus (c. 800 to c. 860),[18] a portion of the clergy of Lyons launched a movement of opposition to Amalarius severe enough to secure his condemnation for heresy in September, 838. Meanwhile Agobard had written three books against Amalarius: the brief tract, *On Divine Psalmody*[19] (see our translation below), a more comprehensive treatise on *The Correction of the Antiphonary*,[20] and a vigorous critique[21] of Amalarius' *magnum opus*, the *Liber officialis*.[22] In an almost

[14] *De divisione imperii Francorum inter filios Ludovici* (MGH:EpKA, 3.223–226; MPL 104.287B–292B), c. late 831.
[15] *De comparatione regiminis ecclesiastici et politici* (MGH:EpKA, 3.226–228; MPL 104.291C–298B), between April 13 and June 1, 833.
[16] "Manifesto" (MGH:Scriptores, 15.274 f.; MPL 104.307C–315B), between June 1 and 24, 833. This is the first six chapters of what is usually entitled *Liber apologeticus* (see next note).
[17] *Liber apologeticus pro filiis Ludovici pii imperatoris adversus patrem* (MGH: Scriptores, 15.276–279; MPL 104.315B–320C), mid-November 833. This title is reserved for chs. 7–13 (see preceding note). Agobard also prepared a brief statement confirming his presence at Louis's deposition, *Chartula porrecta Lothario in synodo Compendiensi* (MGH:Leges, 1.369; MPL 104.319D–324A), November, 833.
[18] M. Manitius, *Geschichte der lateinischen Literatur des Mittelalters* (Munich: Beck, 1911), 1.560–567; also Cabaniss, "Florus of Lyons," to appear in a forthcoming issue of *Classica et Mediaevalia*.
[19] *De divina psalmodia* (MPL 104.325C–330A), 835–838. This may be construed as an introduction to the following and not as a separate work.
[20] *De correctione antiphonarii* (MGH:EpKA, 3.232–238; MPL 104.329B–340A), 835–838.
[21] *Contra libros quatuor Amalarii* (MPL 104.339A–350B), 835–838.
[22] J. M. Hanssens, ed., *Amalarii episcopi opera liturgica omnia, Liber officialis* (*Studi e Testi*, 1.139; Città del Vaticano: Biblioteca Apostolica Vaticana,

puritanical vein Agobard insisted that in church only Biblical compositions, nothing humanly devised, should be sung, and they without "theatrical intonations and showy melodies."[23] "As in the catholic creed we profess our faith," he states, "not with our own expressions but with those of the apostles, as in the Lord's Prayer we pray not with our own words but with those of our Lord and Saviour himself, so also in the office of divine praise let us sing, not human compositions, but, according to the apostle, divine and spiritual psalms, hymns, and canticles."[24]

Agobard was restored to his function and to imperial favor after the condemnation of Amalarius. He died June 6, 840, two weeks before the emperor's death. But it was Amalarius who won the field, for, apart from two or three followers, Agobard produced no school of thought. Indeed, he was virtually forgotten until 1605, when Papire Masson discovered the manuscript on which most of our knowledge of Agobard depends.[25] On the other hand, Amalarius has been copied, excerpted, and edited from his own day to the present. Such is the irony of history.

Of our selections for translation, Agobard's sermon provides an excellent illustration of the bishop's general approach to theology and his method of presenting it to his people. Above all, it demonstrates the strong Biblical interest of the school of Lyons. The brief statement concerning psalmody brings us to the heart of the never-ending controversy about the authority of Scripture in liturgical practice, one which the later Puritans noised abroad so long and so loudly. Both the works show Agobard, anything but subtle and retiring, as a man of plain, forthright common sense.

Manuscripts. Bibliothèque Nationale (Paris), 2853, saec. ix, contains all the prose works of Agobard except his *Contra libros*

1948). See also Hanssens, "Le Texte du 'Liber Officialis' d'Amalaire," *Ephemerides Liturgicae*, 47 (1933), 113–125, 225–424, 493–505; 48 (1934), 66–79, 223–232, 549–569; 49 (1935), 413–435. Also Cabaniss, "The Personality of Amalarius." (*Church History*, 20 [1951] 34–41); "The Literary Style of Amalarius: A Note." (*Philological Quarterly*, 31 [1952] 423–426); *Amalarius of Metz* (Amsterdam: North-Holland Publishing Co., 1954).

[23] *De correctione antiphonarii*, XII (MPL 104.334C): "theatralibus sonis et scenicis modulationibus. . . ."
[24] *Ibid.*, XIX (MPL 104.338D–340A). The Biblical reference is Eph. 5:19.
[25] Described in MPL 104.9B; MGH:Scriptores, 15.274; MGH:EpKA, 3.150.

IV Amalarii. Bibliothèque de Lyon, 618 (ex 535), saec. xii, contains *Contra libros IV Amalarii* and one of Agobard's other treatises. These two are all-important; five other MSS. contain works already found in these two. Three MSS. have probably been lost. The three "poems" attributed to Agobard may belong to other authors.[26]

Editions. Editio princeps (based on BN 2853 only): *Sancti Agobardi episcopi ecclesiae Lugdunensis opera. Quae octingentos annos in tenebris delituerant, nunc e PAPIRII MASSONI jurisconsulti bibliotheca proferuntur. Accesserunt binae epistolae Leidradi non antea excusae.* Parisiis: Excudebat Dionysius Duvallius, sub Pegaso, in vico Bellovaco, MDCV, cum privilegio regis. In the very year of publication this edition was placed on the Index "donec corrigatur." This condemnation presumably still stands, as it did in the 1929 edition of the Index.

The second edition (the fundamental one) is that of Étienne Baluze, Paris, Chez Muguet, 1666, 2 vols. Based on both BN 2853 and B. de Lyon 618 (ex 535), it is provided with copious notes of great usefulness.

There have been no other true editions. Abbé Migne republished Baluze's edition in MPL 104.29D–352B, with Baluze's notes together with Masson's preface, life of Agobard, and brief synopses of the works. Passages of varying length have been issued in three or four other collections. The treatises which are edited in various volumes of MGH are indicated in the notes to this Introduction.

Neither the *Sermon* nor *On Divine Psalmody* have been edited or published later than MPL, for which reason that text was employed in the ensuing translation, although in preparing the English version of the *Sermon* constant reference has been made to a photostatic reproduction of BN 2853 in our possession. The MPL printing is faulty in a number of places. Most of these have been quietly corrected, but a few of the more striking ones are noted.

Translations. Until now there have been no complete translations of any of Agobard's works into any language, although a number of extracts have been rendered here and there by writers dealing with the bishop.

[26] They are: *De translatione reliquiarum sanctorum martyrum Cypriani, Sperati, et Pantaleonis ad urbem Lugdunensem* (MGH:PLAC, 2.544 f.), among the works of Florus; MPL 104.349C–352B), c. 807 or 808; *Epitaphium Caroli magni imperatoris* (MGH:PLAC, 1.407 f., MPL 104.349BC), c. 814; and the acrostic *Agobardo pax sit* (MGH:PLAC, 2.118 f.); L. Traube, *Karolingische Dichtungen* (Berlin, Weidmann, 1888, 152–155), undated.

Brief Bibliography. 1. P. A. Klap, "Agobard van Lyon," *Theologisch Tijdschrift*, 29 (1895), 15–48, 121–151, 385–407; 30 (1896), 39–58, 379–401, 469–488.

2. J. Leonardi, *Agobard von Lyon und seine politische Publizistik* (Vienna, Lichtner, 1927).

3. Mgr. Bressolles, *Saint Agobard Évêque de Lyon* (Paris, Librairie J. Vrin, 1949). Completed in 1933, this was deposited as a typescript in the Bibliothèque de l'Institut Catholique (Paris) and in some private libraries. It was finally prepared for the press in 1947 and published two years later.

4. Allen Cabaniss, *Agobard of Lyons: Churchman and Critic* (Syracuse, Syracuse University Press, 1953). The Bibliographical Note, 98–113, contains full reference to all books by and about Agobard to date. This book is a complete reworking and rewriting of a PH.D. thesis, "Agobard of Lyons: A Ninth Century Ecclesiastic and Critic," University of Chicago, 1939, which carries extensive translations and annotations. The last chapter, "Agobard's Thought," was lithoprinted by the University of Chicago Libraries in 1941 for private distribution.

Other Agobardian materials by Cabaniss are: "Agobard of Lyons" (*Speculum*, 26 [1951] 50–76); "Agobard and Amalarius: a Comparison" (*Journal of Ecclesiastical History*, 3 [1952] 125–131); "Saint Agobard as Art Critic," *Studies Presented to David Moore Robinson*, ed. G. E. Mylonas and D. Raymond (Saint Louis, Washington University, 1953), 2.1023–1028; "Agobard of Lyons: Rumour, Propaganda, and Freedom of Thought in the Ninth Century" (*History Today*, 3 [1953] 128–134), reprinted as "Agobard of Lyons" in *Diversions of History*, ed. Peter Quennell (London, Allan Wingate, 1954), 41–51.

Agobard of Lyons: On the Truth of the Faith and the Establishment of All Good—An Exhortatory Sermon to the People[27]

THE TEXT

I. Hearken, our brothers, household of Christ, flock of the supreme shepherd, people of his pasture, and sheep of his hand. Enter the gates of the everlasting King with confession, and his courts with hymns,[28] that it may be said to you, "Behold now, bless the Lord, all you servants of the Lord, that stand in the house of the Lord, in the courts of the house of our God.[29] Seek the Lord while he can be found: call upon him while he is near."[30] How near indeed he is! "For in him we live and are moved and have our being."[31] He is deep in all minds, around all bodies; he fills up within, surrounds without, bears up below, covers above.[32] But the time will come when he who is now so near cannot be found. Why will he not be found who is everywhere and who is nowhere absent? Because there will not be time for seeking the Lord, but only for suffering of punishments by those who do not find him now. Do what the psalmist says, "Let all thy works give thanks to thee, O Lord, and let all thy saints bless thee."[33] Bless him with them and give thanks to the Lord with all his works.

II. It is not needful for you to wander from place to place, from this kingdom to another, to seek the Lord.[34] Offering

---

[27] The MS. title is simply "Agobard's Sermon" (*Agobardi sermo*).
[28] Phrases from Ps. 100 (99, V).
[29] Conflation of Ps. 134:1 and Ps. 135:2 (133:1 and 134:2, V).
[30] Isa. 55:6.   [31] Acts 17:28.
[32] Reminiscent of St. Patrick's "Breastplate" (a hymn). For "around all bodies" MPL has *cunctis corporibus interior*, but the MS. clearly reads *cunctis corporibus exterior*, which provides a better parallel for "deep in all minds" (*cunctis mentibus interior*).
[33] Ps. 145:10 (144:10, V).
[34] This moderate reproof of the custom of pilgrimage is of a character

himself to you freely, he says, "Behold, I stand at the door and knock; if anyone hears my voice and opens the door, I will come in to him and eat with him, and he with me."[35] What was ever so sweet, so pleasant? Besides he adds, "He who conquers, I will grant him to sit with me on my throne."[36] See, he wishes to come in to you that you may dine with him. May it not irk you to open the door! Not only does he wish to eat with you in your mind, but he also wishes to lift you up to his throne to sit with him. What more should one desire to whom such things are promised? Yet the Lord promises more: "If anyone loves me, he will keep my word, and my Father will love him, and we will come to him and make our home with him."[37] Let your loins therefore be girded and let the lamps in your hands be burning, and be you like men awaiting their Lord when he returns from the marriage, that when he shall come and knock they may immediately open up for him.[38] Blessed are those servants to whom the Father and the Son come to make their home. But woe to those who drive away from themselves such a guest, for unto a malicious soul wisdom shall not enter; nor dwell in the body that is subject unto sin. For the holy spirit of discipline will flee deceit, and remove from thoughts that are without understanding.[39] Be therefore unwilling to ponder vain things, be unwilling to long for things that will perish; moreover, avoid silly and old wives' fables, and train yourselves in godliness.[40] Open to the Lord who is knocking, that he may come in to you and eat with you and make his home with you. He does not knock silently, but as he knocks he says to every one, "Open to me, my sister, my lover, my dove, my spotless one."[41] "But, applying every effort, provide in your faith virtue and in virtue knowledge."[42] Since by reflecting on faith and hope you increase in knowledge and understanding of God, you do not live worthlessly or fruitlessly. Thus you keep the Lord as your guest.

III. Faith is that whereby we believe[43] one almighty God, Father, Son, and Holy Spirit, true Trinity, true Unity.[44] O

similar to Agobard's disapproval of employing representations ("pictures") in worship as well as to his rejection of all but Scriptural words in the musical parts of the divine office.

[35] Rev. 3:20.   [36] Rev. 3:21.   [37] John 14:23.   [38] Matt. 25:1–13.
[39] Wisdom 1:4, 5.   [40] I Tim. 4:7.   [41] S. of S. 5:2.   [42] II Peter 1:5.
[43] "Fides est qua credimus...." Note that Agobard differentiates *faith* and *belief* and suggests that faith is the instrumentality or means of belief, a quasi-Lutheran position, if one may use anachronistic terminology.
[44] Note here and in the remainder of the paragraph phrases from the *Symbolum quicunque*.

what genuine Trinity wherein none is born of himself, none proceeds from himself, but one from another! That is to say, the Son is begotten of the Father, the Holy Spirit proceeds from the Father and the Son. It appears, therefore, without doubt that there is one who has begotten, another who has been begotten, another who proceeds from both. O what genuine Unity, wherein there is not one Spirit of the Father, another of the Son, but one of both! Nor does he proceed first from the Father into the Son, then from the Son to diffuse the gift of charity into the hearts of believers; but at once from both. There is not one Godhead of the Father, another of the Son, another of the Holy Spirit, but one Godhead of the three; and for that reason truly one God. For if it were one and another, it would not be one. There is therefore one Godhead, one eternal, one majesty, one mightiness, one will, one activity, one affection, one glory. Since there is distinctly one person and another person—therefore the Trinity; but since there is not one thing and another thing—therefore the Unity. Because he who is the Son is not himself the Father, nor is he who is the Father himself the Son or the Holy Spirit—therefore genuine Trinity; yet because what the Son is the Father is and what the Father and Spirit are the Son is—therefore genuine Unity.[45]

Neither the power nor the will of the Father preceded the birth of the Son. So there was nothing to precede the procession of the Holy Spirit. We acknowledge the Father as the begetter of the Son; moreover, as maker of heaven and earth and of all things visible and invisible.[46] We acknowledge the Son as only-begotten of the Father, God of God, light of light, very God of very God, begotten, not made, *homoousios* with the Father (that is, of the same substance with the Father), by whom were made all things in heaven and on earth, through whom the angels praise the Father's majesty, whom the dominions worship, and before whom the powers, heavens, and virtues of the heavens tremble.[47] We acknowledge the Holy Spirit as the lifegiver, proceeding from the Father and the Son, with the Father and the Son together to be worshiped and glorified, who spoke through the prophets. We acknowledge the three together as giving grace, Father, Son, and Holy Spirit, undivided without

---

[45] The MS. reads *Trinitas*, but the MPL correction *Unitas* is undoubtedly proper.
[46] This sentence and the next two are derived from the Nicene Creed. The Greek word *homoousion* appears in the MS. in Latin letters as *homousyon*.
[47] Phrases from early Prefaces of the Mass.

confusion, everlasting without time, equal without difference; one Lord, great and praiseworthy beyond degree, of whose greatness there is no end and of whose wisdom there is no measure; great, indeed, not in size but in worthiness; who, while he is nowhere by mass of body, is nowhere absent by uncircumscribed substance.

IV. From the heavens and in the heights all angels, all virtues, sun and moon, stars and light, the heavens of heavens, and the waters which are above the heavens praise this true Trinity, this true Unity, this one God. Because he himself spoke and they were made; he commanded and they were created. From the earth they praise him, dragons and all deeps, fire, hail, snow, ice, stormy winds, mountains and hills, fruit trees and all cedars, beasts and all cattle, serpents and flying birds, kings of the earth and all peoples, princes and all judges of the earth, young men and maidens, old men and the younger ones, for his name is exalted. His glory is above heaven and earth, and his praise is in the assembly of his saints; praised, indeed, in his saints, in the firmament of his power, in his virtues, according to the abundance of his greatness, with sound of trumpet, with psaltery and harp, with timbrel and dance, with strings and pipe, with well-sounding cymbals, with cymbals of joyfulness.[48]

V. Since therefore all these creatures, rational and irrational, ceaselessly praise God, how should men, made in the image and likeness of God and called to the praise of his glory, be slow or dull or indifferent? Those creatures indeed always praise the Lord. But let us praise him at least frequently, even if we cannot always do so, we to whom it is declared by the apostle, "You are a chosen race, a royal priesthood, a holy nation, a people of possession, that you may proclaim the virtues of him who called you out of darkness into his marvelous light." [49] And by the prophets: "Tell of all his wonderful works, declare his zeal among the nations, make known his deeds among the peoples." [50] About such virtues and marvels, the words of Holy Scripture thus assert, "Who makes the winds his messengers and a flaming fire his minister. Who set the earth on its foundation; it shall not be shaken forever.[51] Who laid its cornerstone,

---

[48] Phrases from the Psalms of Lauds, 148, 149, 150.
[49] I Peter 2:9.
[50] A catena of passages from I Chron. 16:8, 9, 24 (I Para. 16:8, 9, 24, V); Ps. 105:1, 2 (104:1, 2, V); Isa. 12:3.
[51] Adapted from Ps. 104:4, 5 (103:4, 5, V).

when the morning stars together praised him and all the sons of God shouted for joy.[52] By his power the seas were gathered together and by his understanding he smote the proud.[53] Who stretches out the north wind over void and hangs the earth upon nothing. Who binds up the waters in his thick clouds and they do not break forth together below.[54] Who draws up the drops of rain" (or as another translation says, "the numberless tricklings of the rain").[55] "Who has measured the waters in the hollow of his hand and marked off the heavens with a span. Who has weighed the fabric of the earth with three fingers and weighed the mountains in a measure and the fields in a balance.[56] Whose throne was fiery flames and its wheels burning fire. A swift stream of fire issued from his face. Thousands of thousands serve him and ten thousand times a hundred thousands appear before him."[57] For all the hosts of heaven attend him not only on the right but also on the left, out of whom the prophet saw a spirit emerge which said, "I will go forth and will be a lying spirit in the mouth of all his prophets,"[58] that is, prophets of the king beguiled and to be beguiled to go up to the place where death was made ready for him.

VI. Since the holy man Job was enviable, the prince or great one of the host on the left desired that he [Job] might be surrendered to him [Satan] by the Lord, not for the purpose of testing what was done through him [Satan] while that one [Job] was unwilling, but to condemn what he [Satan] sought in the abundance of his own malice. Aflame with fire of envy, the prince of this host on the left also approached the first man, made well and good by the good God,[59] beguiled him, made him a liar, and subjected him to every manner of corruption. Thrust down from the society of angels, he [Satan] made him [Adam] his companion and, dragged away from angelic light, subdued him to his own darkness, rendering him liable to

---

[52] Job 38:7. [53] Job 26:12. [54] Job 38:9.
[55] Job 36:27. Here the "other translation" is no doubt an Old Latin version. In his writings Agobard demonstrates considerable familiarity with different versions, possibly also with Greek, and perhaps even with Hebrew. See a presentation of the "evidence" in Cabaniss, *Agobard of Lyons*, 116–118. In *Contra objectiones Fredegisi*, 9 (MPL 104.164D–165A), Agobard mentions the following: the LXX, Latin translations of the LXX, the versions of Aquila, Theodotion, and Symmachus, Jerome's Vulgate, and Latin versions other than Jerome's. Cf. note 45 below.
[56] Isa. 40:12. [57] Dan. 7:9, 10.
[58] I Kings 22:22 (III Kings 22:22, V).
[59] Cannot one almost hear the French, "le bon Dieu"?

eternal death. But to repair so great a fall, so great a wound, the Lord, supremely good and kind, sent his own Son, God the Word, to become flesh (that is, true man) and to dwell among us (that is, in perfect humanity, which he assumed for us from us, that is, from the holy Virgin prepared and preserved[60] for this purpose); moreover, to dwell corporeally, not spiritually, as in other holy ones, that is, by the gift of grace, as it is written, "He who is united to the Lord is one spirit." [61] For although they are united to the Lord and God dwells in them, it does not thereby come to pass that they are gods by nature; [62] in Christ, however, dwells all the fullness of the Godhead bodily, so that he is God in very substance. The humanity which he undertook can be nothing other than God and the unique Son, since the only-begotten became flesh in order to be true God, true man, one God. And although flesh is one thing, deity another, he is not one person in the flesh, another in the Godhead, but one Christ in both, God-man, the reality and integrity of each nature remaining. Humanity was not changed into divinity, nor divinity converted into humanity. One Christ of both is thus God and is worshiped with the Father and the Son, as we said above, just as he was worshiped before the Word was made flesh. For unchangeable Deity, who in his incarnation took our infirmity that he might die, could be neither diminished nor increased.[63]

VII. Our one Lord Jesus Christ, true God and true man, came therefore to the Passion that he might endure all those things foretold of him by the Scriptures. Wherefore, arrested, bound, scourged, mocked, and hanged on the cross, when the hour came for him by his own power to lay down his life with power to resume it, he says, crying with a loud voice, "It is finished," and, with head bowed, he gave up the spirit.[64] Having been born of a true birth, he endured a true passion of true flesh, he endured true death; and by means of a true resurrection of the flesh "he presented himself alive to the disciples by many proofs, appearing to them during forty days and speaking of the kingdom of God." [65] He ate and drank in

[60] Mgr. Bressolles, *Saint Agobard Évêque de Lyon*, 126, n. 1, asks if this word does not contain an allusion to the dogma of the Immaculate Conception.
[61] I Cor. 6:17.
[62] On the idea mentioned here consult E. Kantorowicz, "*Deus per Naturam, Deus per Gratiam*: A Note on Mediaeval Political Theology" (*Harvard Theological Review*, 45 [1952] 253–277).
[63] An allusion to Spanish adoptionism. See note 81 below.
[64] John 19:30.   [65] Acts 1:3.

their presence, not by reason of necessity, but to show forth his power.[66]

"As they were looking on, he was lifted up, and a cloud took him out of their sight. And while they were gazing into heaven as he went, behold, two men stood by them in white robes, who also said, 'Men of Galilee, why do you stand looking into heaven? This Jesus, who was taken up from you into heaven, will come in the same way as you saw him going into heaven.'"[67] Wherefore at the right hand of God he sits in that flesh which he assumed for us, and he will come in glory to judge the living and the dead, whose Kingdom shall have no end.[68] Verily he is the propitiation for our sins, he who is the faithful witness, the firstborn of the dead, the Prince of the kings of the earth, the Lamb of God who takes away the sins of the world;[69] who is thus with the Father praised by the angels: "To him who sits upon the throne and to the Lamb be blessing and honor and glory and might forever and ever."[70] When he shall come in his own and the Father's majesty, he shall be so feared by those whom he is to judge that they will say to the mountains and rocks, "Fall on us and hide us from the face of him who is seated on the throne, and from the wrath of the Lamb; for the great day of his wrath has come, and who can stand?"[71]

When that has been accomplished, all the elect of all nations, tribes, peoples, and tongues shall be standing before the throne in the presence of the Lamb, clothed with white garments and with palms in their hands. They shall cry with a loud voice, "Salvation to our God who sits upon the throne, and to the Lamb."[72] Of them it is said, "These are they who have come out of the great tribulation; and they have washed their robes and made them white in the blood of the Lamb. Therefore are they before the throne of God, and serve him day and night within his temple; and he who sits upon the throne dwells above them. They shall hunger no more, neither thirst any more; the sun shall not fall upon them, nor any scorching heat; for the Lamb, who is in the midst of the throne, will direct them, and he will guide them to springs of living waters; and God will wipe away every tear from their eyes.[73] And ever-

---

[66] Luke 24:43.   [67] Acts 1:9–11.
[68] Phrases from the Nicene Creed.
[69] A catena of passages from I John 2:2; 4:10; Rev. 1:5; John 1:29.
[70] Rev. 5:13.   [71] Rev. 6:16, 17.   [72] Rev. 7:10.
[73] Rev. 7:14–17. Is there an internal allusion to Ps. 23:2 (22:2; V)?

lasting joy shall be upon their head; they shall obtain joy and gladness, and sorrow and sighing shall flee away."[74]

This city of God (that is, the total society of all the saints) "has no need of sun or moon to shine upon it, for the brightness of God has enlightened it, and its lamp is the Lamb."[75] To it shall be said: "Injustice shall no more be heard in your land, devastation or destruction within your borders; salvation shall overspread your walls, and praise, your gates. The sun shall be yours no more for light by day, nor shall the brightness of the moon give light to you; but the Lord will be to you for everlasting light, and your days of mourning shall be ended. Your people shall be all righteous; they shall inherit the land forever."[76] "The nations shall see your just one, and all the kings your illustrious ones; and a new name shall be cited for you, which the mouth of the Lord has named. You shall be a crown of glory in the hand of the Lord, and a diadem of sovereignty in the hand of your God. You shall no more be termed 'Forsaken,' and your land shall no more be termed 'Desolate'; but you shall be called 'My delight is in her,' and your land 'Inhabited'; for in you the Lord is delighted, and your land shall be inhabited. For a young man shall dwell with a virgin, and your sons shall dwell in you. And the bridegroom shall rejoice over the bride, and your God shall rejoice over you."[77] "Nothing unclean shall enter it, nor anyone who practices abomination or falsehood,"[78] nor foolish virgins, who did not take oil with them[79]; none except those who have been inscribed in the Lamb's book of life, and they shall reign forever and ever.[80]

VIII. These noble testimonies of Holy Scripture demonstrate the unity and equality of the one sitting upon the throne and the Lamb, that is, the Father and the Son, as also there is said to be one great day of their wrath. For he remained equal to the Father even after he was made less than the Father.[81] Wherefore also the holy fathers, that is to say, the doctors of the church, have handed down a very brief hymn which we add to psalms, antiphons, and responsories: "Glory be to the Father, and to the Son, and to the Holy Ghost; as it was in the beginning, is now, and ever shall be, world without end."[82]

---

[74] Isa. 35:10.   [75] Rev. 21:23.   [76] Isa. 60:18–21.   [77] Isa. 62:2–5.
[78] Rev. 21:27.   [79] Cf. Matt. 25:1–13.   [80] Rev. 21:27.
[81] Possibly an allusion to Spanish adoptionism, as in note 63 above. Agobard's treatise, "Against the Dogma of Felix of Urgel," is one of our chief sources of information about the archheretic and his doctrines. Consult Cabaniss, "The Heresiarch Felix" (*Catholic Historical Review*, 39 [1953] 129–141).   [82] The familiar lesser Doxology.

Since the elect of all peoples and tongues are said to stand before the throne in the presence of the Lamb, and since one "Salvation" only is sung to him who sits upon the throne and to the Lamb, and since they equally illuminate their city,[83] this fact is demonstrated, namely, that we acknowledge the Father and the Son and to be one even after he, when made less, became obedient unto death, the death of the cross. "Therefore God has highly exalted him and bestowed on him the name which is above every name, that at the name of Jesus every knee should bow, of things in heaven, on earth, and in the underworld, and every tongue confess that Jesus Christ is Lord in the glory of God the Father." [84] It shows to what height the exalted head lifts his body, as well as the unity of the head and body, that is to say the bridegroom and the bride. Wherefore it is said, "He has clothed me with the garments of salvation, he has covered me with the robe of righteousness, as a bridegroom decked with a garland, and as a bride adorned with her jewels." [85] For he has stated that he is both bridegroom and bride. This great unity is that inestimable and unutterable good which eye has not seen, nor ear heard, nor has it entered the heart of man what God has prepared for those who love him[86]; for the Lamb is indeed the bridegroom of his own flesh, the shepherd of his own sheep. He is, moreover, a lamb in the Passion, lion in the resurrection, eagle in the ascension,[87] also the cornerstone,[88] and the stone hewn from the mountain not with hands which has become a huge mountain filling the whole earth.[89] This is the Kingdom which shall never be destroyed, nor delivered to another people, but shall itself stand forever.[90] Of this unity and unutterable elevation of head and body, the prophet Daniel speaks: "I saw in a vision of the night, and behold, with clouds of heaven there came as it were a son of man, and he came to the Ancient of Days and they presented him before him. And to him he gave power and honor and kingdom, and all peoples, tribes, and languages shall serve him; his power is an everlasting power, which shall not be borne away, and his kingdom one that shall not be destroyed." [91]

IX. This unity and elevation of head and body, still future

---

[83] Cf. Rev. 7:9, 10; 21:23.   [84] Phil. 2:9–11.
[85] Isa. 61:10.   [86] Cf. I Cor. 2:9.
[87] Three non-Scriptural allusions perhaps derived from art; consult Cabaniss, "Saint Agobard as Art Critic."
[88] Eph. 2:20, and elsewhere.
[89] Dan. 2:34, 45.   [90] Dan. 2:44.   [91] Dan. 7:13, 14.

in splendor and in reality, must even now, with every effort of affection, be held in faith and in hope. The apostle commends this highly: "He who descended is he who also ascended above all the heavens, that he might fill all things. He granted that some should be apostles, some prophets, some evangelists, some pastors and teachers, for the equipment of the saints for the work of the ministry, for the building up of the body of Christ, until we all attain to the unity of the faith and knowledge of the Son of God, to mature manhood, to the measure of the age of the fullness of Christ; so that we may no longer be children tossed to and fro, and carried about with every wind of doctrine by the cunning of men, by craftiness in the circumvention of error. Practicing the truth with charity, let us rather grow up in every way in him who is the head, Christ, whose whole body joined together by every joint with which it is supplied, according to the working of each part properly, makes growth of the body unto the upbuilding of itself in love." [92] Again: "The head, from whom the whole body, supplied and knit together through its joints and ligaments, grows unto increase." [93] And in another place: "With eagerness maintain the unity of the Spirit in the bond of peace. There is one body and one Spirit, just as you were called in one hope of your calling, one Lord, one faith, one baptism. One God is the Father of all, who is above all and through all and in us all." [94] Similarly, concerning the unity of the members: "For just as the body is one," he says, "and has many members, and all the members of the body, though they are many, are one body, so also is Christ. For in one Spirit we were all baptized into one body, Jews or Gentiles, slaves or free, and all have drunk in one Spirit. For the body is not one member but many." [95]

X. Moreover, the apostle teaches that the mediation of the mediator between God and man, our Lord Jesus Christ, yokes every elect creature to the Father, so that by this ineffable unity of spirit there is no distinction of race, condition, or sex, but that the one household and city of God is made as well of angels as of men, and that of this great and marvelous unity the one head is Christ: "Do not lie to one another, putting off the old man with his practices and putting on the new, who is being renewed in knowledge after the image of him who created him; where there is not Gentile and Jew, circumcision and uncircumcision, barbarian and Scythian, slave and free, but

[92] Eph. 4:10–16.   [93] Col. 2:19.   [94] Eph. 4:3–6.   [95] I Cor. 12:12–14.

Christ is all and in all."⁹⁶ And again: "As many of you as were baptized into Christ have put on Christ. There is neither Jew nor Greek, there is neither slave nor free, there is neither male nor female; for you are all one in Christ Jesus." ⁹⁷ Elsewhere: "But I want you to understand that the head of every man is Christ; the head of a woman, the husband; and the head of Christ, God." ⁹⁸ And likewise: "For all things are yours, and you are Christ's, and Christ is God's." ⁹⁹ In another place: "He is the image of the invisible God, the first-born of all creation; for in him all things were created in the heavens and on earth, visible and invisible, whether thrones or dominions or principalities or authorities, all things were created through him and in him. He is indeed before all things, and in him all things hold together. He is the Head of the body, the church, who is the beginning, the first-born from the dead, that in everything he may be the one holding pre-eminence. For in him all the fullness was pleased to dwell, and through him all things were reconciled to himself, pacifying through the blood of his cross things whether on earth or in heaven."¹ And yet again: "For in him the whole fullness of deity dwells bodily, and you have been completed in him, who is the Head of all rule and authority." ²

XI. For this ineffable unity the mediator between God and man, the God-man himself, Christ Jesus, prayed the Father at the time of his Passion, saying: "Sanctify them in the truth; thy word is truth. As thou didst send me into the world, I have also sent them into the world. And for their sakes I consecrate myself, that they also may be consecrated in truth. But I do not pray for these only, but also for those who are to believe in me through their word, that they may all be one; even as thou, Father, in me, and I in thee, that they also may be one in us, that the world may believe that thou hast sent me. The glory which thou hast given me I have given them, that they may be one even as also we are one. I in them and thou in me, that they may know that thou hast sent me and hast loved them even as thou hast also loved me. Father, I desire that they also, whom thou hast given me, may be with me where I am, to behold my

⁹⁶ Col. 3:9-11. Cf. Agobard's rather poignant version of one of these passages in his *Adversus legem Gundobadi*, 3 (MPL 104.115A): "Where there is neither Gentile nor Jew, circumcision nor uncircumcision, barbarian nor Scythian, Aquitanian nor Lombard, Burgundian nor Alaman, slave nor free, but Christ is all and in all."
⁹⁷ Gal. 3:27, 28.   ⁹⁸ I Cor. 11:3.   ⁹⁹ I Cor. 3:22, 23.
¹ Col. 1:15-20.   ² Col. 2:9.

glory which thou hast given me because thou hast loved me before the foundation of the world." [3]

When this very great and very sublime unity shall be accomplished, the apostle shows most earnestly when he says, "As in Adam all die, so also in Christ shall all be made alive. But each in his own order: Christ the first fruits, then those who are Christ's who have believed in his coming. Then the end, when he shall have delivered the Kingdom to God and the Father, when he shall have laid waste every rule and authority and power. For he must reign until he has put all his enemies under his feet. But the last enemy, death, shall be destroyed. For he has put all things under his feet." [4] Yet again: "Lo, I tell you a mystery. We shall indeed all arise, but we shall not all be changed, in a moment, in the twinkling of an eye, at the last trumpet. For the trumpet will sound, and the dead will be raised uncorrupted, and we shall be changed. For this corruptible must put on incorruption, and this mortal put on immortality. When this mortal shall have put on immortality, then shall come to pass the saying that is written, 'Death is swallowed up in victory. O death, where is thy victory? O death, where is thy sting?' The sting of death is sin; the power of death, the law. But thanks be to God, who has given us the victory through our Lord Jesus Christ." [5] One does not arrive at this victory except by striving, for he should not be crowned unless he shall have striven lawfully.

XII. Of this unity the portion still on pilgrimage here on earth has adversaries against whom it fights unremittingly, because all who wish to live devoutly in Christ Jesus suffer persecution. First, there are the devil and his angels, our enemies, against whom the apostle wishes us to be armed: "Put on the armor of God, that you may be able to stand against the wiles of the devil. For our struggle is not against flesh and blood, but against princes and powers, against the rulers of the world of this darkness, against spiritual ones of wickedness in the heavenly places. Therefore take the armor of God that you may be able to withstand in the evil day, and having been perfected in all things, to stand. Stand therefore, having girded your loins with truth, and having been clothed with the breastplate of righteousness, and having shod the feet for the preparation of the gospel of peace; in all things taking

---

[3] John 17:17–24.   [4] I Cor. 15:22–27; cf. Ps. 8:6; Eph. 1:22.
[5] I Cor. 15:51–57. Note how the Latin of verse 51 differs from the Greek. Cf. Isa. 25:8; Hos. 13:14.

the shield of faith, with which you can quench all the fiery darts of the most evil one. And take the helmet of salvation and the sword of the Spirit, which is the word of God, praying at all times in the Spirit, by means of all prayer and supplication."[6]

Secondly, there are men publicly persecuting, of whom the Lord himself speaks: "Behold, I send you as sheep in the midst of wolves; so be wise as serpents and innocent as doves. Beware of men. For they will deliver you up in councils, and flog you in their synagogues, and you will be dragged before governors and kings for my sake, for a testimony to them and the Gentiles."[7] There are also other persecutors who hound with enmities, grudges, rejections, accusations, injuries, contentions, and various severities. Against them one should fight, not with weapons, but with forbearance and endurance; as the apostle teaches that we ought to be patient toward everyone and the Lord commands us not to resist evil. "If anyone shall strike you on the right cheek, offer him the other also."[8] And again: "Love your enemies, do good to those who hate you, and pray for the ones persecuting and falsely accusing you,[9] so that you may be sons of your Father who is in the heavens."[10] Still further: "If you will forgive men their trespasses, your Heavenly Father will forgive your offenses; but if you will not forgive men, neither will your Father forgive your trespasses."[11]

Thirdly, there are enemies of the faith of whom the apostle says, "In the last times some will depart from the faith, giving heed to the spirits of error and doctrines of demons, by the pretension of ones speaking a lie."[12] Against them one should fight, not with corporeal, but with spiritual weapons, namely, by examples, by authority of the Scriptures, by reasonings[13] of faith and truth. Finally, there are daily enemies, whom we can avoid neither by place nor by times, whom the apostle enumerates: "Do not gratify the desires of the flesh. For the flesh lusts against the Spirit, and the Spirit against the flesh; for these are opposed to each other, so that you may not do whatever things you would. But if you are led by the Spirit, you are not under the law. Now the works of the flesh are plain, which are fornication, impurity, licentiousness, idolatry, sorceries, enmities, strifes, jealousies, anger, brawls, dissensions, partisanship, envy, murders, drunkenness, carousings, and things like these; which I warn you, as I warned you before, that those

---

[6] Eph. 6:11–18. [7] Matt. 10:16–18. [8] Matt. 5:39.
[9] Luke 6:27, 28. [10] Matt. 5:45. [11] Matt. 6:14, 15.
[12] I Tim. 4:1, 2. [13] Observe Agobard's mention of reason.

who do such things shall not attain the Kingdom of God."[14] Against them one must fight not only by reason, but also by exertion, abstinence, continence, and vigils,[15] as the apostle informs us by his own example: "I pommel my body and subject it to slavery, lest perchance preaching to others I myself should be disqualified."[16] Wherefore near the end of his life, while instructing a disciple, he boasts with this assurance: "As for you, be watchful, strive in all things, do the work of an evangelist, fulfill your ministry. For I am already diminished and the time of my dissolution is at hand. I have fought a good fight, I have finished the race, I have kept the faith. Henceforth there is laid up for me a crown of righteousness, which the Lord, the righteous judge, will award to me on that day, yet not only to me but also to all who love his appearing."[17]

XIII. Amid all these things let the believer beware that he not presume altogether or even in part on his own powers, but on God's help, to arrive at the culmination of goodness and to persevere in good works, as the Lord says, "Apart from me you can do nothing."[18] The apostle also: "It is God who is at work in you, both to will and to accomplish for good favor."[19] And again: "By grace you have been saved through faith, and that not of yourselves."[20] Still further: "Not that we are able to consider anything by us as though from us, but our sufficiency is from God."[21] The Lord says, "No one can come to me unless the Father who sent me shall draw him."[22] God does in man many good things which man does not do; but man does no good things which God does not show man how to do. For truly men do their own will, not God's, when they perform that which displeases God. But when they do what they will so that they serve the divine will, it is his will by which what they will is foreseen and decreed although they do voluntarily what they do. God loves us as we shall be by his grace, not as we are by our own merit. God foresees, foreknows, assists, and rewards in us his own goodness. No one is good but God alone, who is not good with the goodness of another. Men, however, are good, not by their own goodness, but by the goodness of God, who is the fount and source of goodness; nay, rather, who is goodness, from whom comes all good, and without whom there is nothing good.[23]

[14] Gal. 5:16–21.
[15] See note 13 above.
[16] I Cor. 9:27.
[17] II Tim. 4:5–8.
[18] John 15:5.
[19] Phil. 2:13.
[20] Eph. 2:8.
[21] II Cor. 3:5.
[22] John 6:44.
[23] Observe the allusion to predestination, a doctrine hotly controverted and defended in the ninth century.

XIV. This, the faith and hope of the catholic church (which is the pillar and bulwark of the truth[24]), has been preached in the Law and the Prophets, in psalms and hymns, proclaimed by apostles, attested by martyrs, explained by teachers. Whatever is contrary to this faith, and whatever things are discordant and different are foolish, profane, and vainly spoken. They profit much for wickedness, and for that reason are the doctrines of demons and antichrists, of whom the apostle says, "Little children, it is the last hour; and as you have heard that antichrist is coming, now many antichrists have come."[25] Of them another apostle says, "These are grumblers, malcontents, walking according to their own passions, and their mouth speaking pride."[26]

Of them all the head is Antichrist, of whom the apostle warns, "Now concerning the coming of our Lord Jesus Christ and our assembling unto him, we beg you, brethren, not to be quickly shaken from your reason or excited either by spirit or word, or by letter as if sent from us, as though the day of the Lord were present. Let no one deceive you in any way. For unless the rebellion comes first and the man of sin is revealed, the son of perdition, who opposes and exalts himself above everything that is called divine or that is worshiped, so that he takes his seat in the temple of God, displaying himself as though he were God. Do you not remember that when I was still among you I told you these things? Now you know what is restraining him so that he may be revealed in his time. For the mystery of wickedness is already at work; only that he who now restrains it will restrain it until he is done away from the midst. Then that wicked one will be revealed, whom the Lord Jesus will slay with the breath of his mouth and by the brightness of his own coming will destroy him whose coming is, by the activity of Satan, with all power and with pretended signs and wonders, and with all deception of wickedness for those who are perishing, because they did not receive the love of truth so as to be saved. Therefore God will send upon them the working of error, that they may believe a lie, and all be condemned who did not believe the truth, but consented to unrighteousness."[27] Of that time the Lord also says in the Gospel, "Then there will be great tribulation, such as has not been from the beginning of the world until now, nor will be. And unless those days had been shortened, not all flesh would be saved;

[24] I Tim. 3:15.
[25] I John 2:18.
[26] Jude 16.
[27] II Thess. 2:1–12.

but for the sake of the elect those days will be shortened. Then if anyone says to you, 'Lo, here is the Christ!' or, 'There he is!' do not believe it. For false Christs and false prophets will arise and show great signs and wonders, so that if possible even the elect may be led astray. Lo, I have told you beforehand."[28]

Of Antichrist the prophet Daniel foretells thus: "He shall speak words against the Most High and shall wear out the saints of the Most High and shall think that he can change the times and the laws; and they shall be given into his hand for a time, times, and half a time. But judgment shall decree that dominion shall be taken away and consumed and destroyed to the end. But the kingdom and the dominion and the greatness of the kingdom which is under the whole heaven shall be given to the people of the saints of the Most High, whose kingdom shall be everlasting."[29] And again: "Out of one of them came forth a little horn. It became great toward the south, toward the east, and toward the host. It was magnified even to the host of heaven. Some of the host and some of the stars it cast down and trampled upon them. It magnified itself even up to the prince of the host. It took away from him the continual sacrifice and overthrew the place of hallowing. The host was given to it as well as the continual sacrifice for sins. And truth will be prostrate, yet it will act and it will prosper."[30] Still further: "After their rule, when transgressions shall have increased, a king bold of countenance and understanding intentions shall arise. His power shall be strengthened but not by his own forces; and beyond what can be believed he shall lay waste everything and shall be successful and shall act. He shall kill mighty men and the people of the saints as he will. Cunning shall be directed in his hand and his heart shall magnify, and in abundance of all things he shall destroy many. He shall rise up against the prince of princes, but, by no hand, he shall be broken."[31] Yet more: "The king shall do according to his will. He shall be exalted and magnified against every god, and shall speak astonishing things against the God of gods. He shall be guided till the indignation is accomplished, for what is determined has been accomplished. He shall give no heed to the god of his fathers, and he shall be in the desires of women; he shall not give heed to any other gods, for he shall rise up against all things."[32]

[28] Matt. 24:21-25.
[29] Dan. 7:25-27.
[30] Dan. 8:9-12 (very obscure in Latin, Greek, and Hebrew alike).
[31] Dan. 8:23-25.
[32] Dan. 11:36, 37.

In the Apocalypse it is written: "I saw a beast rising out of the sea, having seven horns and ten heads, and ten diadems upon its horn and a name of blasphemy upon its heads. The beast that I saw was like a leopard, and its feet like a bear's, and its mouth like a lion's mouth. To it the dragon gave his power and great authority. I saw one of its heads as though wounded to death, but its deathblow was healed, and the whole earth marveled after the beast. They worshiped the beast, saying, 'Who is like the beast, and who can fight against it?' To it was given a mouth uttering haughty things and blasphemy, and to it was given authority to act for forty-two months; and it opened its mouth in blasphemies against God, to blaspheme his name and his dwelling and those who dwell in heaven. To it also was given to make war with the saints and to conquer them."[33] And further: "Then I saw another beast arising from the earth; and it had two horns like a lamb's and it spoke like a dragon. It exercised all the authority of the first beast in its presence, and made the earth and its inhabitants worship the first beast whose death wound was healed. It worked great signs, as even to make fire come down from heaven to earth in the sight of men; and by the signs which are granted it to do in the presence of the beast, it deceived those who dwell on earth."[34]

Yet more: "I will tell you the mystery of the woman, and of the beast which has seven heads and ten horns that carries her. The beast that you saw was, and is not, and is to ascend from the abyss, and will go to perdition. The dwellers on earth whose names have not been written in the book of life from the foundation of the earth will marvel, beholding what was and is not. This is the mind which has wisdom: the seven heads are seven hills on which the woman is seated. They are also seven kings; five have fallen, one is, the other has not yet come, and when he comes, he must remain a short time. The beast that was and is not, it is an eighth but it is of the seven, and it goes to perdition. The ten horns that you saw are ten kings who have not yet received royal power, but they receive authority as kings for one hour after the beast. These have one mind and will give over their power and authority to the beast. They will make war on the Lamb and the Lamb will conquer them, for

---

[33] Rev. 13:1–7. Agobard does not follow exactly the Latin or Greek text. This seems to be a clear case of erroneous quotation from memory or perhaps a paraphrase (see note 96 above and notes 83, 85, and 11 below).
[34] Rev. 13:11–14.

he is Lord of Lords and King of Kings, and those with him are called and chosen and faithful." [35] And again: "I saw the beast and the kings of the earth and their armies gathered to make war against him who sat upon the horse and against his army. The beast was captured, and with it the false prophet who in its presence worked the signs by which he deceived those who received the mark of the beast and who worship its image. These two were thrown alive into the lake of fire of burning brimstone. The rest were slain by the sword that issues from the mouth of the one sitting upon the horse." [36] Still further: "When the thousand years are ended, Satan will be loosed from his prison and will come out and will deceive the nations which are at the corners of the earth, Gog and Magog, and will gather them for battle; whose number is like the sand of the sea. They went up over the height of the earth and surrounded the camp of the saints and the beloved city; but fire came down from God out of heaven and consumed them, and the devil who deceived them was thrown into the lake of fire and brimstone, where the beast and the false prophets will be tormented day and night forever and ever." [37]

XV. Here there are said to be three: the devil and the beast which is Antichrist and the false prophet who will display in pretended signs and wonders all the power of Antichrist. The two beasts, by the action of the devil, are pre-eminent in the whole body of the lost. But the devil is indeed the author and cause of all evil, although invisible to men living after the flesh. He is also a murderer from the beginning.[38] All the evils which he has engaged in he has accomplished and still accomplishes through men. That first evil, however, which he perpetrated, the deception of the first human beings, he wrought through the serpent, because there was no man through whom the first humans might be deceived. Through the serpent he spoke to Eve, through Eve to Adam. Then through Cain he killed Abel. Thereafter all evils sprouted forth, and iniquities increased and still increase, until they reach the pinnacle of evil, namely, when, God permitting and ordaining, the devil should adopt a vessel most suitable to himself, that is, a man, a condemned and corrupted one, or rather the chief of the corrupted ones, who will grow up into such great wickedness that man may display himself as the worst of all creatures, and regard himself as though he were God, and rise up against everything and exalt

[35] Rev. 17:7–14.
[36] Rev. 19:19–21.
[37] Rev. 20:7–10.
[38] John 8:44.

himself and boast that he is above everything that is called divine and that is worshiped as divine. Of him it has already been said by the Lord: "Upon earth there is not a power which may be compared with him who is made that he might fear nothing. He beholds everything high; he is king over all the sons of pride." [39] That we may know that this is spoken of him is shown earlier: "Though the sword shall reach him, it cannot avail; nor the spear, nor the breastplate." [40]

XVI. That there is one body of all the lost[41] (whose head is Antichrist himself) is shown in the place where it was said, "The members of his flesh are cleaving together." [42] And again: "His body is as it were molten shields, shut up closely with scales covering it. One is joined to another and no breath indeed pierces them. One is joined to the other and clasping each other they shall not be separated." [43] Concerning that body and its head, the devil or Antichrist, the prophet Ezekiel speaks: "Behold, I am against you, Pharaoh, king of Egypt, the great dragon that lies in the midst of the streams and says, 'Mine is the river and I made it myself.' I will put a hook in your jaws and make the fish of your streams stick to your scales. I will draw you out of the midst of your streams, and all your fish will stick to your scales. I will cast forth into the wilderness you and all the fish of your streams." [44]

Here is a statement about his power drawn from a Hebrew translation of The Psalms: "In the depth of his frenzy the wicked shall not seek him; neither is God in all his thoughts. His ways prosper at all times; thy judgments are far away out of his sight; he looks down upon all his foes. He speaks in his heart, 'I shall not be moved from generation to generation; I shall have no adversity.' His mouth is filled with cursing, deceits, and greed; under his tongue are fraud and iniquity. He also sits in ambush near the entrances in hiding places that he may murder the innocent. His eyes stealthily watch the strong men; he lurks in secret like a lion in a covert; he lurks that he may seize the poor when he draws him into his net. The crushed one submits and rushes violently with his own energies." [45]

---

[39] Job 41:33, 34.   [40] Job 41:26.   [41] The doctrine of *corpus diaboli*.
[42] Job 41:23.   [43] Job 41:15-17.   [44] Ezek. 29:3-5.
[45] Ps. 10:4-10 (9:25-31, V). Here is an instance of another version which seems to be based on the Hebrew text. If Agobard was not facile enough with Hebrew, his bright young deacon Florus was. Cf. Florus, *Opuscula adversus Amalarium*, I, 10 (MPL 119.79A): "Care must be taken lest the sacred volumes be polluted by the extremely ignorant author of those errors [Amalarius], for he consistently discusses them with Hebrews, but

XVII. Another psalm sets forth the nature of this body of the devil and Antichrist and what remains for it in the future: "Why do you boast of mischief, O man, who are mighty in wickedness?" and so forth.[46] The book of Wisdom also speaks of this body of the lost, how at the end of time the man weighted down with everlasting miseries achieves a late and fruitless repentance, "Then shall the righteous stand in great steadfastness," and the other words which follow.[47] "Therefore have we erred from the way of truth, and the light of righteousness hath not shined unto us, and the sun of understanding rose not upon us. We were wearied in the way of wickedness and destruction; we have gone through difficult ways, but the way of the Lord we have not known. What hath pride profited us, or what hath vaunting riches brought us? All those things are passed away like a shadow, and as a messenger hastening by and as a ship that passeth over the billowing water."[48] That there is one body composed of lost angels and men, destined for a common doom, the Lord shows in the Gospel where he says that at the judgment he will declare, "Depart from me, you cursed, into the eternal fire which has been prepared for the devil and his angels."[49] At the end of his book, the prophet Isaiah says of the doom of malevolent angels and men, "They shall go forth" (that is, the saints) "and look on the corpses of the men that have lied against me; their worm shall not die, and their fire shall not be quenched, and they shall be an abhorrence of sight to all flesh."[50]

In the Gospel this punishment and place of punishment is called "outer darkness," where that servant is cast who is convicted, not of fraud, but of unprofitableness, because he did not wish to increase the talent he had received by banking it;[51] and where another was cast, bound hand and foot, who was present at a wedding not clothed in a wedding garment.[52] Often in the Scriptures the same place is called Sheol, as in Proverbs, "The path of life is above the wise man, that you may avoid deepest Sheol;"[53] and as the righteous king Hezekiah says to the Lord, "Sheol shall not thank thee, death shall not praise thee."[54] And in the psalm, "In Sheol who shall give thee

because he has no familiarity with their language or their literature, he often, so I hear, corrupts those things which are proper." Consult also the paper, "Florus of Lyons," to appear in a forthcoming issue of *Classica et Mediaevalia*.

[46] Ps. 52:1 (51:3, V). [47] Wisdom 5:1. [48] Wisdom 5:6–10.
[49] Matt. 25:41. [50] Isa. 66:24. [51] Matt. 25:30.
[52] Matt. 22:13. [53] Prov. 15:24. [54] Isa. 38:18.

praise?"[55] Again: "The dead shall not praise thee, O Lord, nor those that go down into Sheol."[56] Blessed Job says, "All my works go down to deepest Sheol."[57] It is also designated by other names, as again blessed Job says to the Lord, "Let me alone that I may lament a little before I go (and I shall not return) to a land gloomy and covered with darkness of death, a land of misery and gloom, where is the shadow of death, and where dwells no order, only everlasting dread."[58] What is meant by the phrase "gloomy land" if not the enclosed land of Tartarus?[59] Not improperly is Sheol denominated a land, for those who have been seized by it [by him?] are firmly held. He therefore who is banished from the presence of the busy Judge is detained in a "land of misery and gloom," because outside grief tortures those whom, divided from the true light within, blindness darkens; that avenging flame of sins accomplished has no consuming power or light.

XVIII. Yet one must know that, as "in the Father's house are many rooms"[60] for diversity of worth, so dissimilarity of offense subjects the damned in the fires of Gehenna to different punishments. This Gehenna by no means burns all with one and the same quality, although there is only one Gehenna. These punishments torture beyond strength the ones plunged into it; and even while extinguishing in them the bulwark of life the punishments keep them alive that the end may punish life, seeing that one may live forever without cessation of torment, for one hastens through tortures toward an end, but failing he endures without end. It becomes therefore for wretched ones a deathless death, an endless end, a ceaseless cessation, since death lives, the end ever begins, and cessation knows not how to cease.[61] There also light does not shine for encouragement, but rather blazes upon someone to torture him. For by the light of the flame the condemned ones will see in torment along with themselves their own posterity, whose love they have offended. For the increase of their own damnation, the Creator afflicts them also with the death of the very ones whose life they loved in the flesh contrary to his commandments. This place of punishment is called a lake, too, but one in which there is no water, as Zechariah suggests: "You have by the blood of your

---

[55] Ps. 6:5 (6:6, V).   [56] Ps. 115:17 (113:25, V).   [57] Job 17:16.
[58] Job 10:20-22.
[59] See the relevant remarks by Cabaniss, "The Harrowing of Hell, Psalm 24, and Pliny the Younger: A Note" (*Vigiliae Christianae*, 7 [1953] 65-74).
[60] John 14:2.   [61] Cf. Gregory the Great, *Moralia in Iob*, 9.48.

covenant set your captives free of the lake in which there is no water." [62] And by righteous king Hezekiah: "Those who go down into the lake shall not hope for thy truth." [63] The depths of the lake are called the bottom of the lake and the depths of the abyss. [64]

XIX. You therefore, purified by the water of Baptism and honored by the Christian name and sealed with the sign of salvation, ponder carefully, examine earnestly if we have anything we rightfully fear, if there is anything we ought with all solicitude of mind to avoid; and let us henceforth by no means neglect to consider, as the holy psalm teaches: "For I confess my iniquity and I meditate on my sin." [65] Again: "I know my transgression and my sin is ever before me." [66] Moreover, let us therein fill not only our minds with meditation but also our tongues with speech. So far as other temporal dangers are smaller, by so much the less may they disturb us. But so far as they are greater, by so much the more may they disquiet, afflict, and vex us with profound sorrows, sighs, and groans, that it may happen to us as it is written: "O Lord, pierce my flesh with thy fear, for I am afraid of thy judgments." [67] Ponder faithfully what blessed Job admits of himself: "I was in terror of God as of waves billowing over me, and I could not have borne his majesty." [68]

If he who so feared could ever fill his mind with vain thoughts or his tongue with indifferent words, cast the eyes of your mind upon the regions round about and consider the mortals of our times. [69] What do you see them intent on; what do they think, say, and do? How many are there who try to obey what the apostle enjoined: "Let no evil talk come out of your mouth, but only such as is good for edifying faith, that it may impart grace to those who hear." [70] Again: "Let the word of Christ dwell in you richly in all wisdom as you teach and admonish one another in psalms and hymns and spiritual songs, as you sing

---

[62] Zech. 9:11.   [63] Isa. 38:18.
[64] For a modern man, this paragraph inevitably conjures up recollections of Jonathan Edwards' famous sermon, "Sinners in the Hands of an Angry God."
[65] Ps. 38:18 (37:19, V). The beginning of this paragraph has a few words from the baptismal liturgy.
[66] Ps. 51:3 (50:5, V).   [67] Ps. 119:120 (118:120, V).
[68] Job 31:23.
[69] A good homiletic device, indicating that Agobard is keeping his present congregation and its circumstances before his mind.
[70] Eph. 4:29.

with thankfulness in your hearts to God. Whatever you do, in word or deed, do everything in the name of the Lord Jesus, giving thanks to God and the Father through him." 71 Again: "What then, brethren? When you come together, each one of you has a psalm, a lesson, a revelation, a tongue, an interpretation. Let all things be done for edification." 72 Still further: "So whether you eat or drink, or whether you do anything else, do all to the glory of God." 73 Utterly so indeed, as the Lord says, "The good man out of the good treasure of his heart brings forth good." 74 As, therefore,75 it is quite true that he who has a treasury of goodness in his heart cannot do otherwise than think and speak good, so he who speaks empty and useless things shows that he himself is empty and void of spiritual grace. For if he were not, he would hasten and doubtless would edify in faith and in thanksgiving to the glory of God those who hear him.

XX. Lo, you have now heard good things, which you ought to love and desire with your whole heart; you have also heard evil things, which you ought to flee with your whole strength and with all exertion. Consider, therefore, the difference between the love of perishing things and the fear of transitory injury and danger. It must be fully understood that as to love unlawful and disorderly temporal goods is sin, so to fear inordinately is also sin; so great a sin that, reckoned among other sins, it excludes one from the Kingdom of Heaven and adjudges one to eternal penalties, as we read in the Apocalypse: "As for the cowardly, the faithless, the polluted, as for murderers, fornicators, sorcerers, idolaters, and all liars, their lot shall be in the lake that burns with fire and brimstone, which is the second death." 76 Moreover the blessed apostle Peter teaches that one should not only not fear persecutors, but also should not consider as an injury whatever ill the persecutors can inflict, joining together two witnesses, a psalm, and the prophet Isaiah, saying: "The eyes of the Lord are upon the righteous, and his ears toward their prayers. But the face of the Lord is against evildoers." And, "Who is there to harm you, if you shall be imitators of the good?" 77 This, too, the Lord enjoins by

---

[71] Col. 3:16, 17.
[72] I Cor. 14:26.
[73] I Cor. 10:31.
[74] Matt. 12:35.
[75] MPL has *ego*, but the MS. clearly reads *ergo*.
[76] Rev. 21:8.
[77] I Peter 3:9–14. The first internal quotation is from Ps. 34:15, 16 (33:16, 17, V), but the second is from Peter, not from Isaiah, as Agobard states.

the prophet: "Fear not the reproaches of men, and do not be dismayed at their revilings. For the worm will eat them up like a garment, and the moth will eat them like wool; but my deliverance will be forever."[78] Likewise also, speaking in his own person in the Gospel, he commands: "Do not fear those who kill the body, and after that have no more that they can do."[79]

XXI. Not to fear the persecutors of the body is a great gift of God as the Lord demonstrates when he speaks through Jeremiah: "But you, gird up your loins; arise and say to them everything that I command you. Do not shrink in dread from their face, for neither will I make you fear their face. I, behold, I give you this day as a fortified city and as an iron pillar, and as a bronze wall, against the whole land."[80] Similarly, also, he says to Ezekiel: "Behold, I have made your face stronger than their faces, and your forehead harder than their foreheads. Like adamant and like flint I have made your face; fear them not, nor be dismayed at their looks, for it is a rebellious house."[81] Since to fear an enemy who can inflict only bodily injury is a grave fault, the psalm therefore directs us to pray thus: "Hear my prayer, O God, when I entreat; preserve my life from dread of the enemy,"[82] as though to say, "From dread of the enemy set me free, and subdue me to fear of you alone."[83] Another psalm says, "Since many are fighting against me, from the height of day I shall be afraid, but I shall put my trust in thee,"[84] or, as it were: "Many indeed are fighting against me. Yet, made strong by the help of your grace, hoping in you, I shall fear not their great number but your sublime light."[85] Those therefore who fight against me cannot scan the height of day, of which the twelve apostles are the shining hours.[86]

XXII. The secure ones, they who truly trust in the Lord, speak thus of themselves: "In God I will praise my words, in God I have put my trust. I will not fear what flesh may do to me."[87] Again: "The Lord is my helper,[88] I shall not fear what

---

[78] Isa. 51:7, 8.   [79] Luke 12:4.   [80] Jer. 1:17, 18.
[81] Ezek. 3:8, 9.   [82] Ps. 64:1 (63:2, V).
[83] Obviously Agobard's own paraphrase; cf. notes 96 and 33 above, notes 85 and 11 below.
[84] Ps. 56:2, 3 (55:3, 4, V).
[85] Again, quite clearly Agobard's own paraphrase; cf. notes 96, 33, and 83 above, note 11 below.
[86] The MS. has *ore* which MPL rightly interprets as *horae*.
[87] Ps. 56:4 (55:5, V).
[88] Probably a vague recollection of Ps. 30:10 (29:11, V) and similar passages.

man may do to me." [89] For, as the apostle asks, "Who shall bring any charge against God's elect?" [90] And again: "Who shall separate us from the love of Christ? Tribulation, or distress, or persecution, or famine, or nakedness, or peril, or sword? As it is written, 'For thy sake we are killed all the day long; we are regarded as sheep for slaughter.' No, in all these things we are conquerors, because of him who loved us." [91] For that reason Christians do not fear tribulations, but even glory in them, knowing that tribulation works patience, and patience approval, and approval hope, yet hope does not bewilder them because the love of God has been spread abroad in their hearts by the Holy Spirit who was given to them. They deem it all joy when they fall into various trials; they have come to know without equivocation that by tribulations and anxieties they are brought together, weighed, purified, as gold and silver in a furnace, not as chaff or hay.[92] For this purpose the Heavenly Father applies to them the fire of tribulation to wash away filth, not to turn them to ashes. In the psalm therefore the voice of the saints exclaims: "Thou, O God, hast tested us; thou hast tried us by fire as silver is tried. Thou didst bring us into the net; thou didst lay afflictions on our back; thou didst place men over our heads; we went through fire and through water; yet thou hast brought us forth unto refreshment." [93] These are the things they bear in various tribulations. They often endure as superiors those persons placed over them whom they know to be inferiors. They endure not only tribulations but also trials by fire and water, both in adversity and in prosperity. They are altogether on guard lest the fire consume them or the water ruin them. But at length, passing through fire and water, that is, through prosperity and adversity, they are brought forth into refreshment, where they no longer fear any enemy or suffer any trouble, because eternal refreshment and eternal repose last forever.[94]

XXIII. But in order to arrive there, what should be done by all believers amid so many ills transitory and permanent, those to be borne and those to be avoided, but what our Lord and Redeemer, our Liberator and Governor, enjoined when he

[89] Ps. 56:11 (55:11, V).   [90] Rom. 8:33.
[91] Rom. 8:35–37. The internal reference is Ps. 44:22 (43:22, V).
[92] Phrases derived from Rom. 5:3–5; James 1:2; Ezek. 22:18–22; I Peter 1: 6, 7; I Cor. 3:12, 13; and similar passages.
[93] Ps. 66:10–12 (65:10–12, V).
[94] Not only Biblical, but also liturgical reminiscences; cf. second *Memento* of the Canon of the Mass.

taught his disciples, "Watch at all times, praying that you may be held worthy to escape all these things that will take place, and to stand before the Son of man." [95] Likewise, also, when he warned them of his own immediate suffering, he says, "Pray that you may not enter temptation." [96] For having been asked earlier by the Pharisees when the Kingdom of God was coming, he added in reply, "One ought always to pray and not lose heart," [97] illustrating this by a parable of the Unjust Judge and the Importunate Widow.[98] In another place, when he told them about a man demanding bread just then to be given to him by another man, he suggested, "I tell you, Ask, and it will be given you; seek, and you will find; knock, and it shall be opened to you. For everyone who asks receives, and he who seeks finds, and to him who knocks it will be opened." [99] A little later: "If you then, although you are evil, know how to give good gifts to your children, how much more will your Father give from heaven the good Spirit to those who ask him?" [1]

XXIV. Concerning persistence or, rather, importunity in prayers, in which believers ought to be solicitous and eager, the entire Holy Scripture of the Old and New Testaments is full of examples and precepts, in which, so incomprehensibly to men, some things which Almighty God had promised would come to pass he delayed that they might be obtained through prayers. For instance, when the apostle Peter was arrested by Herod and thrust into prison, prayer was offered to God by the church without interruption.[2] Paul exhorted his listeners, "Pray at all times in the Spirit, therein keeping alert with all perseverance and supplication for all the saints, and for me, that utterance may be given to me in opening my mouth boldly to make known the mystery of the gospel, for which I discharge my embassy in this chain, that in it I may speak boldly as I ought." [3] In another place he speaks similarly: "Continue steadfastly in prayer, being watchful in it with thanksgiving; praying for us also, that God may open to us a door for the word, to declare the mystery of Christ, on account of which I am bound, that I may make it clear as I ought to speak." [4]

XXV. That each one ought to be attentive in prayer, not only for himself and for the saints, but also for all men, the same

---

[95] Luke 21:36.
[96] Luke 22:40, 46, and parallels.
[97] Luke 18:1.
[98] Cf. Luke 18:2–8.
[99] Luke 11:9, 10.
[1] Luke 11:13.
[2] Cf. Acts, ch. 12.
[3] Eph. 6:18–20.
[4] Col. 4:2–4.

blessed Paul gives commandment: "First of all, then, I urge that supplications, prayers, intercessions, and thanksgivings be made for all men, for kings and all who are in high positions, that we may lead a quiet and peaceable life, in all godliness and purity." [5] He shows that this should be done not only at all times, but also in all places, when a little later he adds, "I desire then that in every place men should pray, lifting up pure hands without anger or quarreling; also that women be in apparel modestly and gravely adorned." [6]

XXVI. One should above all understand that as prayer should be without wrath and contention, so also without doubt, but with confidence and faith. This is illustrated in many places, but especially where Peter says to his Lord: "'Rabbi, look! The fig tree which you cursed has withered.' And answering them, Jesus said, 'Have faith in God. Truly I say to you, that whoever shall say to this mountain, "Be taken up and cast into the sea," and shall not doubt in his heart, but shall believe that what he shall say will come to pass, it will be done for him. Therefore I tell you, whatever you shall ask in prayer, believe that you shall receive them, and they will come to you.'" [7] Blessed James also teaches that one should pray in this manner: "If anyone ask wisdom of God who gives to all men generously and does not reproach, it will be given to him. But let him ask in faith, doubting nothing, for he who doubts is like a wave of the sea that is driven and tossed by the wind. For that person must not suppose that he will receive anything from the Lord. A double-minded man is unstable in all his ways." [8]

The great abundance of God's sweetness evinces a mighty faith and confidence. To him it is declared in another psalm, "Thou, O Lord, art good and gracious and of much mercy to those calling on thee." [9] By the prophet we are told: "Loose the bonds of wickedness, undo the crushing bundles, let those who have been brought to naught go free, and break every yoke. Share your bread with the hungry, bring the homeless poor into your house. Then shall your light break forth like the dawn and your healing shall spring up speedily; and your righteousness shall go before you, and the glory of the Lord shall join you. Then you shall call, and the Lord will hear you; you shall cry, and he will say, 'Here I am.'" [10] In these verses it is clearly manifest that he who reverently listens to the Lord is

---

[5] I Tim. 2:1, 2.   [6] I Tim. 2:8, 9.   [7] Mark 11:21–24.
[8] Free citation of James 1:5–8.   [9] Ps. 86:5 (85:5, V).
[10] Isa. 58:6–9.

mercifully listened to by the Lord. Another translation begins these verses of the prophet thus: "Loose the bonds of forcible securities, let the vanquished go unto release, and rend in pieces every wicked writing, and in sum, while you are still speaking, he will say, 'Here I am.'"[11] Let what is especially needful to be proclaimed be heard and fulfilled.

XXVII. The almighty and merciful Lord gently announces this abundance of his own sweetness by the prophet Ezekiel: "Return and repent from all your transgressions, and iniquity shall not be your ruin. Cast away from you all your transgressions which you have committed, and make for yourselves a new heart and a new spirit. For why will you die, O house of Israel? For I do not wish the death of the one dying, says the Lord. Turn and live."[12] So also Isaiah asserts: "Let the wicked forsake his way, and the unrighteous man his thoughts; and let him return to the Lord, and he will have mercy on him, and to our God, for he is great to pardon."[13] This gentleness of mercy the Lord offers through the same prophet: "Remember these things, O Jacob and Israel, for you are my servant; O Israel, you will not be forgotten by me. I have swept away your transgressions like a cloud and your sins like mist; return to me, for I have redeemed you."[14] And again: "I, I am he who blots out your transgressions for my own sake, and I will not remember your sins."[15]

XXVIII. As for those who shall neglect these most sweet summonses of God in the present time while he can be found and while he is near, the time will come of working no longer, but of receiving each one according to his works, hearing the bitter reproaches: "I have called and you refused, have stretched out my hands and there was no one who heeded; you have ignored all my counsel and would have none of my reproofs; I will therefore laugh at your calamity."[16] To them then shall be that fruitless conversion of which the Lord speaks to everyone through the prophet: "Turn, and you will see what there is between the righteous and the wicked, and between one who serves God and one who does not serve him. For behold, the day will come, burning like an oven, and all the arrogant and evildoers will be stubble; and the day that comes shall burn them up, says the Lord of hosts, which will leave

---

[11] Source unidentified, but it appears to be a local paraphrase by Agobard or by some of his associates. See notes 96, 33, 83, and 85 above.
[12] Ezek. 18:30–32.   [13] Isa. 55:7.   [14] Isa. 44:21, 22.
[15] Isa. 43:25.   [16] Prov. 1:24–26.

them neither root nor branch. But for you who fear my name the sun of righteousness shall rise, with healing in its wings. And you shall go forth, and you shall leap like calves from the stall. And you shall tread down the wicked, when they will be ashes under the sole of your feet, on the day when I act, says the Lord of hosts." [17]

[17] Mal. 3:18 to 4:3.

Agobard of Lyons: On Divine Psalmody[18]

THE TEXT

A stupid and wicked sophist, well known to everyone for his very stupidity and wickedness,[19] has lately sallied forth and does not cease[20] to torture our holy church of Lyons by word and by writings, as though it were not performing the solemnities of divine praise in the correct manner or according to the custom and usage of the fathers. It has therefore become necessary to assemble and arrange the entire sequence of sacred offices which are celebrated in church meetings by the accustomed ministry of singers throughout the whole cycle of the year, as it is, by the grace of God, carefully and fully preserved in the same church in the book which is usually designated by the term *antiphonary*. The formula was established earlier by the pious and orthodox father[21] whose most approved faith and teaching in the service of our Lord God was made known to all as declared weightily and frequently. Thus all the peace-loving and farsighted sons of the church, into whose hands the text of the same book has come, most truly and clearly recognize that the aforesaid church of Christ has, under the governance and protection of the same Lord Christ, by no means deviated from the straight path of the faith. On the contrary, it guards the

---

[18] No title given in the MS.
[19] Amalarius of Metz, *locum tenens* of the see of Lyons during Agobard's exile, 834 (or 835)–838.
[20] "*Nuper . . . erupit . . . sed etiam . . . lacerare non cessat. . . .*" These words imply that Agobard was still in exile and that Amalarius was still in control of the church of Lyons, hence between the years 834 and 838.
[21] Leidrad, bishop of Lyons, c. 798–815, under whose tutelage Agobard began his ecclesiastical career. Those, however, who attribute the little tract to Florus, deacon of Lyons, consider this to be Agobard himself. See the discussion in Cabaniss, *Agobard of Lyons*, 107.

custom of the fathers which ecclesiastical appointment requires and thereby differs in no wise from the ancient use of the church of God, yet does not despise a different custom of anyone if certain that it is commendable. According to the apostle, however, it follows those things which are most useful and excellent. For he says, "It is my prayer that your love may abound more and more, with knowledge and all discernment, so that you may approve what is excellent, that you may be pure and blameless for the day of Christ."[22] In another place: "That you may prove what is the good and acceptable and perfect will of God."[23] Elsewhere: "But earnestly desire the better gifts."[24] And again: "Do not be children in thoughts."[25]

Moreover, the venerable councils of the fathers decree that vulgar psalms[26] should not at all be sung in the church and that "nothing put together in poetic fashion"[27] should be employed in the divine praises. Among others blessed Pope Gregory [the Great] teaches that things should not be loved for the sake of their locations, but rather places for the sake of the good things there. Recommending to us very strongly that as we ought not to strive after things because of their locations, so also not because of any persons or customs of the times, he was not afraid to restrain under the threat of anathema certain things in the Roman church itself which were reprehensible in its

---

[22] Phil. 1:9, 10.   [23] Rom. 12:2.
[24] I Cor. 12:31.   [25] I Cor. 14:20.
[26] Baluze's note on these words is as follows (MPL 104.327D): "They are taken from the last canon of the Council of Laodicea which reads: 'In church it is not appropriate to sing vulgar psalms or for noncanonical books to be read, but only the holy books of the New or Old Testament.' The canon therefore prohibits ecclesiastical use of vulgar psalms, that is, those composed by unofficial or unskilled persons. For the custom had prevailed (see the remarks on the canon of Laodicea by Justellus and Henry Valesius in their edition of Eusebius' *Church History*, VII, 24) that many persons had composed psalms and hymns in Christ's honor and had caused them to be sung in church, as is proved by many passages in Eusebius. For this reason the Council of Laodicea forbade the singing of such psalms in church, believing it unworthy of God's majesty if Christian folk should praise God with words other than those of the Holy Scriptures." The influence of this theory of hymnody is quite evident in some of the churches of the Reformation. The date of the Council of Laodicea is after 381.
[27] This phrase is quoted from the acts of the first Council of Braga (561), among the works of St. Martin of Braga, on which see C. W. Barlow (ed.) *Martini Episcopi Bracarensis Opera Omnia* (Papers and Monographs of the American Academy in Rome, 12, New Haven, Yale University Press, 1950), 112.

holy offices and services, as his decrees plainly show.[28] But if the aforesaid sophist would strive humbly and obediently to ponder, he would not be reduced to the folly of defending as though they were Holy Scripture the words of any men whose names and thought and faith he did not know, and of trying to explain them by fanciful and facetious allegories. Surely if he wished to meditate on something sound, it would suffice to correct and silence him that as day by day at Mass nothing but divine rhetoric is generally uttered, so also night by night at the sacred vigils offered to God the same rule ought certainly to be observed. Surely the same Almighty Lord is praised at both times and each time serves the one Lord to whom it is said, "Thine, O Lord, is the day, thine also the night; thou hast framed the dawn and the sun."[29]

But the stupid and vain labor of that one casts into the prudent, less disputatious, God-fearing ones a major anxiety, so that to avoid growths and errors of that kind they cling more vigorously and more carefully to divine authority and statutes of the church. This very wholesome care for the faith and method of observance, namely, that in God's temple and before the divine altar only the melody of divine eloquence be rehearsed, is most strongly commended to us also by the authority and examples of the Old Testament, as in the book of Chronicles where one reads that blessed David, king and prophet of God, first established in tabernacle or temple the choirs of Levites praising the Lord, and delivered to them by divine providence inspired utterances, psalms, hymns, and canticles, his own as well as those of others who prophesied

[28] Gregory the Great, *Decreta*, IV, indict. 13, epist. 44: "In this holy Roman church over which divine Providence has willed to set me, a most reprehensible practice has arisen, whereby certain singers are chosen for the ministry of the sacred altar and serve in the diaconate because of the melodious quality of their voice. It was agreed that they be relieved of the obligation of preaching and concern for the charitable work of the church. Whence it comes to pass very often that in the sacred ministry a pleasing voice is sought while a harmonious life is neglected, and the singer as servant of the Lord vexes the laity by his morals although he charms them by his voice. Wherefore by this present constitution I decree that in this diocese ministers at the sacred altar must not sing at all, excepting only that they may render the lesson from the Gospel at solemn Mass. I decree that psalms and other lections be offered by subdeacons or, in case of necessity, by those in minor orders. And if anyone shall attempt to oppose this my decision, let him be anathema." Cited by Agobard, *De correctione antiphonarii*, XV (MPL 104.336BD).

[29] Ps. 74:16 (73:16, V).

along with him, and decreed that they should be sung both morning and evening amid the divine burnt offerings and sacrifices.[30] It is fitting that this custom, handed down from the holy prophets, preserved most carefully by the fathers who came afterward, even to the time of the New Testament, when it was necessary for that temple to be destroyed, it is fitting that this custom be continued with devout reverence. It is therefore especially needful that we truly desire to celebrate the divine praises without even the least offense and hesitation.

Let us apply ourselves wholly to divine words in which there is no error, no ambiguity; as the same book of Chronicles reveals of the aforesaid Levites, the ancient singers of divine praise: "The Levites also, that they stand every morning for the purpose of thanking and praising the Lord, and likewise at evening, as well for the offering of the whole burnt offering as on sabbaths and new moons and other feast days."[31] Again at the dedication of the Temple under Solomon it is said: "So the king and all the people dedicated the house of the Lord. The priests stood at their posts; the Levites also, with instruments for songs to the Lord, which King David made for praising the Lord—for his mercy is forever—singing the hymns of David by their hands."[32] Similarly, at the repairing and purification of the same Temple under Hezekiah, it is written, "Hezekiah and the princes commanded the Levites to praise the Lord with the words of David and of Asaph the seer who praised him with great gladness."[33] Likewise, under Josiah at the celebration of the Passover, the book says, "Moreover the singers, the sons of Asaph, stood in their places according to the command of David and Asaph and Heman, and Jeduthun, the king's prophets."[34]

How solemnly and conscientiously this was established, how sweetly and reverently it was to be imitated among the other eminent things of the blessed David, the book of Ecclesiasticus thus recites in praise of him: "In every work he made confession to the holy and most high one with the word of glory; with his whole heart he praised the Lord and loved God who made him and gave him power against enemies. He caused singers also to

---

[30] I Chron., chs. 23 to 25 (I Para., chs. 23 to 25, V).
[31] I Chron. 23:30, 31 (I Para. 23:30, 31, V). Note that the word translated as "on new moons" is *kalendis*.
[32] II Chron. 7:5, 6 (II Para. 7:5, 6, V).
[33] II Chron. 29:30 (II Para. 29:30, V).
[34] II Chron. 35:15 (II Para. 35:15, V).

stand before the altar and caused sweet melodies by their voice. He also gave beauty to the festivals, and adorned the times until the end of his life, that they might praise the Lord's holy name and extol God's holiness every morning."[35] In the book of Samuel also this spiritual grace of singing is prophesied by the same most holy king: "David the son of Jesse spoke, the man on whom appointment rested as the anointed of the God of Jacob, the illustrious psalmist of Israel, 'The Spirit of the Lord has spoken by me, and his word is upon my tongue.' "[36]

There is therefore no doubt that each instructed believer will freely assent to such holy authority and such evident truth. But if any contentious and stubborn person attempts to disagree, and should wish to drink from a muddy stream rather than from the purest spring, he should take care that he not become ill with that most ruinous debility which a certain one of the ancient fathers wisely and briefly warned should be avoided, observing that when truth has been despised the one who imagines he is complying with custom is either envious and spiteful toward the brethren to whom truth is revealed or ungrateful toward God by whose inspiration His church is set in order.

[35] Ecclesiasticus 47:9–12. [36] II Sam. 23:1, 2 (II Kings 23:1, 2, V).

IDEALS OF THE PRIESTHOOD

Anonymous: Address to the Clergy

INTRODUCTION

THE LITTLE DOCUMENT HERE TRANSLATED AS "Address to the Clergy" was selected for inclusion, not because it bears the mark of a great author's name, but because of its intrinsic value. No critical text has been discovered and no translation into any vernacular has been made aside from a brief summary in French.[1]

The form is that of an address by a bishop to his diocesan clergy on their duties as priests, and, as such, comparison is invited with the selection from Theodulph of Orléans which has the same purpose. The sermon has survived in many versions and under many names, including no name at all, usually incomplete, so that it is difficult to determine, if not impossible, what is original and what is the addition of later times.

In 1832, Cardinal Angelo Mai published[2] an "Exhortation to Presbyters" found in a Vatican manuscript and this was reprinted in Migne's *Patrologia latina* among the works of Pope Eutychianus (275–283).[3] Eutychianus is thus the earliest of the many writers to whom the authorship has been ascribed, but no one would now maintain that Eutychianus wrote the sermon and it is by no means clear that in this form we have the original version. Under the heading, "Commonitory of any bishop to his subordinate presbyters and other ministers of any ecclesiastical order," another version was also printed by the Abbé Migne

---

[1] G. Morin, "L'auteur de *l'Admonition Synodale* sur les devoirs du clergé" (*Revue Bénédictine* 9 [1892] 99–108), by far the best discussion of the document.

[2] Angelo Card. Mai, *Scriptorum veterum nova collectio* (1832), 6.2.124–126.

[3] MPL 5.163–168.

among anonymous works of the eighth century.[4] Here the total is divided into 47 articles and about the last third is missing. As a "Sermon of Pope Leo IV" (847–855), another and shorter version was printed by Labbe,[5] but Leo IV was certainly not the author, nor did he lay claim to be, for he inserts the words, "As we have found written elsewhere,"[6] that is, this pope made use of material which pleased him. Indeed, Monsignor Duchesne[7] denies that any pope could have written such a document: the distinctive Roman usage is not found, the diocese is one with rural parishes, and the author calls himself vicar of the apostles, not of Peter.

Among the *Capitula Synodica* of a synod held in 852 by Hincmar of Reims, the first five[8] show dependence upon our text. Regino of Prüm (d. 915) put into the second book of his *De ecclesiastica disciplina et religione Christiana*, ninety-five questions to be asked by bishops or their subordinate officers during diocesan visitations, and almost all of these are also derived ultimately from the same source.[9] Henceforth, the little address was in common use in all Western churches. Baluze placed still another version at the end of his edition of Regino.[10] From a Codex Neresheimensis, copied in 1009, the booklet came to be regarded as the work of Ulrich, Bishop of Augsburg from 923 to 973,[11] and there has been considerable debate as to whether he was the true author, those scholars who concerned themselves with Ulrich being universally agreed, it would appear, that it is genuinely his, while those who took the trouble to study the history of the *sermo* itself have uniformly ranged themselves on the opposite side.[12]

Nearly all of the text was incorporated by Rathier of Verona

---

[4] MPL 96.1375–1379, using a text based on E. Martène, *Veterum scriptorum et monumentorum . . . amplissima collectio* (Paris, 1724–1733) 7.1.
[5] P. Labbe, *Sacrorum conciliorum nova et amplissima collectio* (Paris-Venice, 1759–1798), 11.1075, reprinted in MPL 115.675–684.
[6] *Sicut alibi scriptum invenimus* (MPL 115.673).
[7] L. Duchesne, *Liber pontificalis* 2.135, note 13.
[8] MPL 12.773–792.   [9] MPL 132.185–191.   [10] MPL 132.445–458.
[11] MPL 135.1071–1074, text here translated.
[12] Alfred Schroeder (KL 12.197–219); Ulrich Schmid, *Ulrich, Bischof von Augsburg* (Augsburg, 1st ed., 1901; 2d ed., 1904), and his article (CE 15.123); Max Manitius, *Geschichte der lateinischen Literatur im Mittelalter* (Munich, 1925), 2.203–210, all regard it as genuinely Ulrich's. Against this view, see A. Bigelmair (LTK 10.365–368); A. Hauck (NSH 12.59) and his *Kirchengeschichte Deutschlands* (Leipzig, 1920) 3.47, note 6; Clemente Schmitt (EC 12.722 f.). Bigelmair cites also A. M. Koeringer, *Sendberichte* 1 (1907) 23, note 2, but we have not seen this.

into his *Synodica ad Presbyteros*, composed for delivery in Lent, 966.[13] Even after the Counter Reformation the *sermo* continued to be reissued, ostensibly, of course, as a new composition, e.g., in a Roman pontifical by Agostino Patrizzi, Bishop of Pienza,[14] and in another Roman pontifical.[15]

This was the more surprising as there are in the document touches undeniably very old: women are to be excluded from priests' residences; there are to be nightly offices; unworthy penitents are not to be publicly recommended to the bishop; part of penance may be remitted by alms done by another; Communion is to be taken three times a year; men are urged to refrain from sexual intercourse with their wives at the times of festivals of the church; the festivals are to begin to be celebrated in the evening (*vespera ad vesperam*) after the manner of the Jewish Sabbath; and priests are to commit the *Symbolum Quicumque* to memory. All these features point to an early period.

As late as 1881 a text similar in character to that attributed to Pope Leo IV was found by W. Wattenbach[16] in a Berlin codex of Gratian's *Decretum* and accepted by him as a genuine work of Gratian until he was at once corrected by P. Ewald.[17] From this recital it will be clear that the date of composition must antedate the year of Leo's death, which occurred in 855, and that there is a strong probability of a Gallican origin.

In 1892, Dom Morin[18] reported that in a Munich codex (5515–Diess. 15, saec. xii) of the *Speculum Ecclesiae* of Honorius of Autun (d. 1152),[19] which is a collection of sermons for different occasions, there appeared a "*sermo beati Caesarii episcopi ad clerum*" and that this sermon proved to be our *sermo synodalis*. This had not earlier appeared in either the editions of the works of Honorius or in those of Caesarius. The new attribution appeared highly plausible to Dom Morin and he pointed out in the text characteristic usages of words, phrases, and topics found in other works of Caesarius of Arles (c. 469–542). It would appear that since Dom Morin no one has devoted much study to the problem of authorship and we print the document here as anonymous without prejudice to the question of who the author really was. The *sermo* certainly deserves the honor of a critical edition.

[13] MPL 136.553–568; see principal editions commented on by the Ballerini.
[14] MPL 132.458 f., part 3.
[15] *Ibid.*, part 4, 259–262.   [16] *Neues Archiv* 6.192.
[17] *Ibid.*, p. 652.   [18] See note 1, above.   [19] MPL 172.1103.

Anonymous: Address to the Clergy

THE TEXT

Brother presbyters and priests,[20] you are co-workers of our order.[21] We, however, though unworthy, hold Aaron's place, and you those of Eleazar and Ithamar.[22] We perform the duties of the office of the twelve apostles; you correspond to the seventy disciples. We are your shepherd; you the shepherds of the souls entrusted to you. We shall render to the Chief Shepherd, the Lord Jesus Christ, an accounting with respect to you; you, one concerning the people entrusted to you. And therefore, my very dear friends, look to your danger. Let us admonish and beg your brotherhood to give heed to our admonition, carefully considering your common salvation. Keep in mind what we suggest to you and be zealous in the performance of your work.

First of all, let us admonish you that your life and character be blameless, that is, that your cell be near a church and that you keep in it no women.[23] Every night rise at the nocturns. Chant your course at the prescribed hours. Perform religiously the celebration of Masses. Take the body and blood with fear and reverence. Wash and wipe the holy vessels with your own hands. Let no one sing a Mass without having fasted. Let no one sing without the amice, the alb, the stole, the fanon, the planeta. Let these vestments be clean and never put to other uses. Let no one presume to sing Mass in an alb which he uses at other times. Let no woman approach the altar of the Lord or

---

[20] The word used is *sacerdotes*.
[21] The order of bishops.
[22] See Num. 3:32; 4:28.
[23] Doubtless derived from Canon 3 of the Council of Nicaea. See below Theodulph, text, note 29.

touch the Lord's chalice. Let the corporal[24] be very clean, the altar covered with clean linens. Let nothing be placed on the altar except the capsae[25] and the relics, or perhaps the four Gospels, and the pyxis with the Lord's body for the sick. Let the other objects be stored in a clean place.

Let each church have a complete Mass book, lectionary, and antiphonary. Let a place be prepared in the sacristy or near the altar where the water can be poured out when the sacred vessels are washed, and let a clean vessel with water hang there, and there let the priest[20] wash his hands after Communion. Let the churches be well covered and roofed, and let a nave often be built. Let no one sing Mass outside the church in homes or in places without roofs. Let every presbyter have a cleric or scholar to read the epistle or lesson and to give the responses to the Mass, one with whom he may sing the psalms. Let no one sing Mass alone.

Let no one sing Mass clad in those shoes which in the country we call *sporones*,[26] or with knives hanging outside, because this is not proper, and contrary to the church's rule.

Bless the chalice and the offering with the straight cross, that is, not in a circle and with changes of fingers, as many of you do, but with two fingers drawn together and the thumb between them, by which the Trinity is symbolized, and take pains to make this sign properly. For not otherwise can you bless anything. Visit the sick and restore them, and according to the apostle anoint them with holy oil,[27] and give them Communion with your own hand. And let no one presume to hand over Communion to a layman or woman to be carried to the sick.

Let none of you demand a reward or a gift for baptizing infants or restoring the sick or burying the dead. See that no infant dies without Baptism through your neglect. Let none of you be drunk or quarrelsome because the Lord's servant ought not to quarrel. Let none of you bear arms in strife because your arms should be spiritual. Let none of you be a slave to the sport of dogs or birds.

Let none drink in the taverns. Let each one of you preach to his people from the Gospel or the apostle on the Lord's Day and

---

[24] Either an ancient Eucharistic vestment, or, as here, the cloth on which the consecrated elements are placed during Mass and with which the unused remains are covered.
[25] The capsae and *buxis* or pyxis were *ciboria* or receptacles for the Host.
[26] That is, shoes fitted with spurs.
[27] James 5:14, the only Scriptural passage to which allusion is made.

feast days, according to his ability. You ought to preach the Lord's Word. Care for the poor, the pilgrims, and the orphans, and invite them to your table. Be hospitable that others may get a good example from you.

Every Lord's Day, before Mass, bless the holy water from which the people are sprinkled and keep a vessel for this purpose alone. Do not give holy vessels or priestly vestments as a pledge to a merchant or tavern keeper. Let none of you demand usury and lend money for your own profit. Know that the wealth and properties which you acquire after the day of your ordination belong to the church. Let no one acquire a church without our knowledge and consent. Let none obtain a church through secular authority. Let no one leave the church to which he is assigned and move to another for the sake of gain. Let no one hold several churches without assistance from other presbyters. Let no church ever be divided into several. Let no one receive at a Mass the parishioners of another unless when on a journey or when it is agreeable. Let no one sing Mass in another's parish. Let no one invite a penitent to eat flesh and drink wine except in so far as for the present he is giving alms. Let no one presume to baptize other than on the eve of Easter and Pentecost unless because of the danger of death. Let each have baptismal fonts, and if he cannot have these of stone, let him have them of some other vessel, prepared for this purpose, used for nothing else. See that to all your parishioners you recite the Creed and the Lord's Prayer. Tell your people that the fast of the four seasons and of the rogations and of the greater litany should be kept completely. On the fourth feast before Lent invite the people to confession and impose penance upon them according to the character of the sin, not out of your heart but as it is written in the penitential.[28] Four times a year, that is, on the Lord's birthday, the day on which the Lord's Supper was eaten, on Easter, and Pentecost, admonish all the faithful to be present at the Communion of the Lord's body and blood. At fixed seasons exhort married men to abstain from intercourse with their wives. Bestow gifts after Mass upon the people on feast days. Let no one wear the clothing of the laity. Let no one presume to sell or exchange or alienate in any manner the wealth, possessions, or right of the church.

[28] See John T. McNeill and Helena M. Gamer, *Medieval Handbooks of Penance*, in "Records of Civilization" 29 (New York, Columbia Press, 1938).

Teach that the Lord's Day and other feasts should be free from servile labor from evening to evening. Prevent singing and dancing of women in the nave of the church. Forbid, with Almighty God as witness, the devilish incantations which the common folk are wont to make in the night over the dead and the raucous laughter in which they indulge. Do not communicate with those who have been excommunicated. Let no one presume to sing a Mass for them, and announce this also to your people. Let none of you go to wedding feasts. Proclaim to everyone that no one should marry without the public celebration of the marriage. Completely prohibit elopement, both that no one should approach a woman near of kin, and that no one should marry one betrothed to another. Make swineherds and other shepherds attend Mass, at least on the Lord's Day. Let godparents say, or have said, the Creed and the Lord's Prayer to their godchildren. Let the holy chrism always be kept under wax and seal on account of certain unfaithful ones. We take care to admonish you concerning the ministry entrusted to you that each of you, if it can be done, should hold to the exegesis of the Creed and the Lord's Prayer in accordance with the tradition of the orthodox written in their works, and let him fully understand it, and then, if he knows, let him carefully give instruction in sermons to the people entrusted to him. If not, let him at least hold to it and believe it. Let him understand well the prayers and the canon of the Masses, and if not, let him at least be able to produce it from memory and clearly. Let him be able to read well the Epistle and Gospel, so that he may be able to make its literal sense clear. Let him know how to pronounce the words of the psalms and their divisions in proper fashion by heart with customary rhythms. Let him memorize, as we said above, the speech of Bishop Athanasius on the faith of the Trinity, of which the opening words are "Whosoever will."[29] Let him at least know how to read well the exorcisms and the prayers for making the catechumen, also for consecrating the baptismal font, and the other prayers concerning male and female, when several are to be baptized together; for giving aid to the sick, also the order of reconciliation to the church, according to the manner canonically preserved, and of anointing the sick, and also the prayers proper to this same necessity. Likewise, the order and prayers to be recited at the funerals of the dead. Likewise, let him memorize the exorcisms and the

---

[29] The so-called Athanasian Creed or *Quicumque*.

blessing of salt and water. Let him know the chant both for the night and the day.

Let him understand the minor calculation, that is, the added days, those that run together in regular fashion, the end of the paschal period, and the rest, if possible. Let him have a martyrology and a penitential. We desire, however, very dear brothers, that what you have received from our handing it down to you, you should zealously endeavor to fulfill with good works so far as human weakness suffers, with the help of our Lord Jesus Christ, who, with the Father and the Holy Spirit, lives and reigns as God forever and ever. Amen.

Theodulph of Orléans: Precepts to the Priests of His Diocese

INTRODUCTION

OF THE LIFE OF THEODULPH OF ORLÉANS LITTLE can be said beyond conjecture. Born, certainly, in the mid-eighth century—the place is unknown—he was most probably a native of Spain and a Goth by race. That he had a daughter named Gisla can be demonstrated from the poem of seventeen elegiacs which he wrote to her,[1] but what became of his wife, if he had one, and all details concerning his life before the last decade of the century, are veiled in mist. He must have entered a monastery, for we find him abbot of the celebrated Benedictine establishment, Fleury-sur-Loire, but the date is missing. By 794 he had joined the court of Charlemagne, where he became second in importance as a literary figure to Alcuin himself, and the first poet of the Carolingian age. In that year he attended the Synod of Frankfort at which the adoptionists Felix and Elipandus were condemned, and Alcuin[2] is authority for the statement that he was already Bishop of Orléans, though the usual date of his appointment by Charlemagne to the see is about 798.

As bishop he exhibited strong interest in the reform of the clergy and people and in the establishment of schools. This much can be deduced from the two works on the priestly office, of which our selection is the first. They were first edited by Baronius, who dated them, quite wrongly, in 835, long after Theodulph's death; they appear really to belong to the early years of his pontificate. In 798, with Leidrad of Lyons, he was

---

[1] *Carmina* 3:4 (MPL 105.326 f.).
[2] The testimonies from Alcuin, Eginhard, Hincmar of Reims, Lupus of Ferrières, the Life of Louis the Pious, and the *Chronicon Vetus*, are collected in MPL 105.189–192.

sent as a *missus dominicus*, or royal ambassador, to southern France where he had a chance to observe the need for reforms in the law courts of the Frankish kingdom and produced the poem "Against the Judges" (*Versus contra iudices*),[3] contending for greater leniency in the courts and the greater morality in the judges.

In 811 he was among the witnesses of Charlemagne's will but was involved in the year 818 in the revolt of Bernard, king of Italy, with the result that he was proscribed, ejected from his see, and relegated to imprisonment at Angers. There he died, September 18, 821, perhaps poisoned, as has been claimed. That he had been restored to the see of Orléans before his death is alleged by some, but he was succeeded by Jonas in 818 and the restoration is unlikely. The epitaph taken from his tomb reads: "In this stone are preserved the ashes of one formerly abbot and bishop over the people."[4]

Theodulph is now better known for his poems than for anything else he wrote or did.[5] The most famous of them is the celebrated *Gloria, laus et honor, tibi sit, rex Christe redemptor* of thirty-nine elegiacs, which has passed into the Roman liturgy for Palm Sunday, and in the successful translation by John M. Neale, "All glory, laud, and honor, to Thee, Redeemer, King," set to the stirring music of Melchior Teschner, has become a familiar hymn in many Protestant hymnals.[6]

Besides a work *On the Holy Spirit*,[7] in which the doctrine of the double procession prominent in the "Filioque Controversy" is defended, and another *On the Order of Baptism*,[8] Theodulph wrote the two prose works, already mentioned, on the theme of the priestly office: *Precepts to the Presbyters of his Diocese*[9] and the *Capitulary to the Same*.[10] We offer a translation of the former document made from the text of Jacques Sirmond (Paris, 1656) as reprinted in Migne's *Patrologia latina* 105.191–208.

[3] H. Hagen, *Theodulfi de judicibus versus* (Berne, 1882).
[4] MPL 105.192:
   Illius cineres saxo servantur in isto
   Qui quondam populis praesul et abba fuit.
[5] The *carmina* in seven books are in MPL 105.283–376, with additional poems 377–380; MGH, PLAC, 1, pt. 2, 437–581.
[6] *Carmina*, Bk. 2, no. 3, MPL 105.308 f.; *Analecta Hymnica* 50.160; Ruth Messenger, *The Medieval Latin Hymns* (Washington, Capitol Press, 1953), p. 29.
[7] *De spiritu sancto* (MPL 105.239–276).
[8] *De ordine baptismi* (MPL 105.223–240).
[9] *Capitula ad presbyteros parochiae suae* (MPL 105.191–208).
[10] *Capitulare ad eosdem* (ibid. 105.207–224).

This work, of course, bears comparison with the preceding selection, the "Address to the Clergy," written by an unknown bishop, possibly Caesarius of Arles. It would appear from a number of correspondences that Theodulph had seen one of the versions of the "Address" and used it as a model, but he adds much of value and in no sense is a slavish imitator of his predecessor. In addition, the work is far superior from the literary and intellectual point of view.

The *Precepts* similarly show relationship to the penitentials, and sections 26, 30, 31, and 36 of the *Precepts*, as well as two sections of the Capitulary, are included in the McNeill-Gamer book on the penitentials.[11] Some have claimed that Theodulph was opposed to the penitentials and was originator and guide of the antipenitential party heard at the Council of Chalons. While Theodulph in the *Precepts* rises to a height considerably above that of many of the penitentials, it is clear that he has much the same motives which animated the authors of the penitentials, namely the improvement of the moral and spiritual character of clergy and people.

The following works should be consulted: L. Baunard, *Théodulphe, évêque d'Orléans* (Paris–Orléans, 1860); Cuissard, *Théodulphe, évêque d'Orléans: sa vie et ses œuvres* (Orléans, 1892). See also A. S. Napier, *An Old English Version of the Capitula of Theodulph Together with the Latin Original*, in "Early English Text Society" 150 (London, Kegan Paul, 1916). B. Thorpe prints "Ecclesiastical Institutes" in his *Ancient Laws of England* 2.394–443, that is, an Anglo-Saxon version of the first capitulary (the *Precepts*). E. Power, "Corrections from the Hebrew in the Theodulfian MSS. of the Vulgate" (*Biblica* 5 [1924] 223–258), shows that the emendations are not too happy.

[11] John T. McNeill and Helena M. Gamer, *Medieval Handbooks of Penance*, in "Records of Civilization" 29 (New York, Columbia Press, 1938), pp. 395–397.

Theodulph of Orléans: Precepts[12] to the Priests of His Diocese[13]

THE TEXT

Theodulph to our brothers and fellow presbyters, the priests[14] of the diocese of Orléans.

1. I beg you, my most beloved brothers, to labor with the most watchful care with regard to the progress and improvement of the people subject to you, so that, by showing them the way of salvation and instructing them by word and example, we shall bring back fruitful harvests to our Lord Jesus Christ with his aid, you from their progress, and ourselves from yours. I beg your brotherhood, also, that you read carefully these chapters[12] which I have briefly laid down for the improvement of life, and commit them to memory, and that by reading them and the Holy Scriptures you may regulate the morals and improve the life of the people put under you, and with them, the Lord being your helper, you may strive to reach the heavenly Kingdom. You ought to know truly and always to remember that we, to whom the care of governing souls has been entrusted, will render an accounting in regard to those who perish through our neglect, but in regard to those whom by word and example we shall have gained, we shall receive the reward of eternal life. For to us the Lord has said, "You are the salt of the earth."[15] Because if a faithful people is God's food, we are the spice of his food. Know that your rank is second to our rank and is almost joined to it. For as the bishops hold in the church the place of the apostles, so the presbyters hold the place of the other disciples of the Lord. The former hold the rank of the chief

---

[12] *Capitula*, so called from the itemized form of the work.
[13] *Parochia* (parish) is often used for diocese in the medieval period.
[14] In this selection the word "priest" usually is *sacerdos*.
[15] Matt. 5:13.

priest[16] Aaron, but the latter the rank of his sons. For this reason you ought to be mindful always of so great authority, mindful of your consecration, mindful of the holy unction which you have received in your hands, that you do not lower this authority, nor nullify your consecration, nor defile with sin the hands besmeared with holy oil, but preserving purity of heart and body, offering to the people an example of proper living, you may offer to those over whom you are in charge guidance to the heavenly kingdoms.

2. You ought to be continually reading and constantly at prayer, because the life of the righteous man is taught and equipped by reading, and by constantly reading a person is fortified against sin, according to him who said, "In my heart have I hidden thy word that I might not sin against thee."[17] For these are the arms, namely, reading and prayer, by which the devil is defeated; these are the means by which eternal blessedness is obtained; with these arms vices are suppressed; upon these foods virtues are nourished.

3. But, also, if there be any interruption in reading, the hands should then be used, because "idleness is the enemy to the soul"[18] and the ancient enemy easily carries off to vices the one whom he finds free from reading or praying. By the use of reading you will learn how you should live and how to teach others; by the use of prayer you will be able to be of value both to yourselves and to those united with you in love. By the operation of the hands and the chastisement of the body, you will both deny nourishment to the vices and will supply your own needs and have something to offer for the needs of sufferers.

4. When you come, according to custom, to a synod, carry with you clothing and books, and holy utensils, with which to perform your ministry and the office united with it. Bring with you some two or three clergy with whom you may celebrate the solemnities of the Masses, in order that it may be proved how carefully, how zealously, you perform God's service.

5. Let the bread which you offer to God for sacrifice be baked either by yourselves or by your servants in your presence, in clean and careful manner, and let it be carefully observed that the bread and the wine and the water, without which Masses cannot be celebrated, be kept very clean and handled with care, and that nothing be found in them of poor quality,

---

[16] *Pontifex*.   [17] Ps. 119:11 (118:11, V).
[18] A quotation from Benedict, *Regula Monachorum* 48 (MPL 66.703).

nothing not approved, according to the passage of Scripture which says, "Let the fear of the Lord be with you and do everything with diligence." [19]

6. Let women never approach the altar when the priest is celebrating Mass, but let them stand in their own places and there let the priest receive their offerings as he will offer them to God. For women ought to be mindful of their weakness and of the infirmity of their sex, and therefore fear to touch anything holy in the ministry of the church. These even laymen ought to fear, lest they undergo the punishment of Uzzah,[20] who was willing to touch in an unusual fashion the Ark of the Lord but, struck by the Lord, died.

7. Let a priest never celebrate Mass alone,[21] because as it cannot be celebrated without the salutation of a priest, the response of the people, the admonition of the priest, and again the response of the people, thus it ought never to be celebrated by one man alone. For there should be people to stand around him, to receive his salutation, to give responses to him, and to recall to him that saying of the Lord: "Wherever two or three shall be gathered in my name, there also am I in their midst." [22]

8. We frequently see in churches harvested crops and hay piled up,[23] and for this reason we wish it to be thoroughly observed that nothing should be stored in a church except ecclesiastical vestments and holy vessels and books, lest by chance if businesses are being carried on other than should be, we may hear from the Lord, "My house shall be called a house of prayer, but you have made it a brigands' cave." [24]

9. In these regions in olden times use was made of the church for burying the dead, and often places set apart for divine worship and prepared for offering sacrifices to God were made into cemeteries or *polyandria*.[25] For this reason I want this practice henceforth to be abandoned and no one to be buried in a church, unless perchance such a person be a priest, or some righteous man, who on account of the merit of his life acquired by living in such a way a place for his dead body. Let bodies,

---

[19] II Chron. 19:9 (does not follow LXX, Vulgate, or any Protestant Bible).
[20] The Latin is *Oza*. Cf. II Sam. 6:6–8.
[21] This prohibition is not now observed in the Roman Catholic Church.
[22] Matt. 18:20.
[23] Apparently tithes, not harvest-home decorations.
[24] Matt. 21:13.
[25] A Greek word ("places for many men") = "cemetery." See H. Leclercq, "Polyandre," in DACL 14.1349–1355, where this is the second example cited, the only one in this sense.

however, which in olden times were buried in churches never be cast out, but let the tombs which are visible be lowered more deeply into the earth, and, a paving being built over them, and no trace of the tombs being visible, let the respect for the church be preserved. Where, however, there is such a great number of corpses that this is hard to do, let this place be considered a cemetery and the altar be taken hence and set up where sacrifice can be offered to God reverently and purely.

10. You ought not to gather in the church for any other cause except for praise of the Lord and for carrying on his service. Controversies, however, and tumults, and vain speaking, and other proceedings should be entirely forbidden in that holy place. For where the name of God is invoked, sacrifice is offered to God, and as without doubt angels congregate there in great numbers, it is dangerous to say anything or do anything there which is not fitting to the place. For if the Lord cast out[26] from the Temple those who bought and sold the victims which were to be offered to himself, with how much greater anger will he cast out thence those who defile with lies, vain speaking, jokes, and trifles of this sort, the place set for divine worship?

11. The celebrations of Masses ought never to take place elsewhere than in a church,[27] not in just any houses or in mean places, but in a place which the Lord shall choose, according to the passage of Scripture: "See that you do not offer your burnt offerings in any place which you see, but in a place which the Lord shall choose to place his name there." [28]

12. Let no woman live with a presbyter in a single house. Although the canons[29] permit a priest's mother and sister to live with him, and persons of this kind in whom there is no suspicion, we abolish this privilege for the reason that there may come, out of courtesy to them or to trade with them, other women not at all related to him and offer an enticement for sin to him.

13. You should take care to refrain from drunkenness, and

[26] Matt: 21:12 f.
[27] Masses are now, of course, offered, as occasion demands, in places not formally dedicated as churches, but the altar and its equipment, set up especially for this purpose, is dedicated by appropriate ritual.
[28] Deut. 12:13 f.
[29] The canons referred to are doubtless a revision of Canon 3 of the Council of Nicaea (see C. J. Hefele, *History of the Councils of the Church*, tr. by H. W. Oxenham, 1.379–381) and a similar canon of the Synod of Elvira (*ibid.*, 1.148).

to preach that the people under your care should refrain, and that you should never go through the taverns eating and drinking, nor travel around through houses and villages out of curiosity, nor attend feasts with women or with any impure persons, unless some head of a household, perhaps, shall invite you to his home and, with his wife and children, wishes to rejoice with you in spiritual joy, and to receive the refreshment of your words and to offer you carnal refreshments in the duty of love, for it is fitting that, if at any time any of the faithful gives you the refreshment of carnal foods, he should be given spiritual refreshment by you.

14. Let no presbyter persuade the faithful of the holy church of God belonging to the parish of another presbyter to leave their own church and come to his church and give their tithes to him, but let each one, content with his own church and people, never do to another what he would not wish to be done to himself, in accordance with the passage in the Gospel: "Whatsoever you wish men to do to you, do these same things to them."[30] Moreover, whoever shall contravene these established principles, or shall attempt to struggle against these warnings of ours, let him know that he will lose his rank or that he ought to be kept in prison for a long time.

15. This we absolutely forbid, that none of you attempt to entice over or receive a cleric[31] subordinate to another, because there is a heavy punishment for this act in the sacred canons.

16. If any presbyter shall be found to be giving a bribe or to have given one to any man, cleric or lay, so that he may steal away the church of another presbyter, let him know that for this theft and keen covetousness, either he will lose his rank or he ought to be kept in the toils of prison a long time doing penance.

17. If a sick infant shall be brought to any presbyter for baptism from the parish of another, let the sacrament of Baptism by no means be denied him. Should anyone refuse to grant this office upon request, and the infant should die without the grace of Baptism, the one who did not baptize him shall know that he shall render an accounting for his soul.

18. Let no presbyter presume to employ for other purposes a chalice or a paten or any sacred utensils set apart for divine worship. For whoever drinks from a consecrated chalice anything other than the blood of Christ which is received in the sacrament, and holds a paten for any other function than for the ministry of the altar, must be deterred by the example of

---

[30] Matt. 7:12.   [31] Subordinate clergy.

Belshazzar,[32] who, when he took the vessels of the Lord for common purposes, lost his life and his kingdom as well.

19. If any of the presbyters wishes to send his nephew or other relative to school, in the church of the Holy Cross,[33] or in the monastery of Saint Aignan,[34] or of Saint Benedict,[35] or of Saint Lifard,[36] or in others of those monasteries which it has been granted us to rule, we grant him permission to do so.

20. Let the presbyters keep schools in the villages and hamlets, and if any of the faithful desires to entrust his small children to them to be taught their letters, let them not refuse to receive and teach them, but let them teach them with the greatest love, noticing what is written: "They, however, who shall be learned shall shine as the splendor of the firmament, and they who instruct many to righteousness shall shine as the stars forever and ever."[37] When, therefore, they teach them, let them demand no fee for this instruction, nor take anything from them, except what the parents shall offer them freely through zeal for love.

21. Since, therefore, the pages of all the Holy Scriptures are crammed full of the instruments of good works, and on the fields of the Holy Scriptures can be found the arms with which vices may be suppressed and virtues nourished, it has pleased us to insert into this our prescript[38] the opinion of a certain father[39] about the instruments of good works which contains with great brevity what ought to be done and what avoided.

"In the first place, to love the Lord thy God from the whole heart, the whole soul, and the whole power,[40] then,

[32] Cf. Dan., ch. 5. The Latin is *Baltassar*.
[33] Now the Cathedral of Orléans, though the present church is much later in date. On the diocese of Orléans, see DACL 12.2678–2719.
[34] St. Anianus or Aignan, fifth bishop of Orléans, succeeded Evurcius. He defended the city against Attila in A.D. 451. He is commemorated in the *Martyrologium Hieronymianum* on November 17. His relics were destroyed by Huguenots in 1562. The Church of St. Aignan was founded in Orléans as a Benedictine abbey in 617. See Mario Scaduto, "Aniano di Orleans, S." in EC 1.1288; DACL 12.2685; C. Duhan, *Vie de S. Aignan, évêque d'Orléans* (Orleans, 1877).
[35] Doubtless the celebrated Benedictine abbey of Fleury on which see H. Leclercq, "Fleury-sur-Loire," in DACL 5.1709–1760; G. Chennesseau, *L'Abbaye de Fleury à St. Benoît-sur-Loire* (Paris, 1931).
[36] St. Lifard, abbot of Meung-sur-Loire, is commemorated in the *Martyrologium Hieronymianum* on 3 June. See EC 9.356.
[37] Dan. 12:3. This noble passage represented to early medieval schoolmen the highest ideal obtainable.
[38] *Capitulare*.
[39] The father is Benedict, *Regula Monachorum* 4.   [40] *Virtute*.

thy neighbor as thyself. Then, not to kill; not to commit adultery; not to steal; not to covet; not to give false testimony; to honor all men, and what anyone does not want to be done to himself, not to do to another. To deny himself to himself that he may follow Christ. To castigate the body, not to embrace pleasures; to love fasting; to restore the poor; to clothe the naked; to visit the sick; to bury the dead; to be helpful in tribulation; to comfort the sorrowing. To keep oneself separate from the doings of this life. To place nothing before the love of Christ; not to execute anger; not to reserve a time for wrath; not to hold treachery in the heart; not to give false peace; not to cease loving. Not to swear, lest perchance you swear falsely. To utter truth from the heart and lips; not to return evil for evil; to do no wrong, but to suffer one done to oneself in patience. To love enemies, not to curse those who curse you, but rather to bless. To bear persecution in return for justice. Not to be proud, drunken, gluttonous, drowsy, lazy, grumbling, a disparager. To place one's hope in God. When he sees something good in himself, let him connect it with God, not himself, but let him always know that the bad has been done by himself and let him attribute it to himself. To fear the Day of Judgment; to dread hell; to desire life eternal with every spiritual desire; to keep death daily before one's eyes. To guard the actions of one's life at every hour. To know that in every place God is certainly watching. To dash at once evil thoughts as they come into one's mind to Christ and to lay them before one's spiritual elder. To guard one's mouth from evil or wicked speech; not to love to speak much; not to speak vain words or those fit to laugh at; not to love much laughter or hilarity. Gladly to hear sacred readings, to dwell continually in prayer, to confess daily in prayer to God one's own past misdeeds with tears and groans. To reform from the very misdeeds themselves of another, not fulfill the desires of the flesh. To hate one's own will, to obey the teachings of the priest and teacher in all things, even if he himself does otherwise—which God forbid—mindful of that precept of the Lord: 'Do what they say, but do not do what they do.' [41] Not to wish to be called holy before one is, but first to be it so that it may be said more truly. To fulfill daily with deeds the teachings of God, to love purity, to hate no one, not to have jealousy or envy, not to love strife, to avoid self-exaltation, to

[41] Matt. 23:3.

respect those older and to love those younger. In love of Christ to pray for enemies. To return to peace with those who disagree before the sun sets, and never to despair of God's mercy."

See, these are the tools of the spiritual art which, when they have been employed by us unceasingly, night and day, and on the Day of Judgment are marked again, we shall be recompensed by the Lord with that reward which he himself has promised: "Which eye has not seen, nor ear heard, nor has it ascended into the heart of man, which God has prepared for those who love him." [42]

22. The faithful must be reminded that all of them together, from the least to the greatest, should learn the Lord's Prayer and the Creed,[43] and they must be told that upon these two propositions the whole foundation of the Christian faith rests and unless anyone shall remember these two propositions and believe them with his whole heart, and repeat them very often in prayer, he cannot be catholic. For it has been established that none shall be anointed, nor baptized, nor be lifted up from the water of that fountain, nor can he hold anyone before the bishop to be confirmed, unless he has committed to memory the Creed and the Lord's Prayer, save only those whose age has not yet taught them to speak.[44]

23. They must be told that every day he who cannot pray more often should at least pray twice, that is, in the morning and evening, saying the Creed or the Lord's Prayer or the "O Thou who hast fashioned me,"[45] or even, "God, be merciful to me a sinner," and, "Thanks be to God," in return for the provisions of daily life and because He has deigned to create him after his own image and distinguish him from the beasts. When this has been done and God the sole Creator has been adored, let him call upon the saints that they may deign to intercede on his behalf with the divine Majesty. Let those near a church[46] do this in a church; he who, however, is on a journey or for some reason is in the forests or the fields, wherever the morning or evening hour itself finds him, let him do so, knowing

---

[42] I Cor. 2:9; Isa. 64:4.
[43] Probably the Apostles' Creed, on which see Ivo of Chartres.
[44] These last, doubtless, can only receive baptism and unction.
[45] A prayer which has not survived in either the Roman missal or breviary of our day. It apparently was based on the Septuagint Version of Isa. 27:11.
[46] *Basilica* appears here to have no more special meaning than "church."

that God is present everywhere, as the psalmist says: "In every place of his dominion" [47] and "If I should ascend into heaven, thou art there," [48] etc.

24. On the Lord's Day, however, because on it God established light, on it rained manna in the desert, on it the Redeemer of the human race voluntarily for our salvation rose again from the dead, on it he poured forth the Holy Spirit upon his disciples, there should be so great an observance that besides prayers and the solemnization of the Masses, and those things which pertain to eating, nothing else should be done. For if there should also be need of sailing, or traveling, permission is given provided that on these occasions the Mass and prayers are not passed by. Each Christian must come on the Sabbath Day to church with lights; he must come to the night vigils or to the morning office. He must come also with offerings for the solemnization of Masses. And while they come to church, no case should be pleaded or heard, no lawsuits may be held, but the time must be free for God alone, namely, in the celebration of the holy offices, and in the offering of alms, and in feasting spiritually on praise of God with friends, neighbors, and strangers.

25. They must be exhorted to love hospitality and to refuse to furnish shelter to no one, and if by chance they should supply shelter to anyone, not to take pay from him, unless perhaps the recipient gives something of his own accord.[49] They must be told how many have pleased God through the duty of hospitality, as the apostle says: "For by this some have pleased God, having received angels under their roof." [50] And again, "Hospitable without grumbling." [51] And the Lord himself will say at the Judgment, "I was a stranger and you made me your guest." [52] Let them know also that whoever loves hospitality receives Christ in the guests.[53] For that limitation of hospitality is not only inhuman but even cruel, in which a guest is never

---

[47] Ps. 103:22 (102:22, V).   [48] Ps. 139:8 (138:8, V).

[49] Monastic establishments of the present day sometimes admit travelers to their hospitality, but make no charge. "Guests should place in the alms box near the exit at least as much as they would pay in an hotel." So Baedeker, *Southern Italy* (Leipzig, 1930), p. 19, apropos of Monte Cassino Abbey.

[50] Heb. 13:2 (loosely quoted).

[51] I Peter 4:9.   [52] Matt. 25:35.

[53] In 1931 the translator sat for some time in the cell of the abbot of the Camaldolese convent above Frascati. He apologized for keeping the abbot from his duties. Said the abbot: "A monk has no duties greater than to care for guests. *In hospitibus Christus adoretur!*"

received unless the one who gives the hospitality is first paid, and what the Lord has bidden to do in regard to receiving the Heavenly Kingdom, let this be done in regard to receiving earthly possessions.

26. You must preach also that the faithful beware of perjury and to refrain from it absolutely, knowing that this is a great crime both in the Law[54] and the Prophets,[55] and prohibited in the Gospels.[56] For we have heard that some people think this crime of no importance and somehow place upon perjurers a small measure of penance. They ought to know that the same penance should be imposed for perjury as for adultery, for fornication, for homicide, and for other criminal vices. If anyone, however, who has committed perjury or any criminal sin, and, being afraid of the pain of long penance, is unwilling to come to confession, he ought to be expelled from the church, from both Communion and association with the faithful, so that no one eats with him, nor drinks, nor speaks, nor takes him into his house.

27. They must be told to abstain from false testimony, knowing that this also is a very serious crime, and forbidden by the Lord himself on Mt. Sinai, when the same Lord said: "Thou shalt not give false testimony," [57] and, "A false witness will not be unpunished." [58] Let whoever has done this know that he must be purified by such penance as was stated above concerning perjury, or he must be condemned by the same condemnation and excommunications as was stated. They must be told that it is the highest—I shall not say stupidity but—wickedness, to incur guilt for so great a crime on account of a desire for silver and gold, or clothing, or any other thing, or, as very frequently happens, because of drunkenness, so that he be kept in close confinement for seven years, or be expelled from the church, as the Lord says, "What does it profit a man if he shall gain the whole world and cause the loss of his soul?" [59] Although he may seem more cruel to others, let him really be cruel to himself.[60]

28. We exhort you to be ready to teach the people. He who knows the Scriptures, let him preach the Scriptures, but he who does not know them, let him at least say to the people what is

---

[54] E.g., Lev. 19:12.   [55] E.g., Isa. 48:1; Jer. 5:2; 7:9.   [56] Matt. 5:33.
[57] Ex. 20:16.   [58] Prov. 19:5.   [59] Matt. 16:26.
[60] The meaning of this sentence (*Quippe cum aliis videatur plus existere, sibimet crudelis existat*) seems to have little connection with the preceding and we suspect it of having gotten out of place.

very familiar, that they "turn from evil and do good, seek peace and pursue it, because the eyes of the Lord are upon the righteous and his ears are turned to their prayers," [61] etc. No one can therefore excuse himself because he does not have a tongue which he can use to edify someone. For when he shall see anyone in error, he can at once, to the best of his ability and powers, by arguing, pleading, reproving, withdraw him from his error and exhort him to do good works. But when, with the Lord's help, we assemble together for a synod, let each man know how to tell us how much he has accomplished with help from the Lord, or what fruit he has accomplished. And if any man perhaps needs our aid, let him tell us this in love, and we with no less love will not postpone bringing aid to him as we are able.

29. You ought to admonish the faithful to be constant and zealous in prayer. The prayer, however, ought to be of this kind that, when the Creed has first been said, as if the constant foundation of his faith, let him say, whoever he is, three times the "O Thou who hast fashioned me, have mercy upon me" [45] and three times the "O God, be merciful to me a sinner," [62] and let him complete it with the Lord's Prayer. If, therefore, the place and time should permit,[63] let him pray to the holy apostles and martyrs to intercede for him, and, having armed his forehead with the sign of the cross, let him lift up his hands and eyes with his heart and give thanks to God. But if the time should be insufficient to do all this, let so much suffice: "O Thou who hast fashioned me, have mercy upon me," [45] and "O God, be merciful to me a sinner," [62] and the Lord's Prayer, but with groaning and contrition of heart.

30. For every day in our prayer to God, either once or twice or more often as we can, we ought to confess our sins, as the prophet says: "I have acknowledged my sin to thee, and my unrighteousness I have not hid. I said, 'I shall confess against myself my unrighteous acts to the Lord,' and thou didst forgive the guilt of my sin." [64] For when confession has been made to the Lord in prayer with a groan and tears, the Fiftieth [65] or the Twenty-fourth [66] or the Thirty-first [67] Psalm should be recited, or others pertaining to the same subject, and so the

---

[61] Ps. 34:14 f. (33:15 f., V) inexactly quoted.
[62] Luke 18:13.
[63] *Exegerit* means "demand" but, "permit" is required.
[64] Ps. 32:5 (31:5, V).
[65] Ps. 51.
[66] Ps. 25 (R.S.V.).
[67] Ps. 32 (R.S.V.).

prayer should be completed. Because the confession which we make to priests brings us also this support that, having received from them salutary advice, we wash away the stains of sins by the most wholesome observance of penance, or by silent[68] prayers. But the confession which we make to God alone is helpful in that in so far as we are mindful of our sins, so far does the Lord remember, and, on the other hand, so far as we forget them, so far does the Lord forget them, as the prophet says: "And thy sins shall I not remember."[69] You,[70] however, be mindful of what David the prophet is recorded as having done, when he said, "Since I know my iniquity and my sin is ever against me."[71]

31. Confessions should be made concerning all sins committed in either deed or thought. There are eight chief vices, from which hardly anyone can be found free. The first is gluttony, that is, voracity of the belly; second, fornication; third, languor or sadness; fourth, avarice; fifth, vainglory; sixth, envy; seventh, anger; eighth, pride.[72] When, therefore, anyone comes to confession, he should be diligently asked how or when he has committed the sin which he confesses he has done, and according to the measure of the deed ought the penance to be indicated to him. He ought to be persuaded that he should even make confession of wicked thoughts. He ought also to be directed to make his confession of the eight principal vices, and the priest ought to mention each one of them by name and to receive confession about it.

32. The hungry should be filled, the thirsty should be given drink, the naked covered, the sick and those in prison visited, and the strangers taken in, as the Lord says: "For I was hungry and you gave me to eat; I was thirsty and you gave me to drink,"[73] etc. For all these things, each one ought to do spiritually in himself and fulfill them bodily in others, because all these are almost of no value for gaining life eternal, if anyone lives lustfully, proudly, enviously, and, not to repeat each of them individually, in vice and without control, and lacks other

[68] The text here reads *mutuis* which we emend to *mutis*.
[69] Jer. 31:34.   [70] The word is singular.   [71] Ps. 51:3 (50:5, V).
[72] This list follows principally, not that of Gregory the Great (*Moralia* 26.28, MPL 76.364), but that of John Cassian (*Collationes* 5.2, CSEL 13.121, 17.81), and differs from Cassian in putting *tristitia* and *accedia* together and then adding *invidia*. On this topic, see John T. McNeill and Helena M. Gamer, *Medieval Handbooks of Penance*, in "Records of Civilization" 29 (New York, Columbia Press, 1938), pp. 18–20.
[73] Matt. 25:35.

good works. Therefore, he who sees that he does not possess the Christ who said, "I am the living bread which came down from heaven,"[74] and does not have love, which is the food of the soul, is hungry indeed, but if by good works he unites himself with Christ and fills himself with the sweetness of love, he has fed his hungry self completely. He who lacks the flowing water of the teaching of the Holy Spirit and the Holy Scriptures, is thirsty, but if he waters himself on the stream of God's Word, and saturates his soul on the sweetness of the spiritual cup, he gives his thirsty self to drink. He who sees himself bare of righteousness or of other evidences of good works, and puts on righteousness or other virtues, clothes his naked self without a doubt. If he lies on the bed of his vices, and labors with the sickness of his iniquity, he is sick, indeed, but if from the mire of vices he goes to confession and through the laments of penance he is freed from the bonds of sins, and goes to the light of good works, he visits his sick self and himself in prison without a doubt. If on the highway of this life he sees himself laboring and beset with the inclemency, as it were, of the stormy weather of his vices, and that he does not have a shelter of good works, let him know that he is a man on a journey in need of shelter, but if he leads himself to a house of virtues, and betakes himself to the shelter of their protection, he receives a stranger indeed. Since he shows all these kindnesses to himself in spiritual fashion, in himself he feeds, gives to drink, clothes, visits Christ, whose member he is.

33. The faithful of God's holy church should be warned that they teach their sons and daughters to show obedience to their parents, as the Lord says: "My son, honor thy father"[75]; for the parents also themselves ought to act moderately toward their sons and daughters, as the apostle says: "And you, parents, do not provoke your sons to wrath."[76] For they should be told this, that if they wish to be sparing in parental affection to the hurt of their sons, the Lord does not permit these things to go unpunished unless, perhaps, worthy penitence is shown and because it is easier for the sons to accept a flogging from the parents than to incur God's anger.

34. The people should be admonished that it is true love which loves God more than oneself and a neighbor as oneself, and which does not wish to do to another except what one wishes to be done to oneself, and more things which would be

---

[74] John 6:41 ("living" added).
[75] Ecclesiasticus 7:29 (Vulg.), 7:27, R.V., loosely.   [76] Eph. 6:4.

long to recount. For whoever thinks that love is only in drink and in food, and in the giving of aid and the receiving of things, makes an error of no moderate proportions, as the apostle says: "The kingdom of God is not food and drink."[77] For when they do these very things with love, they are good, and to be accounted among virtues.

35. They who are intent upon business and trade are to be admonished not to desire earthly gain more than eternal life. For he who thinks more of earthly matters than about the salvation of his soul wanders far from the path of truth, and, according to a certain wise man,[78] in his lifetime has destroyed his innermost parts. Here as elsewhere must be followed the apostolic saying, "And let no man transgress and wrong his neighbor in business,"[79] for God is the protector from all these things. For as by those who are excessively concerned with labor in fields and other toil to acquire food and clothing and the other things necessary for human needs, tithes and alms must be given, so this also must be done by those who engage in commerce involving these necessities. For to each man God has given skill by which he may be fed, and each man, of his skill, from which he derives the necessary support of his body, ought to supply support to his soul which is the more necessary.

36. One week before the beginning of Lent confessions should be given to the priests, penance received, quarrels reconciled, and all disputes settled, and from their hearts they ought to forgive debts, so that they may freely say, "Forgive us our debts as we also forgive our debtors."[80] And so, entering upon the blessed Lenten season, they may, with clear and purified minds, approach the holy Easter, and through penitence may renew themselves, which is a second baptism. For as Baptism cleanses sins, so does penitence. And because after Baptism the sinner cannot be baptized again, this remedy of penitence has been given by the Lord that through it in place of Baptism sins committed after Baptism may be washed away. For the Holy Scriptures show that sins can be forgiven in seven ways[81]: First,

---

[77] Rom. 14:17.
[78] Ecclesiasticus 10:10 (Vulg.), 10:9 R.V.
[79] I Thess. 4:6.
[80] Matt. 6:12.
[81] The seven remissions here discussed are indebted directly to Caesarius of Arles, *Hom.* XII (MPL 76.1075), and through him, indirectly, to John Cassian (*Collationes* 20.8, CSEL 13.561 ff.), and through him, ultimately, to Origen's *Second Homily on Leviticus* (MPG 11.418), where the list is Baptism, martyrdom, almsgiving, forgiveness of others, conversion of sinners, fullness of love, penance with tears. See McNeill and Gamer, *op. cit.*, 99, note 5.

in Baptism, which has been given on account of the forgiveness of sins. Secondly, by martyrdom, according to the words of the psalmist: "Blessed is he to whom the Lord imputes no sin,"[82] because, according to what the same David says, "Blessed are those whose iniquities are forgiven and whose sins are covered."[83] Sins are forgiven through Baptism; they are covered through penitence; they are imputed not through martyrdom. Thirdly, by alms, according to Daniel, who says to the heathen king Nebuchadnezzar, "Redeem thy sins with alms in mercies to the poor,"[84] and this: "Water quenches burning fire and alms quench sin."[85] And the Lord in the Gospel: "But give alms and behold, all things pure are yours."[86] Fourthly, if anyone forgives the sins of the one who sins against him, according to this: "Forgive and it will be forgiven to you,"[87] and this: "So also your Father will forgive you your sins, if you forgive anyone from your hearts."[88] Fifthly, if through his preaching anyone should, by the exercise of good works, convert others from their error, in accordance with what the apostle says: "If anyone should make a sinner to turn from the error of his way, he will save his soul from death, and will cover a multitude of sins."[89] Sixthly, through love, according to this: "The love of God covers a multitude of sins"[90] through Jesus Christ our Lord. Seventhly, through penitence, according to what David says: "I turned in my affliction, while it is transfixed with a thorn."[91]

37. Lent itself, however, ought to be kept with highest observance, so that in it the fast never be broken except on the Lord's Days, which are excepted from fasting, because those days are the tithes of our year, which we ought to pass through with all devotion and sanctity. Let there be in them no occasion for breaking the fast because at another time it is customary to dispense with the fasting for the sake of love, but this should not be then. Because at another time, whether to fast or not is based on the wish and judgment of the individual, but at this time a failure to fast is to transcend the will of God. And to fast

---

[82] Ps. 32:2 (31:2, V).
[83] Ps. 32:1 (31:1, V). The argument seems to be that as martyrs are called "blessed," so "blessed" means martyr, though, of course, many examples could be cited of the application of the word to persons not martyrs in the usual sense.
[84] Dan. 4:27 (4:24, V).   [85] Ecclesiasticus 3:33 (Vulg.), 3:30 (R.V.).
[86] Luke 11:41.   [87] Luke 6:37.
[88] Matt. 6:14, loosely.   [89] James 5:20.   [90] I Peter 4:8.
[91] Ps. 32:4 (31:4, V). Both the Hebrew and the Latin are obscure.

at another time is to get a reward for the one who fasts, but at this time, except for the sick and the little children, whoever does not fast shall gain punishment for himself because these same days the Lord has consecrated to holy fasting through Moses and through Elijah and through himself.

38. On the days of the fast, alms should be given, so that anyone, if he does not fast as he ought, may distribute food and drink to the poor, because to fast and to keep the food for lunch until dinner is an increase, not of recompense, but of foods.

39. Many who think they are fasting have the habit of eating as soon as they hear the bell for nones, but they should not believe that they are fasting if they should eat before the office of vespers. For one must go to Masses, and hear the solemnization of Masses and office of vespers, and also give alms, before approaching food. If anyone should be so limited of necessity that he cannot attend Mass, he should break his fast having shown respect to the vesper hour and having completed his prayer.

40. On those days there should be abstention from every pleasure and they must live soberly and chastely. He who can abstain from eggs, cheese, fish, and wine, gains great credit for virtue; he, however, who cannot abstain from them, either because some illness comes or some sort of work, may make use of them. Only let the fasting continue until the celebration of vespers; and let him take wine, not to get drunk, but to restore his body. To abstain, however, from cheese, milk, butter, and eggs, and not to fast [on wine],[92] is foolishness to the highest degree, and bereft entirely of rationality. For getting drunk on wine and profligacy are forbidden, not milk and eggs. The apostle does not say, "Do not take milk and eggs," but "Do not get drunk on wine in which there is profligacy." [93]

41. On each Lord's Day in Lent the sacraments of the body and blood of Christ should be taken by all except those who are excommunicated, and on the Lord's Supper, and on the day of preparation, on the eve of the Passover, and on the day of the Lord's resurrection, should be communicated to absolutely all, and all those days of the Passover week should be kept with equal sanctity.

42. On these days of fasting there should be no lawsuits, no quarrels, but one should continue in the praise of God and doing necessary work. For the Lord reproves those who engage

---

[92] Words in brackets are necessary.   [93] Eph. 5:18.

in quarrels and lawsuits in the time of Lent and who demand debts from debtors, speaking through the prophet: "Behold, on the day of your fasting your pleasures are to be found, and you keep looking for all your debtors. Behold, you fast for lawsuits and for quarrels, and you strike wickedly with your fist." [94]

43. One should abstain from wives on these most consecrated days, and live chastely and piously, so that these holy days be passed with heart and body made holy, and so arrive at the holy day of Pascha because fasting is of little value if defiled by the marital act, and what prayers, vigils, and alms do not recommend.

44. The people must be admonished to approach the most sacred and holy sacrament of the Lord's body and blood with no delay and never to refrain from it, but with all diligence to choose a time when for a little they abstain from the marital act and cleanse themselves from vices, adorn themselves with virtues, be continually in almsgiving and prayers, and so approach so great a sacrament. Because, as it is dangerous for an impure person to approach so great a sacrament, so also it is dangerous to abstain from it for a long time. Except for the list of those who are excommunicated, let them take Communion, not when they please but at specified times, and for those who live devoutly and in holy fashion let them do this almost every day.

45.[95] Let it be ordained that when special Masses are celebrated by priests on Lord's Days, they should not take place in public in such a way that the people can hear them and particularly so that they do not draw themselves away from the public solemnization of Masses according to the canon at the third hour. For some people have a very bad practice in that when, on Lord's Days or on other holy days, they look to hear Masses—they may be Masses for the dead or for other purposes, which are privately celebrated by priests—and then from early morning through the whole day they give themselves to drunkenness and feasting and vain speaking, rather than to serving God.

46. On account of which care must be taken that all come together in public to holy mother church to hear the solemniza-

[94] Isa. 58:3 f.
[95] From this point on the codex which Sirmond had been following became seriously corrupt. At the end (MPL 105.208) is printed another, better version of these two final chapters, united as one, found by him in a *Codex Suessionicus* of Theodulph. We have adopted for the translation this longer variant as it obviously provides a purer text and is far more interesting.

tion of Masses and preaching. Likewise, it is decreed that in a city in which a bishop[96] has been established, all the presbyters and people, both of the city and of its environs, in vestments, should stand with devout heart at that Mass itself until the benediction of the bishop and Communion, and afterward, if they wish, they may with permission revert to their own rank, after the benediction and Communion have been received. And the priests should diligently watch out that neither in the oratories nor the monasteries in the countryside, nor in churches in the countryside, should they presume to celebrate Masses before the second hour except with great caution, and with the doors locked, so that the people may not at all be able to take occasion to absent themselves from the public solemnities, from the Mass or preaching of the bishop, but all of them, the priests of the suburbs as well as those assigned to the city, and all the people, as we said above, may come together with them for the public celebration of Masses, and nobody except little children and the sick, though they may have heard a Mass, both in the cities and in the parish churches, may presume to eat and drink before the completion of the public office.

If anyone should try to transgress these statutes, let him be brought before the canonical judges until he give satisfaction.[97]

---

[96] This word in no way invalidates our belief that the second variant is by Theodulph. He means by "decreed" the act of some higher ecclesiastical authority, papal or conciliar.

[97] Here (MPL 105.206–208) is printed a later summary of the chapters, amounting in bulk to something less than a fifth as much material as in the selection translated.

The Venerable Bede: On Bishop Aidan

INTRODUCTION

IN THE BRIEF NOTE[1] WHICH CONCLUDES THE CELE-brated *Ecclesiastical History of the English People* the author identifies himself as Baeda (rendered in modern speech as Bede), a *famulus* or servant of Christ, and a presbyter in the monastery of the blessed apostles Peter and Paul which is at Uiuraemuda (today Wearmouth) and Ingyruum (now Jarrow).[2] He was born, he says, in the territory of the same monastery, that is, in lands afterward belonging to the monastery which was founded in his childhood, but at the age of seven was given by relatives to be educated by the most reverend Abbot Benedict[3] and later to Ceolfrid.[4] Henceforth, he had spent the whole of his life in the monastery, devoted entirely to

---
[1] Bede, *Hist. Eccl.* 5.24 Plummer's ed., 1.356–60, tr. in part, *ibid.* ix–x. On the life and works see the admirable sketch by Plummer, *ibid.* ix–lxxix.
[2] The two monasteries were both founded by Benedict Biscop: that at Wearmouth, dedicated to St. Peter, in 674, with Eosterwine (d. 686, succeeded by Sigfrid who d. 688–689) in charge; that at Jarrow, dedicated to St. Paul, in 681 or 682, with Ceolfrid in charge. It was intended to operate the two establishments as two parts of the same monastery, but as Abbot Benedict was frequently absent or engaged in other business, in actual practice the two priors were abbots in all but name.
[3] Benedict Biscop (c. 628–689–690), a monk at Lérins about 665, was appointed by Pope Vitalian (657–672) to conduct Theodore of Tarsus to Canterbury in 668. He made six visits to Rome, studied Roman ecclesiastical usages, and brought back a rich store of vestments, books, pictures, etc. See Bede's *Hist. Abbatum* 1–13, Plummer's ed., 1.364–377.
[4] Ceolfrid, born in Northumberland, c. 642, died at Langres, France, en route to Rome, September 24, 716. He became prior at Wearmouth in 674, of Jarrow in 682, abbot of both in 688. Intending to spend the rest of his life in Rome, he resigned in 716, but never reached the Eternal City. His successor as abbot was Hwaetbert, who survived Bede.

meditating on the Scriptures, and amid the observance of monastic discipline and the daily charge of singing in the church he ever held it sweet either to learn or to teach or to write. In his nineteenth year he was made deacon,[5] in his thirtieth presbyter, in each instance by Bishop John[6] at the request of Abbot Ceolfrid. From the time he became presbyter to his fifty-ninth year, when he completed the *Ecclesiastical History*, he had endeavored, for his own use and that of his brethren, to make brief notes on Holy Scripture out of the works of the venerable fathers or in conformity with their meaning and interpretation. Then follows a list of his works up to that time, thirty-five titles in all, and the following beautiful prayer:

"I pray thee, good Jesus, that as thou hast graciously granted me to drink in with delight the words of thy knowledge, so wouldst thou mercifully grant me someday to reach thee, the fount of all wisdom, and to appear forever before thy face."[7]

As the completion of the *Ecclesiastical History* is dated by Bede himself in 731, his birth must have occurred in 672 or 673, his entrance into the monastery in 679 or 680, his ordination as deacon in 691 or 692, and to the priesthood in 702 or 703. Aside from this, we can say that he had made at least one visit to Lindisfarne,[8] was at York in 733,[9] and was probably also at some time in Canterbury.[10] That he had been in Rome, as claimed by some,[11] is exceedingly unlikely, as he never mentions such a visit, but one must not assume from the statement above that he never left the monastery at all. It has generally been believed that he was the lad, later a priest at Jarrow, who, except for Ceolfrid, was the sole survivor of the plague at Jarrow, as told, so touchingly, in the anonymous *History of the Abbots*.[12]

---

[5] The eleven years as deacon should not be regarded as indicating deficiency in Bede. The medieval diaconate had not become, as its modern counterpart now is, merely a preliminary step to the priesthood. Many prominent ecclesiastics never advanced beyond the diaconate, e.g., Paul the Deacon (Warnfrid), Paschasius Radbertus, abbot of Corbie, while Gregory the Great advanced to the papacy from the diaconate.
[6] John, Bishop of Hexham, in whose diocese the monastery was located. See the many references to him in Plummer's index (2.484).
[7] *Hist. Eccl.* 5.23 (end), Plummer's ed. 1.351.
[8] See the preface to the life of Cuthbert written before 721.
[9] *Epist. ad Ecberctum Episcopum* 1 and 17.
[10] This is suggested by M. L. W. Laistner, *Trans. of the R. Hist. Soc.*, 4th ser., 16.92. Certain rare books were known to both Bede and Aldhelm.
[11] See Plummer l.xvi f.   [12] *Hist. Anon. Abbatum* 14 (Plummer 1.393).

From the works it is abundantly demonstrable that Bede was a most profound scholar, a diligent student, not only of the Scriptures and the fathers, but also of at least a limited number of pagan writers as well.[13] Throughout his long life he was constantly engaged in study, in teaching, and in writing, never neglectful of the devotional duties of priest and monk, a good friend to all with whom he came into contact. He died at Jarrow on Wednesday, May 25, 735, Ascension Day. The circumstances of his passing are movingly described in a letter of his pupil Cuthwin, a lector, to another lector, Cuthbert, also Bede's pupil.[14]

It is not to be supposed that the constant application to him of the title "Venerable" means that Bede does not rank as saint.[15] How he came to enjoy this title, so peculiarly his own, is not certain. Three accounts exist. In the first, Bede, blinded by old age, is induced by detractors to preach in chapel on the false supposition that there is a congregation before him, whereupon, as he finishes, the angels cry out, "Amen, very venerable Bede." In a second version, Bede is on a journey in a rocky defile and it is the stones that cry out, "Amen, venerable father." The third variant tells us that the monk who was preparing Bede's epitaph was unable to complete the hexameter and left it unfinished overnight:

"*Hic sunt in fossa Bedae . . . ossa.*"
("Here in the grave are the bones of . . . Bede.")

In the morning it was found that the angels had supplied the apt word "*venerabilis*" to complete the line.[16]

Of the fifty-two titles attributed to Bede either by manuscripts of the works themselves or by allusion to works no longer extant, ten may be dismissed as spurious or probably so. Seven may be classed as scientific (on metrics, grammar, natural history, or chronology). Those on chronology, the *De Temporibus* and the *De Temporum Ratione*, show Bede's preoccupation with the date of Easter. Of the theological works, fourteen are commentaries (Genesis, Samuel, Kings, Ezra-Nehemiah, Proverbs, Canticles, Habakkuk, Tobit, Mark, Luke, two on Acts, the

---

[13] See Laistner, *loc. cit.*
[14] *De obitu Baedae*, text in Plummer l.clx–clxiv, tr. *ibid.* lxxii–lxxvii.
[15] The process of canonization has involved, at least until recently, elevation, successively, to the lower grades of *venerabilis* and *beatus* before reaching that of *sanctus*.
[16] Plummer l.xlviii–xlix.

Catholic Epistles, and the Apocalypse). The others, including hymns, homilies, are on Scriptural passages, pastoral theology, and various topics.

The historical works, nine in number, include lives of Saint Felix, Saint Anastasius, and two, one of them in verse, of Saint Cuthbert; the *Letter to Plegwin* on the six ages of the world; the *Letter to Albinus* which accompanied a copy of the *Ecclesiastical History*; the *History of the Abbots of Wearmouth and Jarrow*, not to be confused with the anonymous *History of the Abbots*, and lastly, the great work for which Bede is best known, the *Ecclesiastical History of the English People*, in five books.

Our selection has been chosen from this and is intended to be representative, not only of Bede's historical writing at its best, but as well a typical account of a medieval English cleric.

The Latin text of Bede's works appears in the twelve volumes of John Allen Giles's *Patres Ecclesiae Anglicanae* (London, Oxford, and Paris, 1843–1844), and in Joseph Stevenson's *Bedae Opera Historica Minora*, published by the English Historical Society (London, 1841). They also appear in Migne's *Patrologia latina*, vols. 90–95. By far the best edition of the historical works is, however, that of Charles Plummer (Oxford, Clarendon Press, 1896), in two volumes, which has a fine introduction, critical and exegetical commentary, and provides critical texts of the *Historia Ecclesiastica Gentis Anglorum*, the *Historia Abbatum*, and the *Epistola ad Ecgberctum*, all by Bede, as well as of the anonymous *Historia Abbatum*. Our translation was made from this superior text. The Old English version was published by Thomas Miller, Early English Text Society (London, Trubner, 1890–1898). Mention should also be made of J. E. King, *Baedae Opera Historica*, Loeb Classical Library (London, Heineman; New York, Putnam, 1930), two vols.; G. F. Browne, *The Venerable Bede: His Life and Writings* in "Studies in Church History" (London, S.P.C.K., 1919); Henry Martin Gillet, *Saint Bede the Venerable* (London, Burns, Oates, and Washbourne, 1935); Putnam Fennell Jones, *A Concordance to the Historica Ecclesiastica of Bede* (Cambridge, Mediaeval Academy, 1929); M. L. W. Laistner, "Bede as a Classical and Patristic Scholar" (*Trans. of the R. Hist. Soc.*, 4th ser., 16 [1933], 68–94); Alexander Hamilton Thompson, *Bede, His Life, Times, and Writings* (Oxford, 1935).

The Venerable Bede: On Bishop Aidan

THE TEXT

3. This Oswald,[17] then, when he came to the throne, desired that the whole nation over which he began to rule should be imbued with the grace of the Christian faith. Having already made many an attempt to overthrow the barbarians, he sent to the elders[18] of the Scots, among whom as an exile he had himself experienced the rite of Baptism,[19] together with the knights who were with him, to ask that he should be sent a bishop by whose teaching and ministry the nation of the Angles which he ruled should both learn the gifts of the Lord's faith and receive the sacraments. Not long afterward he obtained what he asked for, for he received Bishop Aidan, a man of the highest humility, piety, and self-abnegation, possessing zeal for God,[20] though not fully with respect to knowledge. For he was wont to celebrate Easter Sunday after the custom of his own race, as we have often mentioned, from the fourteenth of the moon to the twentieth. This was the date when the northern province of the Scots, and the whole of the nation of the Picts, used to celebrate Easter Sunday in those days, believing that by this observance they were following the writings of the saintly and

[17] St. Oswald (605–642), King of Northumbria, was slain in battle with Penda of Mercia.
[18] Alderman. Throughout this selection the "Scots" are always the inhabitants of Ireland, not of modern Scotland.
[19] Simeon of Durham (1.18) says that Oswald's parents were not Christians, but the *Life of Oswald* represents his mother Acha as a Christian.
[20] The Anglo-Saxon version of Bede omits the rest of this chapter, with, as Plummer (2.124, *ad loc.*) says, "equal good taste and feeling." See Plummer (2.348–353) for an excellent discussion of the differences between the Celtic and Roman dates for the celebration of Easter. In *Hist. Eccl.* 3.17 (p. 161, Plummer) Bede says he detests Aidan's use of the Irish system of chronology.

praiseworthy father[21] Anatolius—whether true or not, it is very easy for any learned man to see—but the Scottish tribes, which dwelt in the southern parts of the island of Ireland, had at the admonition of the bishops of the Apostolic See long before learned to observe Easter according to the canonical rite.[22]

When the bishop, then, arrived at court, the king assigned to him a place for his episcopal see on the island of Lindisfarne,[23] where he himself asked it. This place, of course, on account of the ebb and flow of the tide, is washed about twice daily, like an island, by the waves of the sea, and twice made contiguous to the land when the shore is again uncovered.[24]

Humbly and gladly hearkening in every way to the bishop's teachings, the king expended every effort to establish and extend the church of Christ in his kingdom. Often it happened that—a most beautiful thing to behold—when the bishop, who knew the language of the Angles imperfectly, was preaching the gospel, the king himself stood there as the interpreter of the heavenly word to his generals and ministers,[25] because, of course, during his long exile he had completely mastered the language of the Scots. After that, more men began to come daily from the region[26] of the Scots to Britain and to those provinces of the Angles over which King Oswald ruled, to preach with great devotion the word of faith, and when the newcomers were men of episcopal rank,[27] to minister, to those

---

[21] Anatolius, bishop of Laodicea in the third century, on whom see Eusebius (*Hist. Eccl.* 7.32. 14–20); for the text of the *Canon Paschalis*, see MPG 10.207–231, but this document is assigned by G. Krüger (NSH 1.167) to the sixth century. See B. Krusch, *Studien zur mittelalterlichen Chronologie* (Leipzig, 1880) 311–327; Plummer 2.191.

[22] In A.D. 631 delegates from a South Ireland synod, held probably in 630, visited Rome for consultations on the Easter question, and upon their return the Roman Easter was adopted in another synod in 632 or 633 (Plummer 2.125).

[23] William of Malmesbury (*Gesta Pontificum*, ed. Hamilton, p. 266) tells us that Lindisfarne, a small island, was chosen by Aidan because he sought for quiet and freedom from crowds such as would be present at York (see Plummer 2.125 f.).

[24] Carts could approach the island at such times (*Vita Anon. Cudb.* 44, 46, cited by Plummer, 2.126).

[25] The Anglo-Saxon version calls them "aldermen and thanes."

[26] Not only Ireland but Iona as well.

[27] *Sacerdotali . . . gradu*, probably alludes to the Irish system of nondiocesan bishops attached to monasteries. On *sacerdos*, see Plummer's note (2.55 *ad* 1.28). The ambiguity of this word is to be found not only in the Christian writers of England but in the fathers and early medieval writers of all regions of Latin Christendom.

who believed, the grace of Baptism. In many a place a church was erected; folk joyfully flocked to hear the Word; by royal munificence possessions were bestowed, and lands for the founding of monasteries; the children of the Angles were being instructed by Scottish teachers, together with their more advanced studies and the observance of monastic rule.

For they were monks, especially those who came to preach. Bishop Aidan was himself a monk, and was sent from the island called Hii,[28] of which the monastery, among nearly all those of the northern Scots[29] and among all those of the Picts, for a long time held the chief position and was put in charge of the rule of their people. This island, of course, owns the sway of Britain, being separate from it by a small strait, but by the gift of the Picts who inhabit those parts of Britain, it was long ago handed over to the Scottish monks because by their preaching they had received the Christian faith.

[Chapter 4 describes the history of Iona.]

5. From this island, then, from the company of these monks, Aidan, having received episcopal rank, was sent to the province of the Angles to instruct it in[30] Christ. At that date[31] Segeni,[32] abbot and presbyter, was in charge of this monastery. Among other teachings of how life ought to be lived, he[33] left to his clergy a most wholesome example in his abstinence and chastity. His doctrine was particularly recommended to all by the fact that he himself taught nothing different from the way he lived with his monks. He desired to seek nothing of this world, to love nothing. Everything given him by the kings or the wealthy of this world he was soon glad to give to the poor who came to beg from him. He used to journey about through all the cities and countryside, not on horseback[34] but on foot, unless greater necessity compelled him to ride. Whenever he

---

[28] Iona, a corruption of the form used by Adamnan, *Ioua insula*, (see Plummer 2.127), which was stereotyped by the mistaken fancy that the name was derived from the Hebrew word *iona* (dove), supposed to be an allusion to the name of Saint Columba.

[29] Of northern Ireland.

[30] One MS. has "on Christ's behalf."

[31] Aidan died August 31, 651 (Bede 3.14 end), in the seventeenth year of his episcopate (*ibid.* 3.17), and the Synod of Whitby, which was held before July 664, was in the thirtieth year of the *Episcopatus Scottorum*, so Aidan must have been consecrated before July, 635.

[32] Seghine, abbot of Iona, 623–652 (Reeve's ed. of Adamnan's *Life of Columba*, pp. 373 f.) See Plummer, 2.113.

[33] Aidan, not Segeni, of course.

[34] Cf. 3.14 for the story of the horse given him by Oswyn.

saw, as he walked, either rich or poor, turning at once to them, he would summon those not of the faith to the sacrament of receiving faith; or if he saw the faithful, he would strengthen them in that faith itself and would arouse them by word and deed to perform acts of charity and good works.[35]

So greatly did his life differ from the slothfulness of our time[36] that everyone who walked along with him, whether tonsured or lay, was obligated to meditate, that is to give attention either to the reading of Scripture or the learning[37] of psalms. This was his daily work, and the work of all who were with him, no matter to what places they came. And if by chance it turned out, as it rarely did, that he was invited to a king's banquet, he went with one cleric or two, and after he had taken a little refreshment, he hurried quickly away to read with his monks or to pray. Stimulated by his example, the religious[38] in that period, both men and women, established the yearly custom, except during the period of Easter to Whitsunday when there is a remission of fasting,[39] of prolonging their fasting on Wednesdays[40] and Fridays to two o'clock in the afternoon.[41] Never was he silent before men of wealth out of respect or fear, if they were in any way at fault, but he would reprove them with sharp rebuke. He would never give money to those powerful in this world unless to provide food for any of them who happened to be his guests, but instead he would dispense, as we have said, for the use of the poor those largesses of money which he was given by the rich, or he would spend them for redeeming those who had been unjustly sold. Finally, the many whom he had brought back with this payment, he afterward made his pupils, and by teaching them and instructing them he even raised them to the rank of priest.[42]

They say, moreover, that when King Oswald had asked for

[35] This passage may have influenced Chaucer's description of the parson in the Prologue to the *Canterbury Tales*.
[36] That is, in the decay of Bede's own day.
[37] *Discendis*, but in one MS. the first *s* is erased, and saying psalms would be more practicable during a walk than learning them. On the use of the psalter in the British Isles, see Plummer's excellent note (2.137–139).
[38] Those under a rule.
[39] From Easter to Pentecost, the most festal season of the year.
[40] The name of Wednesday in Irish, *cetain*, "the first fast," commemorates the custom. It was in memory of the Lord's betrayal.
[41] To the ninth hour, from which our word "noon" is derived, having been moved back to midday because this fasting proved too rigorous.
[42] *Ad sacerdotalem . . . gradum*, perhaps even to the rank of bishop.

a bishop[43] from the province[44] of the Scots, to minister the word of faith to himself and his nation, there had first been sent another man of rather strict spirit, who, after preaching for some time to the nation of the Angles with little success, and not being gladly heard by the people, returned home and reported to the council of elders, that he had not been able to succeed in teaching the nation to which he had been sent because they were untamable people, hard and barbarous of heart. But the elders, so they say, began a long discussion in council as to what should be done, desiring to afford the nation the salvation for which they were asked but grieving that the preacher whom they had sent had not been received. Then Aidan said, for he was himself present at the council, to the bishop[45] involved in the discussion, "It seems to me, my brother, that you have been harder than is just in dealing with unlearned hearers, and that contrary to the teaching of the apostle, you have not first offered them the milk of softer doctrine, until gradually nourished on God's Word, they should be strong enough to take the more perfect teaching and to make God's teaching more sublime." When they heard this, all who sat there turned their gaze upon him and, after thoroughly discussing his remarks, decided that he was worthy of the episcopate and should be sent to instruct the unbelieving and the untaught who was himself above all else proved to be endowed with that grace of discernment which is the mother of virtues. So, ordaining him, they sent him to preach. When he had time to do so, he demonstrated that, as earlier he was endowed with humble insight, so later he was also possessed of the other virtues.

6. Instructed, then, by the teaching of this bishop,[45] King Oswald, together with the nation of the Angles over which he was the head, not only learned to hope for the kingdoms of the heavens unknown to their forebears but also received, from that same one God[46] who made heaven and earth, earthly kingdoms beyond any of his predecessors. At last he brought under his sway all the nations and provinces of Britain, which are divided into four[47] tongues, those of the Britons, the Picts, the Scots,

[43] *Antistes*, clearly bishop in context and philology, both.
[44] The Anglo-Saxon version has "of Scotta ealonde," usually Ireland, but here Iona.
[45] *Sacerdotem*—the Anglo-Saxon version calls him "bishop."
[46] Though one MS. has *domino*, the Anglo-Saxon version has "gode."
[47] Bede (1.1) speaks of five languages in Britain, but this includes Latin as the ecclesiastical tongue.

and the Angles. Raised to this lofty height of royal power, he was—a remarkable thing to say—no less humble before the poor and strangers, no less kind and generous. Finally, it is said that one time, when on the holy day of Easter he had sat down to dinner with the above-mentioned bishop, and there was put on the table before him a silver platter filled with royal food, and he was about to stretch forth his hands to bless the bread, there suddenly entered that servant[48] of his who had been entrusted with the duty of receiving the needy, and told the king that a large crowd of poor had come from every direction and were sitting in the courtyard, asking alms from the king. He at once gave direction that the repast set before him be given to the poor, and that the platter be broken up, and divided among them in small bits.[49] When he saw this, the bishop who was sitting there rejoiced at such a deed of piety and, taking his hand, said, "May this hand never grow old." And it turned out in accordance with the prayer of his blessing, for when he was slain in battle, and his hand and arm were severed from the body, it came to pass that they remain to this day uncorrupted. Finally, in the royal city which is called Bebba[50] from the name of a former queen, they are preserved in a silver receptacle in St. Peter's Church, and are venerated with worthy honor by all.

Through the efforts of this king, the provinces of the Deri[51] and the Bernicii, which up to that time were often at odds with each other, remain in peace and unity, and are as one people fashioned together.

He was the nephew of King Edwin[52] by his sister Acha, and it was fitting that so great a precursor would have from his own blood such an heir of his religion and royal power.

[Chapters 7–9 omitted. In Chapter 9, Bede recounts the death of Oswald in battle at Maserfelth, in Shropshire, in his thirty-eighth year, on August 5, 642.]

10. At that time there came another man from the nation of

---

[48] Later, the king's almoner.
[49] The fragments of the dish would serve as well as minted silver in that period.
[50] Bebbanburh, Bebburgh, Babbanbusch, Babbanburch, Bamburth, Bambrught, now Bamborough, was founded by Ida. It is not certainly known whose queen Bebba was.
[51] Or Deiri.
[52] Edwin (585–633), King of Northumbria, son of Ella of Deira. He was slain at Hatfield near Doncaster by Cadwallon of North Wales and Penda of Mercia.

the Britons, as they say, journeying near that same place where the above-mentioned battle was finished, and he saw a little spot that was greener and lovelier than the rest of the field. His intelligent mind began to reflect that there was no other cause of this unusual greenness than that some man of more holy character than the rest of the army had been slain there. And he carried away some of the dust from that place, tied up in a linen cloth, with the thought that the dust would prove efficacious for the healing of the sick. Pursuing his journey, he arrived at a certain village at evening, and entered a house in which the villagers were at a feast. Received by the owners of the house, he took his seat with them at the banquet, hanging the linen package containing the dust he had brought on a pillar of the wall. When later they were giving their attention to feasting and drinking, with a large fire burning before them, it happened that sparks flew upward and ignited the house's roof which was made of thatch, and filled everything at once with flames. When the banqueters saw this, they were instantly terrified, and fled outside, not being able to do anything to save the burning house from being consumed. When the house was burned down, only the pillar on which the package of dust was hanging, remained safe and unharmed from the flames. At the sight of this miracle they were greatly surprised and, inquiring diligently, they found that the dust had been taken from that spot where the blood of King Oswald had been shed. When these miraculous occurrences were made known and published abroad far and wide, many people began to frequent that spot every day, and began to receive the grace of healing for themselves and their families.

INDEXES

GENERAL INDEX

Aaron, 140, 383
Abbots, 166
Abel, 161, 351
Abelard, 250
Abimelech, 203, 275, 276
Abiogenesis, 325
Abraham, 159, 226–228, 232–234, 239, 240, 249, 250, 276, 281
Acha, 404, 409
Achish, 276
Acta Sanctorum, 107
Actium, 195
Actor, 56
Acts, 402
Acts of Peter, 74
Adalhard, 90, 91, 193
Adam, 73, 110, 230, 253, 266, 312, 338, 345, 351
Adamnan, 406
Address to the Clergy, 371–378
Adoptionism, 193, 211, 216, 328, 339, 341
Adultery, 71
Ælbert, 192
Ælfric of Eynsham, 111, 116
Aemiliana, 179
Aeschylus, 187
Africa, 39, 44
Agabus, 80
Agobard of Lyons, 20, 149, 157, 211, 216, 217, 242, 328–367
Agrippinus of Carthage, 43, 44
Aidan, Bishop, 20, 404–410
Aignan, St., monastery of, 387
Aix, Council of, 214, 215, 219
Aix-la-Chapelle, 212, 221
Alban of Saint Martin, 254
Albinus, 192, 193, 300

Alcuin, 16, 192–210, 300, **379**
Aldhelm, 401
Alexander Severus, 62
Alexander the Great, 249
Alexandria, 63
Alexandrian Church, 84
Alexianus, 62
Allegory, 17, 63, 291, 292, 295
Almighty God, 157, 159, 161, 172
Almoner, 409
Alms, 295, 397
Alteration, 25, 69
Amalarius of Metz, 149, 152, 170, 193, 252, 330, 331, 352, 363
Amann, E., 26, 316
Ambrose of Milan, 29, 41, 85, 92, 107, 111, 121, 132, 134, 135, 137, 139, 140, 212, 289, 290
Amos, 285
Amphilochus of Iconium, 85
Amulo of Lyons, 148, 151, 157
Anagogical sense, 291
Ananias, 198
Anastasius, Saint, 403
Anatolius of Laodicea, 405
Ancient faith, 49
Ancient of Days, 342
Andrew, Saint, 47, 180
Angel (angels), 41, 47, 60, 77, 78, 104, 125, 132, 174, 175, 234, 264, 281, 353, 402
Anger, 393
Angers, 380
Angles, 404–406, 408, 409
Anianus, Saint, 387
Anicii, 179
Anonymus Cellotianus, 112
Anonymus Mellicensis, 113

Anselm of Bec, 285
Anselm of Laon, 253
Anthelmi, J., 26, 60
Antichrist, 158, 261, 348, 352, 353
Antioch, 87
Antiochus, 83
Antiochus Epiphanes, 249
Antiphonary, 330
Antiphons, 341
Antiquity (*antiquitas*), 25, 36, 38, 39, 43, 44, 73, 78, 89
Antistes, 43
Antwerp Index, 115
Apelles, 64
Apocalypse, the, 175, 403
Apocrypha, 298, 301
Apollinarianism, 84, 265
Apollinaris, 26, 38, 49, 51–54, 59
Apollos, 199
Apostle (apostles), 38, 43, 47, 48, 75, 80, 195, 298, 306, 348, 382
Apostles, Twelve, 374
Apostles' Creed, the, 20, 316, 323–327, 389
Apostles of Christ, 76
Apostolic doctrine, 46
Apostolic letter, 43
Apostolic See, 43, 183, 190, 405
Apostolic succession, 33
Aquila, 338
Arand, L. A., 162
Arcadius, 88
Archangels, 41, 264
Archdeacon, 162
Arian heresy, 39, 216
Arianism, 84
Arians, 40, 56, 84, 262
Ariminum, 40
Aristotle, 64, 197, 325
Arithmetic, 196
Arius, 38, 73, 210
Ark of the Lord, 384
Artemas, 195
Asaph, 366
Ascension Day, 402
Asia, 43, 83, 257
Assyrians, 160
Athanasian Creed, 60
Athanasius, 26, 40, 42, 72, 83–85, 210, 377
Atlas, 187
Atticus of Constantinople, 85
Attila, 387
Augmentum fidei, 27
Augustine of Canterbury, 181
Augustine of Hippo, 18, 19, 26–30, 34, 43, 44, 48, 53, 61, 64, 77, 78, 80, 81, 85, 92, 105, 107, 111, 115, 127, 128, 135, 140, 141, 144, 145, 149–151, 160–162, 167, 173, 174, 179, 212, 218, 221, 247, 255, 260, 289, 301
Augustinianism, 29, 87
Augustus, 200
Auvergne, 221
Avarice, 393

Baal, 205
Babylon, 175
Backes, L., 117
Baeda, 400
Bakhuizen van den Brink, J N., 13, 109, 114–116, 130
Baleus, J., 193
Ballerini, the, 373
Baluze, E., 33, 332, 364, 372
Baptism, 95, 99, 108, 123, 124, 147, 173, 175, 271, 272, 282, 306–308, 327, 328, 355, 375, 380, 386, 395, 396, 404, 406
Baptism, second, 395
Baptism and anointing, 99, 131
Bardy, G., 34
Barlow, C. W., 364
Barnabas, 198
Baronius, C., 32, 379
Bartholomaeus of Laon, 285
"Bartramus Strabus," 114
Basilica, 389
Basilisk, 72
Basil of Caesarea, 83, 84
Basle, 114
Bassus, 83
Batiffol, P., 182
Battles, F. L., 112
Baunard, L., 381
Baxter, Richard, 31
Beast, the third, 249
Beatitudes, 320, 322
Beatus, 402
Beauvais, 285, 314
Bebba, 409
Bec, 314
Beckmann, J., 286
Bede, Venerable, 16, 20, 92, 212, 400–410
Bedjan, P., 53
Belgian Index, 115
Belief, 335
Bellarmine, R. Card., 32, 252
Bellona, 40
Belshazzar, 387
Benedict, Saint, monastery of, 387
Benedict Biscop, Abbot of Wearmouth, 400
Benedict XIV, 32
Benedict of Nursia, 166, 300, 383, 387
Benedictines of St. Maur, 181, 255, 256

Berengarius of Tours, 18, 92, 112, 244, 251, 253
Berengar of Liége, 251
Bernard, King of Italy, 380
Bernard of Clairvaux, 250, 253
Bernicii, 409
Bernold of Constance, 316
Bertheau, C., 31
Bertramus, 19, 113–116
Besula, 85
Bezalel, 69
Bible, 16, 79, 169
Biblical exegesis, 91, 181, 193
Bigelmair, A., 372
Bindley, T. H., 34
Birckmann, A. and F., 255
Bishop (bishops), 42, 44, 166, 194, 199, 201, 203, 210, 246, 374, 382, 398, 404, 405, 407, 408
Bithynia, 222
Bliemetzrieder, F. P., 316
Bliss, J., 181
Body of Christ (the church), 65
Boethius, 162, 297
Boffito, G., 220
Boileau, J., 116, 117, 130
Boileau-Despréaux, N., 116
Bolland, J., 183
Bon Dieu, le, 338
Boniface, Bishop, 128
Botte, B., 132
Bousfield, M. A., 32
Bradwardine, Thomas, 150
Braga, Council of, 364
Brandenburg, Margrave of, 114
Bread, display, 203
Bressolles, Monsignor, 333, 339
Britain, 112, 406, 408
British Museum, 112
Britons, 408, 410
Browne, G. F., 403
Bruylants, 142
Bullinger, H., 114
Burchard of Worms, 315
Byzantine government, 180

Cabaniss, A., 153, 211, 264, 266, 270, 272, 330, 331, 333, 338, 341, 342, 353, 354, 363
Cadiou, R., 61
Caelestius, 27, 38, 73, 81, 89
Caelian Hill, 180
Caesar, 239, 269, 270
Caesarea, 84
Caesarius of Arles, 16, 29, 373, 381, 395
Cain, 161, 351
Calvin, John, 150, 151
Calvinists, 116
Camaldolese convent, 390

Canaan, 45
Canaanites, 45
Cana of Galilee, 304
Cannes, 23
Canon, the, 38, 79, 298, 364
Canonization, 402
Canon law, 20, 301, 315
Canon of catholicism, 33
Canons, 364, 386
Canterbury, 400, 401
Cappadocia, 62, 84
Cappuyns, D. M., 29, 112
Capreolus of Carthage, 30, 85, 86, 88
Capua, 314
Carolingian age, 193
Carolingian empire, 215
Cartagena, 183
Carthage, 43
Carthage, Council of, 27
Cassander, George, 31
Cassian, John, 17, 26, 28, 29, 53, 393, 395
Cassiodorus, 30, 301
Catenae, 16, 150
Cathedral School of York, 192
"Catholic," 38
Catholic, the, 25
Catholic bishops, 79
Catholic Christians, 39, 48
Catholic church, 25, 38, 48, 54, 59, 77, 78, 82, 242, 326, 348
Catholic doctor, 130
Catholic Epistles, 403
Catholic faith, 36, 37, 51, 54, 59, 66, 77, 79, 308
Catholics, 43, 44, 48, 51, 61, 77, 78
Celestine I, 29, 87
Celibacy, 110
Cellot, L., 112
Celsus, 63
Censors, Roman, 32
Ceolfrid, 400, 401
Cephas, 199
Cerinthus, 257, 261, 263
Chadwick, O., 28
Chaeremon, Abbot, 28
Chalice, 375
Chalons-sur-Marne, 251, 381
Charlemagne, 90, 114, 192, 193, 212, 221, 329, 332, 379, 380
Charles Martel, 329
Charles the Bald, 91, 109, 110, 112, 118, 122, 146, 147, 216
Charlier, C., 153
Chartres, 314
Chasseneuil, 212
Chaucer, G., 407
Chennesseau, G., 387
Cherubim, 264

Chief Shepherd, 374
Children of Israel, 96
Choisy, E., 93
Chosen vessel, 48, 198
Chrism, 325, 377
Christ, 37, 40, 41, 45, 46, 50, 52, 54, 55, 56, 58–60, 77, 80, 89, 94, 95, 97, 102, 104, 105, 107, 109, 128, 136, 137, 139, 185, 240, 244, 257–259, 261, 262, 265, 270, 273, 275, 306, 312, 319, 320, 326, 334
Christ as Head, 73
Christian, the, 17
Christian doctrine, 32
Christian era, 292
Christian ministry, 20
Christian religion, 63, 70
Christian teaching, 52
Christian unity, 18
Christiani, L., 28
Christ Jesus, 54, 195, 272, 343, 344
Christmas, 20
Christmas, H., 115
Christology, 26, 57, 87
Christotokos, 53
Christ's baptism, 58
Christ's birth, 58
Christ's body, 84, 302
Christ's body (the church), 208
Christ's body and blood, 94, 96, 101, 106, 109–111, 114, 118–147, 386, 397
Christ's conception, 58
Christ's flock, 47, 50, 75
Christ's mother, 60
Christ's sheep, 51
Christ the Saviour, 209
Christ's tooth, 285
Christs, two, 53, 54, 59
Chronicles, 365
Chrysostom, John, 84, 92, 187, 194, 212
Church, the, 17, 319
Church, the (Roman Catholic), 33
Church, universal, 33
Church of Christ, 39, 71, 99
Church of God, 60
Church of England, 31
Church of Saint Mary, Ephesus, 83
Cicero, 24, 38, 63
Circumcision, 204, 222, 281, 282
Circumcision party, 206
City of God, 341
City of God (Augustine's), 161, 255
Claudius of Turin, 16, 17, 19, 157, 211–248
Clausier, E., 182
Clement, 110
"Clementine Recognitions," 110
Clement of Alexandria, 205
Clermont, 285, 315

Clivus Scauri, 180
Cochlaeus, J., 255
Cologne, 114, 249
Columba, Saint, 406
Colvenerius, G., 301
Comba, E., 220
Comforter, the, 305
Commonitory, 24
Commonitory, The, 24, 26
Communicatio idiomatum, 58
Communion, 95, 375, 391, 398
Commutation, 122
Company of Apostles, 47
Confession, 393
Confessor (confessors), 41, 42, 62, 73, 84
Congar, M. J., 32, 33
Consensus, 25, 38, 78, 89
Constantine the Great, 40
Constantinople, 180, 183, 272
Constantius II, 40
Consubstantial, 55, 258
Contempt for the world, 310
Conversations at Malines, 32
Conversion, 122
Cooper-Marsdin, A. C., 23
Corbie, 16, 18, 90, 91, 109, 112, 118, 151, 401
Corinthians, 214, 218, 219
Corpus diaboli, 241, 352
Council of Arles, 43
Council of Carthage, 27, 43, 44
Council of Chalcedon, 60
Council of Ephesus, 23, 30, 83–85, 88
Council of Toledo, 183
Council of Trent, 115
Council of Valence, 152
Councils, 79, 109, 346
Counter Reformation, 373
Creation of the world, 196
Creator, 94, 156, 243, 245, 262, 263, 304, 317, 325, 389
Creed, 376, 377, 389
Cretans, 195, 199, 205
Crete, 195, 199, 205
Crusades, 286
Cuissard, 381
Cuno of Siegburg, 249–251, 253, 254
Curtius, E. R., 259
Cuthbert, lector, 402
Cuthbert, Saint, 401, 403
Cuthwin, lector, 402
Cyprian, 43, 44, 47, 78, 83, 85, 92, 217, 243, 332
Cyril of Alexandria, 23, 83–85, 87
Cyril of Jerusalem, 120, 135
Czapla, B., 23

D'Achery, L., 286
Damascus, 198

Damned, the, 27
Daniel, 247, 396
Daniélou, J., 61
Daris, J., 256
David, 104, 125, 203, 219, 254, 275, 279, 365-367, 393, 396
Davis, H., 179
Day of Judgment, 304
Deacon (deacons), 73, 90, 180, 192, 210, 401
Decalogue, 306
Decian persecution, 61
Decreta, 42
Definitiones, 42
Definition of the church, 32
DeGhellinck, J., 316
DeHenin, A., 301
Deity, 59, 339
De la Bastide, M.-A., 116
DeLabriolle, P., 33, 34
De la Taille, M., 111
DeLetter, P., 26, 27, 29
Demetrianus, 217, 243
Demons, 308
DeMontfort, Berthade, 315
DePlinval, G., 26
Deri, 409
Deuterogamy, 201
Deuteronomy, 219
Deutsch, S. M., 286
Deutz, 251, 255
Devil, 76, 345, 352, 383
Diabolus, 208
Diaconate, medieval, 180
Dialectic, 196
Diekmann, G. L., 272
Dionysius of Alexandria, 62
Disciples, 382
Disciples, seventy, 374
Divine canon, 43, 78, 82
Divine grace, 27
Divine law, 62, 75, 76, 79
Divine truth, 17
Divine Word, 188
Divinity of Christ, 53
Docetism, 57
Docimus, 85
Doctrine, Catholic, 32
Doctrine, Christian, 26
Doctrine, true, 25
Dods, M., 161
Dog-headed creatures, 110
Dölger, F. J., 139
Dominions, 264
Domitian, 257
Donatist heresy, 39, 45, 48
Donatus, Aelius, 190, 261
Donatus (not the Great), 43
Donatus the Great, 38, 39, 49

Douai, 115
Double procession, 19, 109
Doxology, lesser, 341
Dragon, 270, 271
Draught of fishes, 244
Driver, G. R., 53
Dructeramnus, 213, 218, 221
Duchesne, L., 148, 149, 372
Duckett, E. S., 194
Dudden, F. H., 182
Duhan, C., 387
Dümmler, E., 194, 219, 220, 252
Dungal, 215-217, 219, 241, 242, 246, 247
Duns Scotus, 113
Durand, U., 93

Eagle, 259, 260
Eanbald, 193
Easter, 376, 395, 404, 407, 409
Ebion, 257, 261
Ebrueil, 212
Ecclesiastes, 255
Eclanum, 81
Ecumenical faith, 77
Ecumenicity, 25, 36, 38, 78, 89
Edwards, Jonathan, 355
Edwin, King, 409
Egbert of York, 192
Eginhard, 379
Egypt, 159, 265
Elagabalus, 62
Elders, 41, 199, 210
Eleazar, 374
Elect, 27
Elijah, 397
Elipandus of Toledo, 211, 379
Eliphius the martyr, 254
Ella of Deira, 409
Elvira, Synod of, 385
Ember Saturday, 143
Engelmodus, 90
Envy, 393
Eosterwine, 400
Ephesians (Epistle), 193, 218
Ephesus, 23, 83-85, 200
Epigenesis, 70
Epimenides of Crete, 205
Epiphanius, 53, 62
Epiphany, 20, 272, 304, 305
Epirochius, 24
Episcopus, 59, 68, 144
Epistle and Gospel, 377
Er, 289
Erasmus, 31
Eriugena, John Scotus, 18, 112, 113, 115, 116, 149, 151, 152, 170, 264
Eternal death, 47
Ettlinger, E., 113

Eucharist, 18, 91, 99, 107, 108, 110, 112, 113, 251, 256, 271, 375
Eucharistia, 130
Eucharistic controversy, 301
Eucharistic presence, 251
Eucherius of Lyons, 24
Eunomius, 38, 75, 210
Euphorbus, 212
Eusebius of Caesarea, 62, 63, 210, 364, 405
Eusebius of Vercellae, 42
Eutychianus, 371
Eutychius of Constantinople, 180
Evangelist, 246
Evans, E., 64
Eve, 266, 351
Ewald, P., 179, 181, 373
Excerpta of Vincent, 25, 30, 58
Excommunication, 47
Exergesis, 17
Exegetes, 190
Exodus, 218, 219
Exra-Nehemiah, 402

Fabricius, J. A., 117
Fahey, J. J., 117
Faith, 27, 47, 73, 335
Faith, hope, and love, 301, 307, 308-310
Faith of the fathers, 71
False doctrines, 61
False prophets, 75
Fasting, 323, 396-398, 407
Fast of four seasons, 376
Fatalism, 78
Father, the, 19, 53, 55, 102, 132, 257, 258, 269, 278-281, 318-320, 324-327, 341, 342, 344, 345, 354, 378
Fathers, the, 16, 31, 36, 73, 90, 109, 301, 364
Faustus of Riez, 27, 230
Felicianism, 216
Felix, Saint, 403
Felix of Urgel, 211, 212, 328, 341, 379
Felix I, 84, 85
Felix II, 84, 85
Fichtenau, 113
Fides, 73
Fifth part added, 96, 97
Figure, 92, 94, 101, 118
Filioque, 19, 109, 326, 380
Filuccius, 88
Firmilian of Caesarea, 62
First Scots Confession, 258
Fisher, John 114
Five senses, 282
Five wounds, 281
Flaccus Albinus, 192
Flacius Illyricus, 315

Fleury-sur-Loire, abbey of, 379, 387
Flodoard of Reims, 111
Florentina, 183
Florilegium, 30
Florus of Lyons, Deacon, 149, 151, 153, 157, 330, 332, 352, 353, 363
Foreknowledge, 156, 157
Foreordination, 155-157
Forgiveness, 321, 395
Formula of Vincent, 18, 25, 31, 32, 38
Fornication, 393
Forster, Froben, 194
Foulque of Anjou, 315
Fourth Gospel, 257, 258
Frankfort, Synod of, 379
Frankish empire, 192, 211
Frankland, 170, 212
Franz, A., 281
Franzelin, J. B. Card., 32
Fredegisus of Tours, 329, 338
Frederick of Cologne, 251-253
Frend, W. H. C., 38
Frudegard, 92
Fulda, 16, 20, 151, 300
Fulgentius of Cartagena and Ecija, 183
Fulgentius of Ruspe, 48, 111, 144, 212

Galatia, 222
Galatians, the (people), 46, 47, 224, 225
Galatians (Epistle), 17, 218, 221
Galderich of Laon, 286
Galilee, 340
Gallia Narbonensis, 328
Gallican liberties, 315
Gallic bishops, 29, 87
Gallic clergy, 28
Gallo-Greeks, 222
Gamer, H. M., 376, 381, 393, 395
Gansvoort, Wessel, 256
Gardiner, F., 194
Gardiner, Stephen, 115
Gaskoin, C. J. B., 194
Gasquet, F. A. Card., 180
Gast, H., 93
Gaul, 241
Gaul, Southern, 26, 29
Gauls, 222
Gaye, R. K., 197
Gehenna, 354
Geiselmann, J., 117
Gelasian sacramentary, 142
Gelasius, 48
Gem, S. H., 111
General council, 79
Genesis, 197, 218, 285, 402
Gennadius, 23, 24, 34, 74
Gentiles, 48, 158, 206, 221, 226, 227, 234, 235, 270, 271, 294, 324, 343
Geoffroy of Chartres, 314

INDEXES

Geometry, 196
Gerberon, Gabriel, 251, 252
Gerbert of Aurillac, 92, 112
Gervasius, Saint, 107
Gessius Marcianus, 62
Gezo of Tortona, 93
Giles, J. A., 403
Gillet, H. M., 403
Gisla, 379
Gliozzo, C., 93, 117
Gloss, 16
Gluttony, 393
Gnosticism, 74
Gnostics, 64
Goar, Saint, 251
Godhead, 96
God of peace, 80
Gods, 273
God's glory, 54
God's grace, 292, 303, 308, 363
God's husbandry, 71
God's people, 51
God's temple, 73, 77
God's Word, 52, 53, 57, 96, 131, 137, 250
God the Creator, 74
God the Father, 142, 253
Gog and Magog, 158, 351
Gordianus, 179
Gospel, 307, 321, 396
Gospels, 75, 77, 291, 375, 391
Gottschalk, 19, 90, 111, 151, 152, 154–156, 301
Goulart, Simon, 115
Grace, 30, 63, 73, 77, 78, 100
Grace and free will, 27
Graceless ones, the, 29
Grace, prevenient, 27
Grammar, 196
Granderath, T., 32
Grant, R. M., 13, 32
Gratian, 315, 373
Gratian (emperor), 41
Greece, 84
Greek, 51, 61, 90, 99, 304, 305
Greek (not the language), 238, 344
Greeks, 109, 137, 222, 272
Gregorian sacramentaries, 142
Gregorio Magno, S., church of, 180
Gregory of Nazianzus, 83, 84, 287, 295
Gregory of Nyssa, 83, 84
Gregory of Tours, 180, 184, 190
Gregory Thaumaturgus, 62
Gregory the Great, 16, 17, 20, 92, 179–191, 212, 245, 285, 298, 354, 365, 393, 401
Gregory II (Pope), 180
Grisar, H., 179, 182
Grotius, Hugo, 31

27—E.M.T.

Guardian of the apostle, 247
Guggenheimer, K., 316
Guibert of Nogent, 17, 19, 285–299
Guizard, L., 316
Gundobad, 328, 344

Habakkuk, 402
Hadrian's mausoleum, 181
Hagen, H., 380
Haimo of Chalon-sur-Saône, 217
Haistulf, 301
Halifax, Lord, 32
Ham, 45
Hanssens, J. M., 149, 330
Hardenberg, Albert Rizaeus, 115
Hardie, R. P., 197
Hardouin, Jean, 116
Harlot, 68
Harris, J. R., 205
Harrold, C. F., 32
Hartmann, L. M., 181
Hauck, A., 301, 372
Hausherr, P. M., 93
Head, the (Christ), 241
Heaven, 47, 53
Hebrew, 61
Hebrew (language), 338, 352, 396, 406
Hebrews (Epistle), 193, 194, 219
Hebrew truth, 276
Hefele, C. J., 201, 385
Hell, 354
Heman, 366
Heracleides, 53
Heresy (heresies), 23, 26, 29, 44–46, 50, 79, 214, 241, 272
Heretics, 36, 37, 43, 45, 50, 73, 116, 169, 264, 265
Héribert, Saint, 252
Heribert of Cologne, 254
Heribrand of Liége, 251
Hériger of Lobbes, 92, 112
Hermogenes, 64
Herod, 359
Hesiod, 187
Hesychius, 92
Heurtley, C. A., 34, 60
Hewison, J. K., 24, 34
Hezekiah, 355, 366
Hii, 406
Hilary, 28, 29, 32, 40, 42, 88, 212
Hilary of Poitiers, 65, 92
Hincmar of Reims, 110, 151, 152, 154, 156, 157, 166, 372, 379
Historical sense, 291
Hodgson, L., 53
Holy Church, 42
Holy Cross Church, 387
Holy, Holy, Holy, 60

Holy of holies, 96
Holy orders, 273
Holy Saturday, 272
Holy Scripture, 38, 78, 95, 157, 163, 172, 186, 249, 255, 265, 337, 341, 359, 365, 382, 387, 394, 403
Holy Spirit, 16, 18, 19, 33, 43, 52, 55, 86, 95, 97, 100, 101, 103, 105, 119, 123–125, 165, 190, 200, 222, 225, 254, 257, 262, 263, 267, 271, 273, 304, 306, 307, 310, 313, 325–327, 336, 341, 358, 378, 380, 394
Homiliarium, 193
Homoousians, 262
Homoousios, 55, 72, 336
Honorius of Autun, 373
Honorius II (Pope), 254
Horace, 24, 48, 299
Hosea, 285
Hosius of Cordova, 201
Howorth, H. H., 182
Hrabanus, 300
Hürter, H., 33
Huguenots, 387
Hugues, Vicomte of Chartres, 315
Humility, 37
Hwaetbert, 400

Ibn Hazm, Abu Muhammad Ali, 254
Idleness, 383
Idolatry, 195, 242
Ignatius, 38, 55
Illusion, 57
Images, 19, 329
Immaculate Conception, 339
Incarnation, 26, 30, 53, 54, 58, 251, 253, 285, 329
Index Expurgatorius, 116
Initium fidei, 27
Innocent I, 81
Intercession of the saints, 215
Interpretation, 17, 38
Iona, 405, 406
Ireland, 405
Irenaeus, 78, 135
Isaac, 227
Isaac, Abbot, 90
Isaiah, 356
Ishmaelites, 214
Isidore of Seville, 92, 111, 130, 183, 211
Israel, 235, 306, 361, 367
Italy, 241, 242
Ithamar, 374
Ivo of Chartres, 20, 314–327, 389

Jacob, 227, 265, 361, 367
James the apostle, 161, 308
Jannes and Jambres, 46
Jarrow, 16, 400–403

Jeduthun, 366
Jerome, Saint, 16, 23, 40, 42, 48, 61, 62, 64, 92, 111, 112, 138, 190, 194, 195, 197, 199, 202, 207, 209, 212, 221
Jerusalem, 237, 291, 306
Jesse, 367
Jessing, J., 34
Jesus Christ, 56, 195, 206, 257, 271, 324
Jew, 74, 107, 108, 238, 266, 344
Jewish myths, 206
Jewish rite, 223
Jews, 50, 52, 64, 104, 108, 145, 158, 204, 225, 234, 238, 244, 250, 254, 264, 270, 271, 275–277, 279, 285, 294, 305, 328, 343
Joachim of Fiore, 253, 259
Job, 185, 187, 189, 191, 247, 253, 259, 270, 338, 354
John, 47, 57, 255, 257–268, 262, 263, 265, 267, 271, 275
John of Antioch, 83, 87
John of Hexham, 401
John's Gospel, 301
Johnson, L. P., 70
John the Baptist, 257, 258, 272
John the Deacon, 183
John the Evangelist, 208
John the Faster, 184
Jonas of Orléans, 211, 215, 216, 219, 241–243, 245–248, 380
Jones, C. W., 180
Jones, P. F., 403
Jordan, 304
Joseph, 267
Joshua (Book), 217, 219
Josiah, 366
Jovinian, 38, 75
Judä, Leo, 114
Judah, 135, 289, 298
Judah (Jewish people), 277
Judaizers, 204, 223
Judas, 285, 298
Judea, 249
Judges (Book), 217, 219
Judgment Day, 36, 388, 389
Judith, 160
Judith (empress), 330
Jülicher, G. A., 34
Julia Mammaea, 62
Julian of Eclanum, 81
Julius Caesar, 214
Julius I, 85
Julius II, 214
Julius Verus Philippus, 62
Jupiter, 242
Justellus, 364
Justin Martyr, 135
Justin II (emperor), 180
Justus, Abbot, 213, 218

INDEXES 419

Kantorowicz, E., 339
Keil, H., 190
Kenney, J., 110
Kenosis, 84
Kermartin, 314
Kierzy, 151, 152, 166
Kihn, H., 32, 34
Kingdom, 258, 271, 308, 309, 313, 320, 340, 345, 347, 359, 382
Kingdom of Heaven, 77, 246, 296
King, J. E., 403
King (God), 323
Kings (Books), 215, 218, 219, 254, 402
Kirk malignant, 258
Kist, N. C., 256
Klap, P. A., 333
Knox, John, 34
Knox, R., 169, 279
Koch, H., 23, 24, 34, 74
Koch, W., 26
Koeringer, A. M., 372
Krüger, G., 34, 405

Labbe, P., 84, 85, 372
Laistner, M. L. W., 150, 151, 401–403
Lamb, the, 98, 102
Lamb of God, 244, 340–342, 350
Lamentations, 91, 285
Lanfranc of Bec, 112, 314
Languor, 393
Laodicea, Council of, 364
Laon, 252, 285
Last Judgment, 175, 313
Lateran Council, 113
Latin, 51, 408
Latin bishops, 40
Latin church, 19
Latourette, K. S., 150
Lauds, 337
Laurentius, 162
Laville, L., 219
Law, the, 77, 309, 348, 391
Lawrence of Liége, Saint, 251
Lazarus, 311
Laziness, 20
Leander of Seville, 180, 181, 183, 185, 189
Lebreton, J., 34
Leclercq, H., 182, 384, 387
Leclercq, J., 315
Lectionary, 375
LeFrois, B. J., 270
Lehmann, P., 30
Leidrad of Lyons, 212, 213, 328, 363, 379
Lent, 221, 373, 395, 397, 398
Leo I the Great, 60, 212, 272
Leo IV, 372, 373
Leo IX, 112
Leo XII, 32

Leonidas, 61
Leontius, 88
Leprosy, 52
Lerina, 23
Lérins, 16, 23, 26, 30, 78, 400
LeSaint, W. P., 201
Levites, 365, 366
Leviticus, 213, 215, 218, 395
Licinianus of Cartagena, 181
Lietzmann, H., 143
Lights of Cappadocia, 84
Lindisfarne, 401, 405
Lion of the tribe of Judah, 244
Litany, greater, 376
Liturgy, 193, 301
Lobbes, 114
Logeman, H., 167
Logismos, 201
Lombard, Peter, 99
Lombards, 180
Loofs, F., 26, 87
Lord, the, 37, 50, 56, 58, 78, 81, 248
Lord Christ, 46, 303
Lord God, 50, 60, 63, 65
Lord Jesus Christ, 126, 145, 304, 307, 323, 327, 343, 348, 374, 378, 382
Lord of Glory, 58, 77
Lord Saviour, 77, 246
Lord's body, 285, 289
Lord's body and blood, 168, 272, 398
Lord's Day, 128, 375–377, 390, 396, 398
Lord's flesh, 53
Lord's name, 37, 61
Lord's Prayer, 20, 119, 316–323, 331, 376, 377, 389, 392
Lord's Supper, 93, 376, 397
Lord's Table, 145
Lord's Word, 376
Lothair, 148, 216, 301
Louis the Pious, King, 212, 213, 216, 218, 221, 328, 330, 379
Love, 31
Lower Pannonia, 51
Lucan, 211
Lucifer, 255
Lucretius, 24, 75, 298
Lupus of Ferrières, 151, 379
Lupus of Troyes, 24
Luther, 17, 150, 271, 335
Lyons, 148, 149, 152, 154, 155, 157, 328, 363

Mabillon, J., 32, 90, 113, 183, 300
Macarius Scotus, 110
Maccabees, the, 249, 250
MacDonald, A. J., 112
Macedonianism, 84
McNeill, J. T., 31, 291, 376, 381, 393, 395

Macedonius, 38
Madoz, J., 23, 24, 30, 33, 34
Magdeburg Centuriators, 115, 122
Magi, 304
Magic, 301, 328
Magicians, 308
Magisterium, 33
Magog, 158, 351
Mai, A. Card., 248, 371
Mainz, 300, 301
Malines, 32
Mameranus, N., 93
Man (Christ), 281
Man of God, 107
Manichees, 56, 57, 231, 266
Manitius, M., 149, 151, 217, 219, 220, 253, 255, 256, 301, 330, 372
Manna, 46, 103, 125, 126, 140
Marcion, 64, 257, 261
Marcus, R. E., 34
Marinus, 88
Marius Mercator, 24, 34, 73
Mark, 402
Markward of Deutz, 254
Martène, E., 93, 100, 372
Martial, 211
Martin, J., 117
Martin of Braga, 211, 364
Martin of Tours, 300
Martyrdom, 41, 61, 395, 396
Martyrology, Roman, 24
Martyrs, 44, 62, 73, 84, 85, 107, 348, 396
Mary, 52, 53, 58, 59, 94, 119, 132, 210, 257-259, 261, 262, 266, 267, 277, 285
Mary ever virgin, 100, 266
Mary, Queen of Scots, 34
Mass, the, 93, 107, 281, 286, 336, 358, 365, 374-377, 384
Mass book, 375
Masseron, A., 314
Masses, 377, 383, 385, 390, 397, 399
Massilia, 26
Masson, Papire, 331, 332
Mater Ecclesia, 66
Matthaeus Flacius, 115
Matthew, 91, 218
Maurists, 255, 256
Maurus, Saint, 300
Maximus of Turin, 212
Meiderlin, Peter, 31
Meinrad-Prenzer, P., 193
Melanchthon, 31, 115
Melk, 113
Mercury, 242
Mere man, 52
Merlet, A., 315
Messenger, Ruth, 380
Messiah, 325

Metacism, 190
Michael, 181
Micrologus, the, 316
Migne, J. P., 33, 93, 116, 192, 194, 286, 301, 371, 380, 403
Miller, 26
Miller, E. W., 256
Miller, L. F., 13
Miller, T., 403
Milman, H. H., 85
Miracles, 95
Missal, 111
Missale Romanum, 142, 272
Mitrovitz, 51
Modern, 162
Mollat, G., 301
Monks, 406
Monodies, 286
Monotheism, 52
Montanus, 65
Monte Cassino, 254, 390
Moors, 214
Moral alteration, 54
More, Sir Thomas, 114
Morin, G., 26, 112, 371, 373
Moses, 49-52, 65, 75, 124, 159, 229-233, 235, 237, 248, 397
Most High, 268
Mother church, 78
Mother of God, 59
Mount Sinai, 233, 306, 391
Moxon, R. S., 26, 32, 33, 42, 60, 62
Müller, J., 256
Mystérion, 99, 131
Mystery, 95, 98, 119, 120, 131, 273

Naegle, A., 117
Napier, A. S., 381
Nativity, 301
Nazareth, 275
Nazarites, 202
Nazianzus, 84
Neale, J. M., 316, 380
Nebuchadnezzar, 396
Neill, S. C., 31
Neo-Caesarea, 62
Nero, 107, 257
Nesle in Picardy, 314
Nestorian Church, 53
Nestorian heresy, 210
Nestorianism, 211
Nestorius, 26, 38, 52-54, 59, 83, 86, 89
New Corbie, 91, 193
Newman, J. H. Card., 32
New Testament, 75, 94, 122, 126, 144, 307, 319, 359, 364, 366
Nibridius of Narbonne, 213
Nicaea, Council of, 210, 374, 385

Niceno-Constantinopolitan Creed, 19, 210, 326, 336, 340
Nicopolis, 195
Noah, 45, 247
Novatian, 38, 43, 74
Numbers, 219
Nykl, A. R., 254

Objectiones Vincentianae, 28, 30, 74
Odilmannus Severus, 91
Oecolampadius, 114
Office of bishop, 51
Old Latin, 135, 174, 338
Old Testament, 49, 75, 94, 96, 101, 144, 234, 291, 301, 359, 364, 365
Ommanney, G. D. W., 26
Onan, 289
Optatus, 48
Oracles of God, 75
Orange, Synod of, 29
Orbais, 151
Order of nature, 133
Orgar of Mainz, 301
Origen, 60–64, 135, 212, 395
Orléans, 387
Orthodox churches, 19
Osiander, 255
Oswald, King, 404, 405, 407–410
Oswyn, 406
Other gods, 49, 51
"O Thou who hast fashioned me," 389, 392
Ott, M., 117
Otto, M., 301
Outler, A. C., 13, 162
Ovid, 24, 42
Oxenham, H. W., 385

Pagan classics, 90
Pagan gods, 242
Pagans, 50, 64, 158, 244
Paidagōgos, 237–239
Pamelius, J., 301
Pannonia, 51
Pantaleon, 332
Paraclete, 267, 305
Pardulus of Laon, 151, 152, 154, 170
Paris, Council of, 216
Parlement at Paris, 116
Parma, 193
Pascha, 128, 398
Paschal I, 214, 219, 247
Paschasius Radbertus, 18, 90–113, 116, 129, 135, 140, 301, 401
Passion, the, 95, 101, 102, 104, 128, 130, 137, 144, 147, 276, 278, 342, 344
Passover, 306, 366, 397
Pastoral Epistles, 194
Pastoral ministry, 20

Patrick, Saint, 334
Patrimonium Petri, 181
Patripassians, 262
Patrizzi, A., 373
Pauline Epistles, 301
Paulinus of Nola, 42
Paul, Saint, 45, 46, 48, 55, 57, 66, 76, 89, 102, 106, 118, 124, 141, 147, 150, 155, 193, 194, 198, 199, 221–223, 230, 238, 242, 298, 309, 310, 359, 400
Paul of Samosata, 75
Paul the Deacon, 179, 401
Paulus Orosius, 211
Pavia, 107
Pearl cult, 259
Pelagians, 19, 26, 48, 73, 81
Pelagius, 27, 38, 73, 81, 89
Pelagius II (Pope), 180
Peltier, H., 93, 117
Penance, 245, 246, 271, 273, 391, 395
Penda of Mercia, 404, 409
Penitence, 108, 394, 395
Penitentials, 381
Pentateuch, 77, 218, 219
Pentecost, 20, 301, 305–307, 376, 407
Peregrinus, 23, 24, 34, 36
Perjury, 391
Persecutions, 305
Perseverance, 27
Person, 53, 56, 57
Peter, Saint, 47, 55, 57, 74, 194, 199, 206, 222, 223, 235, 242, 246, 288, 359, 372, 400
Peter of Alexandria, 83, 84
Peter the Venerable, 250
Petri, Suffridus, 113
Pétrof, D. K., 254
Pez, B., 112
Pharaoh, 352
Pharisees, 248, 276, 359
Philemon, 193, 194, 214, 218
Philip I of France, 315
Philippians, 218
Philip the Arab, 62
Phinehas, 140
Photinus, 26, 38, 49–52, 54, 59
Photius of Constantinople, 109
Physician, 322
Picts, 404, 406, 408
Pierius, 62
Pilate, 269
Piolanti, A., 117, 286
Pius IV, 115
Placidius, 91
Plato, 63, 64
Plegwin, 403
Pliny the Younger, 354
Plummer, C., 400–407
Plumpe, J. C., 13, 66

Pohle, J., 26, 29, 92, 93
Poirel, R. M. J., 24, 34
Poisoners, 75
Polyandria, 384
Pompeius, 44
Pontius Pilate, 325
Poole, R. L., 216, 220
Porphyry, 52, 63
Possevinus, A., 193
Power, E., 381
Powers, 41, 264
Prael, John, 114
Praepositi, 68
Praxeas, 64
Praxeis, 201
Prayers in Mass, 142
Preacher, the, 20
Predestinarianism, 78
Predestination, 27, 30, 78, 109, 155, 347
Prefiguration of Christ, 135
Pre-Reformation, 315
Presbyter, 23, 41, 59, 61, 90, 194, 200, 202, 300, 371, 374, 375, 382, 385, 386, 400, 401
Pride, 393
Priests, 73
Primate of Africa, 85
Principalities, 264
Priscillian, 38, 74, 75
Prodigal Son, 254
Progress, 25, 69, 70
Proof texts, 76, 77
Prophets, 38, 41, 50, 75, 80, 309, 348, 391
Prosper of Aquitaine, 26, 28, 29, 83, 88
Protasius, Saint, 107
Protestant Bibles, 135
Protestants, 19
Proverbs, 402
Providence, 50, 52, 365
Prudentius of Troyes, 151
Psalmist, 270
Psalms, 75, 219, 241, 316, 341, 364, 365
Psalter, 136
Pseudo-Augustine, 121
Pseudo-Dionysius, 264
Pseudo-Messiah, 74
Puiset, Chateau de, 315
Puritans, 331
Pusey, E. B., 34
Pythagoras, 212
Pyxis, 375

Quadrivium, 196
Quaternity, 59, 60
Quennell, P., 333
Quicumque Vult, 26, 60, 373, 377

Rabanus Maurus, 20, 99, 112, 133, 151, 152, 155, 171–173, 193, 212, 213, 217, 300–313
Raby, F. J. E., 29
Rainy, R., 26
Rathier of Verona, 93, 372
Rational soul, 53
Ratramnus, 18, 19, 90, 92, 97, 105, 109–147, 151, 301
Ratus, Guillaume, 93
Rauschen, G., 34
Reason, 346
Rebaptism, 42, 43, 45
Redeemer, 56, 173, 304, 317, 326, 358
Redemption, 118
Reformation, 18, 19, 32, 33, 315, 364
Reformers, 19, 114, 258
Regino of Prüm, 372
Reiner von Lüttich, 256
Relics of saints, 285
Religious haven, 37
Reliquiae Pelagianorum, 26
Remigius, 148, 149
Reply to the Three Letters, 148–175
Responsories, 341
Resurrection, 272, 305
Revelation, 49
Revelation (Apocalypse), 253
Revised Standard Version, 147, 276, 279, 311, 320
Revised Version, 394
Richardson, E. C., 23
Richer of Sens, 314
Ridley, Glocester, 115
Ridley, Nicholas, 115
Ripoll, 30
Risala, the, 254
Rocholl, R., 256
Rock, the, 244
Rogations, 376
Roman breviary, 389
Roman Catholic Church, 258, 384
Roman Catholics, 32, 116
Roman Catholic writers, 92
Roman church, 43, 115, 162, 272, 364, 365
Roman Empire, 40
Roman missal, 389
Romans, the, 238
Romans (Epistle), 214, 218
Rome, 179, 193, 245–247, 315, 400, 401, 405
Ross, W. D., 197
Rota, A., 316
Rouen, 116
Rouse, R., 31
Rudolph, 300
Rufinus, 29, 62–64, 212
Rufinus, Saint, 91

INDEXES 423

Rule for interpretation, 78
Rule of Faith, 79
Rule of Saint Benedict, 166, 167
Rule of Vincent, 26
Rules of exegesis, four, 291
Rupert of Deutz, 17, 249–282
Ruth, 218, 219

Sabbath, 229, 373, 390
Sabellianism, 110
Sabellians, 262
Sabellius, 38, 73
Sacerdos, 38, 40, 41, 43, 50, 57, 62, 69, 73, 79, 82, 83, 86, 202, 374, 382, 405, 407
Sacerdotalis, 203
Sacerdotium, 51
Sacramentary, 142, 193
Sacrament of the Lord's Supper, 95
Sacraments, 97, 106, 121, 131, 132, 134, 175, 271, 272, 304, 307, 398, 407
Sacraments, seven, 99
Sacred Heart, 280
Sacred Host, 255
Sacrifices, 96
St. Germain, monastery of, 285
St. Honorat, 23
St. Lifard, monastery of, 387
Ste. Marguerite, 23
St. Médard, monks of, 285
St. Peter's Church, 409
Saints, 44, 281
Sallust, 24, 40
Salmasius, C., 252
Salvation, 95, 271, 309
Salvian, 37
Samaritan, 74
Samuel (Books), 215, 218, 219, 402
Sanctus, 402
Sanctus, the, 60
Saracens, 215
Sardica, Council of, 201
Satan, 76, 338, 348
Saturn, 242
Saviour, 53, 54, 56, 75, 76, 127, 146, 173, 243, 303, 304, 325
Scaduto, M., 387
Schism, 39, 79, 241
Schmid, U., 372
Schmidt, L., 316
Schmidt, M., 31
Schmitt, C., 372
Scholastics, 99
Schools, 387
Schroeder, A., 372
Schrörs, H., 149
Schuster, M., 75
Scots (Irish), 404–406, 408
Scribes, the, 248

Scriptures, 16, 17, 20, 24, 25, 31, 36, 45, 58, 60, 63, 74, 76, 79, 86, 90, 92, 99, 102, 107, 109, 111, 115, 169, 172, 174, 189, 204, 287, 291, 292, 294, 295, 299, 300, 301, 331, 339, 346, 353, 384, 385, 391, 401, 407
Scudder, J. W., 256
Scythian, 343
Seals, 41
Second Helvetic Confession, 266
Second Person, 255
Sects, 241
Segeni, 406
Semi-Pelagians, 19, 26–30, 64, 78, 88, 148
Seneca, 211
Seniores, 41
Septuagint, 97, 107, 129, 136, 209, 279, 280, 384, 389
Seraphim, 264
Sermo, 133
Serpent, 255
Servant of the servants of God, 183
Servetus, Michael, 151
Seven-branched candlestick, 42, 43
Sevenfold light, 43
Seven remissions, 395
Severus, Saint, 251
Sheol, 353, 354
Shewring, W. H., 190
Sichard, J. B., 34
Sicily, 180
Sieber, A., 316
Siegburg, abbey of, 251
Sigebert of Gembloux, 113
Sigfrid, 400
Silvester II, 92, 112
Silvia, 179
Simeon, 108, 277
Simeon of Durham, 404
Simon Magus, 74, 194, 199
Sirmium, 51
Sirmond, J., 93, 380, 398
Sixtus of Siena, 114, 193
Sixtus III, 23, 28, 30, 87
Smalley, Beryl, 276, 291
Socrates, 50
Soissons, 90, 212
Solomon, 97, 169, 366
Song of Songs, 253, 402
Son of God, 56, 57, 60, 77, 165, 230, 245, 257, 258, 275, 343
Son of Man, 58, 101, 126, 141, 165, 229, 275, 279, 359
Son of the Virgin, 60
Sons, two, 54
Sons of God, two, 53, 308

Sons of the Kingdom, 44
Souter, A., 69
Southwell, J. A., 61
Spain, 211
Speratus, 332
Spirit, the, 31, 47, 127, 165, 225, 305, 343, 346
Spontaneous generation, 325
Sporones, 375
Spotless Lamb, 75
"Stabat Mater," 277
Stephen I, 43
Stevenson, J., 403
Stock, J., 34
Suarez, Francisco, 113
Suau, P., 183
Successors of apostles, 43
Suger of Saint-Denis, 250
Sulpicius Severus, 24, 40
Superstition, 241, 243
Symbol, 118
Symmachus, 338
Synagogues, 346
Synod of Frankfort, 193
Synod of Orange, 29, 162
Synod of Vercelli, 112
Syrus of Pavia, 107

Talbot, C. H., 192
Tarsilla, 179
Tartarus, 173, 175
Taylor, H. O., 151
Taylor, W. F., 113
Teacher of the Gentiles, 48
Te Deum, 47, 60, 266
Temple, 77, 238, 278, 366
Terence, 24, 38
Tertullian, 36, 64, 65, 75, 78, 79, 135
Teschner, M., 380
Theodard, Saint, 251
Theodemir, 19, 212–215, 218, 241, 245
Theodore of Tarsus, 400
Theodosius, 24
Theodosius II, 50, 83, 85
Theodotion, 338
Theodulph of Orléans, 16, 20, 193, 211, 371, 374, 379–399
Theognostus, 62
Theophilus of Alexandria, 83, 84
Theophrastus, 64
Theotokos, 53, 58
Third Ecumenical Council, 83
Thomas Aquinas, 113, 150, 190, 191
Thompson, A. H., 403
Thorpe, B., 111, 381
Thrones, 264
Tiberius II (emperor), 180
Timotheus of Alexandria, 84
Timothy, 68, 69, 72, 89, 200, 206, 310

Tithes, 384
Titus (Epistle), 16, 193, 194
Titus (person), 195, 198, 206
Tobit, 402
"Tome" of Leo the Great, 60
Tonsure, 110
Tours, 16, 112, 192, 193, 212, 300
Tradition, 77
Transubstantiation, 122, 286
Traube, L., 332
Trial by ordeal, 328
Tribunicia potestas, 200
Tridentine faith, 251, 252
Trinity, 26, 30, 52, 54, 59, 60, 73, 110, 247, 251, 254, 255, 262, 263, 307, 329, 336, 337, 375
Trinity of the unity, 73
Trithemius, Joannes, 113, 193
Trivium, 196
Tropological sense, 291
Tropologies, 285
True catholic, 65
Truth, the (Christ), 94, 101, 107, 172, 174, 185, 242, 310
Truth (*veritas*), 92, 111, 118–120
Tschackert, P., 31
Tullie Leucorum in Prima Belgica, 24
Turin, 213, 242
Twelve, the, 222
Tychicus, 195

Ulrich of Augsburg, 372
Unction, 383
Unity, 336
Universal church, 43
Universal council, 39
Universitas, 25, 38
University of Ghent, 112
Unknown God, 206
Urban II, 314
Uzès, 329
Uzzah, 384

Vadian, Joachim, 114, 115
Vainglory, 393
Valentinian, 24
Valentinus, 49
Valerius, Saint, 91
Valesius, Henry, 364
Vandals, 85
Vasquez, 252
Vatican Council, 32
Venerable, 402
Veneration of images, 215, 242, 243
Venerius of Massilia, 88
Ventriloquists, 287
Verbum, 133
Vercelli, Synod of, 112
Vergil, 224

INDEXES

Veritas, 92, 111, 118
Vermigli, Peter Martyr, 115
Verona, 62
Vespers, 397
Vestments, 374, 400
Vetus, Latinum, 190
Vetustas, 25, 38, 73
Vices, eight chief, 393
Vincent, 17, 19, 23–89, 148, 202, 210
Vincent, formula of, 18, 25, 31, 32, 38
Vincentian canon, 33
Vine, A. R., 38, 87
Virgin, 54, 55, 58, 101, 112, 125, 134, 138, 145, 244, 253, 257, 259, 260, 270, 325, 339
Virgin birth, 91
Virginity, 285
Virginity, perpetual, 265, 266
Virgin Mary, 18, 53, 100, 103, 142, 143, 145, 230, 325
Virtues, 264
Visigothic embassy, 183
Vitalian, 400
Vitalis, 28
Vlimmerus, J., 93
Vulgate, 97, 107, 129, 136, 174, 190, 200, 203, 209, 223, 225, 232, 235, 270, 275, 276, 277, 279, 280, 320, 338, 384

Wala, 91
Walafrid Strabo, 114, 151, 217
Warfield, B. B., 26
Warin, 91
Warnefrid, 179, 401
Wattenbach, W., 194, 373
Wearmouth, 400, 403
Wenilo, 166
West, A. F., 194
West Franks, 110
Whitby, 179, 406
White, H. J., 207

White, T. H., 259
Whitsunday, 407
Whittingham, W. R., 116
Wilkinson, J. T., 32
William of Champeaux, 251–253
William of Malmesbury, 405
William of Palestrina, 252
Williams, A. L., 254
Willibrord, 192
Willis, G. G., 38
Wilmart, A., 110, 153
Wilson, H., 34
Wilson, H. A., 142
Winzet, Ninian, 34
Wisdom, 238
Wisdom (Christ), 197, 210
Witzel, George, 31
Wolff, O., 256
Wolfger of Prüfening, 113
Wolfsgruber, C., 182
Word, God's, 16, 19, 53, 54, 55, 57, 58, 81, 108, 339, 408
Word, the, 53, 54, 56, 57, 58, 84, 95, 102, 119, 197, 198, 255, 259–267, 318, 325
Wordsworth, J., 207
Worms, 115, 315
Würzburg, diocese of, 32
Wyclif, John, 112, 252

Xenophon, 64

York, 192, 401
Young, J. J., 29
Yves, Saint, 314
Yves Hélory, 314

Zeus, 195
Zion, 291
Zöckler, O., 183
Zosimus, 81
Zurich, 115

BIBLICAL REFERENCES

Genesis	Genesis—*continued*	Genesis—*continued*
1:3 263	9:22 45	49:10 270
1:6, 7 263	12:3 227	Exodus
2:17 230	15:6 226	8:6, 16, 21 48
3:3 .... 230, 232, 273	17:8 303	20:3–17 306
3:4 273	18:18 227	20:4, 5 242
3:14 232	22:16, 17 159	20:16 391
3:18 71	22:18 .. 227, 249, 270, 281	25:31–40 43
3:19 320	38:6–10 289	31:1–5 69
9:18, 25 45	46:12 289	

Exodus—continued
32:33 174
34:23 237

Leviticus
10:8 202
18:5 228
19:12 391
22:14 96
22:16 98

Numbers
3:32; 4:28 374
6:2–5 202
21:5 46
22:21–30 185

Deuteronomy
12:13, 14 385
13:1 .... 49, 63
13:2 49
13:3 50
13:5 238
16:21 190
18:15 235
19:15 258
21:23 229
32:7 .... 36, 169
32:8 174

I Samuel
21 276
21:1–6 203
21:13 276

II Samuel
6:6–8 384
23:1, 2 367

I Kings
18:22, 25, 40 205
22:22 338

I Chronicles
16:8, 9, 24 337
23 to 25 366
23:30, 31 366

II Chronicles
7:5, 6 366
19:9 384
29:30 366
35:15 366

Job
1:21 312
3:2 187

Job—continued
3:5 187
3:7 187
6:7 188
7:15 187
7:19 188
7:20 188
9:13 187
10:20–22 354
12:13 262
13:26 188
17:16 354
26:12 338
27:6 188
31:16–20 188
31:23 355
36:27 338
38 261
38:7 338
38:9 338
39:27–29 259
39:30 260
41:5 270
41:9 270
41:15–17 352
41:23 352
41:26 352
41:33, 34 352

Psalms
6:5 354
8:6 345
10:4–10 352
16:9 279
17 174
18:25, 26 173
19:4, 5 267
22:6 325
22:16 58
23:2 340
24 .... 274, 354
25 392
26:5 258
30:2 165
30:10 357
30:12 279
32 392
32:1 396
32:2 396
32:4 396
32:5 392
33:9 263
34 .... 275, 276
34:8 135
34:14, 15 392
34:15, 16 356
36:9 165
36:11, 12 317
38:18 355

Psalms—continued
41:1 277
41:4 164
44 91
44:22 358
45:1 .... 260, 265
45:2 267
45:16 246
46:10 36
49:12 317
51 392
51:3 .... 355, 393
52:1 353
55:8 209
56:2, 3, 4 357
56:11 358
57:6, 7 280
57:8 279
59:8 107
62:5–7 309
64:1 357
66:10–12 358
68:18 273
69:20 277
73:27 159
74:16 365
76:6 311
78:25 .... 104, 125
78:39 317
84:2 98
85:11 260
86:5 360
95:10, 11 159
100 334
103:17 159
103:22 390
104:4, 5 337
104:14, 15 136
104:26 270
105:1, 2 337
107:23, 24 293
108 280
108:1, 2 .... 279, 280
109:16 277
111:10 320
115:3 94
115:17 354
119:11 383
119:14 258
119:120 355
119:176 165
134:1 334
135:2 334
139:8 390
145:10 334
148 337
148:2–4 263
149 337
150 337

Proverbs

1:24-26	361
3:1	36
9:5, 17	68
9:4, 13, 14, 15-18	68
10:23, 27	320
13:3	169
15:24	353
17:6	169
19:5	391
21:28	280
22:10	169
22:17	36
22:28	67, 169
23:1	97, 129
26:10	169

Ecclesiastes

10:1	48
10:8	67

Song of Solomon

5:2	335

Isaiah

6:3	60
7:9	145
12:3	337
14:27	229
25:8	345
27:11	389
29:13	207
33:16, 17	259
35:10	341
38:18	353, 355
40:5	265
40:8	261
40:12	338
43:25	361
44:21, 22	361
45:11	160
48:1	391
51:7, 8	357
53:10, 11	281
55:6	334
55:7	361
57:1	277
58:3, 4	398
58:6-9	360
60:18-21	341
61:10	342
62:2-5	341
63:5	277
64:4	389
64:6	271
66:24	353

Jeremiah

1:17, 18	357
2:2	71

Jeremiah—*continued*

3:14	71
5:2	391
7:9	391
7:11	278
13:27	71
31:32	71
31:34	393

Lamentations

4:20	135

Ezekiel

1:21	100
3:8, 9	357
17:24	157, 158
18:4	165
18:25	174
18:30-32	361
18:32	74
22:18-22	358
29:3-5	352
39:8	158

Daniel

2:34, 35, 44, 45	342
4:27	396
5	387
7	249
7:9, 10	38
7:13, 14	342
7:25-27	349
8:9-12	349
8:23-25	349
11:36, 37	349
12:3	387
13:42	157

Hosea

8:9	71
13:14	345

Habakkuk

2:4	226
3:11	261

Malachi

3:6	157
3:18 to 4:3	362

Zechariah

9:11	355

Judith

9:4, 5	160

Wisdom

1:4, 5	335
2:21, 22	274
5:1	353

Wisdom—*continued*

5:6-10	353
8:1	264
10:21	185
12 to 14	263

Ecclesiasticus

3:33	396
6:35	169
7:29	394
8:9, 11, 12	169
8:14	67
10:10	395
23:30	161
24:15, 16	71
24:30	264
32:4	269
39:20	161
47:9-12	367

Susanna

42	157

I Maccabees

1:54-57	250

Matthew

2:16	275
3:2	155
3:12	66
4:5, 6	77
5:5	320
5:13	382
5:16	302
5:33	391
5:39	346
5:45	346
6:3	318
6:6	318
6:9-13	318
6:12	395
6:14	396
6:14, 15	346
6:16	318
6:32-44	318
6:34	321
7:7	78, 156
7:12	386
7:15	75, 76
10:16-18	346
10:22	303
11:28	208
11:29	277, 318
11:30	318
12:8	229
12:34	71
12:35	356
13:24, 25, 37	68

Matthew—continued

13:38............44
13:45, 46..........259
14:13-21..........318
16:4..............71
16:18.........200, 246
16:19............246
16:26............391
18................320
18:6..............246
18:8...............39
18:20.............384
19:12..............61
21:12.............385
21:13.....278, 384, 385
22:13.............353
22:21........239, 270
22:37.............196
22:37-40..........309
23:2..............248
23:3..........248, 388
24:21-25..........349
24:23.............326
24:1-13......335, 341
25:15..............69
25:30.............353
25:33.............326
25:35......203, 390, 393
25:41.............353
26:26......122, 134, 276
26:27.............130
26:28......122, 126, 276
26:39.............278
27:46.............278

Mark

2:28..............229
4:24..............107
6:32-44...........318
8:38...............71
11:21-24..........360
14:23.............130
14:24........122, 126
16:16.............308

Luke

2:25..............108
2:35..............277
3:6...............265
3:8...............234
4:29, 30..........275
6:27, 28..........346
6:29..............204
6:30..............312
6:37..............396
7:47..............237
9:10-17...........318
10:27.........196, 309

Luke—continued

11:3..............119
11:9........78, 156, 358
11:10.............359
11:13.............359
11:41.............396
12:4..............357
15:24.............165
16:8..............298
16:19-31..........311
18:1..............359
18:2-8............359
18:13.............392
18:34.............275
19:10.........165, 265
21:34.............318
21:36.............359
22:17.............130
22:19......103, 126, 130, 134, 147
22:20.............126
22:40, 46.........359
22:42.............278
23:2..............270
24:39.............143
24:43.............340
24:52.............274

John

1:1........260, 261, 262
1:1-3, 14.........257
1:1-14............198
1:2...............262
1:3...........258, 263
1:4...............165
1:5...............246
1:7...............258
1:9...............246
1:14.......95, 263, 265, 267, 325
1:29..........244, 340
1:29, 36...........75
2:1-11............267
3:3...............310
3:13...............58
4:1...............187
4:10...............66
4:24..............263
5:25..............165
6:5-14............318
6:14..............304
6:41......119, 321, 394
6:44..............347
6:49..............105
6:50..............133
6:51.......94, 101, 133
6:52.........126, 276
6:53...101, 126, 275, 302
6:54..............104

John—continued

6:55......101, 104, 138
6:56..............101
6:61, 62..........127
6:63...127, 141, 142, 147
6:66..............127
7:32, 45, 46......276
7:34..............270
7:35..............270
8:1-11............276
8:3-11............208
8:34.........166, 195
8:36..............166
8:39..............227
8:44..............351
8:56..............233
8:58, 59..........276
10:1-8.............79
10:12..............75
10:30, 31.........277
11:47, 53.........277
12:23.............279
13:1..............274
13:35.............310
14:2..............354
14:6..............198
14:15.............310
14:23.............335
14:30.............278
15:5.........119, 347
16:6, 7...........274
17:17-24..........345
18:6.........278, 280
18:36.............269
19:30.............339
19:33.............271
19:34.........138, 271
20:22, 23.........273
21:20.............257
21:24.............258

Acts

1:3...............339
1:9-11............340
2:1-4.............305
3:22..............235
7:14, 15..........265
8:5-24.............74
8:9-24............199
9:1-9.............198
9:15..........48, 198
10:44-46..........225
11:27-30...........80
12................359
13:2..............198
13:9-11...........225
17:23.............206
17:28.............334
19:1-6............225

INDEXES

Acts—*continued*
20:17 200
20:28 .... 144, 200
21:10–12 80

Romans
1:1 195
1:17 .... 95, 226
1:19, 20 .... 155, 263
1:25 .... 156, 243
1:32 289
2 to 4; 11 223
3:19 235
4 227
4:2 228
4:3 226
5:3–5 358
5:5 .... 226, 244
5:14 73
6:3 272
6:4 326
6:9 .... 98, 139, 279
6:11, 13 123
6:19 298
7:13 54
7:24 321
8:3 230
8:9 .... 100, 141
8:15 322
8:33 358
8:35–37 358
8:38 264
9:21 162
10:10 323
11:22 158
11:32 235
12:2 364
13:10 310
13:14 238
14:14–23 206
14:17 395
16:17, 18 46

I Corinthians
1:10 .... 80, 118
1:12 199
1:25 325
2:6 274
2:8 .... 58, 274
2:9 .... 342, 389
2:14 297
3:7 100
3:9 71
3:12, 13 358
3:16, 17 .... 73, 77
3:22, 23 344
4:13 89
4:15 107
5:7 306

I Corinthians—*continued*
5:11 72
6:17 339
6:18 322
9:13 202
9:27 347
10:1–4 124
10:3 103
10:3, 4 135
10:4 .... 125, 141, 244
10:11 160
10:17 146
10:31 356
11:3 344
11:19 66
11:26 147
11:27 .... 207, 302
11:28 106
11:29 106
12:7–11 226
12:8 273
12:12–14 343
12:27 146
12:28 80
12:31 364
13 20
13:12 260
13:13 308
14:3, 37 49
14:20 .... 261, 364
14:26 356
14:33 80
14:36, 37, 38 81
15:22–27 345
15:51 327
15:51–57 345
15:53 327

II Corinthians
3:5 347
3:6 .... 165, 236
3:17 166
5:4 278
5:7 99
5:16 244
5:21 230
6:16 303
11:13 76
11:14, 15 76
12:2 48
13:8 .... 164, 169

Galatians
1:1 223
1:6 223
1:6, 7 46
1:8 .... 46, 47
1:9 .... 47, 74
2:11–14 223

Galatians—*continued*
2:12 206
2:20 228
3 224–240
3:1 .... 223, 225
3:2, 3, 4 225
3:5, 6 226
3:7, 8, 9, 10 227
3:11 226
3:12 228
3:13 229
3:14, 15 232
3:16 .... 227, 232
3:19, 20 233
3:21 235
3:21–23 235
3:24–26 237
3:27 .... 238, 344
3:28 .... 238, 344
3:29 240
5:6 308
5:16 48
5:16–21 347
5:25, 26 48
6:1 168
6:7 107

Ephesians
1:7 138
1:21 264
1:22 345
1:23 65
2:3 271
2:8 347
2:11, 12 235
2:20 342
3:10 264
4:3–6 343
4:5 87
4:8 273
4:10–16 343
4:11 273
4:15 73
4:29 355
5:14 165
5:18 397
5:19 331
6:4 394
6:11–18 346
6:12 264
6:18–20 359

Philippians
1:9, 10 364
1:18 288
2:5, 6 318
2:8 280
2:9–11 342
2:13 347

Philippians—*continued*
2:28.................280
3:6..................229
3:19............204, 206
3:20.................320

Colossians
1:12, 13.............175
1:15–20..............344
1:16.................264
1:18..................73
2:9.............278, 344
2:10, 15.............264
2:19.................343
3:9–11...............344
3:16, 17.............356
4:2–4................359

I Thessalonians
4:6..................395
4:8...................80
5:17.................323

II Thessalonians
1:6, 7...............226
2:1–12...............348

I Timothy
1:19...............46, 74
2:1, 2...............360
2:4..................167
2:8, 9...............360
3:2..................200
3:15.................348
4:1, 2...............346
4:2..................262
4:7..................335
5:12..................46
5:13..................46
6:3..................206
6:4, 5................46
6:8.............202, 321
6:17–19..............310
6:20...67–69, 72–74, 175
6:21.................175

II Timothy
1:11..................48
1:19..................46

II Timothy—*continued*
2:16, 17..............46
3:6, 7................46
3:8...................46
3:9...................46
4:3, 4................46
4:5–8................347

Titus
1:10, 11..............46
2:9..................280

Hebrews
1:3..................102
4:11.................160
6:6..................245
6:13, 14.............159
6:17, 18.............159
7:26–28..............129
10:27.................36
10:33, 34............226
11:1.................121
11:6............308, 323
11:38.................40
12:5.................210
12:6.................189
13:2.................390

James
1:2..................358
1:5–8................360
1:17.................161
2:13.................321
2:14, 15, 17.........308
2:19.................324
2:23.................226
5:14.................375
5:20.................396

I Peter
1:6, 7...............358
1:19..................75
2:9..................337
2:21.................129
3:9–14...............356
4:8..................396
4:9..................390
5:1, 2...............200

II Peter
1:5..................335
2:4..................173
2:16.................288

I John
2:2..................340
2:15.................310
2:17.................310
2:18.................348
3:2..................260
3:16.................170
4:10.................340
4:21.................310

II John
10, 11................72

Jude
3....................47
16...................348

Revelations
1:5..................340
1:12..................43
2:7..................100
2:10..................42
3:20.................335
3:21.................335
4:8...................60
5:1–5.................41
5:2...................41
5:5..................244
5:13.................340
6:16, 17.............340
7:9, 10..............342
7:10.................340
7:14–17..............340
12...................275
13:1–7...............350
13:11–14.............350
14:6.................259
17:7–14..............351
18:21................175
19:19–21.............351
20:7–10..............351
21:8.................356
21:23...........341, 342
21:27................341

www.ingramcontent.com/pod-product-compliance
Lightning Source LLC
Chambersburg PA
CBHW031401290426
44110CB00011B/229